AN ANTHOLOGY OF

Classic

AUSTRALIAN
FOLKLORE

AN ANTHOLOGY OF

Classic

AUSTRALIAN
FOLKLORE

*Two Centuries of Tales, Epics,
Ballads, Myths & Legends*

COMPILED BY A.K. MACDOUGALL

This book is for Veronica

The Five Mile Press Pty Ltd
1 Centre Road, Scoresby
Victoria 3179 Australia
Email: publishing@fivemile.com.au
Website: www.fivemile.com.au

First published as
The Big Treasury of Australian Folklore,
1990; reprinted 1992, 1994
A new, revised and expanded edition published 2002
(reprinted 2002), 2004, 2005 (reprinted 2005)
This revised and expanded edition published 2008
Originally conceived and designed
by A.K.Macdougall/Clarion Editions
Text copyright © Anthony Macdougall

Designed by Geoff Hocking
Edited by Emma Borghesi

Printed in China

National Library of Australia Cataloguing in Publication data:
   Macdougall, Anthony,
   Australian folklore.
   Includes index.
   ISBN 978 1 74211 118 6.
   1. Folklore – Australia. I. Title.
   398.20994

Contents

Introduction /6

1: *Aboriginal Myths and Legends* /9

2: *Ships and Seafarers* /19

3: *Convicts and Colonists* /59

4: *Bushrangers* /115

5: *The Squatters* /139

6: *The Gold Rush* /153

7: *Bush Living* /179

8: *The Overlanders* /219

9: *Sheep and Shearing* /239

10: *Into the Unknown* /265

11: *Bush Ballads* /289

12: *The Australian Slanguage* /317

13: *Conflict and Strife* /337

14: *Legends of War* /351

15: *Up and Away: Legends of the Air* /379

16: *Good Sports* /385

17: *Tall Tales—and True* /399

18: *Nicknames* /413

19: *Ragbag* /417

Map of Australia /429

Acknowledgements, Bibliography /430

Index /431

Introduction

COME GOOD TIMES OR BAD, booms or recessions, few Australians question their luck in living in a country where the sun shines most days and the horizons seem limitless. Australians remain a bunch of optimists; it is part of our nature.

Australian folklore reflects this sunny and robust attitude to life. Our recorded history—the basis of any folklore—is short, barely 200 years, but it is rich indeed, full of larger-than-life characters, quirks of fate, and tales and ballads recounted or sung for generations in a language all our own; a blend of dry similes and far-fetched metaphors that still make visitors and Australians laugh out loud. A century ago, when the American humourist Mark Twain visited Australia, he found everything about us amusing, from our accent and our larrikins to our animals—and even our history struck him as one long Tall Story. 'Australian history is almost always picturesque,' he wrote. 'Indeed, it is so curious and strange, that it is in itself the chiefest novelty the country has to offer . . . It does not read like history, but like the most beautiful lies . . . full of surprises, and adventures, and incongruities, and incredibilities; but they are all true; they all happened.'

Shortly afterwards A.B. ('Banjo') Paterson, famous as author of the classic bush ballads *Clancy of the Overflow* and *The Man from Snowy River* decided to collect the old colonial ballads that were in danger of dying out. His book *Old Bush Songs*, published in 1905, rescued much of our folklore from oblivion, helped to give Australia the solid basis of a national literature—and became the starting point for all subsequent collections of Australian ballads. The British and Irish settlers, many of whom were illiterate, brought with them a tradition of folk song. Many of these (English melodies, Scottish border ballads, Irish rebel songs) provided the tunes for our inventive rhymesters; they resulted in some of our best-known ballads, and a nation of city-dwellers has taken these songs to heart. Updating Paterson's collection in the 1950s, when the revival of interest in folksong and folk tales began, Douglas Stewart wrote: 'I should think the Irish did more to set the Australian ballad in motion than any other source one could point to.' He had just come back from Ireland where, while driving him through County Kerry, an Irish friend suddenly started singing *The Wild Colonial Boy!*

The only unique and original part of our folklore is the Aboriginal component. All else—including the language we speak— is derived from overseas, but two centuries has given it a flavour and a character all our own, and it is possibly the only folklore apart from the American that is known widely beyond its own shores.

Even today many Australians find much of their own history dull and colourless, because all the life has been cut out of it. But turn from statistics and sanitized political and economic history to the stories that never made it into the text books—those that live on in our folklore—and Australia bursts into life and colour and song: a world of ballads, yarns and tall stories of drovers and shearers, bushrangers and troopers, bullockies and overlanders, explorers, squatters and selectors, droughts and floods. The bush dominates our folklore and bush characters remain our ideal, embodiments of the Australian qualities of rebellious courage, physical stamina and laconic humour, but our 21st-century national folklore also includes sport and war, two fields of endeavour in which Australians have created legends more familiar perhaps to the younger generations than any bush ballad or yarn. What they all have in common are qualities that warm the heart—and often bring a smile of pride.

What exactly is folklore? Bill Wannan, one of the great collectors of Australian folklore, wrote in the *Australian Encyclopaedia*: 'Folklore is a body of legends, tales, sayings, phrases, ballads, lore and popular allusions held by members of a cultural group ... Like much of the later folklore of North America, that of the non-Aboriginal Australians grew out of a harsh environment, separated by great distances from the lands from which the first settlers (mostly British and Irish) came.' There is a touch of the heroic about many aspects of Australia's past and if folklore romanticizes much of it, it is no bad thing.

So if humour and heroism abound in this anthology, it's no accident. Horror is here also, for Australia was born in pain and injustice, and many of our tales of colonial days are disturbingly macabre. It took Australians fifty years to bring the convict age to an end and two centuries to attempt to make amends to our Aboriginal peoples for past neglect and callousness. But too much of our folk history is fading; and too many traditional heroes are being replaced by stereotypes, 'achievers' motivated by money, many of them with feet of clay; and with every decade that passes our idiosyncratic language loses more of its leaves, though its roots remain strong.

A.K.M.
Binalong, New South Wales, 2008

AUSTRALIAN ABORIGINAL.

1: *Aboriginal Myths and Legends*

ABOUT 40,000 YEARS BEFORE THE COMING of the Europeans—and 36,000 years before the ancient Egyptian civilization reached its peak—our native people established their culture in Australia. They were a nomadic hunting folk who had reached this continent from the Asian landmass—Gondwana—and, in one of pre-history's epic migrations, in time they populated every part of it. When they came the land was rich in vegetation and wild life, but over the millennia the climate changed, turning grassland into desert. When the oceans rose Australia became an island and its inhabitants were marooned here.

The first European voyagers sailing along the continent's forbidding western and northern coasts thought the land was entirely desert, bereft of life, and the English later claimed it as *terra nullius*—empty land: land for the taking. In fact, the Aboriginal people had evolved a remarkable affinity with their surroundings. They were hunter-gatherers without the settled existence that Europeans equated with a culture. They had no supreme monarchs, no villages and no cultivated field, for their surroundings provided all they needed to survive, and Australia's verdant eastern regions, especially, provided food in abundance—fish, birds and animals. The Aborigines had few possessions and no understanding of the British concept of 'property', for their land belonged to all. They were great warriors and inter-tribal battles were common, but they showed no fear when confronted with the first Europeans, and little hostility. Within a generation of settlement they had all but disappeared, for the white man's bullets, European diseases and alcohol took a terrible toll on them. Yet they have obstinately, almost defiantly, refused to die out and their culture is now valued as the one unique element in Australia's own culture.

The Australian Aborigines have no written language. Their myths and legends have been passed down over the millennia by word of mouth, though few of their spoken languages (estimated to have once numbered 250) have survived. Their mythology is collectively called the Dreamtime and tells of the creation of the universe by ancestral beings whose activities in a primordial and featureless landscape resulted in the formation of the terrain and natural phenomena and the establishment of tribal law. The Aborigines consider themselves to be the direct descendants of one or other of these mythological beings and accept responsibility for that part of the country created by their ancestor. This is called an individual's 'Dreaming' or 'Totem' and lays on him or her a close personal link with everything in the environment. There is no question in the Aborigine's mind of the unknown, unseen God of European man. The proof of the Aborigines' beliefs is to be seen in their natural world: its rocks, watercourses, trees and animals. This makes their belief a physically real and living thing, and their secular and ritual life reflects the immediacy of this belief.

These mythological stories, some of them common to many tribes (or peoples), reveal that the Aborigines' ancestors had some of the failings of human beings, and serve as a moral warning to all those who do not strictly observe the tribal code, which is often a harsh one. Many of the stories are familiar to European Australians, and have been for more than a century.

The Making of Fire

In the Dreamtime, Mar was the only one to have fire and he refused to share it with the other Aborigines. They were very angry about this and decided to send Takkanna, the robin, to discover how it was made. One day as Mar prepared to cook his meat, Takkanna watched from behind a bush and saw Mar take the fire from beneath his headdress of feathers to light the grass and sticks. Without being seen, Takkanna pushed a twig into the fire and when it was alight flew away over the country with it.

As he flew, sparks fell from the twig and set fire to the land beneath. When Mar saw his fire had been stolen, he flew into a rage and in the ensuing battle turned into a cockatoo with red feathers on top of his head. Takkana the robin carries to this day his red breast as a reminder of his bravery in bringing fire to the Aborigines.

The Sun-Woman

Each morning as dawn breaks, Wuriupranili the sun-woman lights her torch of bark to carry across the sky and provide light for the day. The red of the sky in the morning is the red ochre with which she decorates her body. At the end of the day when she has reached the western horizon, she again decorates her body with red ochre before extinguishing the flames of her torch of bark and making her underground journey to the eastern horizon again.

The night journey across the sky is made by the moon-man, Japara, who carries the smouldering end of the bark to give a silvery light to the night sky.

How the Sun was Made

'For a long time there was no sun, only a moon and stars. That was before there were men on the earth, only birds and beasts, all of which were many sizes larger than they are now.

One day, Dinewan the emu and Bralgah the native companion were on a large plain near the Murrumbidgee. There they were quarelling and fighting. In her rage, Bralgah rushed to the nest of Dinewan, seized from it one of its huge eggs and threw it with all her force up into the sky. It broke on a heap of firewood there which burst into flame as the yellow yolk spilt all over it. The flame lit up the world below, to the astonishment of everything on it. They had been accustomed to the semi-darkness and were dazzled by such brightness.

A good spirit who lived in the sky saw how bright and beautiful the earth looked when lit up by this blaze. He thought it would be a good thing to make a fire every day, which from that time he has done. All that first night he and his attendant spirits collected wood and heaped it up. When the heap was nearly big enough, they sent out the morning star to warn those on earth that the fire would soon be lit.

They, however, found this warning was not sufficient, for those who slept saw it not. Then they thought they must have some noise made at the break of dawn to herald the coming of the sun and waken the sleepers; but for a long time they could not decide upon to whom they should give this office.

Then one evening they heard the laughter of Gougourgahgah, the laughing jackass, ringing through the air. 'That is the noise we want,' they said. Then they told Gougourgahgah that every morning as the morning star faded and the day dawned he was to laugh his loudest, so that his laughter might awaken all sleepers before sunrise. If he would not agree to do this then no more would they light the sun-fire, but instead would let the earth be ever in twilight again.

But Gougourgahgah saved the light for the world by agreeing to laugh his loudest at every

dawn. He has done this ever since, making the air ring with his loud cackling 'gou-gour-gah-gah, gou-gour-gah-gah, gou-gour-gah-gah-gah'.

When the spirits first light the fire it does not throw out much heat, but in the middle of the day when the whole heap of firewood is in a blaze, the heat is fierce. After that it begins to die gradually away until only the red coals are left at sunset, and they quickly die out (except a few which the spirits cover up with clouds and save to light the heap of wood they collect for the next day).

Children are not allowed to imitate the laughter of Gougourgahgah, lest he should hear them and cease his morning cry. If children do laugh as he does, an extra tooth will grow above their eye-tooth, so that they carry a mark of their mockery in punishment for it. Well do the good spirits know that if ever a time comes when the Gougourgahgah ceases to laugh, then the time has come when no more Daens (warriors) are seen on the land and darkness will reign once again.'

— FROM MORE ABORIGINAL LEGENDARY TALES, 1896,
   CATHERINE LANGLOH PARKER (C. 1855-1940).

The Southern Cross

Mululu, the chief of his tribe, had four daughters and no sons. He was getting old and worried that when he died there would be no-one to protect his daughters. So he called them together and suggested they come with him to the spirit world. He told them he had enlisted the aid of a medicine man who would help them on their journey.

When Mululu died, the daughters set out to find the medicine man, whom they knew had a long silver beard. After a long journey to the north they found him. He had plaited, from the strands of his silver beard, a rope which stretched up into the night sky. The four daughters climbed up the silver rope until they reached their father, who was the bright star we know as Centaurus; and his daughters can be seen close by as the four stars of the Southern Cross.

Uluru

Linga the lizard-man lived in the desert by himself and spent many days making a boomerang. When it was finished he threw it into the air to see if it would fly. It flew a long way and disappeared into the sand hills. Linga followed it and began to dig in the hills, piling up the sand, which is now Uluru, and making the huge holes and chasms that can be seen on the sides of the giant monolith.

The Black Swan

The Wibalu women owned the first boomerangs and would not share them with neighbouring tribes, who consequently decided to take them by force. Two men disguised themselves as white swans, thinking they would distract the women while others in their tribe stole the boomerangs. They were successful, but the furious Wibalu women returned to attack the swans. The swans took refuge on a big lagoon which, unknown to them, belonged to the eagles.

Resentful of the intrusion, the eagles flew at the swans, picking them up in their talons and carrying them off to a distant desert. As they flew, the eagles tore out the swans' white feathers which fell to the ground to become flannel flowers. The swans were finally left to die in the desert, their blood staining their beaks. A flock of crows saw them and, declaring that the eagles were also their enemies, plucked out some of their own black feathers which fluttered down onto the swans to keep them warm. Today, there are only one or two white feathers left on each black swan, to remind them of their terrible ordeal.

The Echidna's Spines

There was an old man called Echidna who lived alone, had nothing to do with others of his tribe and who, mysteriously, never left his hut to hunt. One day it was discovered that he killed and ate the flesh of young men whom he had lured to his hut. The members of the tribe decided to punish and kill Echidna, and so they attacked him with their spears which stayed in his body. Badly injured, Echidna crawled into a hollow log to recover. After a long time, he emerged but his hands and feet had become distorted and short, and had grown claws. That is why today Echidna still carries the spears on his back and can dig very quickly into the ground with his clawed feet when he is in danger.

The Creation of the Jenolan Caves

Mirragan was a hunter who was fishing in a deep waterhole in the Wollondilly River in New South Wales. There he saw a huge creature which was half fish and half snake called Gurangatch. He tried to catch the creature but it escaped by tearing up a valley and in doing so formed the Cox River. Mirragan tried again to catch Gurangatch, but this time he escaped by digging into the mountain and creating an enormous cave.

Mirigan climbed to the top of the mountain and thrust his spear into the cave, causing the blow holes that can be seen in the mountains today. Gurangatch burrowed even further into the mountains and into a deep waterhole on the other side of the mountains, where he was safe.

The Jenolan and Wombeyan caves and the deep waterholes in the Wollondilly and Cox rivers are the result of the battles fought between Gurangatch and Mirragan.

Gayardaree the Platypus

A young duck used to swim away by herself in the creek. Her tribe told her that Mulloka, the water devil, would catch her some day if she were so venturesome. But she did not heed them.

One day after having swum down the creek some distance, she landed on a bank where she saw some young green grass. She was feeding about when suddenly from a hidden place out rushed Biggoon, an immense water rat, and seized her.

She struggled and struggled, but all in vain. 'I live alone,' he said. 'I want a wife.'

'Let me go,' said the duck. 'I am not for you; my tribe has a mate for me.'

'You stay quietly with me, and I will not hurt you. I am lonely here. If you struggle more, or try to escape, I will knock you on the head, or spear you with this little spear I always carry.'

'But my tribe will come and fight you, and perhaps kill me.'

'Not they. They will think Mulloka has got you. But even if they do come, let them. I am ready.' And again he showed his spear.

The duck stayed. She was frightened to go while the rat watched her. She pretended she liked her new life, and meant to stay always; yet all the time she was thinking how she could escape. She knew her tribe was looking for her, for she heard them, but Biggoon kept her imprisoned in his hole in the side of the creek all day. He only let her out for a swim at night, when he knew her tribe would not come for fear of Mulloka.

She hid her feelings so well that at last Biggoon thought she really was content, and gradually he gave up watching her, and instead took his long day's sleep of old. Then came her chance.

One day, when Biggoon was sound asleep, she slunk out of the burrow, slid into the creek and swam away, as quickly as she could, towards her old camp.

Suddenly she heard a sound behind her. She thought it must be Biggoon, or perhaps the dreaded Mulloka, so, stiff as her wings were, she raised herself on them, and flew the rest of the way. She alighted at length, very tired, amongst her tribe. They all gabbled round her at once, hardly giving her time to answer them. When they heard where she had been, the old mother ducks warned all the younger ones only to swim up stream in the future, for Biggoon would surely have vowed vengeance against them all now, and they must not risk meeting him.

How that little duck enjoyed her liberty and being with her tribe again! How she splashed as she pleased in the creek in the daytime and flew about at night if she wished! She felt as if she never wanted to sleep again.

It was not long before the laying season came. The ducks all chose their nesting places, some in hollow trees, and some in mirrieh bushes. When the nests were all nicely lined with down feathers, the ducks laid their eggs. Then they sat patiently on them, until at last the little fluffy, downy ducks came out. Then in a little time the ducks in the trees took the ducklings on their backs and in their bills, and flew into the water with them, one at a time. Those in the mirrieh bushes waddled out with their young ones after them.

In due course the duck who had been imprisoned by Biggoon hatched out her young, too. Her friends came swimming round the

mirrieh bush she was in, and said: 'Come along. Bring out your young ones, too. Teach them to love the water as we do.'

Out she came, with only two children after her. And what were they? Her friends set up a great quacking gabble, shrieking, 'What are those?'

'My children,' she said proudly. She would not show that she, too, was puzzled as to why her children were quite different from those of her tribe. Instead of down feathers they had a soft fur; instead of two feet they had four; their bills were those of ducks; their feet were webbed; and their hind feet were just showing the points of a spear, like Biggoon, who always carried his in readiness for his enemies.

'Take them away,' cried her friends, flapping their wings and making a great splash. 'Take them away. They are more like Biggoon than us. Look at their hind feet; the top of his spear is sticking out from them already. Take them away, or we shall kill them before they grow big and kill us. They do not belong to our tribe. Take them away. They have no right here.'

They made such a row that the poor little mother duck went off with her two little despised children, of whom she had been so proud, despite their peculiarities. She did not know where to go. If she went down the creek, Biggoon might catch her again, and make her live in the burrow, or kill her children because they had webbed feet, a duck's bill, and had been hatched out of eggs. He would say they did not belong to his tribe. No-one would own them. There would never be anyone but herself to care for them. The sooner she took them right away the better.

So thinking, she went away upstream until she reached the mountains. There she could hide from all who knew her and bring up her children. On, on she went, until the creek grew narrow and scrubby on its banks. It was so changed from the broad streams which placidly flowed between the large unbroken plains near her home that she scarcely knew it. She lived there for a little while, but soon she felt too lonely and miserable to live and too unhappy to find food. Even her children grew to realize how different they were from her and so kept away by themselves. Thus pining, she soon died away on the mountains, far from her old noorumbah, or hereditary hunting-ground.

The children lived on and throve, laid eggs and hatched out more children just like themselves, until at last, pair by pair, they so increased that all the mountain creeks had some of them. And there they still live, the Gayardaree, or platypus, quite a tribe apart, for when did ever a rat lay eggs? Or a duck have four feet?

— *CATHERINE LANGLOH PARKER.*

2: *Ships and Seafarers*

Terra Australis

'The Australis Terra is the most southern of all lands and is separated from New Guinea by a narrow strait. Its shores are hitherto but little known . . . and seldom is the country visited unless sailors are driven there by storms . . .'
— CORNELIUS WYFLIET, 1598.

MORE THAN 4,000 VESSELS HAVE BEEN wrecked off Australia's coasts during our short recorded history, victims of storms and shoals and human error. Long before Europeans had suspected the existence of the Pacific Ocean, fables carried from the trade routes of Asia told of an immense continent in the southern latitudes that mapmakers called 'Terra Australis Incognita'—the unknown southern land.

The Portuguese and Spanish

In 1488, the Portuguese navigator Diaz, venturing further south along the western coast of Africa than any seaman had ever done before, rounded the Cape of Good Hope and sailed into the sparkling waters of the Indian Ocean. In 1499 Vasco da Gama, following Diaz's route, returned to Portugal in triumph, having reached India in the previous year, and related tales of a fabulous world of gold and spices and plunder. Seven years before, in 1492, Christopher Columbus—like Marco Polo, a spirited and fearless Italian—had sailed the other way, due west, for he knew the world was a sphere and that he could reach India by this more direct route. Instead, he discovered the Americas, an entire 'New World', as the navigator Amerigo Vespucci (another Italian) termed it.

Enter the Spanish. In 1522, the stricken survivors of Ferdinand Magellan's voyage around the world reported to the Spanish Court that they had found a channel through the islands that form the southern tip of South America. They had sailed through the channel and entered an ocean that dwarfed even the Atlantic in immensity

Magellan's flagship:
a 19th century view

—the Pacific. They had sailed across it to the Philippines and the East Indies—realms of wonder and danger, of potentates and pirates, and trade for the taking.

In 1568 another Spaniard, Mendana, sailed across the broad Pacific and discovered the Solomons. Later in 1577 Francis Drake sailed from England, ostensibly to search for the Great South Land, but in truth to challenge Spain's monopoly; he too returned in triumph having circumnavigated the world. Consumed with missionary zeal to convert the heathen to the Catholic faith, the Spanish navigator Quiros entered the Pacific Ocean from South America in 1605 and reached the New Hebrides.

But it was his lieutenant Torres, making a course for Spain by sailing west, who in 1606 sighted the southern coasts of New Guinea and the northern tip of Australia as he ventured through the straits which separate them. (So secretive were the Spanish that the existence of Torres Strait remained unknown until 1762, when an English fleet took Manila and discovered there Torres' charts and descriptions.)

By coincidence, the Dutch had also sighted Australia in 1606, when Janszoon sailed from Java in the tiny *Duyfken* ('dove'), and discovered the continent's northern coast—and Cape York, which he thought to be an extension of New Guinea.

The Mahogany Ship

Somewhere beneath the sands of Warrnambool on Victoria's south-eastern coast is buried Australia's most enduring maritime legend—the Mahogany Ship, said by some to be either a Spanish galleon or a Portuguese caravel dating from the 1500s. Unless it is a gigantic national hoax in which the locals have joined willingly (something not unknown in Australia!) it could well be the remains of our first shipwreck.

The wreck was first sighted in 1836 by sealers, who reported seeing a ship stranded on the beach to the harbour master at Port Fairy, who then verified its existence. According to descriptions it was a ship of 16th-century design, lying broadside on her stern amongst the sandhills.

Ten years later a bunch of keys of Spanish design and similar vintage were found under five metres of earth on the shores of Corio Bay, Victoria (east of Warrnambool). And, as far north as Cooktown in north Queensland, Aboriginal legends spoke of a cave there containing the skeletons of Europeans clad in 16th-century armour; survivors, perhaps, of a shipwreck who had retreated inland for safety. All these rumours—and some puzzling early maps—sparked conjecture that the Spanish or Portuguese had indeed sailed Australia's southern and eastern coasts centuries before the English and Dutch.

According to legend, a portion of the stern of the Mahogany Ship and the remains of three masts were still visible as late as 1860, and as recently as 1880 folk at Warrnambool maintained they had clambered over the remaining timbers of the ship's deck while sheep grazed near the wreck. But within a few years the encroaching sandhills had buried the remains and all recent excavations have failed to unearth so much as a single nail.

Dutch Courage

The 1600s would belong to the rising Protestant powers, the Dutch and the English, who, having challenged the waning might of Catholic Europe in matters of faith, could only survive by trade; a grim alternative to religion. Their maritime empires would grow along the sea lanes they opened.

In 1616, the Dutch explorer Schouten became the first to sail around the tip of South America into the Pacific (others had chosen the safer channel though the islands, the Straits of Magellan), and he named the stormy cape after his vessel, the *Hoorn*. The same year, another Dutchman, Dirk Hartog, encountered the coast of Western Australia and charted its bare line as far north as the North-West Cape, and returned six years later to its southern tip, Cape Leeuin.

The immensity of the southern continent (New Holland, as they called it) fascinated the Dutch. In 1642 the governor of the Dutch East Indies dispatched one Abel Tasman to explore its southern reaches. Beating across the Great Australian Bight, Tasman made landfall on the island in the south which now bears his name, but which he called Van Diemen's Land in honour of his superior. He then sailed further east, to discover and name New Zealand. But Tasman's report contained little to interest the East Indies Company. The native peoples he had encountered were unfriendly in the extreme, and ferocious, with little to barter. The Europeans' arrival had been premature.

The Gilt Dragon, *1656*

Anthropologists have often been puzzled by the number of fair-haired, blue-eyed Aborigines among tribes on Western Australia's coast. Locals have the answer: they are descendants of the hundreds of European, mainly Dutch, seamen shipwrecked there, some from ships whose names have disappeared from history.

Long before the English supremacy, the Dutch supplanted the Portuguese as the masters of the trade routes from Africa to south-east Asia, their ships beating across the broad northern reaches of the Indian Ocean in search of trade. The *Gilt Dragon*, weighing 600 tons and carrying 194 passengers and crew, was well off-course

when she struck a reef three sea miles off the coast south of the future site of Fremantle in April 1656. Only 68 people managed to reach the shore, of whom eight were selected to sail for Batavia in a small boat to bring help.

Within weeks, two rescue ships arrived at the scene, but no trace of the 60 survivors could be found. A well-armed party from one vessel went ashore and was never seen again.

In 1658, the Dutch East Indies Company sent another two ships to try and recover the *Gilt Dragon*'s treasure. A shore party of 14 men from one ship was left stranded when continual storms forced their vessel to make for the open sea. Tired of waiting for her to reappear, some of the Dutch sailors built boats from sealskins and sailed them to Batavia.

The Batavia *Horror*

The wreck of the *Batavia* and the subsequent mutiny and murders produced the most notorious episode in seafaring history—a tale of lust, bloodshed and betrayal that has few parallels. The *Batavia*, 500 tons and the flagship of the Dutch East India Company, left Holland in October 1628, bound for the Indies. She carried 316 people— crew, soldiers, merchants, women and children—and, in her holds, more than 250,000 guilders in coins. The senior merchant and commander, Francis Pelsaert, soon quarrelled with the *Batavia*'s captain, Adriaen Jacobsz, after the latter tried to force his attention on a woman, Lucretia van der Mylen. Rejected, Jacobsz initially consoled himself with Lucretia's maid, Zwartie Hendrix, until, overcome by his desire for her mistress, he and several confederates one night seized and raped her.

Mutiny was simmering when, at dawn on 4 June 1629, the *Batavia* struck a reef in the Albrohos group of islands and quickly foundered. The survivors managed to reach the islands from where Pelsaert and Jacobsz sailed in a skiff to Batavia (Jakarta) to get help. There the captain was thrown into gaol for his crimes, and Pelsaert was given a ship, the *Sardam*, in which to rescue the survivors

Among the survivors stranded on the Albrohos Islands, untold horrors had ensued. Resigned to a long stay, they had agreed to allow one Jeronimus Cornelisz and his confederates to assume command. Cornelisz was mentally deranged, a religious fanatic who believed that if man committed crimes of lust and murder then God must approve, for man was made in His image. As supplies dwindled, Cornelisz coldly decided to get rid of most of the survivors.

He chose eight women, including the unfortunate Lucretia, as concubines and ordered the rest to be killed. In an orgy of murder, the thugs began slaying 125 men, women and children, often pursuing their victims across the sands into the shallows.

'They also took men, women and children to an island called Seal's island, pretending that they would take care of them; meanwhile the wickedest murderers went along and killed some of the people left behind,' one survivor later recounted to a disbelieving Pelsaert.

Only one section of the survivors managed to challenge Cornelisz: a party of 50 led by a staunch private named Webbe Hayes sailed to a nearby island to provide a refuge for survivors, and fought off three attacks mounted on them by the mutineers.

Only the arrival of Pelsaert and the *Sardam*'s powerful cannon averted Hayes' murder. Over-awed, Cornelisz's group capitulated.

Pelsaert began to exact vengeance at once. Tortured to confess their crimes, Cornelisz and four henchmen were sentenced to death for murder, the penalty for which was the severing of their hands before they were hanged. On 2 October 1629 the bloody executions were carried out, and the bodies were left to rot on gibbets beneath the unrelenting sun. Two of the younger men were left

Francis Pelsaert — and a 17th century view of the murders of the ship's survivors

to fend for themselves on the coast of Western Australia. Departing the islands of death with the survivors and prisoners (many were destined to be tried and executed in Batavia), Pelsaert was to die, a broken man, one year later. Webbe Hayes was rewarded and promoted. Lucretia van der Mylen was to outlive all the main characters in the tragedy, remaining silent on the horrors she had undergone.

The wreck of the *Batavia* has inspired numerous books and recently an Australian opera.

Dampier

In 1688 came the English, the very year that saw the Protestant supremacy begin, and exactly a century after the Elizabethans' destruction of the Spanish Armada in 1588. William Dampier (1652–1715) sailed as one of a group of privateers (freelance men of war who were part-pirate), but unlike his fellows he was a skilled writer and his account of his various voyages, including his experiences along Australia's north-western coasts, became classics of the literature of the sea. His first impressions of the continent were unflattering (one reader has observed that he arrived at the worst time of the year for a visitor, high summer, and that he did not see Australia at her best):

'Being now clear of all the islands, we stood off south, intending to touch at New Holland, a part of Terra Australis Incognita, to see what that country would afford us. Indeed, as the winds were, we could not now keep our intended course without going to New Holland, unless we had gone back again ...

'The 4th of January, 1688 we fell in with the land of New Holland, having made our course due south ...we anchored January the 5th ... New Holland is a very large tract of land. It is not yet determined whether it is an island or a main continent; but I am certain that it joins neither to Asia, Africa nor America. This part of it that we saw is all low even land with sandy banks against the sea; only the points are rocky, and so are some of the islands in this bay.

'Seeing men walking on the shore, we presently sent a canoe to get some acquaintance with them, for we were in hopes to get some provisions ... But the inhabitants, seeing our boat coming in, ran away and hid themselves. In our search we found no water, but old wells on the sandy bays.

'At last we went over to the islands, and there we found a great many of the natives ... All the signs we could make were to no purpose, for they stood like statues without motion, but grinned like so many monkeys, staring onc upon the other.'

Dampier survived being marooned in the Nicobar Islands, from where he made a voyage in a small boat to Sumatra, wrote a justly famous account of his voyage (1697), and then returned to Australian waters in 1699, only to be faced with mutiny and the foundering of his decrepit ship off Ascension Island. He survived both mishaps, returning to England to later command other voyages. He rescued the marooned sailor Alexander Selkirk (who was the inspiration for Daniel Defoe's *Robinson Crusoe*, published in 1711). The early voyages to the South Seas also intrigued the Irish cleric Dean Swift, author of the rich satire *Gulliver's Travels* (1726), who placed one of his imaginary kingdoms, Lilliput, in a part of the map later known as South Australia!

William Dampier

The Zuytdorp

The mystery of the disappearance in the early 1700s of Holland's largest ship, the *Zuytdorp*, somewhere in the Indian Ocean, was solved by a stockman near Shark Bay on the coast of Western Australia in 1927.

Noticing some strange objects at the base of a cliff, he scrambled down to investigate and found on the shore a carved wooden figure and coins, along with part of an old cannon bearing the date 1711. The find entered local lore but was not announced until 1939, when the coming of war postponed investigations. And it was not until 1958 that divers began discovering more relics on the sea floor, all of them confirming that the wreck was indeed that of the *Zuytdorp*. Oddly, no human remains have been discovered, prompting many to think that the entire crew survived and made their way inland where they made contact with natives. But how the great ship came to be driven against the cliffs, so far from its route, remains an unanswerable question.

The Flying Dutchman

For nearly 300 years the folklore of the sea has spoken of a ghostly Dutch brig condemned to sail the oceans until eternity. Some say she originally carried plague, whilst others say her captain was damned to beat ceaselessly against the gales of Cape Horn for some crime he had committed.

In 1881, the future King George V of England and his brother, the Duke of Clarence, recorded in their journals a sighting of the ghost ship from the deck of HMS *Bacchante* off the Australian coast, while en route from Melbourne to Sydney:

'At 4 am the *Flying Dutchman* crossed our bows. A strange red light as of a phantom ship all aglow, in the midst of which the masts, spars, and sails of a brig two hundred yards distant stood out in strong relief as she came up on the port bow. The lookout man on the forecastle reported her as close on the port bow, where also the officer of the watch from the bridge clearly saw her, as did also the quarterdeck midshipman, who was sent forward at once to the forecastle; but on arriving there, no vestige ... was to be seen either near or right away to the horizon, the night being clear and the sea clam. Thirteen persons altogether saw her, but whether it was *Van Diemen* or the *Flying Dutchman* or who else must remain unknown. The *Tourmaline* and *Cleopatra*, who were sailing on our starboard bow, flashed to ask whether we had seen the strange light ...'

Sighting the *Flying Dutchman* was a presage of doom. On the following morning the sailor who had reported the ghost ship fell from the foremast onto the deck and was killed instantly. On arriving in Sydney, the Admiral was struck down with a sudden illness. The last ship's captain to see the doomed *Waratah* as she disappeared into a hurricane off the eastern coast of Africa in 1909 claims he sighted a ghostly sailing ship with old-fashioned rigging following her into the storm ...

James Cook RN

Captain Cook

Lieutenant James Cook, RN, captain of His Majesty's barque *Endeavour*, left Plymouth in August 1769, bound for Cape Horn and the Pacific Ocean, principally to enable the scientists he carried to observe from the island of Tahiti the transit of the planet Venus across the Sun, an event that would not occur again for a century. He was also empowered to search for the 'Continent or Land of Great Extent' reported to exist to the south of established sea routes. In October 1769 Cook sighted the North Island of New Zealand where he made landfall and, then sailing due west, became the first recorded European to sight the east coast

of Australia. Landing at Botany Bay, Cook and his principal scientist Joseph Banks were impressed by the landscape and astonished by the abundance and oddity of the birds, animals and plants. Cook sailed up the Queensland coast, which he meticulously charted, before striking a reef at the mouth of the Endeavour River which forced him to beach and repair his vessel. 'Land Animals are scarce,' Cook later wrote of Australia. 'The sort that is in the greatest plenty is the Kangooroo or Kanguru, so called by the Natives; we saw a good many of them around the Endeavour River, but kill'd only Three, which we found very good eating.' Cook claimed the entire eastern half of the continent of New Holland for Great Britain, calling it 'New South Wales', though no-one to this day knows why he chose the name, for our south-eastern coast bares no likeness to the coast of Wales or even southern Wales.

Cook returned in triumph to England, having discovered the extent of the Australian continent almost by accident. He led two more great voyages of discovery before his death at the hands of natives in Hawaii, but never returned to Australia, and for fifteen years his report of its existence hardly interested the authorities.

Bligh of the Bounty

'Just before Sun rise Mr Christian, Mate, Chas Churchill, Ships Corporal, John Mills, Gunners Mate and Thomas Burkitt, Seaman, came into my Cabin while I was asleep and seizing me tyed my hands with a Cord behind my back and threatened me with instant death if I spoke or made the least noise . . . Mr Christian had a cutlass in his hand, the others had Muskets and bayonet . . . I was forced on deck in my shirt, suffering great pain . . . I demanded the reason for such a violent Act, but I received no Answer but threats of instant death if I did not hold my tongue. . .'

— *LIEUT. WILLIAM BLIGH, RN, CAPTAIN, HMS* BOUNTY, *IN AN ACCOUNT OF THE MUTINY LED BY FLETCHER CHRISTIAN, APRIL 1789.*

1488, 1588, 1688, 1788: the dates sound like a ship's bells or cannon fire guiding Europeans closer and closer to Terra Australis. In 1788 three expeditions dispatched from Europe were approaching the fringes of the Pacific Ocean, all of them destined to leave a mark on Australian history. Two of them were British, commanded by officers of the Royal Navy who would loom large in our early history, and one was French. On 13 May 1787, eight ships loaded with convicts from England's overcrowded jails together with three storeships sailed from England under the command of Captain Arthur Phillip to found a settlement on the sandy shores of Botany Bay. They arrived there on 20 January 1788. Four days later, lookouts sighted strange ships approaching. They were French, the vessels of the Comte de La Pérouse's expedition dispatched by King Louis to explore the Pacific. The French exchanged courtesies with the English, made camp happily at

Lieut. William Bligh, RN, Captain, HMS Bounty

Botany Bay, then in March sailed away—into oblivion! It was the first of the extraordinary coincidences, and eerie disappearances, that haunt Australia's story. (The wreckage of their ships was found 50 years later, at Vanikoro Island, east of the Solomons.)

In December 1787, His Majesty's Ship the *Bounty*, commanded by Lieutenant William Bligh (1757–1817), left England bound for Tahiti. The purpose of this voyage was to pick up samples of the native plant, breadfruit, a staple food considered ideal for England's slaves in the West Indies. The voyage of the *Bounty* would be the most celebrated in British naval history. One wonders why: the *Bounty* was an insignificant ship, a barque of only 215 tons (little larger than a Manly ferry), the ship's company numbered only 34 in all, and the voyage's impact on the history of exploration would be negligible. Yet the voyage and the mutiny which took place were a microcosm of human passion, a drama of several acts each more extraordinary than its predecessor, and which have inspired numerous books and at least three films.

William Bligh had sailed with Cook on the latter's last voyage, as sailing master of the HMS *Resolution*, and had proved himself to be

a skilled cartographer. He was, in time, to prove himself a great seaman and under Admiral Lord Nelson, a brave and fearless officer. Yet
Bligh lacked the power of human understanding and despised his
inferiors and those he saw as fools, alienating them by his savage
tongue until he drove them not once but twice in his long career
to challenge his authority by mutiny. He was, however, no crueller
than other captains of the day in his application of the lash, and neither a sadist nor a brute.

Fletcher Christian, who was later to lead the mutiny on the
Bounty against Bligh, was not the strong and turbulent figure often
represented to us, but rather a simple man who rebelled against the
scorn levelled against him by an insensitive superior. He had been
singled out early for advancement by Bligh, who promoted him to
second in command and acting Lieutenant in March 1788, after ten
weeks at sea, when the *Bounty* was approaching Cape Horn. For
more than a month the *Bounty* battled against the gales of Cape
Horn before Bligh gave up and chose the easier passage via the
Cape of Good Hope, where he took on new provisions before sailing on.

By superb seamanship Bligh ran a course to Adventure Bay on
the southern tip of Tasmania and anchored there in August 1788.
His presence there was completely unsuspected by the colonists at
Sydney Cove. It was here, on Australian soil, that Bligh first fell out
with his officers, accusing them of inattention to their duties.
'Here', wrote the boatswain's mate, Morrison, whose journal now
resides in the National Library in Canberra, 'were sown seeds of
eternal discord between Lieut. Bligh and some of his Officers.' By
October 1788, only days before the *Bounty* reached Tahiti, Bligh,
the Master and the Surgeon were no longer on speaking terms.

To the men of the *Bounty*, Tahiti seemed paradise itself. Its climate and inhabitants restored their spirits and for men who had
not seen a woman for more than a year the native girls appeared to
be the incarnation of beauty. Crew members traded openly with
the natives and some took women; one party of three men deserted and when apprehended were punished by Bligh with a flogging.
(Only a naval court martial consisting of five officers of post-
Captain rank could order the death penalty; flogging was thus the
only corporal punishment Bligh could inflict.)

In early April 1789, the *Bounty*, her 'tween decks crowded with
a thousand breadfruit plants, left Tahiti for Torres Strait and the voyage to the West Indies.

Right:
Bligh in the hands of the mutineers:
from an engraving by Cruikshank

Eighteen days later, on 23 April, she made landfall at the Cook Islands, where a shore party under Fletcher Christian was troubled by natives. Bligh accused Christian of being a 'cowardly rascal' and asked him if he was afraid of a 'set of naked savages'. When natives then stole a boat anchor, Bligh, appalled by the incompetence of his men, called his officers and men 'a parcel of lubberly rascals'.

Then, on 27 April, noticing that a number of coconuts had disappeared, Bligh accused Christian of stealing them and called him a 'damned hound'. During the evening, a distraught Christian confessed to some of the crew

BLIGH'S BOAT ABANDONED BY THE "BOUNTY."

that he was planning to desert. According to one of the many conflicting accounts, a midshipman, Stewart, suggested that Christian instead take over command of the ship and sail back to Tahiti, in which case many would join him. Seven men immediately promised to stand by Christian if he chose to arrest Bligh.

Just before dawn on 28 April 1789, Christian and his followers burst into Bligh's cabin and hustled him on deck before casting him adrift with eighteen of his loyal sailors in the ship's launch, a sturdy longboat, with barely enough provisions to last them a month. Christian had originally offered the cutter, which could hold barely ten men and whose timbers were rotting, but several of his confederates protested. No blood had been shed, but the mutineers patently hoped that Bligh would perish. As one last insult they threw the thousand precious breadfruit plants into the ocean and then swung the *Bounty* back towards Tahiti.

Bligh calmly raised sail and set course for Timor. It would be a voyage of 3600 nautical miles (6000 kilometres in landlubber's terms). Using remarkable seamanship and by enforcing extremes of discipline and rationing, Bligh reached the Queensland coast in May 1789, having lost only one man to a native attack. He and his fellow survivors feasted on rock oysters and caught seabirds, before steering for the Dutch port of Koepang on Timor's south coast, which they entered on 14 June after an epic 41-day voyage. There Bligh dispatched his version of events to the British Admiralty, completed his log of his astonishing voyage (it is now in the National Library of Australia), and awaited a ship for England.

The Pandora

The Admiralty, having determined to bring the mutineers to justice, dispatched HMS *Pandora*, 24 guns, under the command of Captain Edward Edwards, a man whose reputation for harshness far exceeded Bligh's.

The wreck of the Pandora

Reaching Tahiti in March 1791, Edwards found 14 of the crew of the *Bounty* (some of whom greeted him joyfully, thinking they were being rescued) and clapped them in irons in a cage on the warship's deck before beginning a diligent search of the islands for the remaining nine mutineers.

For 86 days, Edwards combed the waters of the South Pacific before giving up and setting a course for the Endeavour Strait between Cape York and New Guinea to return to England.

When searching for a passage through the reefs of Torres Strait, disaster—some would say poetic justice—struck Edwards. The *Pandora* grounded on the Great Barrier Reef on 28 August 1791, and began taking water before keeling over. She sank the next day, her prisoners still locked in their cage. Just before she went under, a humane bosun's mate slipped the lock, allowing a handful to escape. Of the 134 men on the *Pandora*, only 99 survived.

Crammed into the ship's boats, they steered for Timor as Bligh had done, reaching the island in September. At Koepang, Edwards discovered Mary Bryant, her husband and their companions, the successful escapees from Sydney Cove. His vindictiveness was undiminished and he took them back to England with him in confinement, along with the ten surviving *Bounty* mutineers. After a naval court martial in August 1792, four mutineers were acquitted and six were sentenced to death for mutiny. Three of them, Burkett, Ellison and Millward, were hanged from the yardarm of HMS *Brunswick* in Portsmouth harbour; three others, Morrison, Muspratt and Midshipman Heywood, were reprieved, the last-named staying in naval service to eventually become a Captain.

Bligh, completely exonerated, would also climb the naval ladder and serve under Nelson's approving eye—and make another dramatic entry into Australia's story as victim, again, of mutiny, in the Rum Rebellion of 1808.

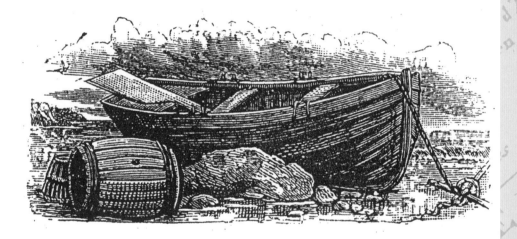

The Pitcairners

But what of Fletcher Christian and the rest of the mutineers? The men arrested by Edwards confessed that after the mutiny Christian had sailed the *Bounty* to Tubuai Island and then returned to Tahiti where the mutineers had quarrelled. Christian had sailed off with eight of the men, six islander couples, a baby girl and ten Tahitian women for an unknown destination. It turned out to be Pitcairn Island, a tiny speck in the Pacific first sighted in 1767 and wrongly plotted on the charts, where the settlers made themselves at home. But isolation and jealousies drove the men to murder, until only one European male was left, John Adams, when an American ship almost accidentally 'rediscovered' Pitcairn in 1809. The numerous descendants of the mutineers, their companions and the native women, the 'Pitcairners', vacated Pitcairn and moved their home in the 1850s to Norfolk Island, where they still flourish.

Mary Bryant

She was the first heroine of Australian history—and of a voyage of escape in a small boat that rivals Bligh's in sheer audacity. But while William Bligh was a trained naval officer with a crew of 18 sailors, Mary Bryant was a convict lass, a fisherman's daughter with little knowledge of navigation; yet she sailed a distance of 3,254 nautical miles from Sydney to Timor, only to be arrested there on her safe arrival.

Sentenced to transportation to Botany Bay for seven years for 'assault and stealing a cloak', Mary Broad was a Cornish girl who arrived with the First Fleet in 1788. She married a fellow convict, William Bryant, a fortnight after their arrival at Sydney Cove. Bryant, a skilled fisherman who had been sentenced for smuggling, was given the duty of catching fish for the settlement; using this freedom of movement, he approached the sympathetic skipper of a Dutch ship in harbour who gave him charts and a compass, quadrant, musket and ammunition. On the night of 28 March 1791, the Bryants, together with their infant son and daughter and seven fellow convicts, stole the governor's cutter and sailed out of Sydney Harbour; their destination was Timor. They progressed up the eastern coast of Australia for 69 days and reached the Dutch colony at Koepang without loss of life on 5 June 1791. There they told the authorities that they were survivors of shipwreck, but Captain Edwards, informed of their arrival, re-arrested them all and transported them back to England. William Bryant and his two children and three of his convict companions died on the way, and on arrival in England the survivors were again arraigned on trial and sentenced to Newgate prison.

James Boswell now enters the story. The fiery Scot, who in 1791 had published his classic biography of his beloved friend Dr Samuel Johnson (it appeared to mixed reviews) and soon afterwards survived a savage mugging in the backstreets he frequently haunted (London after dark was still unsafe), was already an ailing man in his early sixties and was to die only three years later, but his hatred of injustice was undimmed. A brilliant advocate, he devoted his energies to getting Mary and her fellow survivors freed. He succeeded in his self-appointed task late in 1793 and gave Mary an annuity of 10 pounds a year (their odd relationship has inspired much conjecture and a recent stage play). Mary Bryant settled down to life in

Cornwall where she was known as 'The Girl from Botany Bay' and one of the convicts, John Butcher, returned to Australia as a soldier of the New South Wales Corps and bccamc a law-abiding settler on the Hawkesbury.

Flinders and Tom Thumb

As a boy in Lincolnshire, Matthew Flinders (1774–1814) read Daniel Defoe's *Robinson Crusoe*, and dreamed thereafter of going to sea and faraway places. He joined the Royal Navy in 1790, aged sixteen, and the following year accompanied Bligh on the second (peaceful) breadfruit voyage to the Pacific.

In 1794, Flinders volunteered to accompany Governor Hunter to New South Wales, and met on board a surgeon, George Bass, with whom he formed a lifelong friendship. In 1795, Bass and Flinders embarked on a two-year series of voyages to explore the coast south of Sydney, sailing

Mathew Flinders

a tiny boat less than 2.5 metres long which they dubbed *Tom Thumb* as far as Port Hacking, surviving storms and mountainous seas.

In 1798, Bass and Flinders made their epic circumnavigation of Van Diemen's Land in the cutter *Norfolk*, and in 1801 Flinders sailed from England in command of the HMS *Investigator* on his greatest voyage: the circumnavigation of the entire continent. Returning to England in the *Porpoise*, Flinders was shipwrecked 700 miles (nearly 1,200 km) up the Queensland coast, and navigated the ship's cutter back to Sydney to get help for the 94 survivors. Commanding another ship, the tiny and barely seaworthy schooner *Cumberland,* he was attempting another return voyage to England when he had to stop at the French island of Mauritius, where, war having again broken out between France and England, he was kept under confinement until 1810. He was already stricken with a fatal illness but he lived long enough after his release and return to England to hold in his hands the splendid folio edition of his account of his discoveries, which was published in London the day before his death in 1814. It is to Flinders that we owe the first adoption of the name 'Australia' for the continent of 'Terra Australis' that all still referred to as New Holland.

The Wreck of the Neva

'The *Neva* sailed from Cork, Ireland, on 8 January, 1835. B.H. Peck was the master, and Dr Stevenson, RN, the ship's surgeon. She had on board 150 female prisoners and 33 of their children, nine free women and their 22 children, and a crew of 26. Several ships had been wrecked on King's Island, and when a vessel approached it the mate of the watch warned his men to keep a bright look out. He said, "King's Island is inhabited by the bloodiest man-eaters ever known; and, if you don't want to go to pot, you had better keep your eyes skinned." So the look-out man did not go to sleep.

'Nevertheless, the *Neva* went ashore on the Harbinger reef on 13 May, where she unshipped her rudder and parted into four pieces. Only nine men and 13 women reached the island; they were nearly naked and had nothing to eat, and they wandered along the beach during the night, searching amongst the wreckage. At last they found a puncheon of rum, up-ended it, stove in the head, and drank. The 13 women then lay down on the sand close together, and slept. The night was very cold, and Robinson, an apprentice, covered the women as well as he could with some pieces of sail and blankets soaked with salt water. The men walked about the beach all night to keep themselves warm, being afraid to go inland for fear of the cannibal blackfellows. In the morning, they went to rouse the women, and found that seven of the 13 were dead.

'The surviving men were the master, B.H. Peck, Joseph Bennet, Thomas Sharp, John Watson, Edward Calthorp, Thomas Hines, Robert Ballard, John Robinson, and William Kinderey. The women were Ellen Galvin, Mary Stating, Ann Cullen, Rosa Heland, Rose

Dunn and Margaret Drury. For three weeks these people lived almost entirely on shellfish. They threw up a barricade on the shore, above high water mark, to protect themselves against the cannibals. The only chest that came ashore unbroken was that of Robinson the apprentice, and in it was a canister of powder. A flint musket was also found among the wreckage, and with the flint and steel they struck a light and made a fire. When they went down to the beach in search of shellfish, one man kept guard at the barricade, and looked out for the blackfellows; his musket was loaded with powder and pebbles.

'Three weeks passed by before any of the natives appeared, but at last they were seen approaching along the shore from the south. At the first alarm all the shipwrecked people ran to the barricade for shelter, and the men armed themselves with anything in the shape of weapons they could find. But their main hope of victory was the musket. They could not expect to kill many cannibals with one shot, but the flash and report would be sure to strike them with terror, and put them to flight.

'By this time their diet of shellfish had left the survivors weak and emaciated, skeletons only just alive; the anthropophagi would have nothing but bones to pick. Still, the little life left in them was precious, and they resolved not to surrender easily. They watched the savages approaching; at length they could count their number. There were only 11 all told, and they were advancing slowly. As they drew closer, they saw that seven of the 11 were small, only picaninnies. When they came nearer still, three out of the other four were seen to be lubras, and the 11th individual then showed himself to be a white savage, who roared out, "Mates ahoy!"

'The white man was Scott, the sealer, who had taken up his abode on the island with his harem, three Tasmanian gins and seven children.

'They were the only permanent inhabitants; the cannibal blacks had disappeared, and continued to exist only in the fancies of the mariners. Scott's residence was opposite New Year's Island, not far from the shore; there he had built a hut and planted a garden with potatoes and other vegetables. Fresh meat he obtained from the kangaroos and seals. Their skins he took to Launceston in his boat, and in it he brought back supplies of flour and groceries. He had observed dead bodies of women and men, and pieces of a wrecked vessel cast up by the sea, and had travelled along the shore with his family, looking for anything useful or valuable which the wreck might yield. After hearing the story, and seeing the miserable plight of the castaways, he invited them to his home.

'On arriving at the hut, Scott and his lubras prepared for their guests a beautiful meal of kangaroo and potatoes. This was their only food as long as they remained on King's Island, for Scott's only boat had gone adrift, and his flour, tea, and sugar had been all consumed. But kangaroo beef and potatoes seemed a most luxurious diet to the men and women who had been kept alive for three weeks on nothing but shellfish.'

— ADAPTED FROM THE BOOK OF THE BUSH, *1870*,
GEORGE DUNDERDALE *(1822–1903)*.

The story ended happily, for the *Neva's* survivors were later rescued by a ship and taken to Launceston. But the safe passage of Bass Strait remained a challenge to ships' captains, for its waters were strewn with islets and rocks and its seas could be wild in time of storm. In the early hours of darkness on 4 August 1845, King Island at the western entrance of Bass Strait claimed another victim, the sailing ship *Cataraqui*, which struck a reef in a gale; her captain had been unable to establish his correct position by taking a sighting from the stars because of the persistent thick cloud. Of the 415 people (some accounts state 423) aboard her, mainly English immigrants, there were only nine survivors, and one of them gave a graphic description of the horror story to a Melbourne journalist.

The Wreck of the Cataraqui

'Immediately the ship struck, she was sounded, and four feet of water was in the hold. The scene of confusion and misery that ensued at this awful period, it is impossible to describe. All the passengers attempted to rush on deck, and many succeeded in doing so, until the ladders were knocked away by the workings of the vessel; when the shrieks from men, women and children from below were terrible, calling on the watch on deck to assist them. The crew, to a man, were on deck the moment the ship struck, and were instantly employed in handing up the passengers. Up to the time the vessel began breaking up it is supposed that between three and four hundred were got on deck by the extraordinary exertions of the crew. At this time the sea was breaking over the ship on the (sheltered) side, sweeping the decks, every sea taking away more of the passengers.

'About 5 a.m. the ship careened right over . . . washing away boats, bulwarks, spars, a part of the cuddy, and literally swept the decks. At this critical period the captain gave orders to cut away the masts . . . at this time the passengers below were all drowned, the ship being full of water, and the captain called out to those on deck to cling to that part of the wreck which was then above water, till daylight, hoping that the spars would be of some service in making a breakwater under her lee, and thus enable the survivors to get on

The wreck of the migrant ship Cataraqui

shore in the morning. As day broke we found the stern of the vessel washed in, and numerous dead bodies floating around the ships, and some hanging upon the rocks. Some of the passengers and crew (about 200 altogether) were still holding on to the vessel, the sea breaking over, and every wave washing some of them away. Those who were able, continued to cling to the wreck until about four in the afternoon (4 August) when she parted amidships . . . immediately about 70 or a hundred were launched into the tumultuous and remorseless waves! . . . The remains of the upper deck now began to break up and wash away. The survivors now began to collect bits of rope, so as to construct a buoy, with the view of floating it on shore [but it] could not be got nearer than twenty yards [about 20 metres] from the shore . . .

  'Thus [with] the sea breaking over them, the winds raging, and the rain continuing heavy all night, the poor survivors continued clinging to the ship's bow. Numbers died . . . and as day broke the following morning, it discovered only about 30 left alive . . .'

— GEORGE DUNDERDALE.

Only nine survivors made it to the shore, which was strewn with wreckage and bodies, and next day they saw approaching several of the island's settlers, who had noticed wreckage around the coast. As the settlers' own boat had been wrecked, the survivors remained on King Island another five weeks before on 7 September signalling a passing ship, which landed them in Melbourne a week later.

The Lost Ships

'Before any white man had made his abode in Gippsland, a schooner sailed from Sydney chartered by a new settler who had taken up a station in the Port Phillip district. His wife and family were on board, and he had shipped a large quantity of stores, suitable for commencing life in a new land. It was afterwards remembered that the deck of the vessel was encumbered with cargo of various kinds, including a bullock dray, and that the deck hamper would render the vessel unfit for bad weather.

'As she did not arrive at Port Phillip within a reasonable time, a cutter was sent along the coast in search of her; and her long boat was found ashore near the Lakes Entrance, but nothing else belonging to her was ever seen.

'When the report arose in 1843 that a white woman had been seen with the blacks, it was supposed that she was one of the passengers of the missing schooner, and parties of horsemen went out to search for her among the natives, but the only white woman ever found was a wooden one: the figure-head of a ship.

'Some time afterwards, when Gippsland had been settled by white men, a tree was discovered on Woodside station near the beach, in the bark of which letters had been cut, and it was said they would correspond with the initials of the names of some of the passengers and crew of the lost schooner. By their appearance, they must have been carved many years previously. This tree was cut down, and the part of the trunk containing the letters was sawn off and sent to Melbourne. There is little doubt that the letters on the tree had been cut by one of the survivors of that ill-fated schooner, who had landed in the long boat near the Lakes, and had made their way along the Ninety-Mile Beach to Woodside. They were far from the usual track of coasting vessels, and had little chance of attracting attention by signals or fires. Even if they had plenty of food, it was impossible for them to travel in safety through that unknown country to Port Phillip, crossing the inlets, creeks and swamps, in daily danger of losing their lives by the spears of the natives. They must have wandered along the Ninety-Mile Beach as far as they could go, and then, weary and worn out for want of food, yet reluctant to die the death of the unhonoured dead, one of them had carved the letters on the tree, as a last despairing message to their friends, before they were killed by the savages, or succumbed to starvation.'

— *GEORGE DUNDERDALE.*

The Wreck of the Marie

The brigantine *Marie* departed the newly-founded settlement of Adelaide on 7 June 1840 bound for Hobart Town. She carried 26 souls, including passengers, and a cargo of 4,000 English sovereigns, but she struck rocks in Lacepede Bay, on the desolate Coorong coast near present-day Kingston, and she began to break up. All aboard made it to shore, where numerous Aborigines greeted them with hostility. Bribed with silver watches and jewellery, the Aborigines accompanied the survivors on their long walk to the nearest settlement, a whaling station 200 kilometres distant. The group had reached the mouth of Lake Albert and was crossing the broad Coorong in dugouts when the Aborigines turned on them, killing all the Europeans—men, women and children—except for one woman, who swam to safety. She eventually reached the mouth of the Murray, then disappeared. For years afterwards rumours spread of a woman with red hair who was living with the tribes of the Lower Murray. The gold aboard the *Marie* was never found.

Castaways

Hundreds of survivors of shipwrecks reached the Australian coast, where many of them were taken care of by Aboriginal people, and others savagely killed.

On 21 May 1836, the brig *Stirling Castle*, six days out of Sydney bound for Singapore, struck a reef off the Queensland coast, not far from the future Port Bowen. It was the second time the master, James Fraser, had been shipwrecked. All aboard took to three boats: Fraser and his pregnant wife Eliza and 17 men in one, with the two other boats carrying 19 others. After weeks in open boats, the survivors reached an island near the coast, where seven men under the bosun took a boat in which they landed near the Clarence River. There several were killed by Aborigines, whilst others died of starvation; only one of the party survived.

Captain Fraser, his wife Eliza (who had just given birth, though the baby died) and several others reached Great Sandy Island (later Fraser Island) where they were taken to the mainland by Aborigines, while others in the crew set out overland for Moreton Bay (Brisbane), 160 kilometres away, to get help. Soon afterwards, Fraser was attacked by the blacks and speared to death before his wife's eyes, and another crew member was roasted. From Moreton Bay, a search party led by a convict John Graham rescued Eliza Fraser on 11 August. She returned to Sydney and later married a ship's master named Green, with whom she sailed to England.

A year later, the whaler *Carib* was wrecked off the Nuyt's Archipelago and one of the survivors, William Jackman, was captured by tribesmen. Nearly three years later, the whaler *Camilla* put in to a nearby bay for water and Jackman was rescued. His book *An Australian Captive* (published in 1853) was a valuable account of Aboriginal life seen through the eyes of an ordinary Englishman who was the victim of extraordinary circumstances.

Ship's Belles

In 1857, the *Seabelle* was wrecked off Breaksea Spit at the northern end of Fraser Island and was presumed lost with all hands. Within two years, however, rumours reached Brisbane that survivors were living with natives, prompting Captain Arnold to sail from Maryborough in the Coquette to initiate a search.

He found two young European girls, their faces disfigured by tribal markings but otherwise well. The elder one, aged 17 and named Kitty, informed the captain that the tribesmen had killed the rest of the crew and passengers. Both girls were taken to Sydney and placed in the care of an institution, from where their names disappear from history.

Barbara Thompson

One day in October 1849, when HMS *Rattlesnake* lay anchored in a bay near Prince of Wales Island off Cape York, a group of her sailors ashore watched uneasily as a party of natives approached them. Suddenly, one of the natives, paler than the rest and naked but for a palm-frond skirt, cried out, in halting English, 'I am a Christian. I am so ashamed.'

She spoke with an Aberdeen accent. The English sailors shouted to one of their mates, 'Hey, Scottie! We've found a Scotch girl!', and when the Scot took her under his care and began to bathe her, she told him her extraordinary story.

She had been born Barbara Craufurd and had immigrated to Australia with her Scots parents. In 1844, aged 16, she had eloped with a sailor named Thompson and sailed with him in search of a cargo vessel reputed to be stuck fast on a reef in Torres Strait. When their ship was wrecked, she had been the sole survivor and the natives, believing her to be one of their tribe who had come back from the dead, had cared for her ever since. She had even met another European who lived with a tribe on an island to the north renowned for their savagery; they had once killed the entire 20-man crew of a French vessel that had run aground there. Taken aboard the *Rattlesnake* and dressed in clothes donated by the ship's company, Barbara Thompson was taken to Sydney. She later remarried and lived until 1912.

The Wreck of the Dunbar

A giant anchor salvaged from the clipper *Dunbar* stands as her memorial atop 'the Gap'—the high cliffs of Sydney's South Head. It is all that was saved from her wreck, apart from one survivor.

The *Dunbar*, launched in 1853, was one of the fastest sailing ships on the England-Australia route; she was one of a new class known as 'clippers', designed for speed, and cut the voyage from one of 140 days to just 90. She sailed from Plymouth on her second voyage to Sydney Town on 31 May 1857, carrying 121 souls and ample cargo, and had passed Botany Bay after a voyage without incident in the late afternoon of 20 August 1857 when her captain, concerned by worsening weather, decided to make for Sydney Harbour, despite a bitter southerly gale and poor visibility due to heavy rain squalls. Glimpsing the Macquarie Light on South Head, he decided to enter the port just before midnight, but apparently mistook the 'Inner South Head' (the Gap) for the South Head itself. The wind had swung round to the south-east when the *Dunbar*'s mate shouted 'Breakers ahead!' But the ship then struck the rocks below the Gap; with her hull ripped open, her topmasts falling, she healed violently to starboard and went under in the dark and stormy winter night, taking nearly everyone on board with her. Several men including the boatswain and a seaman clung to the cliff face as waves crashed below and over them. Only the seaman, James Johnson, survived; clinging to his foothold for 36 hours until his weak cries were heard, he was hauled to safety on 22 August.

An inquiry attached no blame to *Dunbar*'s captain, for the severity of the storm made it impossible for him to drop anchor; he was an experienced seaman and had chosen not to ride out the storm at sea (as more sensible captains would have done). But a light was soon erected on the Inner South Head, the Hornby Light, and the inquiry recommended that a pilot service should thereafter guide vessels into Sydney Harbour as they had long done at the treacherous entrance to Port Phillip Bay. Soon steam-powered passenger and cargo ships took over from sail, and reduced the dangers of the elements.

The Mystery of the Waratah

The new Blue Anchor Line steamer *Waratah* left Sydney for London in June 1909 carrying 211 crew and passengers and crossed the Indian Ocean without incident. But at Durban a passenger left the ship, explaining he had been haunted by strange dreams of impending doom. The *Waratah* left Durban and was sighted by two passing ships as a hurricane blew up, and she then disappeared. No

trace of her was found despite two searches in the following months by specially-chartered steamers. One captain who had passed the *Waratah* before she disappeared said that he sighted a sailing ship with old-fashioned rigging following the Australian ship into the hurricane and gave his opinion that it was the 'ghost ship', the *Flying Dutchman*.

Birth of a Navy

Australia was the first Dominion to form her own Navy, after decades of opposition to the idea from the Admiralty. Britain's policy changed overnight when the growing threat from German naval construction was understood, and the Royal Australian Navy (RAN) was born in 1911, consisting of little more than the old colonial gunboats and three newly-built destroyers; 'a tin pot navy' as one critic of their cost described them.

But more ships were being built and the RAN's First Fleet proudly steamed into Sydney Harbour in October 1913, consisting of the giant battle-cruiser HMAS *Australia*, three cruisers and three destroyers, soon joined by two small submarines.

The cruiser HMAS *Sydney* sank the German cruiser *Emden* off the Cocos Islands in November 1914 in one of the first naval victories of the war, and both submarines were later lost (AE1 disappeared with all hands off the coast of New Guinea in 1914, and AE2 was sunk after forcing the Dardanelles in 1915). But the rest of the war was an anti-climax for the RAN, with no ships lost and few actions fought.

In the 1920s, most of the ships were sold off or scuttled and many suggested that the RAN was no longer a necessity and should be disbanded. Wiser heads ruled. New cruisers were ordered from British shipyards and at the outbreak of war in 1939 the RAN was a sizeable force: two heavy cruisers and three modern light cruisers (in addition to five ageing destroyers and smaller ships, and the obsolete cruiser HMAS *Adelaide*, which was kept in Australian waters).

Of the five modern cruisers, three were lost in action (*Canberra*, *Sydney* and *Perth*) and two were almost sunk. The *Hobart* was hit off the Solomons by torpedoes which caused high loss of life, and the flagship *Australia* took the heaviest battering of all: she was struck again and again by kamikaze suicide aircraft (which seemed to single out the three-stacker for special punishment) in the great 1944–45 battles off the Philippines, and suffered heavy casualties. Of the five old destroyers of the 'Scrap Iron Flotilla', only two survived the war. No other navy in the world suffered such heavy ship losses in relation to its size.

The first HMAS Sydney

The two cruisers named *Sydney* were among the most famous warships in the Royal Australian Navy and they shared more than their name in common.

The first HMAS *Sydney* was a coal-burning light cruiser of 5,400 tons mounting eight 6-inch guns, and was launched on the Clyde in Scotland in 1912 for the infant Royal Australian Navy. She carried a ship's company of 400 officers and men. Her adversary was a slightly smaller German light cruiser, the *Emden*, armed with ten 4-inch

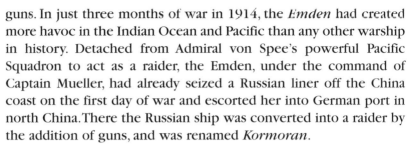

guns. In just three months of war in 1914, the *Emden* had created more havoc in the Indian Ocean and Pacific than any other warship in history. Detached from Admiral von Spee's powerful Pacific Squadron to act as a raider, the Emden, under the command of Captain Mueller, had already seized a Russian liner off the China coast on the first day of war and escorted her into German port in north China. There the Russian ship was converted into a raider by the addition of guns, and was renamed *Kormoran*.

The *Emden* reached the Pacific Ocean in early September 1914 disguised as a British cruiser by adding a dummy fourth funnel— and in just four days sank six allied merchant ships and then one week later shelled the Indian port of Madras, setting alight the huge oil tanks there. On 25 September, the *Emden* appeared off Colombo and in three days sank another four ships and captured a coaler. Hunted by no fewer than sixteen allied warships, she then put into Diego Garcia island for supplies—where the British, lacking a wireless, were unaware war had broken out, and entertained the Germans royally—before steaming for the waters south of India where in a few hours (20 October) she sank four British ships and eight days later steamed into Georgetown on the Malaya coast sinking a Russian and a French warship before escaping.

On the morning of 9 November 1914, her spectacular career came to an end. When she appeared off Cocos Island, the wireless operators had time to report the presence of a 'strange warship' and, to the warships escorting the Australian troop convoy steaming past the islands barely 50 miles away, this brief message meant only one thing: the *Emden* was there. Detached from the convoy, the HMAS *Sydney* steamed for Cocos Island at full speed and hit the *Emden* in a tornado of shells, driving her, burning, onto a coral reef at 11.20 a.m. Captain Mueller was among the many German dead. It was one of the most spirited naval victories of the war.

As for *Kormoran*, she had a less successful career than *Emden*, but while hunting for her fruitlessly three Australian destroyers chugged 270 km (150 miles) up the dark Sepik River in northern New Guinea. The *Kormoran*, apparently out of fuel, later put in to the American island of Guam in December 1914 and was interned. The ship then disappears from history.

HMAS Sydney: *'Missing, Believed Lost'*

By 1941 the second HMAS *Sydney* was the pride of the Royal Australian Navy, a veteran of two years' active service. Originally laid down for the Royal Navy as HMS *Phaeton*, she was a light cruiser of 7,000 tons, completed in 1935, and re-named by the RAN in honour of her predecessor. Sailors say it brings bad luck to re-name a ship. Phaeton was the 'Shining One' of Greek mythology, offspring of Phoebus the Sun, the young god who brought destruction to the coasts of Africa and would have set the world aflame had not Zeus transfixed him with a thunderbolt.

Employed after the outbreak of war in 1939 on nine months of patrol and escort duties, *Sydney* had joined the British Mediterranean Fleet in May 1940. One month later France left the war and Italy entered the conflict, and for a year the fleet fought against great odds. Commanded by Captain John Collins, *Sydney* joined in the bombardment of Italian defences on the north African coast, sank an enemy destroyer on 28 June, fought in the Battle of Calabria, survived murderous air attacks and then tackled two enemy cruisers in a famous action off the coast of Crete on 19 July 1940, sinking one of them, the *Bartolomeo Colleoni*, and damaging the other. She survived six months of constant battle, including steaming into the Adriatic at night to sink enemy shipping, without the loss of a single man and was known as 'Lucky *Sydney*' when she returned to Australian waters early in 1941.

On 11 November 1941, *Sydney*, now commanded by Captain J. Burnett, left Fremantle to escort the troopship *Zealandia* to the Sunda Strait (between Java and Sumatra). She handed over *Zealandia* to a new escort on 17 November and set course for Fremantle. After that, nothing more was heard from her. Concern grew after 22 November, the estimated day of her return, but wireless messages to her brought no response and air searches found no trace of the Australian cruiser.

On 30 November more than 300 German sailors were found drifting in boats off the Western Australian coast near Carnarvon. They were survivors of a German raider disguised as a harmless merchant ship; her name was *Kormoran*. At over 9,000 tons, powered by diesel and armed with powerful hidden guns and underwater torpedo tubes (in addition to two aircraft), *Kormoran* was larger than the Australian cruiser, and nearly as well armed. She had already sunk numerous Allied ships. Over the next few days the story of *Sydney*'s fate was finally pieced together.

At about 4 p.m. on 19 November the *Kormoran*, then prowling for Allied or neutral merchant ships in the Indian Ocean 150 miles (about 250 kilometres) south-west of Carnarvon, Western Australia, sighted smoke on the horizon. It was *Sydney*. When the Australian cruiser was seven miles distant (11 kilometres) she altered course to investigate the suspicious ship, ordering *Kormoran* by searchlight signal to identify herself. The German captain, Detmers, replied that his was a Dutch ship, the *Straat Malakka*. By about 5.15 p.m. the Australian cruiser had drawn closer and was steaming broadside on, barely one nautical mile (about 1,700 metres) from the disguised German ship, demanding further identification. According to the official history of the RAN, *Sydney* was at Action Stations, with all her guns manned, but no one knows—if German accounts are true—why Captain Burnett took his ship so close to an unidentified vessel.

At 5.30 p.m., *Sydney* demanded: 'Show Your Secret Sign'. Knowing the game was up, Detmers dropped his disguise, striking his Dutch flag and hoisting the German war flag and launching torpedoes at the precise moment that his hidden guns opened fire with a tornado of shells. According to German survivors, *Sydney*, cruising at point blank range, was struck in just four seconds by shells, cannon and machine-guns, and then crippled by a torpedo. But the Australian cruiser's X (upper rear) turret fought back, firing salvoes that struck the raider's engine room, starting a fire that was to prove fatal for her. Wracked by explosions, *Sydney* launched her torpedoes to no effect, and drifted away, on fire, to the south. She was last seen as a glow on the horizon that disappeared at approximately 10 p.m.

HMAS Sydney *pursuing the Italian cruisers in the Cape Spada battle, July 1940 (Frank Norton, Australian War Memorial, Canberra)*

But the *Kormoran* was also doomed. Seventy Germans had been killed and as fires approached his fuel tanks and hundreds of mines, Detmers ordered the ship to be abandoned, and his men took to boats, in which some reached the bleak coast, and in which the majority were found drifting. Nothing was ever found of *Sydney* and her 645 officers and men; except an empty life raft. Her loss was the greatest tragedy in Australian maritime history.

But for more than 60 years the tragedy has remained a mystery. Too many questions have never been satisfactorily answered and numerous books have pointed out discrepancies in eyewitness accounts of *Sydney*'s end. (More books have been written about HMAS *Sydney* than any other warship, for her record in war was outstanding and her end inexplicable.) Why did Burnett hazard his ship? Why did *Sydney* not fly off her spotter aircraft to investigate the unknown vessel? As there were no eyewitnesses to the battle other than the German survivors, could they be relied on to tell the truth? Why were there no survivors from the *Sydney*, when the

ship took five hours to sink, while the German survivors were found in full health after eleven days adrift? How could the German war flag have been hoisted without *Sydney* opening fire within seconds? In other words, did *Kormoran* fire the first shots while still under false colours (an act regarded as a war crime)? Was *Sydney* at Action Stations, as the official history avers, or only at cruising stations or Second Degree of Readiness?

A federal parliamentary inquiry that heard evidence for more than a year and released a detailed report on the loss of *Sydney* in 1999 failed to solve the mystery.

The end of the 66-year search and the astonishing discovery of the wrecks of HMAS *Sydney* and *Kormoran* 130 sea miles (over 200 kilometres) off the Western Australian coast in March 2008 is described in more detail on page 428.

HMAS Sydney, *seen before her wartime camouflage was added*
AWM Photo 6400

The 'Scrap Iron Flotilla'

Radio Berlin called them 'Australia's ridiculous collection of scrap iron'. They were five of the oldest destroyers in the Mediterranean Fleet and their Australian sailors called them 'the Crocks'. But they became a legend.

Dating from 1917–18, they were on loan to the Royal Australian Navy from the British Admiralty and were saved from the scrap-iron merchants at the last moment, when the British Navy foresaw a desperate need for destroyers if war came again. Their names were *Stuart*, *Voyager*, *Vendetta*, *Vampire* and *Waterhen*. They were all ageing, thousand-ton V- and W-class destroyers, and their flotilla leader, HMAS *Stuart* (Commander Hector Waller, RAN) was just as old. But they were strongly-built ships and, like all destroyers, faster than a cruiser, capable of 34 knots if their engines could stand the strain. In November 1939 they slipped out of Australian ports, course set for Singapore, but were then ordered to the Mediterranean. The Commander-in-Chief, Admiral Cunningham, wrote soon afterwards: 'The officers and men of these Australian destroyers are magnificent material and quite wasted out here in these old ships. (Rear-Admiral) Tovey has suggested that they might be transferred lock, stock and barrel to five new ships and used at home. They certainly are the most lively and undefeated fellows I have ever had to do with.' But the ebullient Australian sailors were destined to man their old ships for a year of the hardest fighting of the Mediterranean war.

The 'Scrap Iron Flotilla' fought under the legendary 'Hec' Waller separately and together in fleet actions from the Battle of Calabria to the Battle of Matapan (March 1941), made 139 runs in and out of the beleagured fortress of Tobruk (the 'Tobruk Ferry Run'), mostly under cover of night, and served in the Aegean, bringing troops off Crete and bombarding the enemy coast during the Syrian campaign: enough service for the most modern of warships. In all these campaigns, the skies were dominated by enemy dive-bombers. HMAS *Vampire*, her engines almost worn out, was the first to be sent home; exactly one month later (29 June 1941) HMAS *Waterhen*, the beloved 'Chook', was crippled by dive-bombers off Sollum and sank the next day. In mid-July, the *Voyager* limped into Alexandria on one engine and was ordered home; HMAS *Stuart* followed her a month later. HMAS *Vendetta* was the last to leave 'the Med', in October 1941, after nearly two years' active service in the Northern Hemisphere.

This was not the end. In December 1941, Japan struck in the Pacific, and HMAS *Vampire*, based in Singapore, fought in the Malaya campaign; she was sunk off Ceylon with the carrier HMS *Hermes* in April 1942 after taking 13 direct hits from Japanese

bombs. HMAS *Voyager*, ferrying reinforcements to the commandos on Timor, was lost on the Timor coast in September 1942 (her rusting remains can still be seen), and only *Vendetta* and *Stuart* survived the war. *Vendetta* was scuttled off Sydney Heads, graveyard of warships, in 1948.

Yarra's *Last Fight*

HMAS *Yarra* was an Australian-built sloop (a class later known as frigates), twice the size of a corvette but only half the size of a World War II destroyer, and much slower: her speed was barely 17 knots. Launched in 1936, the first of four built at Cockatoo Island for the Royal Australian Navy, she carried three 4-inch guns and 136 officers and men. All four sloops saw an enormous range of service but few could match *Yarra*'s record. Despatched from Australian waters (under the command of Lieut-Commander Harrington) for escort duty in the Red Sea, she was soon in action. During the British invasion of Iran on the night of 24 August 1941, she formed part of a motley flotilla which sailed to seize the three vital Iranian ports at the head of the Persian Gulf. She was the first ship to reach Khorramshahr, sinking the Iranian sloop *Babr* with ten salvoes before steaming up the Karun River to bombard enemy positions and board two gunboats. Recalled to the Pacific, *Yarra* was escorting the last convoy into Singapore on 5 February 1942 when the liner *Empress of Asia*, carrying more than 2,000 reinforcements, was struck by Japanese dive-bombers and left burning and sinking. The *Yarra* rescued 1,800 of the troops from the fire-ravaged ship.

Singapore fell to the Japanese ten days later, and Java fell two weeks later. On the night of 28 February 1942, the last Australian cruiser in Java waters, HMAS *Perth*, with the cruiser USS *Houston*, steamed for Sunda Strait between Sumatra and Java to make a break for home, but just before midnight encountered a 60-ship Japanese convoy. In an hour of unequal battle in the exploding darkness, *Perth* was sunk (with the loss of Captain Hec Waller and 350 of his men), followed soon afterwards by *Houston*, taking four enemy ships with them.

On the next day, 2 March 1942, HMAS *Yarra* (Lieut-Commander Robert Rankin, RAN), left the southern Java waters as sole escort of a small convoy of three small merchant vessels, under orders to make for Fremantle (a four-day voyage) and hopefully elude the Japanese task forces known to be in the area. Just after 6.30 a.m. on 4 March 1942, the *Yarra*, steaming in the Indian Ocean far off the north-west coast of Western Australia, sighted a fleet of warships closing on them fast; their pagoda-like fighting tops identified them as three Japanese cruisers accompanied by two destroyers. With alarm rattles sounding, Rankin ordered 'Signal the convoy to scatter' and addressed his men: 'We don't stand much chance, lads, but we can at least show them how a good ship goes down.' Hoisting battle ensigns and laying a smokescreen, *Yarra* turned to do battle. In less than an hour, all three merchantmen had been sunk and the *Yarra* was devastated by enemy shells, her bridge destroyed and Rankin killed. Her survivors were ordered to abandon ship and for three hours the Japanese circled her blazing hull pouring into her point-blank fire; but she refused to sink.

At 10 a.m. the game little ship finally went under and the enemy fleet steamed from the scene, making no attempt to help survivors. Only 13 of *Yarra*'s men survived, to be rescued five days later from life rafts by the Dutch submarine K11.

Breaking with tradition, Australia's new Collins-class submarines carry the names of past heroes of the Royal Australian Navy to perpetuate their memory: among them are *Collins*, *Farncomb*, *Dechaineux*—and *Waller* and *Rankin*.

Tragic Timor

This small mountainous island north west of Darwin has occupied an importance in Australian history out of all proportion to its size. The Portuguese, in search of the riches of the East, arrived there as early as 1511—only nineteen years after Columbus had discovered America!—and soon established a settlement around the fine harbour of Dili on Timor's north coast. They were followed by their rivals the Dutch, who claimed all the East Indies, established themselves on the south-west coast at Koepang (Kupang) and spent two centuries contesting the Portuguese claim to the island.

William Dampier sought refuge on Timor after being shipwrecked, as did William Bligh, who steered a course for Koepang after his epic open-boat voyage in 1789; as did Mary Bryant and her fellow escapees from Botany Bay. George Grey used the hardy Timor ponies on his expeditions in north-west Australia in the 1840s, and a century later (in the 1930s) Dili became an important refuelling point for Qantas's flying boat service. The stretch of

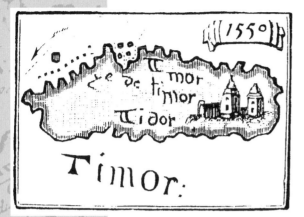

ocean known as the 'Timor Gap' between Timor and Darwin is the widest distance over ocean on the entire England-Australia route.

Early in 1942, as the Japanese tide swept south, a small Australian unit, 'Sparrow Force', mainly recruited from resourceful Western Australian country men, defended Dili before retreating into the mountainous hinterland, rejecting all enemy demands for their surrender. Portuguese Timor's small population was ninety per cent Christian and the native people sustained the Australians, acting as scouts and guides, supplying them with food, bearers and ponies, despite cruel reprisals. It was two months before Darwin picked up the first signals from Sparrow Force's crude wireless, but in the months following ammunition and supplies reached them by air and sea. By early in 1943 when the last commandos were evacuated from Timor, they had killed nearly a 1,000 Japanese for the loss of 26 of their own men.

The 'Nutshell Navy'

At sea, the cost of maintaining the commandos on Timor had been high. The old veteran HMAS *Vendetta*, one of the intrepid 'Nutshell Navy' of small ships that had sustained the commandos, was lost off Betano Bay on the south coast in September 1942, and on 1 December the little corvette HMAS *Armidale*, caught in daylight in the Timor Sea, fought off attack by an entire squadron of dive-bombers and was then set upon by nine bombers, three Zeros, and a torpedo-armed amphibian, which finally sank the game little ship. Of the hundreds of refugees, Dutch native troops and crew members aboard her, only 49 men were later rescued.

For the people of Timor the cost of resistance had also been high. Perhaps 50,000 Timorese died during the Japanese occupation, mainly by starvation, and after the Indonesian invasion of 1975 another 100,000 died or were savagely killed over the next 24 years. This genocide caused anguish amongst Australians and the nation cheered when Australian troops, at the request of the United Nations, landed in East Timor to restore order in 1999. A debt had been redeemed.

It was in the waters to the south of Sunda Strait that another tragedy occurred, when 353 refugees making for Australia drowned when their overcrowded boat foundered on 19 October 2001.

*Britain's coat-of-arms,
symbol of the Crown's
authority*

3: *Convicts and Colonists*

The First Fleet: 1788

HOW DO YOU FOUND A NATION? Take 1,044 people—including 772 convicts—and 11 ships, and place them under the command of an obscure naval officer, and send them to the other end of the earth, to a continent inhabited by stone-age tribesmen. And hope they all survive.

No nation has had a more bizarre birth than modern Australia. Britain's loss in 1783 of the American colonies, to which convicts had long been transported, caused the English government to consider establishing a settlement, and a place of banishment, in New Holland. The whimsical idea of relieving the pressure on England's overcrowded gaols by founding a settlement of convicts at the remote 'Botany Bay' on Australia's eastern coast, discovered by Captain Cook in 1770, prompted many humorous street ballads and at least one opera, called *Botany Bay*, which closed at the Royal Circus Theatre in London on 12 May 1787, one day before Captain Arthur Phillip, RN, governor-designate of New South Wales, led the First Fleet from Portsmouth Harbour and into the Channel for the seven-month voyage to the Antipodes.

While some looked forward to making landfall in a new home 'much warmer than England, and ten times as large', one sceptic, the historian of voyages, Alexander Dalrymple, predicted: 'All that will happen to them is that they will be sent, at the Public Expense, to a Good Country and Temperate Climate, where they will be their own masters.'

How right he was. The climate was one of the healthiest in the world, free of diseases, and when the colony was firmly established the majority of the convicts transported for seven years for minor felonies (today they would be termed 'misdemeanours' and merit nothing but a reprimand and a warning) experienced conditions better than they had imagined, for most were assigned to work as servants or labourers, and in time earned a form of freedom by ticket-of-leave. But those sentenced to 14 years, and the incorrigible criminals and the rebellious amongst them, suffered greater hardship and often cruel punishment. It was a hard and callous age, when children were transported for stealing a few shillings (the First Fleet convicts included 32 children). Even marines and soldiers received 100 or 200 lashes for minor infractions.

Botany Bay: A New Song

Let us drink a good health to our schemers above,
   Who at length have contriv'd from this land to remove,
   Thieves, robbers and villains, they'll send 'em away,
   To become a new people at Botany Bay.

Some men say they have talents and trades to get bread,
   Yet they sponge on mankind to be cloathed and fed,
   They'll spend all they get, and turn night into day—
   Now I'd have all such sots sent to Botany Bay.

There's gay powder'd coxcombs and proud dressy fops,
   Who with very small fortunes set up in great shops,
   They'll run into debt with design ne'er to pay,
   They should all be transported to Botany Bay ...

There's nightwalking strumpets who swarm in each street,
   Proclaiming their calling to each man they meet:
   They become such a pest that without more delay,
   Those corrupters of youth should be sent to the Bay.

There's monopolizers who add to their store,
   By cruel oppression and squeezing the poor,
   There's butchers and farmers get rich in that way,
   But I'd have all such rogues sent to Botany Bay ...

You lecherous whore-masters who practice vile arts,
   To ruin young virgins and break parents' hearts,
   Or from the fond husband and the wife lead astray—
   Yet such debauch'd stallions be sent to the Bay.

There's whores, pimps and bastards, a large costly crew
   Maintain'd by the sweat of a labouring few,
   They should have no commission, place, pension or pay,
   Such locusts should all go to Botany Bay.

The hulks and the jails had some thousands in store,
   But out of the jails are ten thousand times more,
   Who live by fraud, cheating, vile tricks and foul play,
   And should all be sent over to Botany Bay.

Now should any take umbrage at what I have writ,
   Or find here a bonnet or cap that will fit,
   To such I have only this one word to say:
   They are welcome to wear it in Botany Bay.

— *Traditional, 1790.*

Here's Adieu to All Judges and Juries

Here's Adieu to all judges and juries,
    Justice and the Old Bailey too;
    Seven years you've transported my true love,
    Seven years he's transported I know.

How hard is the place of confinement,
    That keeps me from my heart's delight.
    Cold irons and chains all bound round me,
    And a plank for my pillow at night.

If I'd got the wings of an eagle,
    I would lend you my wings for to fly,
    I'd fly to the arms of my Polly love,
    And in her soft bosom I'd lie.

And if ever I return from the ocean,
    Stores of riches I'll bring to my dear;
    And it's all for the sake of my Polly love,
    I will cross the salt seas without fear.

— *TRADITIONAL 1790.*

From an engraving by Thomas Rowlandson, c. 1780

Away with These Whimsical Bubbles of Air

Away with these whimsical bubbles of air,
    Which only excite a momentary stare;
    Attention to plans of utility pay,
    Weigh anchor, and steer for Botany Bay.

Let no-one think much of a trifling expense,
    Who knows what may happen a hundred years hence?
    The loss of America what can repay?
    New colonies seek for at Botany Bay.

O'er Neptune's domain, how extensive the scope,
    Of quickly returning, how defiant the hope.
    The Capes must be doubled, and then bear away,
    Three thousand good leagues to reach Botany Bay.

Of these precious souls who for nobody care,
    It seems a large cargo the kingdom can spare,
    To ship off a gross or two, make no delay,
    They cannot too soon go to Botany Bay.

They go to an island to take personal charge,
    Much warmer than Britain, and ten times as large,
    No custom-house duty, no freightage to pay,
    And tax free they live when at Botany Bay.

This garden of Eden, this new promised land,
    The time to set sail for will soon be at hand;
    Ye worst of land-lubbers make ready for sea,
    There's room for you all about Botany Bay.

— *London street ballad of the 1780s.*

Botany Bay

The best known of all the convict ballads dates not from the 1780s but from the 1850s and was penned by the productive Englishman Charles Thatcher (1838–71).

Farewell to old England for ever,
    Farewell to my rum culls as well;
    Farewell to the well-known old Bailee,
    Where I used to cut such a swell.

Chorus:
    Singing too-ral li-ooral li-ad-dity,
    Singing too-ral li-ooral li-ay;
    Singing too-ral li-ooral li-ad-dity
    Singing too-ral li-ooral li-ay.

There's the Captain as is our Commander,
    There's the bo'sun and all the ship's crew,
    There's the first and second-class passengers,
    Knows what we poor convicts go through.

'Taint leavin' old England we cares about,
    'Taint cos we mispels what we knows,
    But becos all we light-fingered gentry,
    Hops around with a log on our toes.

For seven long years I'll be staying here,
    For seven long years and a day,
    For meeting a cove in an area,
    And taking his ticker away.

Oh, had I the wings of a turtle-dove!
    I'd soar on my pinions so high,
    Slap bang to the arms of my Polly love,
    And in her sweet presence I'd die.

Now, all my young Dookies and Duchesses,
    Take warning from what I've to say,
    Mind all is your own as you touchesses,
    Or you'll find us in Botany Bay.

— *Traditional.*

Farewell to Botany Bay

When the First Fleet dropped anchor in Botany Bay in January 1788, one officer of marines wrote: 'I cannot say from the appearance of the shore that I will like it.' So unpromising appeared the scrubby land fringing the bay that Governor Phillip next day went up the coast in a small boat to search for a better site and, sighting two majestic headlands, decided to investigate their harbour: Port Jackson. He sailed between the rugged cliffs to discover one of the largest, most expansive protected stretches of water in the world, one with numerous bays and inlets. Several miles up-harbour from the Heads he found a wooded cove with a stream of fresh water, which he named Sydney Cove. This, he declared, would be the site for the colony.

Yet 'Botany Bay,' which is today as deserted, barren and lonely as it was in 1788, remained the name for the colony for the best part of 50 years.

Kangaroos and Wallabies

The ships of the First Fleet returning to England took with them the first specimens of kangaroo—and the marsupial astonished the English. The first European to describe them, the Dutchman Pelsaert, described the wallabies (small cousins of the kangaroo) as 'Cats ... creatures of miraculous form, as big as a hare' while Dampier likened them to a raccoon.

THE WONDERFUL
KANGUROO,
FROM
BOTANY BAY,
(The only One ever brought alive to Europe)
Removed from the HAY-MARKET, and now exhibited at the LYCEUM, in the STRAND, from 8 o'Clock in the Morning, till 8 in the Evening.

THIS amazing, beautiful, and tame Animal, is about five Feet in Height, of a Fawn Colour, and diftinguifhes itfelf in Shape, Make, and true Symmetry of Parts, different from all other QUADRUPEDS. Its Swiftnefs, when purfued, is fuperior to the Greyhound: to enumerate its extraordinary Qualities would far exceed the common Limits of a Public Notice. Let it fuffice to obferve, that the Public in general are pleafed, and beftow their Plaudits; the Ingenious are delighted; the Virtuofo, and Connoiffeur, are taught to admire! impreffing the Beholder with Wonder and Aftonifhment, at the Sight of this unparalleled Animal from the Southern Hemifphere, that almoft furpaffes Belief; therefore Ocular Demonftration will exceed all that Words can defcribe, or Pencil delineate.......Admittance, ONE SHILLING each.

Later, the first live kangaroo to reach England was exhibited to the public and described as an 'amazing, beautiful and tame animal, of about five feet in height, of a brown colour … its swiftness, when pursued, is superior to the greyhound …'

So prolific are kangaroos and their brethren throughout Australia that they are a species no longer in danger of extinction.

Strange Creatures

The 'koala bear', which spends its time high in gum trees eating the tips of gum leaves (and nothing else) and then snoozing after this exhausting process, is not a bear at all but a marsupial, related (but not too closely) to the

Koala 'bear'.

wombat, another cute but cantankerous bush dweller that makes its burrows deep underground, sleeps during the day and mostly emerges at night to fossick for roots.

Both creatures fascinated the first settlers, but neither puzzled Europeans more than the amphibian platypus. A platypus caught on the banks of a lake near the Hawkesbury River in 1797 was the first one to be scientifically described, and the first platypus specimen sent to England was regarded by scientists there as a practical joke constructed by the colonists, for it was unlike any creature they had beheld: it had the bill of a duck, a furred body, short legs with claws, and the tail of a beaver!

The Starvation Years

After the arrival of the First Fleet in 1788, no further ships bearing provisions appeared from England. By March 1790, Phillip had sent half the marines and 200 of the convicts to Norfolk Island to ease the colony's food situation and ordered the *Sirius* to sail for China to bring back supplies. Her wreck on Norfolk Island plunged the colony into a deep depression and the governor ordered the half-rations be reduced even further in the hope that some souls might survive at least six months. Fish were plentiful but few of the crops they planted had survived. 'Should we have no arrivals in that time, the game will be up with us,' Surgeon White wrote to a friend in London, though his letter's chances of being delivered were slim:

'In the name of heaven, what has the Ministry been about? Surely they have quite forgotten us … It would be wise by the first steps to withdraw the settlement … The *Supply* tender sails tomorrow for Batavia in hope that the Dutch may be able to send in time to save us; should any accident happen to it, Lord have mercy upon us …'

The Second Fleet

For more than two years, no ship from England reached the colony. But on the evening of 3 June 1790, there was sudden commotion at Sydney Cove: the flag had been hoisted at South Head, signal of an incoming ship. Captain Watkin Tench of the marines was too overcome with emotion to speak, for beating up harbour was a vessel with English colours flying. She was the *Lady Juliana*, first vessel of the Second Fleet, arriving with food and more convicts.

The colony would survive.

True Patriots All

From distant climes o'er wide-spread seas we come,
Though not with much éclat or beat of drum,
True patriots all, for be it understood,
We left our country for our country's good;
No private views disgrac'd our generous zeal,
What urg'd our travels was our country's weal,
And none will doubt but that our emigration,
Has prov'd most useful to the British nation.

— *TRADITIONAL.*

The First Hanging: 1788

On 27 February 1788, a military court sentenced to death three convicts, Thomas Barrett, Henry Lovell and Joseph Hall and ordered a fourth, John Ryan, to receive 300 lashes for stealing 'butter, pease and pork'. At 5 p.m. the marines were ordered under arms and marched to the place of execution, a tree  midway between the male and female convict camps. Surgeon Bowes wrote:

'At a quarter after five, the unhappy men were brought to the place where they were to suffer. A large party of marines were drawn up opposite the gallows and all the convicts were summoned to see the deserved end of their companions. When they arrived near the tree, Major Ross received a respite for 24 hours for Lovell and Hall, but Barrett, who was a most vile character, was turned off after 6 o'clock p.m. He expressed not the least sign of fear till he mounted the ladder, and then he turned very pale and seemed very much shocked. It was sometime before the hangman (a convict) could be prevailed upon to execute his office, nor would he at last have comply'd, if he had not been severely threatened by the Provost Marshall, Mr. Brewer, and Major Ross threatened to give orders to the marines to shoot him …

'Just before Barrett was turned off, he confessed the justice of his sentence, and that he had led a very wicked life … He then exhorted all of them to take warning of his unhappy fate and so launched into Eternity.'

On the next day, after the marines had assembled again near the gallows, the remaining three convicts were reprieved.

Bennelong

Governor Phillip, anxious to establish good relations with the Eora people whose lands he had invaded, decided in December 1788 to kidnap one of them and learn their ways, but his first captive, a man named Arabanoo, died of smallpox six months later. In November 1789 Phillip captured two others, Bennelong and Colebee, but both eventually escaped from European civilization. In late 1790, when Phillip was speared by an Eora at Manly, Bennelong reappeared at the settlement at Sydney Cove to inquire about the governor's health, and when he was assured he would not be detained against his wishes, he became a regular visitor there. A small hut was built for him on the eastern arm of Sydney Cove (now known as Bennelong Point, and the site of the Sydney Opera House), and Bennelong quickly learned English phrases, started wearing English clothes and developed a taste for liquor. When Phillip returned to England late in 1792, he took Bennelong with him, and there introduced him to King George III.

But Bennelong, increasingly homesick, found London society boring, and the climate unhealthy. He sailed for Sydney in 1795 in the *Reliance*, accompanying the new governor, John Hunter. Shipmates included Mathew Flinders and George Bass.

On his return Bennelong grew increasingly quarrelsome and drank to excess. He was often involved in tribal fights and was killed at Kissing Point in 1813.

Miss Molly

Arrested at 14 when riding a stolen horse—and dressed as a boy—a young Molly Haydock was sentenced to hang for theft; but she survived to become Mary Reibey, Sydney's first successful businesswoman, and founder of a colonial dynasty.

Molly Haydock was born near Blackburn in Lancashire in 1777. When she was found riding a stolen mare and protesting that her name was James Borrow, she was thrown into prison in 1791 with

pickpockets and thugs, pretending she was a boy until she was brought before the judge. Anguished pleas for mercy from her family saw her sentence reduced to transportation for seven years and she embarked for Sydney in a female convict transport several months later.

Working as a servant, young Molly caught the eye of an Irish-born former naval office, Thomas Reibey, and married him in 1804. The couple expanded Thomas' fledgling trading activities in partnership with Edward Wills, and when both men died in 1811 Mary Reibey took over the business. With the help of her seven children she expanded into shipping and warehousing, using her canny north country acumen for business so successfully that she became one of the colony's wealthiest citizens. Loved and respected for her donations to charity and involvement in community affairs, she died in 1855, living long enough to see her family established as wealthy pioneers in both New South Wales and Tasmania.

Margaret Catchpole

She was another convict girl—and she died mourned as a heroine. Born at Ipswich, Suffolk, in 1762, the daughter of farm workers, Margaret Catchpole was well-known as a spirited young girl when she rode a horse a long distance to get a doctor for a sick neighbour; according to a popular fictionalized account of her life written by an admirer soon after her death, she saved the lives of the three children of her employer. But when she was barely sixteen she became involved with a young ne'er-do-well and stole a horse to ride to London to see him. She was apprehended, charged with stealing and sentenced to death, but the penalty was commuted to 14 years' transportation.

In March 1801, just before she was to sail for Australia, she escaped from Ipswich jail by climbing a 7-metre high wall with the aid of a rope, but was recaptured and again sentenced to death, and again sentenced to transportation instead.

She arrived in the Colony later in the year, was assigned as a servant for the Palmer family, whose children she nursed and whose property she ran as overseer. She was granted a complete pardon in 1814 and died five years later from an illness (possibly pleurisy) contracted in going out in appalling weather to again help a neighbour.

The Celebrated Mr Barrington

He has been described as one of the most colourful characters who ever came to Australia as a convict—and one of the most charming.

Born near Dublin in 1755, George Barrington embarked early on an acting career, joining a team of strolling players, one of whom at least had a criminal bent: John Price, an Englishman, who was convinced that more money lay in picking pockets. Barrington and Price formed a two-man team, the former posing as a wealthy young fop, the latter as his manservant, and picked pockets at public gatherings with impunity until Price was caught and transported to America. Soon afterwards, Barrington was caught in the act of trying to steal the jewelled snuff box from Count Orloff at Covent Garden. Hauled before Sir John Fielding, the blind magistrate and author of Tom Jones, Barrington was somehow acquitted.

Again caught stealing and this time sentenced to three years in the hulks at Woolwich, Barrington was freed after a year, for all found him a delightful personality. He was again apprehended, while picking pockets at the races at Enfield in 1790, and this time sentenced to transportation to New South Wales. He arrived in Sydney as a convict on the Third Fleet in 1791; the experience made him a reformed character and he was favoured by the governor and in time appointed Constable at Windsor. However, Barrington's mind began to fail and he died in Australia in 1804, mourned by all.

Barrington caught in the act

Thomas Muir and the Scottish Martyrs

The best and noblest privilege in Hell,
  For souls like ours is, Nobly to rebel,
  To raise the standard of revolt and try,
  The happy fruits of lov'd Democracy.

— POEM WRITTEN BY THOMAS MUIR,
  IN EXILE IN SYDNEY.

Thomas Muir, minus one eye: image of a revolutionary

'I have engaged in a grand, a just, and a glorious cause which, sooner or later, must and will prevail,' said Thomas Muir when sentenced to 14 years transportation for his belief in democracy. He was the first and most famous of the Scottish martyrs.

In 1793, when Britain declared war on revolutionary France, men of radical political beliefs went in fear of their lives and liberties. Muir, a young Glasgow lawyer and a member of a Jacobin discussion club, was charged with sedition by a Scottish court, mainly for handing out copies of Tom Paine's *Rights of Man*. The severity of his sentence shocked even English courts.

Within months, other peaceful democrats were sentenced to similar terms: Thomas Palmer, an English Unitarian preacher of Dundee, received seven years and William Skirving, Joseph Gerrald and Maurice Margarot each received a 14-year sentence. Muir and three other martyrs arrived in Sydney in February 1794.

Although treated with leniency, Muir refused to knuckle under, and in 1796 stole a boat and rowed out of Sydney Harbour to board a Yankee trader, the *Otter*, which took him to North America. From California he made his way to Cuba and took a Spanish frigate to Cadiz, surviving en route an attack by British warships which cost him his eye and severely disfigured him. On arriving in Spain, Muir was immediately invited to France where, living in poverty, but free, he died in 1799 at the age of 34.

Both Skirving and Gerrald died in Sydney in 1796, long estranged from Margarot, whom all suspected of double dealing (and who returned in 1810 to England where he died five years later, avoided by his former comrades).

Thomas Palmer finished his sentence, went into the boat-building business in Sydney (constructing his vessels by looking up 'Ships' in the *Encyclopaedia Britannica*) and attempted to sail a refitted Spanish warship back to England. Marooned at Guam when his ship

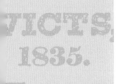

sank, Palmer died of disease there in 1802. Two years later an American sea captain disinterred his body and took it back with him to give it a Christian burial in Boston.

The Irish Martyrs

In April 1798, an Irish convict tilling a field at Toongabbie near Parramatta suddenly threw down his hoe, shouting 'Three Cheers for Liberty!' He was sentenced and flogged on the spot for sedition.

Ireland itself was simmering on the edge of rebellion. Exasperated by England's economic and political domination, the Irish Protestants rose up in May 1798, beginning a bloody five-year insurrection that rapidly involved the mass of the population—the Irish Catholics—and even a French invasion force.

None, in the long run, suffered more than the native Irish. In time 50,000 Irish 'rebels' would be brought in chains to Australia, nearly all of them political prisoners, victims of both the 1798 rebellion and the troubles of the 1820s and 1840s. An equal number would emigrate as a result of poverty and the potato famine. Clinging to their Catholic faith, they would within a century form 30 per cent of Australia's (largely Protestant) population. Their exploits, rebel songs and traditions would mix with those of the English and Scots to form the basis of our folklore. Physically and mentally tough, they would help to found (and later dominate) the Labor Party, while the Irish Protestants were invariably conservatives. Skilled in-fighters in politics, the Irish would produce more Australian prime ministers than any other group: Scullin, Lyons, Fadden, Curtin, Forde, Chifley, McEwen, McMahon, and Keating; and John Gorton had an Irish mother.

'The scene at the landing was one never to be forgotten. The contrast between the old country and the new land to which they had been brought seemed utterly to bewilder them. They were hustled ashore and driven off to the huts like a flock of hunted and frightened sheep. We older prisoners were quite amused at their astonishment at seeing our strange dress of yellow and black. I tried to talk to some of them but could not make out a word of what they said ...'

— *WILLIAM DERICOURT, AN ENGLISH PRISONER DESCRIBING THE ARRIVAL OF IRISH CONVICTS (FROM* OLD CONVICT DAYS*)*

'It was a sorry sight to see so gallant a gentleman submit himself to these vulgar people in authority, and with a silent dignity obey the order given him. For, after all, he and many other prisoners were gentlemen of birth—such as Counsellor Sutton, Dr McCallum and Mr Brennan. They were persons of refinement, whose only crime was love of their native land, and a desire for its freedom. Had they been Englishmen this would have been highly esteemed . . .'

— CAPTAIN WILLIAM EASTWICK, ENGLISH MASTER MARINER DESCRIBING THE ARRIVAL OF GENERAL HOLT AND THE IRISH PRISONERS AT NORFOLK ISLAND.

The Croppies are Rising!

Governor Hunter described the Irish 'Croppies' (who wore their hair close-cropped like the French revolutionaries) as 'diabolical' and 'turbulent' and his successor, Governor King, saw the first 235 Irish political prisoners who arrived in the colony in 1800 as a danger to the settlement.

The long-feared Irish rebellion, born of ill-treatment and desperation, came on 4 March 1804, when a group of convicts near Castle Hill, north-west of Sydney, broke out and seized arms, burning farms as they marched towards Parramatta. Hearing the shouts 'The Croppies are coming!', the Reverend Samuel Marsden, who had flogged too many Irishmen to feel safe in his home, bundled himself into a vessel for Sydney, leaving Parramatta to the volunteers. In Sydney Town, Major Johnston called the New South Wales Corps to arms and marched a body of 50 soldiers overnight to Parramatta, arriving to find no sign of the rebels. After a night of drinking and carousing, the convicts had headed for the Hawkesbury region and it was here, on a hill 13 kilometres from Windsor, that the troops found them next morning. It has been known ever since as Vinegar Hill, site of the only battle, apart from Eureka, ever fought on Australian soil.

Calling on the rebels to surrender, Johnston rode forward to parley with the rebel leader, Cunningham, and suddenly clapped a pistol to the latter's head and arrested him. He then ordered the Corps to open fire. Within minutes, 12 convicts lay dead, six wounded, and another 26 were taken prisoner. Punishment was swift. Nine of the ringleaders were hanged, nine flogged, and 50 others sentenced to long terms at the penal colony at Coal River (Newcastle).

The Floggers

'I was to leeward of the floggers . . . I was two perches from them. The flesh and skin blew in my face as it shook off the cats. Fitzgerald received his 300 lashes. Doctor Mason—I will never forget him— he used to go feel his pulse, and he smiled and said: "This man will tire you before he will fail—Go on."

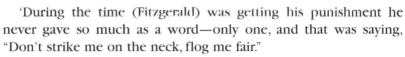

'During the time (Fitzgerald) was getting his punishment he never gave so much as a word—only one, and that was saying, "Don't strike me on the neck, flog me fair."

'When he was let loose, two of the constables went and took hold of him by the arms to keep him in the cart. I was standing by. (He) said to them, "Let me go." He struck both of them with his elbows in the pit of the stomach and knocked them both down, and then stepped in the cart. I heard Dr Mason say that man had strength enough to bear 200 more.

'Next was tied up Paddy Galvin, a young boy about 20 years of age. He was ordered to get 300 lashes. He got 100 on the back, and you could see his back bone between his shoulder blades. Then the Doctor ordered him to get another hundred on his bottom. He got it, and then his haunches were in such a jelly that the Doctor ordered him to be flogged on the calves of his legs. He got 100 there and as much as a whimper he never gave. They asked him if he would tell where the pikes were hid. He said he did not know, and would not tell. "You may as well hang me now," he said, "for you never will get any music from me so." They put him in the cart and sent him to the hospital.'

— *FROM AN OLD ACCOUNT*

The Rum Corps

'Soldiers from the Savoy [military prison] and other characters who have been considered as disgraceful to every other regiment in His Majesty's Service have been thought fit and proper recruits for the New South Wales Corps,' complained Governor Hunter to the Duke of Portland in 1796. His words fell on deaf ears, for England, then at war with France, had no regiments to send in their place.

The New South Wales Corps, formed in 1789 to replace the unhappy marines, was to prove a bane to all the naval governors and a threat to their authority. The officers, in particular John Macarthur, were ambitious and avaricious, the rank and file recruited from the poor of London and not much better characters than the convicts they guarded.

When Bligh attempted to break their officers' monopoly in the colony—particularly in the trading of rum—the corps overthrew him in 1808 and ruled in his stead for two years.

On the arrival of Lachlan Macquarie and the 73rd Regiment in 1810, the corps was shipped back to

England, renamed the 102nd Foot, and soon saw action in the Americas, proving to be good soldiers after all. Nicknamed the 'Botany Bay Rangers', they were commanded in battle by the dashing young Charley Napier who called them 'my gents' and wrote of how the 'officers and men sigh for Botany Bay.' The regiment was disbanded in 1818.

Rum!

Cut yer name across me backbone,
   Stretch me skin across a drum,
   Iron me up to Pinchgut Island,
   From today till kingdom come!

I will eat your Norfolk dumpling,
   Like a juicy Spanish plum,
   Even dance the Newgate hornpipe,
   If you'll only give me rum!

— *Traditional.*

Pinchgut was the rocky outcrop opposite Sydney Cove where, according to legend, convicts convicted of murder were marooned to die of starvation and thirst. In the 1850s it was converted into a fortress defended by cannon—Fort Denison—to repel an expected Russian invasion, but it is now a tourist destination complete with a luxury restaurant. The name 'Pinchgut' is derived either from the convicts' sufferings or from the fact that the harbour narrows here (the two headlands were linked by the giant Sydney Harbour Bridge in 1932).

The Rum Rebellion, 1808

In 1806, Captain William Bligh, hero (of sorts) of the *Bounty* mutiny, was appointed governor of New South Wales, with orders to straighten out the colony. He won the approval of most of the settlers but aroused the animosity of the New South Wales Corps and one of its former officers, John Macarthur, now one of the colony's principal traders. Bligh's patience, which was never great, was soon exhausted and his language and abuse of officers became notorious. His attempt to have Macarthur charged with sedition brought about his downfall.

On 26 January 1808, the twentieth anniversary of the official foundation of the colony, Major George Johnston, pressured into action by his subordinates, called the regiment to arms, and led them uphill from the barracks to Government House, preceded by the band playing 'The British Grenadiers.' Bligh's bodyguard melted away without firing a shot and the only defence mounted was that by Mary Putland, the governor's daughter, who hit one soldier over the head with her umbrella at the doorway. Two others found Bligh in an upstairs bedroom attempting to hide his papers under the bed, though they told all and sundry that he had been trying to hide beneath it.

Informed by Johnston that he was taking over the governor's powers, Bligh was placed in detention and then allowed to leave by ship. The arrival of the new Governor Macquarie in 1810, and the removal of the mutinous regiment, was followed in 1811 by George Johnston's court martial in England. It was a lengthy trial resulting in his being cashiered from the army; a light sentence explicable by what the presiding general called the 'extraordinary circumstances' of the mutiny.

Johnston returned to his estate in Sydney; Bligh, a deeply embittered man, was in time promoted to Admiral of the Blue (Vice-Admiral) but was never again entrusted with another position of authority.

Macarthur's Merinos

John Macarthur (1766–1834), formerly a Captain in the New South Wales Corps, had disposed of his enemy Governor Bligh. A tempestuous man, he had already nearly disposed of his own Commanding Officer, Colonel Patterson, whom he wounded in a duel. But Macarthur is best known as the founder of Australia's wool industry. As early as 1797, when the first Spanish merino sheep arrived in the colony, he had seen that Australian conditions were perfect for farming them. The animals produced a wool of extreme softness

John Macarthur

and were inured to both extreme heat and the rigours of cold winters. (The English breeds, however, produced better meat—fat lambs—for eating.) Having petitioned the London government to grant him land on which to commence breeding merinos, Macarthur was allowed to resign (or sell) his commission and was offered 2,000 hectares of land of his own choosing; he selected the richest pastureland available near Sydney, at Camden. There they flourished.

Macarthur thought it advisable to leave the colony for England after the mutiny of 1808 to avoid arrest and did not return to Sydney and his estates until 1817. In his absence, his wife Elizabeth and nephew Hannibal had successfully established his merino flocks: in the previous year the sheep had yielded 15,000 pounds of the finest wool. By the 1990s, Australia's 160,000,000 predominantly merino sheep were producing 75 per cent of all the world's apparel wool and 40 per cent of the total of all the world's wool.

The word 'merino' later became a term of abuse. When Macarthur and his sons became leaders of the prosperous

'Exclusives' who allied themselves with successive governors in resisting social change, they were ridiculed sarcastically as 'the Pure Merinos' by William Charles Wentworth and other opponents.

A Perfect Little Man

'The young Australian is systematically insolent to the new chum; so is everyone indeed. How I who had pretty well run the gauntlet of London life, was branded and fleeced during the first three months of my residence in Sydney! A new chum is fair game for anyone. Your villainous bullock-driver in the interior, when he cannot by any strategem, get his cattle to budge, culminates his oaths and imprecations by striking the leader of the refractory beasts over the head and grunting from the depths of his stomach: "Oh! You b— new chum! Move on!"

'The Australian boy is a slim, dark-eyed, olive-complexioned, young rascal, fond of Cavendish, cricket, and chuck-penny, and systematically insolent to all servant-girls, policemen, and new chums. His hair is shiny with grease, as are the knees of his breeches and the elbows of his jacket. He wears a cabbage-tree hat with a dissipated wisp of black ribbon dangling behind, and loves to walk meditatively with his hands in his pockets, and, if cigarless, to chew a bit of straw in the extreme corner of his mouth . . . He can fight like an Irishman or a Bashi-Bazouk [Turk]; otherwise he is orientally indolent, and will swear with a quiet gusto if you push against him in the street, or request him politely to move on. Lazy as he is though, he is out in the world at ten years of age, earning good wages, and is a perfect little man, learned in all the ways and byways of life at thirteen . . . for shrewdness, effrontery, and mannish affection, your

London gamin pales into utter respectability before the young Australian. I should add that your thoroughbred gumsucker never speaks without apostrophizing his 'oath' and interlarding his diction with the crimsonest of adjectives . . . One is struck aghast with the occasional blasphemy of his language.'

— FRANK FOWLER (1833-63).

Currency Lads and Lasses

It is said that the paymaster of the 73rd Regiment first described the Sydney-born children of the early colonists as 'Currency', for the local currency, a Spanish dollar with a hole in the middle, was far inferior to good old English 'Sterling'. The local lads adopted the insulting term with delight. *The Currency Lass*, the story of the wooing of a genteel 'native-born' lass, staged in 1844, was the first musical comedy produced in Australia, but the poorer among the currency lads sought wives from among the prisoners of the Parramatta women's prison, or 'Factory', prompting this famous ballad:

The Currency Lads may fill their glasses,
  And drink to the health of the Currency Lasses;
  But the lass I adore, the lass for me,
  Is a lass in the Female Factoree.

— TRADITIONAL.

TAR BOY.

The Old Viceroy

Under the rule of Governor Macquarie (1810–21), the colony thrived. The Scottish soldier was a man of deep humanity who improved the conditions of convicts, established a firm economy (the colony's first bank was founded in 1817), welcomed to Government House the previously despised Emancipists (former convicts whose sentences had expired), encouraged exploration, built churches and public buildings of rare grace (most of them still stand) and saw the colony's population grow threefold during his ten-year administration. During the grim decades ahead, Macquarie's rule was looked back upon as a golden age.

Our gallant governor has gone,
  Across the rolling sea,
  To tell the King on England's throne,
  What merry men are we.

CHORUS:
Macquarie was a prince of men,
*   Australia's pride and joy!*
*   We ne'er shall see his like again;*
*   Here's to the old Viceroy.*

Some governors have heads, I think,
    But some have none at all;
    Cheer up, my lads; push round the drink,
    And drown care in Bengal.

What care we for the skill to scan,
    The bright stars overhead?
    Give us for governor a man,
    Who rules and is obeyed

— *MICHAEL MASSEY ROBINSON, 1821.*

James Hardy Vaux, Prince of Pickpockets — and the condemned cell.

James Hardy Vaux

According to legend, James Hardy Vaux was the only felon transported three times to Australia (though it seems one other convict
shares this garland). He was an unrepentant con-man, a self-
confessed thief whose autobiography (written at Newcastle) provides a remarkable portrayal of London's 'Flash' or petty criminal
life, and a character so well known that he featured as a central
character in a play that, according to legend, was attended by the
entire British cabinet. The play, *Van Diemen's Land*, opened in
London in 1830, and was described as a 'serio-comical, operatical,
melodramatical, pantomomical, characteristical, satirical, Tasmanian,
Australian extravaganza'. Its author confessed that he had taken

'dramatic liberties' in including 'that renowned prig Hardy Vaux, and that notorious fence Ikey Solomons' and had 'Vaux' lead the 'Convict Chorus' in singing the opening refrain:

Never droop, Brother convicts, but keep up the ball,
  For in court, or in cottage, in hovel or hall,
  Mankind, as occasion permits, are Rogues All ...

Vaux was born in Surrey in 1782, into a family connected to the gentry, and joined the navy at 16, deserting soon afterwards. Caught stealing in 1800, he was sentenced to seven years' transportation to New South Wales, during which he used his charm and education to lessen the severity of his exile, returning to England as a secretary to Governor King.

He found London full of opportunities for theft and picking pockets, but was caught again in 1808 and sentenced to death, escaping the noose only by a legal technicality. Vaux's aplomb, however, was severely shaken by his short spell in the condemned cell, with a prisoner who was awaiting the hangman:

'This unfortunate person had been convicted of selling forged banknotes ... As he was known to have carried on this illegal and dangerous traffic to a great extent in the town of Birmingham, where he resided, the Bank was determined to make an example of him ... he had no hope of mercy being extended to him; and was consequently in hourly dread of the awful fiat which was to seal his doom, and consign him to a shameful and premature death ... At eight o'clock the doleful sound of the tolling bell announced the awful ceremony, and he was a few minutes afterwards launched into eternity; a woman named Margaret Barrington, for forging and uttering a seaman's will, suffered with him. The fate of this unhappy man, who was of a most inoffensive and gentle disposition and left a numerous family to bewail his loss, affected me much.'

Vaux's ability with the pen soon saw him released from irons, but his first sight of the convict hulk *Retribution* also sobered him:

'Of all the shocking scenes I had ever beheld, this was the most distressing. There were confined in this floating dungeon, nearly six hundred men, most of them double-ironed; and the reader may conceive the horrible effects arising from the continual rattling of chains, the filth and vermin naturally produced by such a crowd of miserable inhabitants, the oaths and execrations constantly heard among them; and above all the shocking necessity of associating and communicating with so depraved a set of beings … I soon met with many of my old Botany Bay acquaintances, who were all eager to offer me their friendship and services, that is, with a view to rob me of what little I had, for in this place there is no other motive …'

Arriving in Australia again in 1810, Vaux married (though he was already married to a wife in England), and had the satisfaction of seeing his lively memoirs published in London in 1819, and then received a conditional pardon the next year. He married for the third time before escaping from New South Wales in 1829, bobbing up the following year in Dublin. Here he was again arrested, this time for forging banknotes, and was again sentenced to transportation, arriving back in Sydney in 1831. Vaux gained his ticket-of-leave five years later, but by now his handsome looks and soft, insinuating manner were losing their effectiveness, and around 1841 he left prison and disappeared from the pages of history, his fate unknown.

A Convict Lament

'Dear Wife,
It's with sorrow that I have to acquaint you that I have this day received my Tryal and have received a hard sentence of Seven Years Transportation beyond the seas …

If I was for any time in prison I would try and content myself, but to be sent from my Native Country perhaps never to see it again distresses me beyond comprehension and will terminate my life …

To part with my dear wife and child, parents and friends, to be no more, cut off in the bloom of my youth without doing the least wrong to any person on earth—O my hard fate, may God have mercy on me …

— Your affec. Husband until death, Thomas Holden'
Holden was a Lancashire weaver convicted in 1812 of 'administering an illegal oath' to another worker in Bolton, Lancashire.

Blue Mountains

For a quarter of a century, the colonists at Sydney were fascinated by a range of mountains that appeared as a line of blue on the western horizon. Convicts who escaped into their fastnesses were never seen again and the first tentative explorers found the terrain an impenetrable barrier, rugged and heavily forested, whose wide expansive valleys ended abruptly in cliffs of sandstone. They were in fact not strictly mountains at all, but part of the high serrated plateau along the east coast known as The Great Dividing Range, or the Great Divide. The bluish haze that gave the Blue Mountains their name was inexplicable; it was later discovered that the mist came from the leaves of the eucalyptus trees that covered them (and which, when processed, would produce an export known around the world: the universal cure-all, eucalyptus oil). To Sydney's north was a fine river, named the Hawkesbury, that flowed through broken country past towering sandstone cliffs (a later visitor, Anthony Trollope, called the river the equal of the Rhine), while to the south an ocean of dark forest reached to the

horizon; this was the bush later called the Bargo Brush, reaching over a tangle of hills called the Razorback. It seemed that Sydney was fated to be a coastal settlement, its interior a 'Great Unknown'.

But in 1813, three explorers set out from the foothills, with Governor Macquarie's blessing, to attempt to cross the Blue Mountains. Their names were Blaxland, Wentworth and Lawson, and they followed not the valleys but the ridges, and beheld at journey's end a vista of rare magnificence: undulating, verdant plains reaching as far as the eyes could see. Within two years the town of Bathurst had been founded, and the opening of the Inland had begun.

The English Martyrs

With victory over France achieved in 1815, England's economy entered a long period of crisis as exports stagnated and domestic prices rose, accompanied by political unrest such as the kingdom had never known. Even in Scotland a worker's rebellion in 1820 saw three of its leaders hanged and beheaded for treason before stunned and silenced crowds. (Scores more, reprieved, were sentenced to transportation to Australia.) A decade of riot and unrest climaxed in 1830 when workers in southern England marched from village to village smashing the machinery of the Industrial

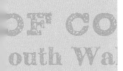

Revolution that was ruining their artisan livelihood. The 'Swing Riots' (Captain Swing was their mythical leader) were suppressed with brutality: 19 workers were hanged and 481 of them transported to Australia.

Though Lord Grey's *Great Reform Act* of 1832 averted revolution by extending the franchise to the middle class, it did little for the poor. And though the hideous list of 200 offences punishable by death in the 1780s had, by 1830, been reduced to 25 or so, the crime of protesting against dreadful working conditions could still result in cruel punishment: the six peaceable and noble Tolpuddle Martyrs of 1836 were sentenced to seven years' transportation as an example to others, but in this case public opinion was outraged and all were pardoned by the monarch in 1838 before returning as heroes to England.

Not all convicts were criminals. Thousands of free-born Englishmen suffered for their political beliefs and found in Australia the democracy that had eluded them in their homeland.

The English notion of personal freedom was translated into strident demands by the colonies for an end to the transportation of convicts and for self-government during the 1840s. Since the 1850s, when the sudden discovery of gold transformed the Australian colonies and ushered in self-government and a remarkably wide franchise (in the gold rush years, an Australian worker often earned as much as members of the prosperous middle-class in England, thus qualifying for the vote) Australians have, in the main, been in command of their own political destinies. Almost by accident Australia became one of the world's first democracies.

BELOW: 'Tolpuddle Martyr' George Loveless — transported for attempting to form a farmer worker's union

GEORGE LOVELESS, Aged 41.

THE RETURNED "CONVICTS."

JAMES BRINE, Aged 25.

THOMAS STANFIELD, Aged 51.

JOHN STANFIELD, Aged 25.

JAMES LOVELESS, Aged 29.

The Seizure of the Cyprus

Come all you sons of Freedom, a chorus join with me,
    I'll sing a song of heroes, and glorious liberty.
    Some lads condemn'd from England, sail'd to Van Diemen's
    Shore,
    Their Country, friends and parents, perhaps never to see more.

When landed in this Colony to different Masters went,
    For trifling offences, t' Hobart Town gaol were sent,
    A second sentence being incurr'd 'e were order'd for to be
    Sent to Macquarie Harbour, that place of tyranny.

The hardships we'd to undergo, are matters of record,
    But who believes the convict, or who regards his word?
    For starv'd and flogg'd and punish'd, depriv'd of all redress,
    The Bush our only refuge, with death to end distress.

Hundreds of us were shot down, for daring to be free,
    Numbers caught and banished, to life-long slavery.
    Brave Swallow, Watt and Davis, were in our noble band
    Determin'd at the first slant, to quit Van Diemen's Land

March'd down in chains and guarded, on the *Cyprus Brig*
    convey'd
    The topsails being hoisted, the anchor being weighed,
    The wind it blew Sou'Sou'West and on we went straightway,
    Till we found ourselves Wind-bound, in gloomy Recherche Bay.

'Twas August eighteen twenty nine, with thirty one on board,
    Lieutenant Carew left the *Brig*, and soon we passed the word
    The Doctor too was absent, the soldiers off their guard,
    A better opportunity could never have occur'd.

Confin'd within a dismal hole, we soon conriv'd a plan,
  To capture now the *Cyprus*, or perish every man.
  But thirteen turn'd faint-hearted and begg'd to go ashore,
  So eighteen boys rush'd daring, and took the *Brig* and store.

We first address'd the soldiers 'for Liberty we crave,
  Give up your arms this instant, or the sea will be your grave,
  By tyranny we've been oppress'd, by your Colonial laws,
  But we'll bid adieu to slavery, or die in freedom's cause.'

We next drove off the Skipper, who came to help his crew,
  Then gave three cheers for liberty, 'twas answer'd cheerly too.
  We brought the sailors from below, and row'd them to the land
  Likewise the wife and children of Carew in command.

The Morn broke bright the Wind was fair, we headed for the sea
  With one cheer more for those on shore and glorious liberty.
  For Navigating smartly Bill Swallow was the man,
  Who laid a course out neatly to take us to Japan.

Then sound your golden trumpets, play on your tuneful note.
  The *Cyprus Brig* is sailing, how proudly she floats.
  May fortune help th' Noble lads, and keep them ever free
  From Gags, and Cats, and Chains, and Traps, and Cruel Tyranny.

— 'FRANK THE POET' (FRANCIS MACNAMARA) (1811-?)

Aboriginal Languages

When Europeans arrived in Australia in 1788 the Aboriginal peoples spoke about 250 different languages (the tribes in Cape York alone spoke 55 of them) but now barely 20 are still spoken. This passage describes words in use in south-eastern New South Wales as late as the 1850:

'The tribes, prior to the coming of the whites, had most of them clearly marked dialects, and inland people found it hard to understand the Tablelanders or the Coast tribes. But the greater communication brought by the invasion of Europeans caused a wider currency and general adoption of various words and phrases. For example, such words as Baal (no or wicked), Budgeree (good), Cobbawn (large), Yabber (food), Waddy (wood), Boori (thunder), Kerang (gumtree), Nerang (small), Cowra (feathers), Nangery (to camp), etc., were common expressions to the Lachlan, Coast, and Argyle Aborigines. The blacks had, apparently, a musical ear for nomenclature. Take, for instance, such words as Cobbadong (Moon in the water); Wombeyan (big kangaroo); Wollondilly (water trickling over rocks); Durran Durra (a messenger); Currabungla (stone in the water); Wingecarribee (flight of birds);

Mulwarrie (long water); Gullen (a swamp); Uabba (go fast); Yulong (a timbered hill), etc.'

— FROM OLD PIONEERING DAYS IN THE SUNNY SOUTH, *1907,*
CHAS. MACALISTER.

The Lash

'Twenty-five lashes! In Australia and Tasmania they gave a convict fifty for almost any little offense; and sometimes a brutal officer would add fifty, and then another fifty, and so on, as long as the sufferer could endure the torture and live. In Tasmania I read the entry, in an old manuscript official record, of a case where a convict was given three hundred lashes—for stealing some silver spoons. And men got more than that, sometimes. Who handled the cat? Often it was another convict; sometimes it was the culprit's dearest comrade; and he had to lay on with all his might; otherwise he would get a flogging himself for his mercy—for he was under watch—and yet not do his friend any good; the friend would be attended to by another hand and suffer no lack in the matter of full punishment.

'The convict life in Tasmania was so unendurable, and suicide so difficult to accomplish that once or twice despairing men got together and drew straws to determine which of them should kill another of the group—this murder to secure the death of the perpetrator and to the witnesses of it by the hand of the hangman!

'Some of the convicts—indeed, a good many of them—were very bad people, even for that day; but the most of them were probably not noticeably worse than the average of the people they left behind them at home. We must believe this; we cannot avoid it. We are obliged to believe that a nation that could look on, unmoved, and see starving or freezing women hanged for stealing twenty six cents' worth of bacon or rags, and boys snatched from their mothers, and men from their families, and sent to the other side of the world for long terms of years for similar trifling offences, was a nation to whom the term "civilized" could not in any large way be applied. And we must also believe that a nation that with it, was not advancing in any showy way toward a higher grade of civilization.

'If we look into the characters and conduct of the officers and gentlemen who had charge of the convicts and attended to their backs and stomachs, we must grant again that as between the convict and his masters, and between both and the nation at home, there was a quite noticeable monotony of sameness.'

— FROM FOLLOWING THE EQUATOR, *1897, MARK TWAIN.*

Port Arthur

The Redcoats

Until 1870, when the last red-coated British troops were withdrawn from Australia, New Zealand and Canada, a succession of regiments served periods of up to four years in the Australian colonies before invariably progressing to India, where many of them died in battle or of disease. The Australian climate was a healthy one but few of the Redcoats, who were themselves subjected to a harsh discipline, enjoyed the monotony of guarding convicts or the depressing nature of their duty. In hearing of a posting to Australia many officers sold their commissions or exchanged them with colleagues whose units were remaining in England or Ireland. Their lonely outposts, often consisting of as few as half a dozen men, reached from Port Arthur in Tasmania to Port Essington in the Northern Territory. Almost no folklore of the regiments exists; the soldiers were mostly illiterate, the officers too bored or overworked to write or record the life they lived or the songs their soldiers sang. There are few reminders of the soldiers' presence other than the mute cannon that still stand on the harbour fortifications, the sturdy barracks they built, a few regimental buttons sometimes unearthed. But their remote bush 'stations' gave Australians the name for country properties.

'The soldiers at the Southern Stockades were chiefly men of the 28th Regiment [North Gloucestershire Regiment, which served here from 1836–42], originally sent out from England in charge of convicts; and I might say here, that the soldiers generally disliked the occupation. In the first place they thought that in being sent out to the wilds of Australia with convicts, they were being punished equally with their prisoners. And it is scarcely to be wondered at, that being thus segregated from friends and home and country, many a weak-minded soldier should have thought to drown his sorrow and discontent in the cup that brings oblivion, at the pubs, and grog-shanties of the early days. Soldiers, in consequence of their being over the convicts, were unpopular in the country, and the author has heard many an old soldier deny strongly that he once wore the Army uniform . . .'
— *CHAS. MACALISTER.*

Port Arthur

The new ruler of Van Diemen's Land, Colonel George Arthur, who arrived in 1824 was a martinet, an army officer noted for his efficiency and belief in harsh discipline, and he left his name to a place that makes the blood run cold: Port Arthur. But Arthur's first problem was the Aboriginal population, which by 1830 had been reduced to barely 2,000 souls, but who were still fighting settlers. He decided to drive them into the Tasman Peninsula in the south-east of the island, but netted only a man and a small boy. The remnants of the Tasmanian Aborigines were later removed to islands in Bass Strait, where the last of them, Truganini, died in 1876.

Arthur considered it inefficient to maintain a prison for the worst offenders at Port Macquarie on the distant west coast and another, for light offenders, at Maria Island off the east coast. He closed them both down and in 1830 founded a new prison settlement at Port Arthur on the Tasman Peninsula south of Hobart, one from which it would be impossible to escape. It grew into an immense complex of stone prisons, workhouses and barracks, and a graceful church, and was run with brutality, following Arthur's orders that prison should be a place of misery for those sentenced to its confines. When Arthur was recalled to England in 1837, the colony went wild with joy. Port Arthur was closed down in 1877 but its ruins stand today and for long were a popular tourist spot. Here a gunman, Martin Bryant, shot 35 sight-seers on an April day in 1996.

Liberty or Death: Mutiny on Norfolk Island, 1834

'Those who were to live wept bitterly, whilst those doomed to die, without exception, dropped on their knees, and with dry eyes, thanked God that they were to be delivered from such a place,' recalled the priest who visited the 30 convict prisoners under sentence of death for the mutiny of January 1834. The 14 who were hanged in two batches soon afterward considered death a release from a living hell, and those who were reprieved cursed their fate.

Under Morisset and his callous lieutenant, Captain Foster Fyans, Norfolk Island reached a depth of human degradation that still defies belief. The floggings and tortures had so destroyed the prisoners' will to live that by late 1833 Governor Bourke, a humane man, was receiving disturbing reports that convicts were drawing straws to choose whom among their fellows would kill them to end their misery. Fyans records the incident when a gang of 16 convicts on road work suddenly manacled their overseer and drew straws, the winner, a man called Fitzgerald, calling another to 'stick him' (Fitzgerald) and cause as little pain as possible. He died two days later and the others were shipped to Sydney for trial, the voyage being a welcome respite from the horrors of the island, though a one-way trip to the gallows.

Rumours of a convict revolt reached the Commandant, together with a list supplied by informers of 200 die-hards who were planning

to murder their goalers and build a launch to sail to America, but Morisset was prostrate with persistant migraine and Fyans merely apprehensive.

On 15 January 1834, an unusually large number of convicts reported sick, and once inside the hospital fell on their guards, struck off their irons, armed themselves with crude weapons, and waited for the soldiers to return from the road gang.

A hundred metres away, thirty convicts mustering near the gate under a detail of 13 soldiers of the 4th Regiment, suddenly leaped upon their guards, who within minutes found themselves surrounded by the mob of 120 convicts, including the hospital gang. The first musket shots brought Fyans running from his cottage on Quality Row; forming a group of Redcoats, he ordered them to open fire on the approaching mob and when the smoke cleared, fifteen rebels lay stretched on the ground and the rest were running into the sugar cane.

Hearing the Kingston melee, a lookout ran to the convicts at Longbridge with the cry 'Turn out my lads—now is the time for Liberty!' A crowd of 80 broke into the tool chest, armed themselves with axes and pitchforks and poured down the road to Kingston, shouting 'Liberty or death!' A few volleys from the troops sent them running. By nightfall, Fyans had rounded up the 200 survivors of the revolt, including 50 wounded. Five convicts were dead.

No guards were killed in the affray (other than two who shot each other by mistake at nightfall) but retribution was terrible. For the next five months, while waiting for a judge to arrive to try the culprits, Fyans and the guards subjected the prisoners to such constant floggings that they wore out the Cats, and the prisoners were chained in irons triple the normal weight.

Judge William Burton, arriving in June 1834, was horrified by the appearance of the prisoners and moved by the manly bearing of one of the ringleaders, Douglas, who said in the dock: 'When a man comes here, his Man's heart is taken from him, and he is given the heart of a Beast.'

On returning to Sydney, Burton convinced Bourke to spare the lives of 16 of the convicted mutineers. The remaining 14 were hanged, dressed in white, on the scaffold overlooking the ocean on Norfolk Island in September 1834.

The Demon: John Price

John Giles Price (1808–57) looked every inch an English gentleman, but Marcus Clarke portrayed him as the heartless Commandant Frere in his classic novel *For the Term of His Natural Life*, and one of his convict charges, obsessed with the sufferings he had undergone at Price's hands, wrote a novel (unpublished) about him called *The Demon*. The historian Robert Hughes called Price 'one of the durable ogres of the Antipodean imagination for more than a century.' Few mourned his passing when convicts in Melbourne bashed him to death at Williamstown quarry and the Melbourne *Age* spoke for many of his victims in its obituary: 'He was a cruel man, and his cruelty came back to him.'

One of the 14 children of a penniless Cornish baronet, Price hungered for the position and power denied him in England, arriving in Hobart in 1836. Physically immense, charming (he married the niece of Sir John Franklin in 1838), a loving husband and father, Price seems to have been what modern psychologists would call a paranoid with schizophrenic tendencies, and an unusually cruel one. Appointed Commandant at Norfolk Island following the 1846 rebellion, Price instituted a reign of terror. He regarded the convicts as beyond salvation, the incarnation of evil. He sentenced one prisoner to be flogged for losing his shoelaces, another got 36 strokes for being cheeky. When the surgeon described one newly-arrived prisoner as 'an inoffensive man with very fine feelings' Price replied cynically: 'Oh, I'll soon take them out of him.' Other prisoners were sentenced to cutting coral on the reefs, up to their waists in water and burdened with 17-kilo leg irons; others were condemned to 14 days solitary confinement for 'being at the privy when the bell rang.'

In 1849 the former chaplain on the island, Thomas Rogers, published a blistering eye-witness account of Price's cruelties and three years later Bishop Willson was so moved by the punishments meted out by Price that he wrote a 30-page report to Governor Denison, damning 'the system which invests one man at this remote place with absolute, irresponsible power.' Price, in tears, begged Willson not to forward the report.

But the British Government had already decided to close down Norfolk Island and remove the intractable prisoners to Port Arthur, the 'new model' prison. Price returned to Hobart, reappearing in Victoria in 1854 as Inspector-General of Prisons. Again, his name became a byword for heartless cruelty. Resuming his characteristic habit of walking amongst the convict working parties unarmed, intimidating his charges by sheer bravado and an aura of power, he visited the quarry at Williamstown on 2 March 1857. When a convict, Dan Kelly, asked him if a recent three-day solitary sentence would affect his forthcoming ticket-of-leave, Price replied in the affirmative. 'You bloody tyrant, your race will soon be run!' Kelly shouted at him.

The convicts began to cluster around Price, abusing him. One threw a clod of earth at him. Price turned as if to run, amid a hail of rocks, and stumbled. As he went down the convicts fell on him, hitting him with their shovels, almost braining him. Price, beyond recovery, died a day later. Seven convicts were hanged for his murder. They were Price's last victims.

Cornstalks

In the early 1800s, newly-arrived English colonists compared the tall, strapping children of the first convicts to cornstalks, 'because they shoot up so quickly'. The native-born white Australians thus added a second nickname to their language.

'Cornstalks' would remain for a century the nickname for New South Welshmen, just as 'Sandgropers' were Western Australians.

When Hamilton Hume, discoverer in 1824 of the mighty river that flows west from the Australian Alps to South Australia, heard that it had been renamed in honour of the Colonial Secretary in London, General Sir George Murray, he explained good naturedly: 'Murray was a General, and I was just a Cornstalk.'

'You cannot imagine such a beautiful race as the rising generation in the colony,' wrote a newly-arrived English official, George Boyes, to his wife from Hobart in the 1820s. 'As they grow up they think nothing of England and cannot bear the idea of going there. It is extraordinary the passionate love they have for the country of their birth ... there is a degree of liberty here which you can hardly imagine ...' Commissioner Bigge, at the same time, reported to London: 'The inhabitants born in the colony are generally tall in person, and slender in limbs ... In their temper they are quick and irascible; they exhibit neither the vices nor the feelings of their [convict] parents ...'

Cabbage Tree Hats

The colonists found the fruit of the cabbage tree plant delicious and the leaves perfect for braiding into straw hats. Soon men of all classes were wearing them during the heat of summer. The Victorian pioneer Edward Curr (1820–89) wrote in his reminiscences (published in 1883) of the squatters of the 1840s: 'Many of these, I noticed, indulged in blue serge shirts instead of coats, cabbage tree hats, belts supporting leather pouches and, in few cases, a pistol, which with breeches, boots and spurs, completed the costume.' The working classes, renowned for their rowdiness whenever they gathered in groups, were known as 'The Cabbage Tree Mob' from the hats they wore, even inside the theatre.

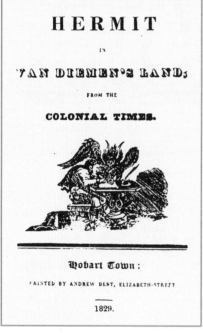

The Sad Fate of Henry Savery

Henry Savery is remembered today as Australia's first novelist and the author of the first collection of literary essays published in the colony. Unfortunately he directed most of his rich talents into forgery and his life became a tragic melodrama.

Born in Bristol, the son of a prosperous merchant, Henry Savery seemed destined for success, but he entered sugar-refining and went bankrupt in 1819. Undeterred, he took up the editorship of the *Bristol Observer* while also running a brokerage and insurance business. In 1822, he made the mistake of re-entering the sugar business and financing expansion by forging fictitious bills drawn on non-existent persons. As his bills bounced and his creditors grew in number, he panicked on hearing of the hanging of a forger in November 1824. Booking a passage to America (with a false cheque), Savery was on board the vessel when the constables rowed out to arrest him. Throwing himself into the sea, he was dragged out and arraigned before the magistrate.

At his trial on 4 April 1825, Savery was sentenced to death, despite an impassioned plea from the prosecutor for mercy: 'The consequences of his crime were limited; the public have suffered

Writing like the devil, Savery appears in this vignette on the title page of his book of essays, published and printed in Hobart in 1829

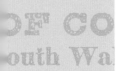

nothing'. He spent nearly three weeks in the death cell before his execution was commuted to transportation to Van Diemen's Land.

Savery arrived at Hobart Town late in 1825 and was assigned as a servant to Captain Thomas, a landowner and bloodstock breeder. Thomas was killed by natives in 1827, and Savery, already 'cutting a dash' and acting the swell, obtained a comfortable position as a clerk with the government before turning his nimble hand in 1820 to writing articles on Tasmanian life for the *Colonial Times* under the nom-de-plume of 'Simon Stukely'. One piece resulted in a libel action.

When the governor complained that Savery had done no work for several months, the author explained that his hand was injured. He had instead been writing his autobiographical novel, *Quintus Sevinton*, in which the transported hero manages to get assigned to his own wife as a live-in servant. It was wishful thinking: when Savery's wife sailed out to join him in 1820 under the guardianship of Algernon Montague, the new attorney-general, she was apparently seduced on the high seas by Montague and departed from Hobart after only a few months. Nevertheless, the novel was published in Hobart in 1830 and reprinted in London two years later.

Savery obtained his ticket-of-leave in 1832, but it was suspended shortly afterwards when he printed a libellous article (not by his hand) in the *Tasmanian*, of which he was temporary editor. Bad luck seemed to dog his life. The end came when he was caught in forgery: sentenced to Port Arthur penal settlement by his old enemy Algernon Montague, Savery cut his throat there in February 1842.

Black Francis

'I knew of several men who got their fifty lashes for being off the premises for only one night. One such man was Charles Smith, assigned in 1836 to Captain Edwards, run-holder of Argyle. He [Smith] was sent for letters to the P.O. and did not return to the farm till next morning. Brought before Captain Allman, J.P., he was awarded fifty lashes for his one night's absence, though the man pleaded illness.

'No doubt the old records, if unearthed, would show scores of such cases. It is not too much to say, that the word of a convict had no value whatever in the view of the magistrates, not even if backed by a St. Peter. The accused very seldom got the benefit of the doubt in the Penal days. The Government floggers at the Penal Stations were generally wretches who volunteered for this brutal work, so as to escape the penalties of the Iron-gang, of which they were often originally members.

'The author particularly remembers two such callous fellows, viz: Billy O'Rourke (the Towrang flogger), and Black Francis—a Negro—the Goulburn castigator, from 1838 to 1841. Billy O'Rourke was a small, wizened-looking object, but muscular, and he revelled in his work. Before he began flogging, he would often say to the man chained up for punishment: "Heavy weather, byes (boys); heavy weather; but aisy now, sure it might be worse."

'Black Francis used to lay the cat on with savage ferocity. He met with a sudden and tragic end—being found one morning "as dead as a door-nail", in the bush near the Run of Water, with three leaden lugs in his carcase. He used to make it his business to inform on some "ticket-o-leave" men (after sometimes sharing their plunder), who were in the habit of robbing teams of spirits, that carriers were taking up-country. On several occasions he had "treed" and flogged his man for the offence referred to. But at last Nemesis overtook him, as stated, and Francis resigned the gentle art of flogging and everything else on this side of the Jordan.

'Some of the convicts, as may be imagined, were made of the sternest human stuff possible, and men of that type never flinched under the lash. On two occasions I saw men—after undergoing, one a flogging of fifty, and the other, seventy-five lashes, bleeding as they were, deliberately spit, after the punishment, in the flogger's face. One of them told Black Francis "he couldn't flog hard enough to kill a butterfly".'
— CHAS. MACALISTER.

Bungaree, King of the Blacks

These were the words inscribed on the brass plate presented to him by Governor Macquarie, who also gave the Aboriginal leader his old military uniform, which Bungaree enjoyed wearing. (He was also a skilled mimic of several governors.) 'A worthy and brave fellow,' Matthew Flinders called him. Bungaree, 'chief of the Broken Bay tribe', sailed with Flinders on his voyage to Moreton Bay (Brisbane) in 1799 and then accompanied him as an interpreter on the Flinders circumnavigation of Australia in HMS *Investigator* in 1802–03, proving a fine companion and a good sailor. He also accompanied the explorer Captain Phillip Parker King

(son of Governor King and destined to be the first Australian-born admiral) in the *Mermaid*, dying in Sydney in 1830 in his fifties, but living on in numerous portraits.

The Myall Creek Massacre, 1838

'You have been found guilty of the murder of men, women and children and the law of the land says whoever is guilty of murder shall suffer death ... may the Lord have mercy on your souls.' The sentencing to death of seven white men for murdering Aborigines was unheard of in 1838. In 50 years of settlement no European had ever been executed for killing blacks, and the condemned were confident of a reprieve. Governor Gipps, an incorruptible man, rejected all pleas for mercy. The law must take its course. The trial became a turning point in Australian history.

The massacre of which the whites were accused was a particularly cold-blooded one. In June 1838, twelve station hands, all former convicts, at William Dangar's Myall Creek property in New South Wales, irritated by constant acts of thievery by local natives, decided to take matters into their own hands. They herded the local encampment of blacks together and coldly slaughtered them all, a total of 28 old men, women and children, before burning the bodies on a fire.

Discovering their charred remains, Dangar's manager insisted on reporting the killing to the police. When local squatters rallied to the killers' defence and paid for counsel, all the suspects were acquitted of murder of the men, and the court broke into cheering when the verdict was announced.

Men and women of character were appalled by the acquittal, which was a slap in the face of English justice. If the British Empire had any claim to respect it was because all its subjects lived under the same system of justice, protected by the same laws whatever the colour of their skin. Angry also were the governor and his attorney-general, an Irishman named Plunkett. 'So much for English justice,' was a frequently heard comment. 'Right, I'll give you Irish justice,' Plunkett pledged. Offering four of the suspects immunity from capital punishment if they turned Queen's Evidence, Plunkett charged the remaining seven (one had escaped) with the murder of the women. After a two-day trial, all were found guilty, and were publicly hanged in Sydney on 18 December 1838.

Spears and Woomeras

'As to the native weapons—the fighting and hunting spears were
barbed at the end with pieces of ironbark, tipped to a point. Those
pieces were glued on with wattle and other gum, and the gum grew
as hard as Portland cement. The Author has known a spear to pen-
etrate the stiff bark of a gumtree at 150 yards [150 metres)] distance and further. The spear-thrower [or 'Woomera'] was much
used by the Argyle tribes.'

— CHAS. MACALISTER.

Boomerangs

'As all Australians know, the blacks used two different
boomcrangs—onc in war and attack, and the other in play. I believe
it was from conning over the shape and "properties" of the
boomerang (a piece of originally green ironbark, myrtle, or myall,
curved and formed by the natives' ingenuity) that Sir Thomas
Mitchell got the idea of making his famous propeller for sea-going
vessels.

'In starting to shape a boomerang, the piece of timber selected
was first drawn through the warm ashes of a smouldering fire, so as
to draw the sap out of the wood and when drying was scraped to
the required article. I knew only one white man capable of making
a serviceable boomerang. The "knulla-knullas", or "boondies" were
ironbark sticks with a heavy knob on the end, used in killing pos-
sums, etcetera, and sometimes in tribal warfare.'

— CHAS. MACALISTER.

Hunting and Fishing

'At stalking game, such as wallabies,
emus, wild turkeys, etc, the "yabbas"
were in their element. A hunter would
creep on his quarry—if, say, a turkey—
undercover of a large bush, which he
had fixed around himself in such a way as to make it seem the bush
was the bush and nothing more. The bush-clad hunter would
patiently creep on the bird till within striking distance—and then a
boomerang would hiss through the air, and a lot of blackfellows and
their gins and piccaninnies would have supper on half-"grilled"
turkey . . . The gins feasted on the scraps the men threw to them
over their shoulders, as a drover sometimes feeds his dog. The gins
were the slaves and drudges …

'The blacks were very clever in water and sometimes caught wild duck in a singular way. One or two young blacks, as I have often seen them, would hide as dusk came on among the rushes along the river bank at likely "duck" reaches along the stream. While the shoal of birds were swimming about near the blacks' hiding place, one of the men would dive silently and keep below the surface of the water a little while, holding a reed or straw in view of the game. If a bird came within reach of the trapper's hand, it was snapped immediately...'

— *CHAS. MACALISTER.*

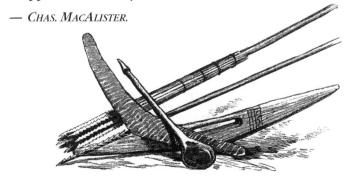

Wanted: Women

'In New South Wales and Van Diemen's Land there are very few women compared with the whole number of people,' explained an advertisement in London in 1833.

This was something of an understatement. The colonies' first census in 1828 had confirmed the alarming suspicion that Australia was almost totally male: for every 100 females there were 333 males vying for their favours, or resigned to bachelorhood—or worse. Despite the colonies' reputation as a 'Sink of Iniquity and Depravity', 217 young women answered the plea to emigrate and arrived in the *Bussorah Merchant* at Sydney to find mobs of men lining the docks in expectation. Carefully chaperoned on the voyage, the women were snapped up by the well-to-do as servants and house-keepers. 'It was like a country fair more than anything else,' a witness recorded of the carnival-like affair, but he forecast that the arrival of female emigrants would be like 'purified gold' on the colonies' morals.

The year before, a ship had brought out 150 young Irish girls from Cork and nearly all were settled in quickly as servants, the Master reported, with only ten of them taking to the streets. But the *Princess Royal* which docked in Hobart in 1832 disgorged some of the toughest women yet seen in the colony, all of them drawn from the prisons of London. Among the 200 females were girls who had been arrested as young as fourteen for stealing food, and most had been brutalized by their experience. The language and behaviour of many of them appalled the straight-laced Governor Arthur, and most of them proved surly servants at best, prompting the abusive term 'a Princess Royal' for a bawdy harridan years afterwards.

As subsidized emigration increased in the 1840s, many credulous young women arrived to find no bed of roses awaiting them, and sometimes no bed at all. As late as 1849, when Caroline Chisholm was fighting her battle to provide care for the new arrivals, a passenger on an emigrant ship recorded that her company consisted of

Caroline Chisholm

'a few poor innocent girls mixed up with the lowest prostitutes from the streets of London'.

Morality improved beyond expectations, but the perfect balance in numbers between males and females was not achieved until the early 1900s. As late as 1900 there were still 110 men in Australia for every 100 women. This abnormal state of the sexes produced on the one hand an aggressive sense of mateship between men; but also, because women were prized, it resulted in female emancipation in Australia decades before Britain and Europe followed her example.

Ben Boyd

Just as the convict age was ending another scoundrel appeared on the Australian scene—a businessman with wild dreams. His name was Benjamin Boyd. Born in Scotland in 1786 he began life as a stockbroker in London and then looked for fame and fortune in the Australian colonies, securing the patronage of high government officials and capital to develop trade with Sydney, using chartered vessels. He arrived in Sydney in his yacht *Wanderer* and soon established a bank there (1843), purchased extensive sheep properties and then entered the whaling industry, establishing a village on Twofold Bay which he called Boyd Town (it still stands). But by 1846 Bold Ben Boyd was in financial difficulties and three years later his bank crashed. Boyd hastily left the Colony in his yacht *Wanderer* for the gold fields of California. He was returning when he went ashore on Guadalcanal Island in the Solomons and promptly disappeared. According to legend, he was eaten by cannibals.

Henry Parkes: Immigrant

The future Sir Henry Parkes, father of Australian federation, hated Australia when he arrived, calling Sydney 'more wicked than I had conceived it possible for any place to be' and begged his friends in England 'by no means to come to this colony.'

'I have been disappointed in all my expectations of Australia,' Parkes wrote to his parents in Birmingham in May 1840, eight months after his arrival, in language many English migrants would have applauded a century later. 'There was no place for the emigrants to go . . . When they left the ship they had to do as best they could,' he wrote, and complained that houses renting at home for 2/6 a week cost 15/- in Sydney. He had obtained a job as labourer on Jamison's estate at Penrith for £25 a year (wages plus food) and was forced to sleep with wife and new-born babe for the first four months there on a sheet of bark off a box-tree, and an old door.

But Parkes, born in 1815, the son of a Warwickshire yeoman, was tough. Returning to Sydney, he set up as an ivory turner in Kent Street in 1844 and, as the debate about transportation intensified, started playing a part in local politics as one of the reformer Robert Lowe's supporters. In 1840, Parkes drew up 'the deliberate and solumn' protest against the continuation of transportation, stating that it is incompatible with our existence as a free colony, desiring self-government, to be the receptacle of another country's felons.' It was the beginning of his political career.

'Sir Henery'

In his later years, white-maned like a tribal elder, Sir Henry Parkes was a cartoonists' delight. By 1850 the unhappy English emigrant had founded a Sydney newspaper, the *Empire*, as a platform for his radical opinions, and launched himself on his amazing career as democrat, demagogue and champion of popular causes, supplanting W.C. Wentworth as a tribune of the people.

Twice bankrupt, thrice married, five times premier of New South Wales, Parkes called for a single, federated Australia as early as 1867 and is justly remembered as the 'Father of Federation'. He entered the New South Wales parliament in 1854 but had to resign to try and save the Empire from bankruptcy.

He was elected again in 1858, only to resign six months later because of insolvency. He stood again in 1860 as a supporter of Robertson's land policy, extended education, intensified immigration and free trade, which became his passion. Thanks to Parkes' efforts, Florence Nightingale was asked to send the first trained nurses to New South Wales.

Insolvent once more, Parkes resigned his seat in 1870 but by 1872 was premier, lasting until 1875. After two more spells as premier, he announced his retirement in 1885, but was called back to

The rising politician — and one who has just fallen: Parkes, seated, and the Reverend John Dunmore Lang

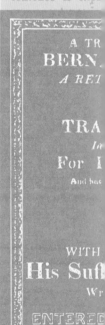

politics, being elected premier two years later, and again in 1889, the year in which, in a famous speech at Tenterfield, he called for a 'great national government for all Australia.'

Parkes was president of the 1891 convention which drew up the Federal Constitution bill. Losing his seat in 1894, he stood again for election at the age of 81 but was unsuccessful and died at his home at Faulconbridge in the Blue Mountains in April 1896. Five years later—on 1 January 1901, the first day of the 20th century—the six Australian colonies became states of a single federation, the Commonwealth of Australia, and Parkes' dream became a reality.

Parkes fathered 11 children by his three wives and managed to find time to write six volumes of poetry.

Chain Gangs, 1840s

'The Towrang convicts were, by regulation, classified into two parties; the "light sentence" [or 7-years' men] being engaged in the lighter tasks, such as looking after the officers' horses, and quarters; driving the Stockade bullock-teams; felling the trees along the road-line; and so on; while the Iron-gang [comprising the 14-years' men and 'lifers'] were hard at it, packing and rolling [building] different sections of the main Southern road between Marulan and Goulburn; making the massive stone culverts, which have so well withstood the ravages of time, and at such-like heavier orders of

labour. The prisoners wore a yellow and black uniform of rough material, and marched in files to their work to the rattle and jingle of their irons. A guard of soldiers with fixed bayonets escorted the men to their allotted toil and stood over them at work. At daybreak in the summer, an hour later in the winter, the prisoners were out and toiled all day like beasts of burden; their food was generally of the coarsest—often barely enough to keep body and soul together. At five in the afternoon they were marched back to camp, and after a supper of salt junk, damper and posts-and-rails tea, they were sent to their sleeping-boxes for the night—members of the Iron-gangs often having to sleep with their fetters on like so many chained dogs . . . generally the scourge of 'discipline' fell heavily on a prisoner for the slightest breach of the rules. Some of the Towrang convicts had been well brought up, amongst them a doctor, chemist, and ex-military officer; while others, as stated, were doing time for trivial offences. . . It seemed to be the chief object of the penal system to increase the depravity it pretended to check . . .'

— *CHAS. MACALISTER.*

The Immigrants, 1840s

They are the unsung heroes of Australia's story. They suffered the horrors and hardships of a three-month voyage under sail in conditions little better than that of a jail, enduring overcrowding, epidemics of fever and disease, the depredations of unscrupulous agents and ship's masters, and the indifference of the inhabitants of the new land. Only the hardiest survived.

Government assistance to immigrants had begun in the 1830s but the Irish famine of the 1840s and the discovery of gold in New South Wales and Victoria in the 1850s transformed the trickle of newcomers into a flood. The 20-year period, a time of great economic hardship and political repression in Britain and Europe, saw nearly 130,000 immigrants and their families arrive in Australia, the majority (about 100,000) being 'assisted passage' migrants from Britain, coming steerage. Many newcomers came from Germany, fleeing oppression. Devout Lutherans in the main, they proved hardy settlers in South Australia, planting vineyards that still flourish.

Death rates were high. In the Layton, sailing from Bristol in 1837, 72 children died on the voyage from measles; as late as 1840 typhus carried away 40 passengers on another ship. Many ships were both unhygienic and unsafe, overloaded by dishonest masters eager to obtain the Bounty paid for each passenger landed safely.

'Late in the afternoon, to our dismay, no less than 150 emigrants swarmed up our sides,' recorded Georgiana McRae (a fee-paying passenger, and proud of it) before her ship sailed from Plymouth in 1850. 'Captain Gatenby astonished me by saying: "If ever we are compelled to take to the boats, only cuddy-passengers will be allowed to embark. The emigrants must stay behind".'

Shipwreck was the horror all emigrants dreaded, particularly during the dangerous passage through stormy Bass Strait. In 1845, the *Cataraqui* ran aground on a reef there; 369 emigrants were drowned, only one surviving. Twenty emigrant ships were lost at sea, victims of storm and shipwreck on the England–Australia passage, and nearly 2,000 people drowned.

No More Convicts!

England had abolished the slave trade in 1807, ordering the Royal Navy to seize any slave ship they encountered on the high seas, and in 1833 proclaimed an end to slavery in the British Empire, paying plantation owners in the West Indies and elsewhere compensation for the liberation of their labourers. But the transportation of convicts continued amid mounting demands that the cruel practice (the 'System') be ended. None were louder in their demands that the far-flung Australian colonies that were now attracting increasing numbers of free immigrants—and some recalled with unease Governor Phillip's bold words of 1787: 'There can be no slavery in a free land, and consequently no Slaves.'

In October 1840, Governor Gipps announced that transportation to Australia would cease, except to Van Diemen's Land and Norfolk Island. (The governor was also ordered to establish British sovereignty over New Zealand before the French got there first.)

The news that transportation was ending came just as the worst drought in memory was beginning, along with Australia's first economic depression that wiped out the fortunes of hundreds of property owners. And in 1842, the year the Bank of Australia collapsed,

came the first democratic elections: for 24 additional members of the Legislative Council of New South Wales.

But in 1849, the British government made the astonishing decision to resume transportation of convicts. Favoured by the landowners, who were desperate for cheap labour, it saw the first flexing of the muscles of ordinary Australians: the colonists' protests were loud and thunderous. The convict ships were blockaded at the wharves and even moderate leaders told the governor that 'it is incompatible with our existence as a free colony desiring self-government to be the receptacle of another country's felons.' The Reverend John Dunmore Lang went further: he called for the establishment of an Australian republic.

In 1850, two days after the Legislative Council had voted to resist transportation of convicts, word arrived that the British government was offering a form of self-government to the colonies, thus defusing an explosive situation. The Port Phillip District would no longer be under remote control from Sydney; it would form the new Colony of Victoria. The territory of the Moreton Bay district would later form the Colony of Queensland. Van Diemen's Land accepted further convicts until 1853 but then became a separate colony, taking the name Tasmania in an attempt to bury her brutal past. The road to self-government over the next decade would be a rocky one but soon the convict era would become an embarrassing memory. It's only enduring legacy surfaces in Australians' intolerance of bullies and oppression of any sort—and their willingness to fight them.

The Scots

The Highland Scots had long been viewed as semi-barbaric by the English, great warriors but prone to clan feuds and constant rebellion. The educated Scots from Edinburgh were notable for their sharp intelligence and keen ambition— these traits, too, caused the English unease. Only ten per cent of Great Britain's population, the Scots were called by William Pitt the 'Hardy Race' and provided three of the first six governors (Hunter, Macquarie and Brisbane); Scots officers took over the running of the New South Wales Corps (Paterson, Johnston, Macarthur) until another Scot (Macquarie) put an end to their business; and Scots produced some of the most formidable explorers of coast and interior (Grant, Murray, Thomas Mitchell, John MacDouall Stuart, John McKinlay, Donald Mackay) and remarkable settlers—among them the pioneer of Gippsland Angus McMillan, and the Archer and Leslie brothers of Queensland.

The first great influx of Scots came in the 1840s, and they were as poverty-stricken as the English and Irish who preceded them. Herded off their lands by their own lairds, who found running sheep more profitable than caring for crofters cultivating crops, the majority of the Scots emigrated to the Americas, but many made the voyage to Australia, stumbling off the vessels speaking their harsh

Governor Lachlan Macquarie   *Reverend John Dunmore Lang*

Gaelic, like the Irish. They were tough folk, clannish in their loyalties and seldom seen to smile. The colourful Presbyterian minister John Dunmore Lang (1799–1878), arriving in Sydney in 1823, was disturbed to discover so few Scots and returned to bring out more (1831), becoming a pioneer of assisted immigration. With the discovery of gold, the trickle of Presbyterian Scots became a flood, and their arrival gave Victoria much of its character. Like the Irish, the Scots, inured to the lonely life, seemed at home in the bush, whereas the bulk of the English migrants, a gregarious people, were happiest in the cities and towns. Denied power in the land of their birth (like the Irish), the Scots sought power and influence voraciously in their new homeland, producing numerous political leaders and colonial premiers. By the early 1900s, the Scots comprised 15 per cent of Australia's population and close to 25 per cent of Australia's rural place names were Scottish, from the Hunter Valley (Maitland, Cessnock, Scone) to distant Perth, and from Maclean and Glen Innes to Mackay and Innisfail. As newspaper owners, publishers (namely Angus & Robertson), writers, engineers, scholars, soldiers, and politicians, the Scots tended to dominate by sheer persistence and doggedness of purpose. When Australia's volunteer army sailed to war in 1914, her prime minister (Andrew Fisher), her governor-general (Sir Ronald Munro-Ferguson) and her

commanding General (William Throsby Bridges) were all Scottish-born; and Bridges' three brigadiers of the 1st Division were named MacLaurin, Sinclair-MacLagan and McCay.

In 1939 Australia's leaders, her governor-general (Lord Gowrie); prime minister (Robert Gordon Menzies); and first divisional commander, Major-General Mackay, were of Scottish stock, as were Canada's.

Advance, Australia Fair!

Andrew Barton Paterson, the son of a Scot, became the nation's best known balladist and author of her unofficial national anthem, *Waltzing Matilda*; Dorothea Mackellar wrote Australia's best loved poem (*I love a sunburnt country*); and a Scottish immigrant school teacher, Peter Dodds McCormick, who arrived in 1855, wrote a song that became Australia's official national anthem. It was first performed at the Highland Society dinner in Sydney on St Andrews Day, 1878, was immediately popular, and was proclaimed our anthem by the Whitlam Labor government in 1974 to replace *God Save the Queen*. This decision was reversed by the succeeding Fraser government, but the game of musical anthems was ended in 1983 by the Hawke Labor government, who quickly reversed the Fraser decision, leaving the public so confused that many still do not know the words, though all know the tune.

Australians all, let us rejoice,
For we are young and free.
We've golden soil and wealth for toil,
Our home is girt by sea.
Our land abounds in nature's gifts,
Of beauty rich and rare,
In history's page let every stage,
Advance Australia fair.
In joyful strains then let us sing,
Advance Australia Fair!

The Blackbirders

In Queensland, proclaimed a separate colony in 1859, lie the graves, now overgrown and forgotten, of 10,000 natives of the Pacific kidnapped from their islands late in the 19th century. They died of neglect and disease rather than brutality, but the Blackbirding era remains another dark, unwritten chapter of our history, one so far avoided by historians and living only in legend and lore.

It began in the 1860s when sugar was found to grow luxuriantly in the Queensland climate. It was a valuable crop, but the industry suffered from a shortage of workers, for Europeans wilted quickly in the humidity of the colony's coastal regions. Black labour was seen as the solution. All attempts by the British government to regulate the 'employment' of islanders and their proper payment and care failed, and the only heroes of the tale remain the ships and men of the Royal Navy who saw the impressments of unsuspecting natives by rogues—the 'Blackbirders'—as no different from slavery, and sought to suppress the trade. More than 50,000 Pacific islanders worked on Queensland plantations until the practice was made illegal following federation in 1901; and one in five of them died on Australian soil.

Captain Bully Hayes

'Of all the rogues, robbers and ruthless killers who dodged the hangman during the first decade of blackbirding, the most colourful scoundrel of the lot was Bully Hayes,' writes Hector Holthouse in *Cannibal Cargoes*. The burly, bearded, brutal slaver met a bloody end, though our folklore sometimes presents him wrongly as a Ned Kelly of the South Seas.

Born in Cleveland, Ohio, William Henry Hayes showed his true metal early, when he ran off with $4,000 stolen from his father. At the age of 20 he headed for California for the 1849 gold rush, stole a ship in San Francisco and sailed for China, smuggling coolies into South America and Australia before settling briefly into business in Adelaide in 1857. Gifted with American charm and a glib tongue, the rogue turned up in New Zealand, married a rich woman (he already had wives in America and Australia) and conned her into financing his purchase of an old schooner which he used for runs to Fiji (during which he took a fourth wife). After gun-running to the Maoris, Hayes went into Blackbirding around 1867. He was under detention in Samoa in 1870 when his old friend Captain Ben Pease arrived there. He left with Hayes on board but the two men fought over a native woman and Pease mysteriously disappeared at sea (according to legend Hayes threw him overboard) from his own ship, the *Water Lily.*

Renaming Pease's ship the *Leonara*, Hayes embarked on an orgy of kidnapping and violence. Manned by a mixed crew of whites and natives, and accompanied by a harem of black women, the *Leonara* sailed from the Solomons to the Gilberts and Marshalls and the Samoas, escaping arrest on one occasion by the USS *Narragansett* because nobody would appear as witness against Hayes. 'He plundered, swindled and kidnapped wherever he went,' wrote one of his American crew, 'and yet no matter where he went, whether among white men, brown men or black, he had friends.' One of his employees was the Australian writer Louis Becke, who sailed with Hayes for more than two years and remembered him for his kindness to his native labourers, who received better treatment than his cut-throat crew.

Finally caught by the tireless HMS *Rosario*, Hayes was charged by the Royal Navy with, according to Becke, 'ninety-seven charges—every count, I believe, except leprosy', but escaped to Guam in a long boat, took ship to San Francisco and there conned a partner named Moody into purchasing a schooner, the *Lotus*, for trading purposes. One night in October 1876, Hayes stole Moody's ship and his wife and sailed for Samoa. He left there with Jenny Moody and two crew members, called at Jaluit in the German Marshalls early in 1877 and was never seen again.

According to rumour, Bully Hayes fought with the mate, was knocked on the head and thrown overboard to the sharks. When the *Lotus* returned to Jaluit minus her captain, the German authorities and ships hoisted bunting to celebrate the rogue's passing, and his murderer conveniently disappeared. Jenny Moody, Hayes' last conquest, died in poverty in Honolulu.

Colourful Captain Cadell

Captain Francis Cadell, pioneer riverboat captain, deserved a better fate than being murdered by his cook's mate somewhere in the South Pacific.

A Scot, Cadell joined a ship for China in 1830 at the age of 17 and then served in the Royal Sovereign in South America, which gave him an opportunity to explore the Amazon. He returned to Scotland to study ship building at Napier's yards, where he had a vessel, the *Queen of Sheba*, built and sailed her to Australia in 1851.

Arriving in Adelaide in 1852, Cadell heard of the government offer of £2,000 to the owner of the first steamer to navigate the Murray River as far as the Darling River junction. In a steamer built in Sydney, Cadell reached Swan Hill in August 1853, soon afterwards forming the River Murray Navigation Company whose three steamers journeyed as far as Albury. Cadell piloted one of them up the Murrumbidgee to Gundagai, and also explored the Darling on his vessel.

By 1861, however, Cadell was bankrupt, and forced to sell his last steamer to the New Zealand Government. By 1870, he was involved in whaling and in trading in the Pacific, and then took up pearling in northern Australia, using natives from the Dutch East Indies as divers. In 1879, while cruising in the Indies in his schooner, *Gem*, Cadell disappeared, and his ship was never seen again.

Rumours persisted for years that he was killed by natives, but Dutch authorities maintained that he was killed by one of his crew for non-payment of wages for five years and the boat then scuttled to cover all traces of the murder.

4: *Bushrangers*

Black Caesar

A USTRALIA'S FIRST 'BUSHRANGER' was a convict of the First Fleet, a giant West Indian black named John Caesar, who absconded from the settlement with a stolen musket and was soon joined in the bush by six or seven other 'bolters'.

Quickly recaptured, he escaped summary hanging because of Governor Phillip's sympathy for him, but he escaped again, earning the colony's gratitude for shooting a feared Aborigine named Permulwy. Every time he was caught, Black Caesar escaped, until his depredations forced Governor Hunter in 1796 to put a price on his head: five gallons of rum to the man who captured him. The bushranger was shot dead soon afterwards by a settler named Wimbow, near Liberty Plains.

Bushranger!

The term 'bushrangers' was common as early as 1805, when it was used in the Sydney *Gazette* to describe a group of suspected highway robbers, possibly escaped convicts, who often waylaid travellers in the bush. Their numbers increased dramatically in the 1820s (a time of severe repression in the Colonies), and in 1830 their depredations were so widespread that the Legislative Council passed the *Bushranger Act* to deal with the problem. Police and soldiers were given almost unlimited powers of search and arrest, and those apprehended faced severe penalties: convicted robbers (and housebreakers) were hanged three days afterwards. It is probably at this time that many bushrangers aroused some sympathy among the poorer members of the populace, for a number of them had originally been victims of injustice, or of a harsh form of justice. Few of them were dangerous and even fewer murderous, but it is puzzling how so many of them became folk heroes, for they preyed on the weak and helpless, while those game enough to fight them, the police troopers and squatters, are now forgotten.

Victoria was plagued by bushrangers in the gold rush years of the 1850s; many of them were found to be former convicts from Van Diemen's Land. Coaches running from Bendigo to Melbourne were often bailed up, and the gold escort from Heathcote to Melbourne was robbed in 1853. One 'Vandemonian', Frank McCallum ('Captain Melville'), was a violent man, and committed suicide in his cell in Melbourne jail in 1857 after a five-year career of robbery.

Bushrangers infested New South Wales a decade later, during the 1860s, and most of them came from among the poor and hard-done-by. Frank Gardiner (1830–1903), who organized the Eugowra Rocks stage coach robbery (1864) served ten years in jail for the crime before reforming his ways; and the exploits of his gang members 'Flash John' Gilbert (a Canadian) and Ben Hall, live on in ballads. Among the most feared bushrangers were a number of psychopaths: the two Clarke brothers, who were apprehended and hanged in 1867 for murdering police troopers in the Braidwood area, and 'Mad Dan Morgan' (1830–65), who carried out a reign a terror, including several murders, in the Riverina and Monaro. When he raided the Macpherson property near Wangaratta, holding the family captive (one of the infants was Christina Macpherson, who later wrote the tune to 'Waltzing Matilda'), he was shot down and killed by a station hand.

An evil man was Morgan, a price was on his head;
The simple bush-folk whispered his very name with dread ...

'Mad' Dan Morgan

The Wild Colonial Boy

There was a wild colonial boy, Jack Donahoe by name,
  Of poor but honest parents he was born in Castlemaine.
  He was his father's dearest hope, his mother's pride and joy.
  O, fondly did his parents love their Wild ColonialBoy.

CHORUS:
So ride with me, my hearties, we'll cross the mountains high
  Together we will plunder, together we will die.
  We'll wander through the valleys and gallop o'er the plains,
  For scorn we to live in slavery, bound down with iron chains!

IIe was scarcely sixteen years of age when he left his father's
    home,
  A convict to Australia, across the seas to roam.
  They put him in the Iron Gang in the Government employ,
  But ne'er an iron on earth could hold the Wild Colonial Boy.

And when they sentenced him to hang to end his wild career,
  With a shout of defiance bold Donahoe broke clear.
  He robbed those wealthy squatters, their stock he did destroy,
  But never a trap in the land could catch the Wild Colonial Boy.

The one day when he was cruising near the broad Nepean's side,
  From out the thick Bringelly bush the horse police did ride.

'Die or resign, Jack Donahoe!' they shouted in their joy.
'I'll fight this night with all my might!' cried the Wild Colonial
Boy.

He fought six rounds with the horse police before the fatal ball,
  Which pierced his heart with cruel smart, caused Donahoe to
  fall.
  And then he closed his mournful eyes, his pistol an empty toy,
  Crying: 'Parents dear, O say a prayer for the Wild Colonial Boy.'

— *Traditional Ballad*

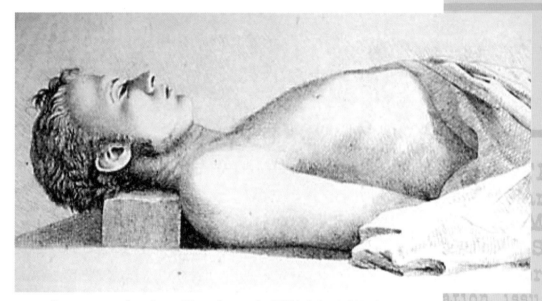

Post-mortem drawing of Donohoe – the 'Wild Colonial Boy'
by Thomas Mitchell

The Wild Colonial Boy, with its thundering chorus, is the best
known bushranger ballad of them all—for there are dozens of ver-
sions, and the hero's name is sometimes Jack Donohoo, Jim Doolan,
or Jack Duggan—celebrates the deeds of the fair-haired, blue-eyed
young Dubliner, John Donohoe (1806–30), who was sentenced to
transportation for life in 1823. He stood only 5 foot 4 inches tall
(163 cm)—'just a handful'—and little is known of his early life
other than that he spent his boyhood in Castlemoine, Ireland (translated into Castlemaine in the ballad), but his exploits in the colony
made him the hero of the oppressed, a cheeky Irish rebel who made
an ass of the hated Governor Darling and met his fate like a man.

Donohoe arrived in Sydney in 1825 and was assigned as a servant
to a settler at Parramatta, but he played up and was sent to join a
chain gang. Assigned to a second settler, Major West, he absconded
with two other Irishmen, Kilroy and Smith, and began holding up

drays on the Windsor Road in December 1827. Lacking horses, the three were caught and sentenced to hang for highway robbery in March 1828, but Donohoe made a break for it on his way to the death cell and took to the bush.

Gathering a gang of Irish and English fugitives, Jack Donohoe led them on a spree for the next 18 months, stealing horses from settlers and bailing up the unwary from Bathurst to the Illawarra and even, according to rumour, as far north as the Hunter. He acquired a will-of-the-wisp renown, eluding Darling's troopers at every turn, and once—according to a report in the *Australian*—rode into Sydney to enjoy a ginger beer.

Aided by dozens of sympathizers (30 of them got prison terms when his confederate, Walmsley, turned informer to save his neck), Donohoe was caught by the troopers near Bringelly in 1830 and gunned down by a bullet in the head. His body was brought to Sydney and the corpse was drawn by Thomas Mitchell, who wrote beneath it Byron's words: 'Fair in Death's face—before—and now.'

Within weeks, ceramic effigies of Donohoe were being sold in Sydney, a mark of his fame. To his admirers then and now he was the 'Wild Colonial Boy'—a son of Ireland taking on the 'System' and making a mockery of it. The ballad of his life and death, with all its variations and changes of name, became our first national song, and its rollicking chorus—in Frank Clunes' words—'was sung with fervour as a kind of national anthem' by succeeding generations of Australians.

Wanted Dead or Alive: Matt Brady

*'It has caused Matthew Brady much con-
cern that a person known as Sir George
Arthur is at large. Twenty gallons of rum
will be given to any person that delivers his
person to me.'*

— (SIGNED) MATTHEW BRADY

Matthew Brady

This was Matt Brady's cheeky response to
Governor Arthur's offer of a £10 reward for anyone delivering the elusive bushranger to the
Law. It was found tacked to the door of an inn
at Cross March in Van Diemen's Land.

Brady was the Bold Jack Donahue of
Tasmania, the wild colonial boy who never
harmed a woman and would shoot any man
who did, mocking the authorities at every turn.

Despite his Irish name Brady (1799–1826)
was a Manchester boy sentenced to seven years
for stealing a basket of food. A constant absconder, and soon sentenced to Macquarie Harbour,
he escaped with 13 others in a whaleboat in
1824. Stealing a settler's guns, the gang took to
the bush (aided and abetted by sympathetic settlers who had once been convicts themselves)
and for nearly two years they roamed at will.

When Governor Arthur raised the reward to
300 guineas and infiltrated informers into the
gang's ranks while intensifying their pursuit, Brady was finally run
to earth. Wounded in the leg in a skirmish, he was captured in 1826
by a settler named John Batman and taken first to Launceston and
then Hobart.

Awaiting trial and the hangman's noose, Matthew Brady was treated like a king by the populace and his cell was filled with flowers
and cakes sent by female well-wishers. To his disgust he was hanged
with the child-killer, 'Monster Jeffries', but the crowd who saw him
meet his end on 4 May 1826 wept and cheered him. 'The government could not expunge his name from popular memory,' writes
Robert Hughes, and Brady became an authentic folk hero, his name
commemorated in Brady's Lookout, the 1,300-metre peak that looks
down, with some contempt, on 'Arthur's Lake.'

Musquito, the Black Bushranger

'With Musquito will be executed tomorrow morning the Van Diemen's Land native, Black Jack, his companion on crime. Black Tom, another villain, was brought up in this town by the late Mr Birch, from whose service Musquito enticed him, but not before he had become addicted to rum and tobacco.

'It may not be known that Musquito was once a civilized black, that is, he had lived for a long period, when he was employed by the police as a tracker, more especially in the pursuit of the last and worst of the bushrangers, Michael Howe. With the downfall of that desperate outlaw, which put an end to free-booting in Van Diemen's Land, Musquito's services were no longer required by the police; and to the shame of the government, who had jeopardized his safety over and over again in his dangerous calling of tracker, was dismissed without any reward. As well (now being only a dismissed police-servant without protection), he suffered much abuse from the low, police-hating element of Hobart Town. This odium was more than he could bear, and exasperated at the indignities he was doomed to undergo, he joined his fortunes with the Oyster Bay tribe, of which in a short time he became leader, and instructor in chief.

'The immediate crime for which Musquito was tried and found guilty, was the murder of two men, named respectively William Holyoak and Mammoa. Black Jack is to be executed for the killing of a person named Patrick McCarthy; but both ruffians are equally guilty of both misdeeds and many other murders of poor, unfortunate stock-keepers in isolated parts of the Eastern coast.'

— *NOTICE IN HOBART TOWN, 24 FEBRUARY 1825.*

Jacky Jacky, the Gentleman Bushranger

William John Westwood was born in Kent in 1820, the son of a farmer, and was well educated. He was transported for forgery to Botany Bay, where he was sent to work for a farmer, a particularly brutal man who flogged his charges. Escaping into the bush, Westwood, who was just twenty, soon afterwards bailed up a parliamentarian on the way to a ball at Government House in Sydney and accompanied him to the function, where he met Governor Gipps and flirted with the ladies. Later he walked into a billiards saloon in Goulburn and challenged the three best players to a game, beating then hands down before announcing his identity and escaping. Later captured, he was sent to Cockatoo Island prison but organized a mass escape and swum across the harbour to Balmain, where he was recaptured. Sentenced to Port Arthur, a place of hell, he organized another mass breakout but was it was unsuccessful and when retaken was sentenced to death by hanging. He had not harmed a single soul.

Captain Thunderbolt

Fred Ward, known to folklore as Captain Thunderbolt, was born in Windsor, New South Wales, in 1836 and started life as a stockman. Thrown into Cockatoo Island prison for being in possession of stolen horses, he escaped with another prisoner in 1863 and embarked on a seven-year spree.

Known for his good looks and cheeky ways, he called himself 'Captain Thunderbolt' when he robbed the toll-house near Maitland at pistol point. He then visited a pub for a snack and then bailed up a man and his sick wife on the road but let them pass unmolested, explaining 'I don't rob sick women'; he then encountered a man and four females, joked that it was unfair that one man had four ladies and he had none, rode past a trooper who had no ammunition left in his pistol and let him go too, and then went back to the pub for tea and regaled the publican's wife with

Frederick Ward – a.k.a. 'Captain Thunderbolt'

his exploits. He was riding away when four troopers rode up to him. A constable held a pistol to Ward's head and said, 'You're my prisoner.' Captain Thunderbolt replied with a laugh, 'Am I?' and spurred his horse forward, escaping into the bush, the troopers in hot pursuit. They gave up when their horses grew too exhausted to ride further.

Captain Thunderbolt was finally pursued on horseback by police near Uralla in New South Wales in 1870 and chased into the Rocky River, where he shot it out on horseback with Constable Walker and was wounded in the affray. Walker dragged Thunderbolt to the bank and rode off to get assistance, but when he returned the culprit was gone. Thunderbolt was found hours later but died before he could be taken to a doctor. He had killed no-one.

Horses

'The chief necessity for a successful career as a bushranger was a good supply of race-horses, and hence it was almost impossible for any person to keep a really valuable saddle horse during this "Reign of Terror", as the newspapers of this district called it. Special raids were organized by members of the gang to obtain a supply of horses, and the bushrangers frequently travelled upwards of two hundred miles [more than 300 kilometres] to secure a horse which had

made a name on the turf ... When leading the race horse Micky Hunter out of his stall Gilbert patted his neck and said, "You're the b-- cove we want." Old Comus and several other horses were taken out of Mr Icely's stables at Coombing. The old horse had had a good career on the course, and had been put aside for stud purposes, and Mr Icely offered a large sum to the bushrangers to leave him alone, but Gilbert said, "There's a good gallop in him yet." But the bushrangers did not devote their whole time to capturing race horses ...'

— *FROM* THE STORY OF THE AUSTRALIAN BUSHRANGERS, *1899, GEORGE BOXALL.*

Ben Hall
(Courtesy: Forbes Historical Museum)

Brave Ben Hall

Ben Hall (1837–65) was a Currency Boy, the son of former convict, and was born at Breeza, New South Wales. His early life was blameless. In 1856 he married Bridget Walsh from Forbes and the couple lived on a cattle property at Sandy Creek in the Weddin Mountains, where they raised a son. Legends abound as to how Ben Hall became a criminal: one story relates that he was wrongly arrested for suspected complicity in a crime, and when released from jail found his farm deserted, his wife gone and his cattle strayed. He was identified as one of Gardiner and Gilbert's gang that held up the gold coach at Eugowra Rocks in June 1862, stealing £14,000; and when Gardiner fled to Queensland, Ben Hall led the gang in Australia's first bank hold-up, robbing the Commercial Bank in Carcoar (near Bathurst) in July 1863. Between February 1863 and April 1865, Ben Hall's gang carried out numerous hold-ups on the roads and raided towns and homesteads 21 times. Hall and Gilbert rode into Bathurst in October 1863 to obtain revolvers, escaping when the alarm was raised by riding through the crowd in the main street, shouting 'Two of us is good enough for forty b-- troopers', and galloped into the timbered country, where they shook off their pursuers. (The local police superintendent, a hapless English baronet, Sir Frederick Pottinger, later accidentally shot himself.) They raided Canowindra three times in late 1863, on all occasions staying overnight at Robinson's Hotel. In December, bold as brass, they bailed up the Burrowa (Boorowa) mail coach and were angry to open the bags and find mainly cheques, which they asked the passengers to cash for them. Next day they rode up to the Burrowa Inn, ordered breakfast and stood drinks all round for their captives while they relieved them of their valuables. In December, Hall and Gilbert stuck up a newspaper editor and his wife in their sulky on the road from Bowning to Binalong (Gilbert swapped hats with the editor), and then bailed up several teams of bullock drivers, who ended up cooking breakfast for them all. They repeated this comedy on successive days before the local squatters decided to form a posse to capture them. So far the bushrangers had not killed anyone and only one of their gang had been shot, and for a while they lay low.

Dunn, Gilbert and Ben Hall

Come all you wild colonials
  And listen to my tale;
  A story of bushrangers' deeds
  I will to you unveil.
  'Tis of those gallant heroes,
  Game fighters one and all;
  And we'll sit and sing, long live the King,
  Dunn, Gilbert and Ben Hall.

Ben Hall was a squatter
  Who owned six hundred head;
  A peaceful man he was until
  Arrested by Sir Fred.

His home burned down, his wife cleared out,
His cattle perished all.
They'll not take me a second time,'
Says valiant Ben Hall.

John Gilbert was a flash cove
And John O'Meally too;
With Ben and Burke and Johnny Vane,
They were all comrades true.
They rode into Canowindra,
And gave a public ball.
'Roll up, roll up, and have a spree,'
Say Gilbert and Ben Hall.

Frank Gardiner was a bushranger
Of terrible renown;
He robbed the Forbes gold escort,
And eloped with Kitty Brown.
But in the end they lagged him,
Two-and-thirty years in all.
'We must avenge the Darkie',
Say Dunn, Gilbert and Ben Hall.

They made a raid on Bathurst,
The pace was getting hot;
But Johnny Vane surrendered,
After Mickey Burke was shot.
O'Meally at Goimbla,
Did like a hero fall,
'The game is getting lively'
Say Gilbert and Ben Hall.

'Hand over all your watches
And the banknotes in your purses.
All travellers must pay toll to us;
We don't care for your curses.
We are the rulers of the roads,
We've seen the troops fall,
And we want your gold and money,'
Say Dunn, Gilbert and Ben Hall

'Next week we'll visit Goulburn
and clean the banks out there;
So if you see the peelers,
Just tell them to beware;
Some day to Sydney city
We mean to pay a call,
And we'll take the whole damn country',
Say Dunn, Gilbert and Ben Hall.

The End of Dunn, Gilbert and Ben Hall: 1865

In October 1864, Ben Hall, who had once more teamed up with the young Canadian, 'Flash Johnny' Gilbert, recruited John Dunn into a gang. Dunn was 17 years old but already widely known as a jockey, and for skipping bail on robbery charges. The trio raided the Rossi property near Goulburn to give Captain Rossi a hiding but found only the servants at home. So instead they stole the Captain's silver, smoked his cigars, drank his liquor and belted out jigs on his piano, before disappearing into the night.

Outside Gundagai they had the misfortune of striking a coach escorted by two of the toughest Mounted Police: Sub-Inspector O'Neill and Sergeant Parry. In a close fight, Gilbert shot Parry and O'Neill nearly knocked Hall senseless with the butt of his gun before the gang made off.

Hall, Dunn and Gilbert now knew that they were doomed men, but in November they rode into Forbes for a drink and in December, when bailing up travellers (including a wedding party) outside Young, they were nearly shot from their saddles when one of their intended victims, the politician William Macleay, stalked them with a rifle.

On Boxing Day 1864, the trio appeared at a dance at Binda. While Ben Hall (no dancing man) stood guard, Dunn and Gilbert enjoyed themselves dancing waltzes and jigs with the best looking women after considerable drinking.

In January the marked men cheekily turned up at a race meeting near Forbes that was attended by Sir Frederick Pottinger (who went out of his way not to arrest them).

On 26 January 1865, the gang staged a hold-up at Geary's Gap, south of Goulburn, and rode on to Collector where Dunn shot a policeman, to Ben Hall's horror. The country was now thick with armed settlers and troopers, but the gang still roamed with impunity.

In February, the trio held up a dray carrying W.P. Faithfull's four sons: Percy, George, Monty and Reggie. Instead of meekly handing over his possessions, the driver whipped his horses into a gallop and, hotly pursued by the bushrangers, made the homestead in safety, his brothers firing at their pursuers.

The net was closing on the trio, but in March they again rode into Forbes after weeks of stealing horses from stations and close brushes with troopers. When his nemesis, Pottinger, died (from a gunshot wound, self-inflicted according to legend), Ben Hall seems to have wanted to give up bushranging for a living. The gang split up.

Hall was alone when a party of troopers, tipped off by Mary Connelly's husband Goobang Mick, caught him asleep near midnight on 5 May 1865. Startled by a sound, Ben woke in a second and rose to his feet, only to be cut down by 27 bullets. His body could barely be recognized when it was carried into Forbes. He was 27 when he died: a bullet for every year.

On 13 May, police, tipped off by Dunn's grandfather, Kelly, surrounded the Kelly house in Binalong where Dunn and Gilbert were sleeping. Gilbert fell dead to a bullet as he tried to escape across a paddock but Dunn, though wounded in the ankle, managed to escape. They caught up with him on Christmas Eve, 1865. Wounded in a gunfight with three troopers, Dunn was carried to Coonamble in intense pain and nursed back to health. He escaped from Dubbo gaol in January 1866 but was recaptured next day. He was hanged in Sydney in March, 1866.

Ben Hall is buried in Forbes cemetery; his grave is still well tended and often visited by those who still sympathize with the plight of a fair man forced into crime. He lies not far from Ned Kelly's sister Kate, who drowned near Forbes in 1898.

Legend has it that his betrayer, Connelly, was torn to pieces by his own dogs; but this seems to be wishful thinking; others remember him living as a butcher in Cobar. Ben's wife, Bridget Hall-Taylor outlived both her men.

Piesley

On 23 March, 1861 an officer of the Bank of New South Wales riding up the mountain track from the Turon River to Tambaroora (near Hill End) was bailed up by two armed men, John Piesley, an absconder from Cockatoo Island, and his confederate and relieved of £565 in banknotes and gold. A new rash of bushranging had begun.

Frank Clune calls Piesley 'the first fair dinkum Australian-born bushranger in the full meaning of the term'. The ex-convict teamed up with Frank Gardiner in holding up travellers from Yass to Cowra and with John Gilbert bailed up the Yass to Gundagai stage coach during his spree.

Piesley was not violent: he wrote a letter while on the run that was published in the *Bathurst Free Press* stating: 'Never in no instance did I ever use violence . . . I love my native land, I love freedom and detest cruelty to man or beast.'

Nevertheless, he shot a man in a drunken brawl, and was tracked down to a homestead near Tarcutta, where he was arrested. He was hanged at Bathurst on 23 March 1862.

Fred Lowry

'Tell 'em I Died Game'

These were the dying words of the bushranger Fred Lowry, shot by police constables when they burst into the hut in which he was hiding in 1863. His first words when hit by a bullet were 'I'm done for! Where's the priest?' He was more than six feet tall (2 metres), and he was only 26 years old when he was shot.

Captain Moonlite

He was the strangest bushranger of them all—and possibly mad. Born Andrew George Scott in Ireland and well educated, he emigrated to Australia, fought as a volunteer in the Maori War (1861–65) before returning to Victoria, where he moved to Bacchus Marsh. There he began studies to enter the Church of England, and worked as a lay reader, often visiting his flock, who regarded him highly. One night a masked man burst into the bank manager's home at Mount Egerton with a gun in his hand. The bank manager recognized the intruder as Scott, and burst out laughing, asking him if this

'Captain Moonlite'

was suitable behaviour for a clergyman. The intruder, who called himself (appropriately) 'Captain Moonlite', tied him up and left him in the schoolhouse, and then took his keys and escaped with £1,000 from the bank's safe. When the manager and schoolmaster were arrested for staging the robbery, Scott turned up give evidence against them, but was eventually arrested for bouncing cheques in New South Wales and sentenced to 18 months in jail. Briefly a free man, he was arrested in Victoria for the bank robbery and lodged in Ballarat Jail, from which he escaped after setting free all the other prisoners in his block; they followed him over the wall. Captured again and imprisoned, Moonlite was released for good behaviour from Pentridge in March 1879, but was soon leading another gang of desperate men. Raiding a property in November 1879, they were surrounded by troopers (one of whom was killed) and all the bushrangers were killed or captured. Scott and one confederate were hanged for murder soon afterwards.

The Last Bushrangers: The Kelly Gang

Oh, Paddy dear, and did you hear
　　The news that's going round,
　　On the head of bold Ned Kelly
　　They have placed a thousand pound.
　　And on Steve Hart, Joe Byrne and Dan,
　　Two thousand more they'd give,
　　But if the price was doubled, boys,
　　The Kelly gang would live.

— *TRADITIONAL BALLAD.*

Edward 'Ned' Kelly (1855–80) exerts an extraordinary spell over Australian history and remains a dominating figure in our folklore. To many he is the wildest colonial boy of them all, the born rebel forced into crime by police victimization, the incarnation of all the wrongs inflicted on the poor Irish; to others he is a simple brute who received his just desserts. Everything about him was original: from his suits of home-made armour to his gift of the gab; from his considerable charm to his feats of horsemanship and enjoyment in dressing up. And his courage in facing death—first, in the shoot-out at Glenrowan, clanking out to fight in his armour after refusing to

NED KELLY, THE BUSHRANGER.

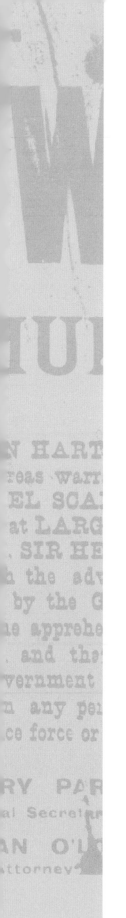

leave his mates in the lurch, and then facing execution with the simple words 'Such is life'—has left him an Australian hero of sorts. The phrase 'Game as Ned Kelly' still lives in the language, and so does 'Such is Life'.

The following report by the journalist and novelist Marcus Clarke (1846–81) is remarkably accurate but repeats the assertion that Ned 'shot the constable' when his brother Dan was being arrested for horse-stealing. Ned protested to his dying day that he was hundreds of miles away at the time.

'On the 26th October 1878, Melbourne was thrown into a state of profound excitement by the announcement that the almost-forgotten crime of old colonial days had been revived, and that a gang of Bushrangers had fought the police in the Wombat Ranges, only 50 miles [80 kilometres] from Mansfield. The details of the business were soon in everybody's mouth, and the history of the criminals became common property.

'In the township of Greta, had lived for some years, a family named Kelly, who occupied themselves in the harmless pursuit of cattle-breeding. Such breeders, however, are known by the name of "cattle duffers", or "bush whackers", their function being rather the stealing of stock than the rearing of it. The Kellys bore a bad name in this district, and the mother and two sons were in prison at one time. An attempt having been made to arrest Daniel Kelly for horse-stealing, his brother Edward shot the constable in the wrist, and the pair fled to the mountains. They made for the pathless wildernesses at the head of the King River, where Power, a bushranger now in gaol, had been accustomed to hide, and for some time baffled pursuit. The residents in and about Mansfield were generally friendly to the young men, and news of the movements of the troopers were "telegraphed" to them by their confederates. At last a body of police, armed with revolvers, a Spencer rifle, and a double-barrelled gun, started from Mansfield, under command of Sergeant Kennedy, and camped for the night at a place called Stringy Bark Creek.

'At dawn the next morning, two of the men, Kennedy and Scanlan, went away to explore, leaving M'Intyre and Lonigan in charge of the camp. M'Intyre foolishly went out to shoot parrots, and the shots were heard by the Kellys, who were up in the mountain. About five o'clock in the evening, the troopers in camp were confronted by four armed men—the two Kellys, [Joe] Hart and [Steve] Byrne. Ned Kelly carried two rifles. M'Intyre was unarmed, and held up his hands in token of surrender; but Lonigan tried to draw his revolver. Ned Kelly instantly fired, and shot him in the temple. He fell dead.

'The bushrangers then compelled M'Intyre to make tea, and questioned him as to the movements of the police. "Did you come out to shoot us?" asked Ned. "We came to apprehend you," said the trooper. "Are you going to shoot us?" Kelly then promised that if the two troopers, who were away, surrendered on their return, their lives would be spared. "If you try to escape," said he, "I will follow you to Mansfield, and shoot you at the police-station. I thought you had been Constable Flood: and, if you had been, I would have burned you alive."

'When Kennedy and Scanlan approached, the bushrangers concealed themselves, and made M'Intyre sit on a log under cover of their rifles. "You had better surrender, sergeant," said he, "We are sur-rounded." Kennedy appeared to think it was a joke, and put his hand to his revolver, when one of the gang fired, but missed him. He then dismounted. Scanlan tried to get his rifle unslung, but was shot down at once. The gang then began firing indiscriminately, and M'Intyre, "Thinking," he said, "that all was over," jumped on Kennedy's horse, and galloped off. After riding two miles in the scrub, his horse fell exhausted, and he took off his boots so as to make less noise in the scrub, and walked to Mansfield, which he reached at three in the afternoon.

Constable Michael Scanlan

'On the 30th of October the body of Kennedy was found, half a mile from the camp where the fatal affray took place. It may be mentioned here, as an instance of the nature of the country, that a party of prospectors lost a horse near the same place, and did not find him for three weeks, although he was in hobbles all the time. The corpse of the unfortunate man presented a horrible appearance. He had been shot through the head, the ball coming out in front and carrying away part of his face. Several bullets were found in the body. A large detachment of police were now ordered up, and the Chief Commissioner arrived to superintend operations in person, but for two months nothing was heard of the gang.

Constable Michael Kennedy

'On the 9th of December they descended upon a station near Faithfull Creek, imprisoned the hands, and then rode down to Euroa, and in broad daylight robbed the bank of £1,900 in notes, gold and silver, but committed no murder. Euroa is a mere village, and only one constable was in the station. The outlaws rode up to the bank, and Ned Kelly, going inside, took possession of the place at the muzzle of his revolver, put the manager, his wife, children and servants to a springcart and drove them to the station. After some display of horsemanship by the robbers—who, like all bush-born

Australians, almost live in the saddle—departed in the direction of the Strathbogie Ranges.

'The reward was now increased to £2,800, and volunteers pressed in from all sides. Black trackers were sent for from Queensland. The township of Mansfield was like a village occupied by hostile troops, but the place swarmed with sympathizers, and it became evident that the stolen money was being freely circulated. Kate Kelly, the bushranger's sister, rode into the ranges and back defiantly, and though several arrests were made and much time and money wasted in fruitless excursions, the outlaws are still at large. The only certain news was contained in a letter sent by Ned Kelly to Mr Cameron, a member of Parliament, stating that he shot Kennedy in fair fight, and that he took to the bush in consequence of being unlawfully imprisoned and hunted down by the police.

Constable Thomas M'Intyre

'The escape of the gang may seem very extraordinary, but only those who have lived in the Australian mountain ranges can understand how easy it is for those familiar with the bush to avoid pursuit. Thickets of impenetrable scrub; huge fallen trees entwisted with creepers into a sort of savage barricade; a sunless gloom of saplings growing less than a foot apart; now and then great rocks split into gullies where a regiment might camp unseen. Suddenly the explorer, parting the branches before him with his hands, finds himself in a little round swamp covered with reeds—an oasis in the desert of civilization. At the other side the "bush" begins again; the ground rises and becomes more open; the spur of the ranges juts out and becomes a cliff. Above the natural pathway are spots where three determined men could bar the progress of an army. The inhabitants of the district will conduct you round a rock where you have camped, perhaps for hours, and show you a cavern, or follow the bed of the creek upwards until they emerge from a plateau from whence they can read the country as from the car of a balloon. Let us add to this fact, that the majority of these inhabitants regard the police as common enemies, and it will not be difficult to understand how the Kellys have been enabled to escape so long. They have been supplied ever since their flight from Greta with intelligence and food, and it is impossible to say how much longer they may not be enabled to elude pursuit.'

Constable Thomas Lonigan

— MARCUS CLARKE (1846-81), JOURNALIST AND NOVELIST.

Ned Kelly's Jerilderie Letter, 1879

The original of this extraordinary literary creation, written in Jerilderie and posted to the politician Cameron, has been lost; but numerous copies were made from it and its authenticity has never been challenged. Ned Kelly, who could barely print his name, apparently dictated it to the one member of his gang who could write. Some colourful excerpts from it appear below:

'. . . those men came into the bush with the intention of scattering pieces of me and my brother all over the bush; and yet they know and acknowledge that I have been wronged, and my mother and five men lagged innocent.

'And is my brothers and sisters, and my mother, not to be pitied also, who have no alternative but to put up with the brutal and cowardly conduct of a parcel of big, ugly, fat-necked, wombat-headed, big-bellied, magpie-legged, narrow-hipped, splay-footed sons of Irish bailiffs or English landlords, known as "Officers of Justice" or "Victorian Police?"

'Some call them honest gentlemen, but I would like to know what business an honest man would have in the police? It is an old saying that it takes a rogue to catch a rogue. A man who knows nothing about roguery would never enter the police force, and take an oath to arrest his brother, sister, father or mother, if required, and obtain a conviction, if possible.

'Any man knows it is possible to swear a lie. If a policeman loses a conviction for the sake of not swearing a lie, he has broken his oath. Therefore he is a perjurer either way.

'What would people say if they saw a strapping big lump of an Irishman shepherding sheep for fifteen bob a week, or tailing turkeys in the Tallarook Ranges for a smile from Julia!

'They would say he ought to be ashamed of himself, but he would be a King compared with a policeman, who, for a lazy, loafing, cowardly billet, deserted the Ash Corner and the Shamrock— the emblem of true wit and beauty—to serve under the flag of a nation that has destroyed, massacred and murdered his forefathers by the greatest of tortures imaginable, such as rolling them downhill in spiked barrels, or pulling out their fingernails and toenails, or on the wheel, while others were transported to Van Diemen's Land to pine their young lives away in starvation and misery, among tyrants, worse than the promised Hell itself.

'All of true blood, bone and beauty who were not murdered on their own soil, or fled to America to bloom again another day, were doomed to Port Macquarie, Toongabbie, Norfolk Island, and Emu Plains; and, in those places of tyranny, many a blooming Irishman,

rather than submit to the Saxon yoke, was flogged to death, and bravely died in service chains, but true to the Shamrock, and a credit to Paddy's Land.

'What would people say if I became a policeman, and took an oath to arrest my brothers and sisters and relations, and to convict them by fair or foul means, after the convictions of my mother and the persecutions and insults offered to myself and my people?

'Would they say I was a decent gentleman? Yet a policeman is still worse, and guilty of meaner actions than that.

'The Queen must surely be proud of such heroic men as the police and Irish soldiers! It needs eight or eleven of the biggest mud-crushers in Melbourne to take one poor little half-starved larrikin to a watch-house.

'I have seen as many as eleven of them, big and ugly enough to lift Mount Macedon out of a crab-hold—more like baboons or gorillas than men—actually come into a court-house and swear they could not arrest one eight-stone larrikin, and them armed with batons and niddies, without some civilians' assistance, and some of them going to the hospital from the effects of hits from the fists of the larrikin; and the magistrate would send the poor little larrikin into a dungeon, for being a better man than such a parcel of armed curs!

'What would England do if America declared war on her and hoisted the green flag? It is all Irishmen who have command of England's armies, forts and batteries. Even her very Life Guards and Beef Eaters are Irish!

'Would they not slew around and fight her with her own arms for the sake of the colour they have not dared to wear for years, to reinstate it, and raise Old Erin's Isle once more from the pressure and tyranny of the English yoke, which has kept it in poverty and starvation, and caused them to wear the enemy's coat?

'What else can England expect?

'Are there not big fat-necked unicorns enough, paid to torment and drive me to do things I don't wish to do, without the public assisting?

'I have never interfered with any person unless he deserved it, and yet there are civilians who take fire-arms against me, for what reason I do not know, unless they want me to turn on them, and exterminate them without medicine.

'I shall be compelled to make an example of some of them, if they cannot find another employment.

NED KELLY AT BAY
FROM A SKETCH DRAWN ON THE SPOT BY MR. T. CARRINGTON.

'If I had robbed and plundered, ravished and murdered everyone I met, young and old, rich and poor, the public could not do any more than take fire-arms to assist the police, as they have done.

'But by the Light that Shines, the pleasure of being pegged on an ant-bed, with their bellies opened, their fat taken out and rendered and poured down their throats boiling hot will be cool to what I will give some of them . . .'

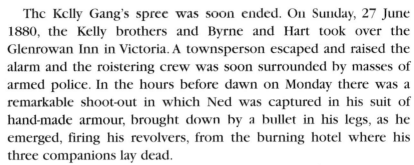

The Kelly Gang's spree was soon ended. On Sunday, 27 June 1880, the Kelly brothers and Byrne and Hart took over the Glenrowan Inn in Victoria. A townsperson escaped and raised the alarm and the roistering crew was soon surrounded by masses of armed police. In the hours before dawn on Monday there was a remarkable shoot-out in which Ned was captured in his suit of hand-made armour, brought down by a bullet in his legs, as he emerged, firing his revolvers, from the burning hotel where his three companions lay dead.

He was placed on trial in Melbourne, found guilty of murder, and hanged on 11 November 1880. 'Such is life.'

Passing Judgement

On passing sentence of death on the murderous Clarke brothers in 1867, the Chief Justice of New South Wales, Sir Alfred Stephen, said:

'I never knew a bushranger—except one who is now suffering sentences aggregating thirty-two years—who made any money by it ...I will read you a list of bushrangers, many of them young men, capable of better things, but who died violent deaths. Piesely executed; Davis sentenced to death; Gardiner sentenced to thirty-two years hard labour; Gilbert shot dead; Hall shot dead; Bow and Fordyce sentenced to death, but their sentences commuted to imprisonment for life; Manns executed; O'Meally shot dead; Burke shot dead; Gordon sentenced to death; Dunleavy sentenced to death; Dunn executed; Lowry shot dead; Vane a long sentence; Foley a long sentence; Morgan shot dead; yourselves, Thomas and John Clarke, about to be sentenced to death; Fletcher shot dead; Patrick Connell shot dead; Tom Connell sentenced to death, but sentence commuted to imprisonment for life; Bill Scott, a companion of yours, believed to have been murdered by you ...The list shows six shot dead and ten wounded ...Unfortunately there were seven constables shot dead and ten wounded in three years since 1863 ...The murders believed to have been committed by you bushrangers are appalling to think of. How many wives have you made widows, how many children orphans, what loss of property, what sorrow you have caused! ... and yet, these bushrangers, the scum of the earth, the lowest of the low, the most wicked of the wicked, are occasionally held up for our admiration! But better days are coming. It is the old leaven of convictism not yet worked out, but brighter days are coming. You will not live to see them, but others will.'

By the end of the 1860s the lawlessness had ended—apart from Ned Kelly's wild eruption—and Australia was soon to become one of the most law-abiding societies on earth, where for a century policemen could walk unarmed.

5: *The Squatters*

The Squatter Kings of New South Wales—
  The Squatter Kings who reign,
  O'er rocky hill, and scrubby ridge,
  O'er swamp, and salt-bush plain . . .
— *FROM A BALLAD BY* **G.H. GIBSON.**

IN 1831 THE MAKING OF LAND GRANTS TO favoured settlers ceased. While the governor in Sydney procrastinated and London ordered settlement confined to the nineteen counties that formed a cosy semi-circle around Sydney stretching only as far west as Bathurst, south as far as the Murrumbidgee, enterprising men rode out to claim the virgin bush for themselves, driving their flocks of sheep and herds of cattle alongside their drays and carts. Those with capital thrived.

'Squatting in its first burst may have been the most romantic episode in all Australian history,' writes an American historian, 'but it was a rough and tumble episode, generally comparable to the occupation of the cattle country in the American West.'

'Not all the armies in England, not a hundred thousand soldiers scattered through the bush, could drive back those herds within the limits of the nineteen counties,' Governor Bourke wrote to the Colonial Office in the mid-1830s as he attempted to impose some system on the settlers' seizure of the hinterland.

Bourke's first attempt to stem the flood was to define certain squatting 'districts' in 1836 where settlers could occupy Crown Land on payment of a fee of £10 annually, irrespective of the area they seized. In 1838, the governor established border police to keep order in the districts and to levy a tax on the number of sheep each squatter possessed, while protecting them from native attacks. But it soon proved impossible to police the squatters. Until the Depression of 1840-43, the squatters of New South Wales waxed rich on the prices their wool brought until speculation and a glutted market wiped out hundreds of them. Those who survived would become the closest thing Australia has to a landed aristocracy—the pioneer families who built their wealth on sheep and cattle. But history and folklore would treat them unkindly, seeing greed and opportunism in their rush to secure the best pickings. Only those whose exertions verged on the heroic would become folk heroes.

The Free Colonies

New Australian colonies were, however, being founded on stronger and fairer foundations, free of convicts, chain gangs and oligarchies. The western half of the continent was still unclaimed by any European power, and France took steps to claim it. Early in 1829, Britain hurriedly sent a warship to the mouth of the Swan River, which the Dutch had explored as early as the 1600s, to claim the remaining half of 'New Holland' for the British Crown, with orders to politely evict any French found there. Two months later the first free settlers arrived from England at the Swan River, where they would found Perth and its port, Fremantle.

In 1836, the first English emigrants landed at the site of Adelaide to establish a Utopian settlement, the 'Province of South Australia'. They were soon joined by Scots, and Cornish miners, and God-fearing German Lutherans (who would plant the vines in the Barossa Valley that grew into a vigorous wine industry). The Province—never a colony—became a model of progress and religious tolerance in an ugly age of intolerance, though one emigrant took the authorities to task for not mentioning the extremities of heat in summer when the hot winds from central Australia leave Adelaide gasping for air in oven-like conditions. And thirty years later, the American Mark Twain wondered why it was called South Australia,

for every colony apart from Queensland extended further south than it did!

It was settled only a year after the establishment of European settlers on the northern shores of Port Phillip Bay—which would grow into the prosperous Colony of Victoria.

Melbourne Founded

John Batman, the founder of Melbourne in 1835

'In 1835 John Batman went to Port Phillip with a few friends and seven Sydney blackfellows. On June 14th he returned to Van Diemen's Land, and by the 25th of the same month he had compiled a report of his expedition, which he sent to Governor Arthur, together with a copy of the grant of land executed by the black chiefs. He had obtained three copies of the grant signed by three brothers Jagga-Jagga; by Bungaree, Yan-Yan, Moorwhip and Marmarallar. The area of the land bought by Batman was not surveyed with precision, but it was of great extent, like infinite space, whose centre is everywhere, and circumference nowhere. And in addition he took up a small patch of one hundred thousand acres [40,468.5 hectares] between the bay and the Barwon, including the insignificant site of Geelong, a place of small account even to this day. Batman was a long-limbed Sydney native, and he bestrode his real estate like a Colossus, but King William of England was a bigger Colossus than Batman—he claimed both the land and the blacks, and ignored the Crown grant.

'Next, John Fawkner and his friends chartered the schooner *Enterprise* for a voyage across the Straits to Australia Felix. He afterwards claimed to be the founder of Melbourne. He could write and talk everlastingly, but he had not the robur and as triplex suitable for a sea-robber. Sea-sickness nearly killed him, so he stayed behind while the other adventurers went and laid the foundations. They first examined the shores of Western Port, then went to Port Phillip Bay and entered the River Yarra. They disembarked on its banks, ploughed some land, sowed maize and wheat, and planted two thousand fruit trees. They were not so grasping as Batman, and each man pegged out a farm of only one hundred acres [40.5 hectares]. These farms were very valuable in the days of the late boom, and are called the city of Melbourne. Batman wanted to oust the newcomers; he claimed the farms under his grant from the Jagga-Jaggas. He squatted on Batman's Hill, and looked down with evil eyes on the rival immigrants . . .'

— GEORGE DUNDERDALE.

Living Off the Land: Gippsland

'The country between the sea and the mountains [of eastern Victoria] was the happy-hunting-ground of the natives before the arrival of the ill-omened white-fellow. The inlets teemed with flathead, mullet, perch, schnapper, oysters and sharks, and also with innumerable water-fowl. The rivers yielded eels and blackfish. The sand shores of the island were honey-combed with the holes in which millions of mutton-birds deposited their eggs in the last days of November in each year. Along many tracks in the scrub the black wallabies and paddy-melons hopped low. In the open glades among the great gum-trees marched the stately emu, and tall kangaroos, seven feet high, stood erect on

their monstrous hind-legs, their little fore-paws hanging in front, and their small faces looking as innocent as sheep.

'Every hollow gum-tree harboured two or more fat opossums, which, when roasted, made a rich and savoury meal. Parrots of the most brilliant plumage, like winged flowers, flew in flocks from tree to tree, so tame that you could kill them with a stick, and so beautiful that it seemed a sin to destroy them. Black cockatoos, screaming harshly the while, tore long strips of bark from the mess-mate, searching for the savoury grub. Bronzed-wing pigeons, gleam-ing in the sun, rose from the scrub, and flocks of white cockatoos, perched high on the bare limbs of the dead trees, seemed to have made them burst into miraculous bloom like Aaron's rod.

'The great white pelican stood on one leg on a sand-bank, gazing along its huge beak at the receding tide, hour after hour, solemn and solitary, meditating on the mysteries of Nature.

'But on the mountains both birds and beasts were scarce, as many a famishing white man has found to his sorrow. In the heat of summer the sea-breeze grows faint, and dies before it reaches the ranges. Long ropes of bark, curled with the hot sun, hang motion-less from the black-butts and blue gums; a few birds may be seen sitting on the limbs of the trees, with their wings extended, their beaks open, panting for breath, unable to utter a sound from their parched throats.

LEADBEATER'S COCKATOO.

' "When all food fails them welcome haws" is a saying that does not apply to Australia, which yields no haws or fruit of any kind that can long sustain life. A starving man may try to allay the pangs of hunger with the wild raspberries, or with the cherries which wear their seeds outside, but the longer he eats them, the more hungry he grows. One resource of the lost white man, if he has a gun and ammunition, is the native bear, sometimes called monkey bear. Its flesh is strong and muscular, and its eucalyptic odour is stronger still. A dog will eat opossum with pleasure, but he must be very hungry before he will eat bear; and how lost to all delicacy of taste, and sense of refinement, must the epicure be who will make the attempt!

'The last quadruped on which a meal can be made is the dingo, and the last winged creature is the owl, whose scanty flesh is viler even than that of the hank or carrion crow, and yet a white man has partaken of all these and survived. Some men have tried roasted snake, but I have never heard of anyone who could keep it in his stomach.'

— *GEORGE DUNDERDALE.*

German Settlers, South Australia, 1839

'The first village we passed was Klemzig, a settlement of Germans who had lately arrived in the colony and who were busy erecting their houses and farming their little gardens. It was a beautiful site in the Australian bush to see the neat and gabled houses with their small windows and large lofts arising after the fashion of the father-land and to see the neat, quiet and respectable figures of the Teutonic occupants, the ancient frau seated at the door of the cottage knitting, the children in their costume with a handkerchief of many colours tied round the head of the girl, the men working with the everlasting pipe in their mouths, all ready with a kind and civil salutation so different from the rough, overbearing manners of our own country men. The South Australian Germans are strict Calvinists and each village has its pastor. They are gregarious people. They seldom set up as individuals in the far bush, living, working and acting for themselves, but they congregate in villages and the herds and flocks often belong to the people in common.'

— *FROM AN OLD ACCOUNT.*

Patrick Leslie, Prince of Bushmen

Patrick Leslie is celebrated in history and folklore as the pioneer and 'rediscoverer' of Queensland's Darling Downs, and a fearless bushman. Born into a family of sturdy brothers, sons of a Scottish laird, he arrived in New South Wales in 1835, accompanied by his brothers George and Walter.

After several years on properties, the brothers decided to look for land of their own in the north of the colony. In 1840, Patrick Leslie, accompanied by a convict companion, rode into the hinterland from Brisbane and beyond the mountains found the lush hill country noted 20 years before by Cunningham which the latter had named the Darling Downs.

Staking out a property, Leslie was joined there by Walter and the latter's sheep herds. However, ruined by the Depression and left deeply in debt, Patrick sold out, buying another property, Goomburra (which he later sold to the brewer, Tooth) and selected the site of Warwick, close to the present border of New South Wales and Queensland.

Soon re-established as the leading pastoralist on the Darling Downs and renowned for his stud breeding of animals, Patrick Leslie was also a strong character 'who more than once backed his arguments with his fists.' But he was a poor businessman. He sold up, moved to New Zealand and returned to spend his last days in Sydney, where he died in 1881, staunchly conservative to the end.

A Squatter of the Olden Time

I'll sing you a fine new song, made by my blessed mate,
  Of a fine Australian squatter, who had a fine estate;
  Who swore by right pre-emptive, at a sanguinary rate,
  That by his rams, his ewes, his lambs, Victoria was made great—
  Like a fine Australian settler, one of the olden time.

His hut around was hung with guns, whips, spurs, and boots
  and shoes,
  And kettles, and tin pannikins to hold the tea he brews;
  And here his worship lolls at ease, and takes his smoke and
  snooze—
  And quaffs his cup of hyonskin, the beverage old chums
  choose—
  Like a fine Australian squatter, one of the olden time.

When shearing time approaches, he opens hut to all,
  And though ten thousand are his sheep, he
  neatly shears them all,
  E'en to the scabby wanderers you'd think no good at all,
  For while he fattens all the great, he boils down the small—
  Like a fine old Murray settler, one of the olden time.

And when his worship comes to town, his agent for to see,
  His wool to ship, his beasts to sell, he lives right merrily;
  The Club his place of residence, as becomes a bush J.P.,
  He darkly hints that Thomson's run from scab is hardly free—
  Like a fine Australian gentleman, one of the olden time.

And now his fortune he has made, to England straight goes he,
  But finds with grief he's not received, as he had hoped to be;
  His friends declare his habits queer, his language much too free,
  And are somewhat apt to cross the street, when him they
  chance to meet—
  This fine Australian gentleman, one of the olden time.

— TRADITIONAL BALLAD.

Squatters

'The squatter travelling along through the country generally takes two horses, leading one and riding the other, and in this way makes very long journeys. The work which Australian horses will do when immediately taken off the grass is very surprising.

'I have ridden forty, fifty and even as much as sixty-four miles a day—the whole weight on the animal's back being over seventeen stone, and have come to the end of the day's work without tiring the horse. According to the distance to be done, and the number of consecutive days during which you require your steed to travel, will be your pace. The fastest which I ever did from morning to evening was eight miles; but six miles an hour will perhaps be the average rate.

'The stories, however, that we hear are very wonderful—for in matters of horseflesh, gentlemen in Australia do not hide their lights under bushels. I have heard men boast of doing ten miles an hour for ten hours running and one very enterprising horseman assured me that he had ridden seventy-five miles in four hours. The bush horses are, generally, not shod—though I would always recommend shoeing for a long journey—and are very rarely stabled. They are expected—to use a bush phrase—to cut their own bread and butter, or, in other words, to feed themselves by foraging. The two paces which are commonly adopted by horsemen in the bush are walking and cantering. Men seldom trot, and consequently many horses altogether lose, or never acquire, the habit of trotting. I have been assured that Australian horses will get over the ground at a fast pace with greater ease to themselves by a continual canter than by changing the pace for a trot. That such a theory is altogether wrong, I have not the slightest doubt. I have found in Australia, as all horsemen know in England, that horses carrying heavy weights will make much longer journeys if made to trot than they can do if required to canter hour after hour. The canter is the easier pace to the man, and therefore it has been adopted. Not uncommonly a horse will knock up with his rider on the road. On such occasions the rider turns into the nearest squatter's station, and borrows another. The fact that everybody's horses, and everybody's saddles and bridles, are always at someone else's house and never at the owner's, is one of the most remarkable and perhaps not least pleasing phases of Australian life. Nevertheless, it tends to some confusion.'

— *FROM* AUSTRALIA AND NEW ZEALAND, *1873,*
   ANTHONY TROLLOPE *(1815-82).*

Squatters versus Selectors

'Unlock the land!' was the cry of the 1850s. 'Free selection for all!' others chanted, and counted the months to the first day of 1861, when, under the new Land Laws of Premier John Robertson of New South Wales ('Honest Jack Robertson'), the 14-year leases granted to squatters in 1847 were to expire, and the land would be opened to all.

But the new buyers, high with hopes but low in capital, found little good land to select. They were generally offered the worst pieces of land from the great stations, or ones that were inaccessible or ones lacking water (river frontages or well-watered creeks). Many—like the Soldier Settlers given blocks in the 1920s—eventually had to give up and sell up. By 1890, a handful of squatting families in Victoria alone owned 809,371 hectares (2 million acres) of the best freehold land in their colony, establishing pastoral dynasties that have lasted to this day: the Armytages and Austins, Chirnsides and Clarkes, McCullochs and Manifolds, Wilsons and Winters. Together with the Falkiners and MacArthur-Onslows of New South Wales, they formed a Squattocracy or Upper Class as secure as any in the Old Country. And their properties, well-capitalized and fertile, were efficient: between 1860 and the early 1890s the number of sheep in Australia rose from 20 million to 100 million, and the weight of wool per sheep rose from 3 pounds (approximately 1.4 kilograms) to 7 pounds (approximately 3.4 kilograms).

For the 'Selectors', many of whom lacked even enough cash after their down payment to purchase tools and implements, life was one of continuous hardship. They were among the true pioneers of Australia, heroes of folk history.

The 'Riverine'

'Prince Warung', the author of the following piece, was an English-born journalist, William Astley (1855–1911), who made his name with tales of the Riverina folk.

'It is a traditional belief with the sturdy people of the Riverine district that theirs was always "an honest man's country"—that in the elasticity of its atmosphere men of the shady sort could not breathe, and their methods would not work. Like many other good old beliefs this particular one had no warrant in fact. What with smuggling and "the rebate system" on the rivers and dummying and "peacocking" on land, I do not think, area for area, a region can be found in Australia where the device that is dubious and the dodge that is dark grew to such luxuriance. Once upon a time of very long ago, that was, of course. At the present day, it is unnecessary to state, the men of the Riverine are as guileless "as they make 'em". The breath of the plains and the rivers is now an exhalation of innocence—of a surety. Such a dodge as is herein related would be of impossible happening now.

'The generation of settlers of which the parentage was in the *Robertson Land Act* was, in truth, a very sad one. Morally speaking, I mean. As far as spirits and tempers went it was jovial and companionable, but the admirable comradeship which, on the surface, marked the country, hid feuds, and hatreds, and duplicities that were so far from admirable as to be detestable. Sometimes the disguise was thrown aside, and "the fine free-hand squatter" showed his teeth clenched menacingly, or the "enterprising selector" forgot his manners and threatened and boasted that he and his class would pick the eyes out of every run in the district, and the heart out of every run-holder. Sometimes the one was in fault, and sometimes the other; oftenest, both were in error. And thus, whether the Riverine sky smiled with exquisite delicacy of blue tint, or frowned with occasional sullenness, or glared brassily, the men who worked and schemed beneath it were driven by the folly and iniquity of the politicians to range themselves in one of two opposing armies, and to spend their energies in cutting one another's throats, instead of combining the eminently useful work of cutting the throats of the legislators.

'It was nothing but natural that some persons and things quite innocent of partisanship should get mixed up involuntarily with these class-battles and animosities; bankers, tradesmen, and clergymen with every wish to remain independent of both sides became entangled with one or the other, or both. So too, the boat-owner, who earned big lump freights from the squatter for wool and stores, but who also made big profits on his own tradings with the selectors and tradesmen. Even the Government officials took sides.'

The Eumerella Shore

There's a happy little valley on the Eumerella shore,
    Where I've lingered many happy hours away,
    On my little free selection I have acres by the score,
    Where I unyoke the bullocks from the dray.
    To my bullocks then I say,
    No matter where you stray,
    You will never be impounded any more;
    For you're running, running, running on the duffer's piece
    of land,
    Free selected on the Eumerella shore.

When the moon has climbed the mountains and stars are shining
    bright,
    Then we saddle up our horses and away,
    And we steal the squatters' cattle in the darkness of the night,
    And we brand 'em at the dawning of the day.

Oh, my little poddy calf,
    At the squatter you may laugh,
    For he'll never be your owner any more;
    For you're running, running, running on the duffer's piece
    of land,
    Free selected on the Eumerella shore.

If we find a mob of horses when the paddock rails are down,
    Although before, they're never known to stray,
    Oh, quickly will we drive them to some distant inland town,
    And sell them into slav'ry far away.

To Jack Robertson we'll say,
    You've been leading us astray,
    And we'll never go a-farming any more;
    For it's easier duffing cattle on the little piece of land,
    Free selected on the Eumerella shore.

— *Traditional Ballad.*

6: *The Gold Rush*

GOLD! GOLD! GOLD! Its discovery in the 1850s eclipsed that of 1849 in California and transformed Australia. The remote colonies soon became the new El Dorado, destination of thousands of fortune hunters, and immigrant families escaping bleak poverty and grey horizons. The mineral changed the course of Australian history.

Hargraves

If one man could be described as the 'gold finder', it was an Englishman, Edward Hammond Hargraves (1816–91). He was a larger-than-life figure: two metres tall (6 foot, 5 inches) and 140 kilos (22 stone). Immigrating to Australia as a 16-year-old boy, he had prospected for gold in California in the 1849 'rush' and was struck by the similarity there of the terrain to the land around Bathurst in New South Wales, quartz country, with myriad gullies and streams. Returning to Australia luckless, he began panning for alluvial gold, using the methods he has learned in California, in the creeks near Bathurst in February 1851 and quickly found some. In April 1851, his partners, Lister and the Tom brothers, went down to Lewis Ponds Creek and there discovered quantities—'payable quantities'—of gold. Hargraves named the site Ophir, after the city of gold in the Bible, and bore the samples to Sydney. There he found the authorities there cautious and non-committal, for others had found gold, though not in large quantities. The authorities feared an influx of lawless gold-seekers; but the discovery was announced on 14 May. In the same month, gold was discovered near Wellington, in the central west of New South Wales, and then on the Turon River north of Bathurst—and the gold rush was on. Hargraves was later rewarded handsomely by the New South Wales government for his discoveries and died a wealthy man.

GREAT BOURKE STREET, MELBOURNE

Victoria the Golden

The Colony of Victoria, whose separation from New South Wales was proclaimed with rejoicing on 1 July 1851, was derided by many north of the Murray as 'a Cabbage Patch': a green and fertile stretch of earth, but with little else to offer. The new Colony, however, got off to bright start. With so many people leaving for the New South Wales goldfields, the government offered a reward to anyone who found gold in Victoria. Thirteen days later a miner called James Esmond found a reef near Clunes. By year's end, gold had also been found at Ballaarat (an Aboriginal name that later became Ballarat) and Sandhurst (later Bendigo, from the Biblical name Abednego)—and within a year more than 100,000 people had poured into Victoria alone.

Gold exports enriched England, too, and the government of Great Britain soon looked on the troublesome Australian colonies with a new respect. Before long, the vaults of the Bank of England in London held so much of the precious metal that gold sovereigns became commonplace in the coinage. In gold, a radical journal in Victoria, proclaimed, 'lies the elements of our future greatness— yes, we shall be a NATION, not a dependency of a far-off country!'

With gold came the lawlessness the government had dreaded: more than a decade of highway robbery and bushranging resulted. The authorities lacked the police and resources necessary to maintain order, and when it tried to coerce law-abiding miners and diggers with iniquitous licences allocated by corrupt officials, the government soon faced open rebellion: at Eureka Stockade in 1854.

Melbourne Booms

'Though Melbourne, in 1855, was a youthful city compared to Sydney, the enormous traffic brought to and fro by the diggings was rapidly taking the Victorian capital to the top of the poll amongst Australian cities. But, as I remember Melbourne in 1855, many parts of what are now busy, populous arteries, had not been cleared of timber. Stumps of trees recently cut down were standing in several streets. The Flemington Road, to wit, was a real bushy neighbourhood. A number of tents, inhabited by recently arrived immigrants, stood around the site of the present big Railway Station at Prince's Bridge, 'ere the owners departed for Bendigo, Ballarat and other rushes . . . Cantlon's "Bull and Mouth" in Bourke Street was the real hive of the wide democracy—the horny-handed . . .'

— *Chas. MacAlister.*

Gold on the Turon

'As every schoolboy knows, the Turon rush broke out in 1851, and it was a 'hummer'; truly an epoch-marking event which set the world ablaze with excitement, and made Australia's name known from pole to pole.

'I first heard of the Turon gold discovery while homeward-bound from Sydney in May, 1851, accompanied by my late brother (Thos. MacAlister), and other carriers. A horseman leading a "packer" overtook us one afternoon at the Bargo River crossing. He said, "I suppose you chaps have heard of gold being found over on the Turon?"

'We answered "No," and naturally asked who had discovered it. Our informant said, "Oh, a man named Hargraves—not long back from California—struck it at Summer Hill Creek. Good and rich, too. I'm making for there now," he added as he rode away. On reaching Goulburn we found a few had already started for the rush, and more making ready, and I quickly resolved to join in the hunt …'

— *CHAS. MACALISTER.*

Hill End and Sofala

In 1851 a huge mass of gold, the 'Kerr Hundredweight', was discovered on the banks of the Turon River north of Bathurst, New South Wales, and a township sprung up there almost overnight. It was named Sofala, after the fabled gold-trading centre in Mozambique, and soon 40 hotels were trading there. And in 1871 more gold was found in the rugged hill country to its north-west, at Hill End and Tambaroora, 900 metres above sea level. Thousands of diggers trekked up to Hill End, where Holtermann's Nugget weighing in at 286 kilograms was found in 1872, but within four or five years most of the gold had given out.

Sofala and Hill End (an hour's drive from it up a steep and twisting mountain road) are now historic sites, but fossickers still go there and find specks and small nuggets. Sofala, which today has the appearance of a town from the American Wild West, has been immortalized in paintings by Russell Drysdale, while the gold rush days at Hill End are preserved in the famed glass-plate photographs commissioned by its most prosperous citizen, the German immigrant Bernard Otto Holtermann, which are now one of the treasures of the Mitchell Library in Sydney. Hill End has been the home of numerous artists, the best-known of whom was Donald Friend.

Holtermann and his 'nugget'

Photographs from Holtermann's Hill End Collection
(Mitchell Library, State Library of New South Wales)

Photograph from Holtermann's Hill End Collection
(*Mitchell Library, State Library of New South Wales*)

SKETCHES AT THE GOLD FIELDS (FROM MELBOURNE PUNCH)

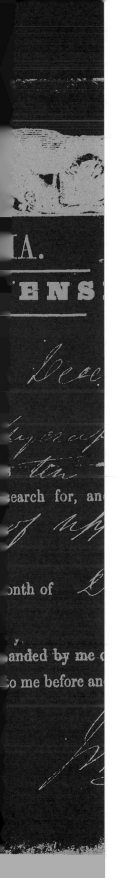

The Miner

The miner he goes and changes his clothes,
  And then makes his way to the shaft;
  For each man will know he's going below,
  To put in eight hours of graft.

CHORUS:
With his calico cap and his old flannel shirt,
  His pants with the strap round the knee,
  His boots watertight and his candle alight,
  His crib and his billy of tea.

The tapman to the driver will knock four and one,
  The ropes to the windlass will strain;
  As one shift comes up, another goes down,
  And working commences again.

He works hard for his pay at six bob a day,
  He toils for his missus and kids.
  He gets what's left over, and thinks he's in clover,
  To cut off his baccy from quids.

And thus he goes on, week in and week out,
  To toil for his life's daily bread.
  He's off to the mine in hail, rain or shine,
  That his dear ones at home may be fed.

Digging holes in the ground where there's gold
  to be found,
  (And most times where gold it is not),
  A man's like a rabbit with this digging habit,
  And like one he ought to be shot.

— *ANONYMOUS.*

Eureka!

Shots were fired and diggers were killed at a place called Eureka
Stockade, in the first and only battle in Australian history between
free men and the armed forces of the Crown.

  Only two months after the discovery of gold in Victoria in 1851,
Lieutenant-Governor La Trobe, concerned at the influx of fortune
hunters and the threat to the colony's social fabric (such as it was)
ordered diggers to pay a licence fee of 30 shillings a month—an
exorbitant cost that many who were heading for the new goldfields
at Buninyong (soon to be the township of Ballaarat) could not pay,
or refused to pay. La Trobe's successor, Hotham, decided to use force
to make the diggers pay 'the bloody tax'. When the mass of diggers

called upon licence-holders to burn their licences as a show of solidarity with them, many did, and under the flag of the Southern Cross the mob vowed to stand together against a tyrannical government. On Sunday 3 December 1854, the redcoats attacked the diggers' stockade on Bakery Hill and the rebellion was over in minutes. Twenty-four ill-armed diggers were killed and five soldiers.

But none of those taken prisoner was found guilty of treason. An injustice had been challenged, and was soon ended. Victor Daley's famous 'Ballad of Eureka' is printed further on in this book.

The flow of wealth in Australia in the 1850s brought riches in which all would share, from the highest to the lowest. A new middle class demanded the democratic freedoms protected by an elected legislature enjoyed by Englishmen in the mother country, and their families demanded the entertainments enjoyed overseas: theatres played to packed houses, and newspapers and journals flourished. Workers were able to down tools and demand better conditions than any enjoyed anywhere else in the world. The '8-Hour Day' became law for stonemasons and builders in Victoria in 1856

HON. PETER LALOR.

and for some workers in New South Wales the following year. By the 1870s, 'Marvellous Melbourne' had overtaken Sydney as Australia's largest and stateliest city, initiating a good-natured, unending, inter-city rivalry that has never changed into mutual admiration.

A 'Bunyip Aristocracy'

When the efforts of the ageing William Charles Wentworth (1790–1871), son of an Irish convict doctor, explorer, fighter for freedom of the press and trial by jury, and champion of the people against autocratic governors, finally achieved self-government for New South Wales, Wentworth proposed an upper house similar to the British House of Lords, one in which nominated members of a local peerage would sit for life. This astonishing proposal aroused the orator Dan Deniehy to ridicule it as 'a bunyip aristocracy' and he talked of how people would respond to having to bow and scrape before a 'Duke of Woolloomooloo'. Notions of a homegrown nobility died, but in all Australian states (Queensland abolished theirs) the upper house (legislative council) remains a chamber of members who for most of the council's existence were not elected by the people and were handsomely paid to do, apparently, very little.

'Vandemonians'

Among the gold-seekers and free immigrants heading for Victoria in the 1850s were numbers from across Bass Strait. Settlers from Tasmania (Van Diemen's Land) had founded Victoria but the new influx included former convicts, many of them hardened criminals—the Vandemonians—who quickly established a bad name for themselves on the gold fields as thieves and claim-jumpers. Some of them even joined the police (the troopers), adding insult to injury.

A GOLD FIELD IN THE "DIGGINS."

Lola Montez

She was the most famous performer to appear before Australian audiences in the 1850s and her scandalous life became even more colourful during her brief stay. Born Maria Dolores Gilbert in 1818 in Limerick, Ireland, she left an unsuccessful marriage to dance on the stage in London under a Spanish name and then progressed in 1846 to Bavaria, where in quick succession she enjoyed a love affair with the composer Liszt and then enchanted the eccentric King Ludwig (whose other passions were to include Richard Wagner's music and building fairytale castles). Forced to flee Bavaria, she visited the Australian goldfields where she enacted on stage a spirited melodrama with a Bavarian setting. When her performance was criticized by the editor of the *Ballarat Times* she accused him publicly of being a drunk and then, succumbing to her Irish temper, took a whip to him in the bar of a hotel. After her Australian success, she went on to the United States where she died soon afterwards, in 1861.

Tambaroora Gold

It was just a year ago, as near as I can guess,
　　When I left dear old Sydney Town in trouble and distress.
　　My friends and sweetheart slighted me and gave me turnips cold,
　　Until a voice cried in my ear, 'Try Tambaroora gold!'

The day I left old Sydney Town, a tear fell from my eye
　　Of all my friends there was not one to say to me goodbye.
　　So I wandered on my journey, and quite soon I did behold,
　　The hills that glittered brightly with bright Tambaroora gold.

I'd not been long upon the fields before I got job,
　　And worked six months for wages with a chap named Dusty Bob.
　　With that a claim I purchased, and while turning up the mould.
　　My pile I soon created with bright Tambaroora gold.

Then I came back to Sydney Town, a regular dashing swell,
　　And strange to say my previous friends all seemed to wish me well.

They lowly bowed and touched their hats as up the street I strolled;
But, thinks I, they don't want Johnny but his Tambaroora gold.

When I walked down the street last night, by someone I was told,
To stand and to deliver up my Tambaroora gold.
I flew into him madly; in the gutter as we rolled,
He cried, 'Spare my days, and Devil take your Tambaroora gold.'

The other day as I strolled out I met Eileen Arvone,
Who once gave me cold turnips when she found my money gone.
Said she, 'Come to my bosom, John, we'll be lovers as of old.'
But says I, 'You don't love Johnny but his Tambaroora gold.'

So all you bold young diggers, attend to my advice,
And don't trust man or woman till you've looked them over twice,
I have travelled for experience and have many a time been sold,
But this time they won't get Johnny or his Tambaroora gold.

— *TRADITIONAL.*

Cobb and Co.

With the gold rush came Cobb and Co., the stage coach company of the American entrepreneurs Freeman Cobb and his partners, which began services in Melbourne in 1854 and to the Victorian goldfields soon afterwards. It was an all-American enterprise: English coaches were not sturdy enough so Cobb and Co.'s coach bodies were made in America of hickory, with leather suspension that took the jolt out of bumping over bush tracks but left some passengers feeling sea-sick. The early drivers were also American, men experienced in handling large teams of horses for companies like Wells Fargo. The coaches returned good profits and a new owner, James Rutherford, extended the services, securing a monopoly on mail contracts. With more gold discoveries in New South Wales, Cobb and Co. transferred its headquarters in 1862 to Bathurst, where it remained for 50 years, along with a coach-building centre. The other coaching services tried to compete with it, unsuccessfully: one offered the 480-km round trip from Goulburn to Cooma and back for 10 shillings, but during the Gulgong gold rush other coaches charged twenty times that amount—£10—for the 33-km journey from Mudgee to Gulgong.

In 1865 Cobb and Co. extended services within Queensland and by 1870 the company was harnessing 6,000 horses a day and their coaches were covering 45,000 kilometres a week; one of them, the 'Leviathan' running between Castlemaine and Kyneton in Victoria, was drawn by a team of 22 horses. The coming of the railways to country areas in the 1870s and 1880s broke Cobb and Co.'s monopoly on transport, although one horse-drawn coach service continued to run as late as 1924; but by then Cobb and Co. had become part of Australian folklore.

The Coachdriver

'Next to the American coach driver I think the Australian professional may take precedence of all the world in skill and daring. The roads in the newest settlements of Queensland are among the very worst to be found in Australia, and the man who undertakes to conduct a coach drawn by four half-broken-in young horses safely for a couple of hundred miles [300 kilometres] over these roads may claim to be a scientific man.

'It does not require much skill or coolness to hold passively a pair of reins attached to the leathery jaws of a sluggish beast peaceably ambling over a road level as a bowling-green; but to sit behind four wild brutes, who are with difficulty restrained at the start by a groom at the head of each, and to keep them firmly under control the instant that are liberated, when they at once attempt to bolt, is a matter requiring coolness, presence of mind, and great judgement.'

— A.J. (WILLIAM ALEXANDER) BOYD.

The Kiandra Rush

And just now I'm longing to see the old places,
I'm longing to visit old Sydney again—
For I'm full of the Snowy's white hills and wild graces;
I'm a broken-down digger on Kiandra plain.'

— *OLD SONG.*

In late winter of 1860, gold was discovered high in the Snowy Mountains and before long 15,000 diggers were staking out claims at Kiandra.

'When the Author's party left Goulburn for the Kiandra rush at the end of January, 1861, the new field some six months in operation, had, according to all accounts, a mighty future ahead of it ... Following his usual practice, the Author, before leaving himself, started two bullock teams loaded to the brim with commodities, for the new Ophir. The freight included four tons of flour ...

'In reading over, from time to time, accounts of the great Klondyke goldfield, away in the frozen regions of the United States [the 1890s Klondike rush in Canada], I am reminded of similar phases which gold-seekers experienced on snow-bound Kiandra. For a time it was impossible without appliances of those days to attempt to dig through the deep snowdrifts—from ten to twenty feet in depth—or to work in the "blinding swarm" of the fast-falling snow, and I have often thought since that the gold won by the Kiandra diggers was a reward well-earned indeed. For three weeks, nine of us, mates together, never left the hut we were camped in except to get a bit of wood, or provender, and we were obliged to shovel the piled snow from the door of the hut every time we opened it....'

— *CHAS. MACALISTER.*

When the Kiandra goldfields petered out, newcomers started making their way to the Australian Alps in winter. It is said that Norwegian diggers were the first to make slides, toboggans and skis—and Australians soon followed. In the years before 1914, chalets and guest houses were built in the Snowy Mountains (the New South Wales and Victorian alps) for holiday makers and skiing was already a popular sport for the wealthy.

The Snowy Scheme

The 'Snowy' became the scene of a mighty endeavour to dam the waters of the New South Wales and Victorian Alps for the generation of electricity, and to then channel the waters into irrigation use. The Snowy Mountains Hydro-Electric Scheme was established in 1949 and employed a work force of more than 100,000, mainly migrants ('New Australians') from 30 countries. Its first stage was completed in 1955 and the monumental project completed within 25 years of its commencement.

Lambing Flat

It was the most violent riot by miners against the Chinese on the new goldfields, and it required a strong military force dispatched, complete with field gun, from Sydney to restore order.

During the 1850s, nearly 20,000 Chinese had entered Victoria and headed for the goldfields. The Chinese had been among the first Asians to make contact with the Australian continent (a wreck discovered off Geraldton in 1968 yielded Chinese artifacts dating from the 11th century). The new wave of Chinese came mainly from southern China and they planned to make their fortune and then return to their homeland and families. As early as the 1840s, when more than a hundred Chinese workers from Canton arrived in Sydney, a police officer described them as an example to the whole community, being 'temperate, frugal, hard-working and law abiding.' But on the goldfields their presence was challenged: the Chinese were successful traders, but they were not accompanied by women, and some were said to smoke opium. When they flocked to Lambing Flat in New South Wales after gold was discovered there in July 1860, the miners were—by November—making life difficult for them. 'The Chinese adopted all kinds of slim tricks to avoid paying the licence fee [the 30 shillings per annum for each miner], which in itself was a real grievance on the part of the whites,' wrote an unsympathetic Charles MacAlister. In 1861, the Europeans evicted the Chinese from their diggings, driving them out as far as Wombat about eight kilometres away, but when they began to trickle back, a riot broke out and dozens of defenceless Chinese were bashed, though there is no record of any deaths. The outraged Governor Young in Sydney dispatched a column of redcoats to the scene, accompanied by artillery, and order was restored. It was one of the ugliest incidents in our history and left such shameful memories that Lambing Flat, soon a thriving township, was renamed Young in honour of the governor who refused to turn a blind eye to racist violence.

When the gold strikes ended, the majority of Chinese returned to their homeland, and in the 1890s the colonies began restricting Asian immigration to Australia. But 30,000 Chinese stayed, and they have been a valued and enduring element in Australian life to this day.

The Gold Escort

'There is something in the word "Gold Escort" which conveys a world of meaning to my mind. Suggestive as it is of troopers, horses, arms, gold bags, van and rear-guards—of semi-military progress through the wild Australian bush, of night camps and bushrangers—it carries with it an idea of a strange kind of existence, such as can only be realized by a participation in the toils and pleasures of a trip from the diggings to the port with the Escort.

'The duty of conveying the gold from a New South Wales diggings to the seaboard has always been fraught with considerable danger to the officers and troopers composing the guard, although at the present day the danger cannot be compared with what it was many years ago, when the diggings, then in the first blush of their discovery, attracted hordes of ruffians of every type of rascality, who depended not only on their own industry for "making a pile",

but on the chances afforded them for rapine, robbery, and even murder, by the necessarily weak police protection, and the facilities which existed for making away with such unrecognizable plunder as alluvial gold.

'In Queensland we have no bushrangers. There are no old convict-shepherds—no bush telegraphs—none of the thousand and one conveniences for securing the safety of these gentry. Queensland is peopled by a peace-loving community, which asks nothing better than to be left in the full enjoyment of its mercantile or rural pursuits, unmolested by bushrangers or police. Nevertheless, the temptation to plunder, where the facilities are great, is such that some men could not resist the impulse, and hence arises the necessity, even in our peaceful land, for an armed and mounted force to take charge of the precious freight on its way to the port of shipment. This escort is usually composed of six or eight mounted white troopers, with a sergeant, a sub-inspector of police, and a couple of black boys, all armed, except the latter, with rifles and revolvers. According to the nature of the country to be traversed, pack-horses or vehicles are used for the conveyance of the gold. Where the country is level, as between Charters Towers, Ravenswood, etc. and Townsville, the shipping port, a coach is employed; but between Etheridge and Cardwell, where the country is mountainous, and the road intersected with rivers and swamps, and strewn for hundreds of miles with basalt, a coach would not stand the work, and pack-horses are the means of conveyance. Each horse is provided with a couple of stout leather bags. The gold, after being weighed at the banks, is put up in parcels as equal in weight as is possible, packed in strong canvas.'

— A.J. (WILLIAM ALEXANDER) BOYD.

Police Troopers

'This man was, I believe, no more than an ordinary policeman. The rural policemen of the colonies, who have to pass over wide districts, are all mounted. But they carry themselves higher, and stand much higher among their fellow-citizens, than do the men of the same class with us. We are apt to separate men into two classes—and define each man by saying that he is or that he is not a gentleman.'

—FROM AUSTRALIA AND NEW ZEALAND, *1873,*
ANTHONY TROLLOPE *(1815-82).*

Queensland was the next colony to experience the excitement of a gold rush. In 1867, gold was discovered at Gympie and miners flocked north. The find saved the new colony from bankruptcy.

The next year, more gold was discovered at Ravenswood, west of Townsville, and in 1872 Hugh Mosman made a strike at Charters Towers. These were preludes to the biggest Queensland rush of all: in September 1873, word got out that a rich discovery had been made on the Palmer River in the north, and within weeks an army of 35,000 diggers were heading for the new Eldorado.

The song below that commemorates the find was sung to the tune of *Ten Thousand Miles Away*—the same tune as that adapted for the theme of the popular 1970s television series, *Rush*.

The Palmer River Song

The wind is fair and free, my boys,
   The wind is fair and free;
   The steamer's course is north, my boys,
   And the Palmer we will see.
   And the Palmer we will see, my boys,
   And Cooktown's muddy shore,
   Where I've been told there's lots of gold,
   So stay down South no more.

CHORUS:
   So, blow ye winds, heighho!
   A digging we will go,
   I'll stay no more down South, my boys.
   So let the music play.
   In spite of what I'm told,

I'm off to search for gold,
And make a push for that new rush
A thousand miles away.

I hear the blacks are troublesome,
And spear both horse and man,
The rivers all are wide and deep,
No bridges them do span.
No bridges them do span, my boys,
And so you'll have to swim,
But never fear the yarns you hear
And gold you're sure to win.

So let us make a move, my boys,
For that new promised land,
And do the best we can, my boys,
To lend a helping hand.
To lend a helping hand, my boys,
Where the soil is rich and new;
In spite of blacks and unknown tracks,
We'll show what we can do.

— TRADITIONAL.

The Golden Gullies of the Palmer

Then roll the swag and blanket up,
And let us haste away,
To the Golden Palmer, boys,
Where everyone, they say,
Can get his ounce of gold, or
It may be more, a day,
In the Golden Gullies of the Palmer.

CHORUS:
Hurrah! Hurrah! We'll sound the jubilee.
Hurrah! Hurrah! And we will merry be,
When we reach the diggings, boys,
There the nuggets see,
In the Golden Gullies of the Palmer.

Kick at troubles when they come, boys,
The motto be for all;
And if you've missed the ladder
In climbing Fortune's wall,
Depend upon it, boys,

You'll recover from thc fall,
In the Golden Gullies of the Palmer.

Then sound the chorus once again
And give it with a roar,
And let its echoes ring, boys,
Upon the sea and shore,
Until it reach the mountains,
Where gold is in galore,
In the Golden Gullies of the Palmer.

— *TRADITIONAL.*

The Digger

'Of the men around me some were miners working for wages, and some were shareholders, each probably with a large stake in the concern. I could not in the least tell which was which. They were all dressed alike, and there was nothing of the master and the man in the tone of their conversation. Among those present at the washing up, there were two Italians, an American, a German, and a Scotchman who, I learned, were partners in the property. The important task of conducting the last wash, of throwing away for ever the stones and dirt from which the gold had sunk, was on this occasion confided to the hands of the American. The gold was carried away in a pannikin by the German. Why should he not have put in his fingers and appropriated an ounce of the fragments to his own use? I know it is mean to suspect; but among us in England checks are necessary. No doubt the German to whom the pannikin was confided was respected far and wide for his honesty. Of the courtesy of all these men it is impossible to speak too highly, or of the civility of the miners generally; and in saying this I do not allude to the demeanour of the men to myself or to other chance visitors, but to their ordinary mode of conducting themselves. The Australian miner when he is in work never drinks—and seems to feel a pride in his courtesy. It must be understood that his is not a submissive deportment, prone to the touching of hats and a silent reverence to his betters, but a manly bearing, which enables him to express himself freely, but which never verges on distasteful familiarity.'

— *ANTHONY TROLLOPE, 1873.*

'The digger proper is generous, bold, reckless, always willing to help a friend or a brother digger, eager in the pursuit of gold, careless of it when he has obtained it. No distance is too great for him to tramp to a new scene of adventure. With his tent and his blanket, his billy and his pipe, he will start a thousand-mile walk as unconcernedly as you or I would walk from our house to the post-office. Patient and plodding, ever hoping, often months without doing more than earning "tucker", he delves on until he either makes his pile, or is laid up ordinary. What Australia would have been without that adventurous pioneer, the digger, it is hard to tell. He penetrates wilds which the foot of the white man has never before trodden. He braves the attacks of savage natives. He takes his chance of fever and ague, hunger, thirst and death. When we consider what untold wealth has been gained to the world by untiring energy and perseverance of the "wandering digger", as he has been called, well may we exclaim, "All honour to that 'wandering digger!' may a rich reward be his mead!" The great and rich cities of Melbourne and Sydney were raised to their present state of greatness by the digger, Gympie, Townsville, Cooktown, Charters Towers, Ravenswood, and the far-off Georgetown and Normanton, all owe their existence to the digger. Where, a few years ago, scarcely a vessel was to be seen, swift steamers, bearing rich freights, now cleave the waves in every direction. Men have grown rich on the profits of trade caused by the labours of the digger. Sweep him from the face of the earth, and we sweep away magnificent cities, thriving towns, enormous trade; and universal ruin would be the result in many parts of the world. San Francisco owed its first existence to the places discovered by the diggers. Both the Old and the New World would have been enormous losers had there been no such person as the "wandering digger". Take him by the hand, paternal

government! Remove restrictions from the labours of this giant, who hath worked such marvels! Study his interests, and you study the interests of the country. Finally, provide him in his old age, who hath nobly served his country when "youth was at the prow, gold at the helm".'

— *A.J. (WILLIAM ALEXANDER) BOYD*

Kingdoms of Pearls

More riches were found. In 1861 James Turner, the captain of the Flying Foam, sailing from Fremantle, gathered from the vicinity of Nickol Bay near Cossack (close to Dampier, Western Australia) nearly a thousand pearl shells and 150 pearls. He later engaged tribesmen to dive for pearls from dinghies for him and when the employment of Aborigines was forbidden by law he imported divers from Timor and Java. Soon 80 luggers were working the coast there.

In 1868, a sea captain named Banner sailing in Torres Strait put into Warrior Island, so named because of the ferocity of the natives, who exacted tribute from passing boats and pursued in outrigger canoes any who refused to pay. (The warriors used bows and arrows—a weapon not used by Australian Aborigines.) He was intrigued to see the islanders wearing strings and ornaments of pearls, and the children playing marbles with pearls. When word of this reached Europeans, the 'pearl rush' was on. The pearl-bearing oyster beds of the island were quickly plundered, but more pearls were soon found and a new industry was born, one that thrived until the decline in world demand for pearl shell in the late-1950s. Christian missionaries arrived to spread the Gospel in the Torres Strait Islands in 1871 and the Islands were annexed by Queensland in 1879.

During the 1890s, Broome on Roebuck Bay in Western Australia became the main pearling port, and Japanese divers were employed there: the cemeteries are filled with their graves, for pearl-diving was a dangerous industry with threats not only from cyclones common in northern waters, but from sharks and paralysis ('the bends'). Australia's largest pearl, the 'Star of the West', was discovered near Broome in 1917; it weighed 6.48 grams. In 1899, a cyclone off Cape York sank or destroyed 50 boats and killed 300 people.

MOUNT ALEXANDER GOLD-DIGGERS AT EVENING MESS.

Prospectin'

'Seen lots o' country? My word I have! I done a lot o' prospectin' in Victoria and New South Wales. I was one o' the first on New Ballarat, or Indigo, Chiltern as is now. From there I went to the Snowy River, an' then I took a notion an' went off to the Port Curtis rush, an' that's how I first come to Queensland. I found a good gully or two at Gympie. After that I travelled over to Western Creek, and done a lot o' prospectin' all the way. I was at Gilberton for a bit, and then at the Cape River. I was at all them little diggings round Rockhampton, and now here I am at the Palmer. I reckon I've about done wanderin'. I've a goodish bit o' gold, an' I'm not so young as I used to be. I reckon I'll settle down soon an' get a good reef as'll keep me comfortable till I kicks the bucket an' passes in my checks.

'Well, I reckon you want to get to sleep now, an' my pipe's out. So good night, mate. The mosquiters is beginning to be deuced bad. I'll just rig up a good old smoke so's we'll be able to get to sleep.'

— *A.J. (WILLIAM ALEXANDER) BOYD.*

Walhalla, Gippsland

'At last we got to the place, very tired and very footsore, and had bedrooms allocated to us in the hotel close to the quartz-crushing machine, which goes on day and night eating up the rock which is dragged forth from the bowels of the earth. The noisy monster continued his voracious meal without cessation for a moment, so that sleep was out of the question. To the residents of the inn the effect was simply somniferous. Their complaint was that from twelve o'clock on Saturday night when the monster begins to keep his Sabbath, to twelve o'clock on Sunday night when his religious observances are over, the air is so burdened by silence that they can neither talk by day nor sleep by night.

''The mining town which has been dignified by the name of Walhalla lies at the bottom of a gully from which the wooded sides rise steeply. Through it meanders a stream which is now, of course, contaminated by the diggings, and pumpings, and gold-washing, and quartz-crushing, which have befallen the locality. Nevertheless it has a peculiar beauty of its own, and a picturesque interest arising in part from the wooded hills which so closely overhang it—but partly also from the quaintness of a town so placed. The buildings, consisting of banks, churches, schools, hotels, manager's houses, and miners' cottages, lie along the stream, or are perched up on low altitudes among the trees. There is something like a winding street through it, which is nearly a mile long—though indeed it is difficult sometimes to distinguish between the river and the street; but there is no road to it from any place in the world; and even the tracks by which it is to be left are not easy of discovery. We went down to it by the "Little Joe", the Little Joe being a hill-side, and I hope I may never have to go down the Little Joe again with a tired horse behind me. We left it by a path as steep, and so hidden that we should never have found it without a guide.

'The great mine at Walhalla when I was there was the Long Tunnel. Shares in the Long Tunnel were hardly to be had for money; but, bought even at most exaggerated prices, gave almost endless interest. I went down the Long Tunnel, and came up again. As usual

I found below a dirty grubbing world. Men were earning between 2 and 3 [pounds] a week, living hardly, though always plenteously; and speculating in gold with their savings. But here, as elsewhere, they were courteous and kind. Their children are all educated, and if churches and meeting-houses may be taken as proof of religion they are religious. I was told that the place contained abut 15,000 inhabitants. I cannot repeat too often that I have never met more courteous men than the gold-miners of Australia.

'We stayed but one night, and then proceeded on our journey, still taking our mounted guide, and for the first ten miles [16 kilometres] were under the special guardianship of the mayor, who was to be looked upon, I was told, as a deputation from the town in honour of my friend. A very pleasant fellow we found the Mayor of Walhalla, and we parted from him in great kindness, even though he did lose the way in the forest, and take us, all for nothing, up and down one mountain side. When he parted from us our trusty trooper was a safer guide.'

— ANTHONY TROLLOPE,
   DESCRIBING WALHALLA IN GIPPSLAND IN 1871-72.

There would be further gold strikes—most notably in Western Australia in the 1890s—but the surface gold was soon plundered and Australia's true wealth for the next century would lie in the land itself: in the wheat fields, and the sheep and cattle stations that stretched from the richly-pastured coastal areas to the edge of the desert plains.

7: *Bush Living*

'Cockatoo' Farmer

'WHY COCKATOO? What, in the name of all that's lovely, has a cockatoo got in common with a farmer? They both appreciate good maize, doubtless, but there, I apprehend, the similitude ends.

'Who first discovered the title of "cockatoo farmer"? Who was the first cockatoo farmer?

'There are certainly two ways in which the name might have arisen. It might have originated with ticket-of-leave men from Cockatoo Island; or it may possibly have been a term of reproach applied to the industrious farmer, who settled or perched on the resumed portions of a squatter's run, so much to the latter's rage and disgust that [newcomers] contemptuously likened the farmer to the white-coated, yellow-crested screamer that settles or perches on the trees at the edge of his namesake's clearing.

'Let a cockie speak for himself.

'Hard at it, as you say. There ain't much rest for the likes o' me. 'Tain't like them swell coves as is able to put on lots o' hands, as eats'em out of house an' home, as farmed don't pay no how with them chaps. Does it pay me? I don't see as it actilly pays nobody.'

— *A.J. (WILLIAM ALEXANDER) BOYD.*

The Stringybark Cockatoo

I'm a broken-hearted miner, who loves his cup to drain,
  Which often times has caused me to lie in frost and rain.
  Roaming about the country, looking for some work to do,
  I got a job of reaping off a stringybark cockatoo.

CHORUS:
  Oh, the stringybark cockatoo,
  Oh, the stringybark cockatoo,
  I got a job of reaping off a stringybark cockatoo.

Ten bob an acre was his price—with promise of fairish board.
  He said his crops were very light, 'twas all he could afford.
  He drove me out in a bullock dray, and his piggery met my view.
  Oh, the pigs and geese were in the wheat of the stringybark
  cockatoo.

The hut was made of the surface mud, the roof of a reedy thatch,
  The doors and windows open flew without a bolt or latch.
  The pigs and geese were in the hut, the hen on the table flew.
  And she laid an egg in the old tin plate for thestringybark
  cockatoo.

For breakfast we had pollard, boys, it tasted like cobbler's paste,
  To help it down we had to eat brown bread with vinegar taste.
  The tea was made of the native hops which out on the ranges
  grew;
  'Twas sweetened with honey bees and was for the stringybark
  cockatoo.

For dinner we had goanna hash, we thought it mighty hard;
  They wouldn't give us butter, so we forced down bread and
  lard.
  Quondong duff, paddy melon pie, and wallaby Irish stew
  We used to eat while reaping for the stringybark cockatoo.

When we started to cut, the rust and smut was just beginning to
  shed,
  And all we had to sleep on was a dog and a sheep skin bed.
  The bugs and fleas tormented me, they made me scratch and
  screw;
  I lost my rest while reaping for the stringybark cockatoo.

At night when work was over I'd nurse the youngest child,
  And when I'd say a joking word, the mother would laugh and
  smile.
  The old cocky, he grew jealous, and he thumped me black and
  blue,
  And he drove me off without a rap—the stringybark cockatoo.

— *Traditional.*

The Jackeroo

When I arrived in Brisbane I thought to cut a dash,
  But I was very soon pulled up by the shortage of my cash;
  I met a Northern squatter who said that he'd take me,
  For forty pounds per annum a jackeroo to be.

I'm a jackeroo, just come from the old countree,
  The squatters here they need not fear that they can humbug
  me.

When I got to the station I saw the super there,
  'Hello!' he says, 'my Johnny Raw, what the d— brings you here?'
  And then I draws myself right up, as straight as I could be,
  'I'm here,' I says, 'to do twelve months, a jackeroo to be.'

I'm a jackeroo, just come from the old countree,
  The squatters here they need not fear that they can humbug
  me.

Oh, first he sent me driving a nasty, jibbing mare,
  He told me that she'd pull the dray without any trouble or care,

But she stuck me up on the road, and I began to holler,
When up the super comes—and calls me a b— crawler.

And a jumped-up jackeroo just out from the old countree:
The squatters here, I'm free to swear, have got the loan of me.
Now, all day while I'm shepherding and taking of the sun,
I sigh and wish within myself that this 'ere lambing was done;
For the flour is bad the tea is bad as well,
And I wish the Northern squatters and their stations were all in hell.

That's the hope of a jackeroo just come from the old countree;
The squatters here, I sadly fear, will see the last of me.

Now, all arriving new-chums, take warning here by me.
Never go to a northern squatter, bush experience to see,
For they will use you strangely and treat you most damnably;
You'll scarcely live a six-months; if you do, then beggar me!

The advice of a jackaroo—not long from the old countree—
The squatters here, 'tis very clear, have had a loan of me.

—'GAMBASINO', 1888.

Women of the West

They left the vine-wreathed cottage and the mansion on the hill,
   The houses in the busy streets where life is never still,
   The pleasure of the city, and the friends they cherished best:
   For love they faced the wilderness—the Women of the West.

The roar, and rush, and fever of the city died away,
   And the old-time joys and faces—they were gone for many a
   day;
   In their place the lurching coach-wheel, or the creaking bullock-
   chains,
   O'er the everlasting sameness of the never-ending plains.

In the slab-built, zinc-roofed homestead of some lately-settled run,
   In the tent beside the bankment of a railway just begun,
   In the huts on new selections, in the camps of man's unrest,
   On the frontiers of the Nation, live the Women of the West.

The red sun robs their beauty, and in weariness and pain,
   The slow years steal the nameless grace that never comes again;
   And there are hours men cannot soothe, and words men cannot
   say—
   The nearest woman's face may be a hundred miles away.

The wide Bush holds the secrets of their longing and desires,
   When the white stars in reverence light their holy altar-fires,
   And silence, like the touch of God, sinks deep into the breast
   Perchance He hears and understands the Women of the West.

For them no trumpet sounds the call, no poet plies his arts—
   They only hear the beating of their gallant, loving hearts.
   But they have sung with silent lives the song all songs above,
   The holiness of sacrifice, the dignity of love.

Well have we held our father's creed. No call has passed us by.
   We faced and fought the wilderness, we sent our sons to die.
   And we have hearts to do and dare, and yet, o'er all the rest,
   The hearts that made the Nation were the Women of the West.

— GEORGE ESSEX EVANS (1863-1909).

Bush Homes

'Slabs, bark, greenhide and dog-leg fences were the leading features of the old bush home, and still are in many places: but in settled districts shingles and galvanized iron have taken the place of bark, and two-rail and wire fences succeed the dog-leg. Neat cottages gleam everywhere in the deep forests, and carts and buggies rattle in the wake of the primordial slide. Yet I doubt if the man in the modern cottage is happier than his progenitor in the little bark hut, whose saddle reposed on a peg in one corner, his bag bunk rigged up in another; who stepped out on a cowhide mat, stood his dampers on a packing-case, and slung his billy on a wire hooked to a blackened trace-chain . . .

'In the early days many a settler's house was built of solid logs and pug. It was roofed with stringybark, the latter being hung with greenhide and held down with poles ("riders" and "jockeys") pegged together. This was, no doubt, a replica of the log cabins of Yankee backwoodsmen. It was a formidable structure, more comfortable than elegant.

'Then there was the mud house. Many squatters in western Queensland lived for years in this kind of dwelling, the walls being built of stiff clay, with grass for binding. Similar structures are still in use west of Windorah, the walls built of earth and tallow, and the floors of ashes and tallow, which set like cement. Currawalla Station, in this neighbourhood, is surrounded by a great wall, eight feet high, built of the same material. The enclosure prevents the homestead being inundated when the flood comes down Farrar's Creek. It is a unique sight to see this place low and dry in the midst of miles of seething waters. The blending of tallow makes the walls waterproof, and also prevents erosion when subjected to a strong current.

'Mention of the log-and-pug recalls that it was from this kind of holding that our wattle trees got their name. The earliest settlers around Port Jackson [on the New South Wales central coast] found these trees handiest for building purposes. The trunks were laid horizontally between uprights, and the interspaces filled with stiff mud, a process known as wattling. They were thus called wattle-houses.

'In the north-west of New South Wales, the dug-out is common, with only the low roof showing above ground. It is cool in summer and warm in winter, besides being free from flies. A fossicker and gardener lived for years in one of these in Mount Browne district. One night, during a heavy storm, a dam alongside burst, and the inrush of water washed him out of his bunk. He escaped through the roof, and spent the night watching the overflow to see that nothing got away. It took him two days to pump his house out; then he had to leave the roof off for a week to let it dry. To dive below like a wombat was his ideal of comfort. But most people look upon the dug-out with horror. As one remarked, "Let's keep on top while we can kick; we'll be underground long enough".'

— *FROM* LIFE IN THE AUSTRALIAN BACKBLOCKS, *1911,*
EDWARD S. SORENSON (1869-1939).

Bullocks

'Our horned cattle amounted in 1813 to 21,513, and in 1821 to 69,149. Our breeds are derived from the Bengal buffalo variety with smooth skins, short snail horns and humpy shoulders; and from the various English breeds that have been at different times imported...

'You will buy well bred two-year-old heifers in calf for eight and ten pounds; milch cows at from twelve to fifteen guineas; young bullocks of two or three years, weighing six or seven hundred pounds, for seven or eight pounds; and old broken-in working bullocks at from ten to thirteen guineas.

'The bullocks are by far the best animals for draught, at least in the present state of things. They do not require the expensive keeping of the horse; are less than a fourth of the price; when any accident befalls them may be slaughtered and salted; and on their getting into years may be fattened for the butcher; while the horse is yearly becoming less valuable, and is ultimately worthy only the price of his hide.

'Oxen are said to be slower than horses, but this depends entirely upon your manner of proceeding. If you select a lively, strong bullock, and teach him a good, quick pace at the commencement, his speed will prove little short of that of the horse. There is no necessity for either corn-feeding, curry-combing or doctoring bullocks, as horses; while, on long journeys, you fetter their forelegs at night and allow them to feed till morning on the adjoining pasture, then yoke them to again, nearly as fresh as ever.

'There has been much disputing about the respective superiority of yokes and harness, but certainly yokes appear to carry away the palm completely. All that you have to procure with respect to them are the two steel bows and the chain, the wooden part being easily made on your own farm; and the whole apparatus is so simple, so cheap and so easily kept in order, compared with the harness, that those who have tried both will not be long in throwing the latter aside.

'I even conceive that the yoke gives greater purchase than the harness, because the power exerted is one which both lifts and impels; while the neck is the strongest part of the bullock and the yokes do not impede the motion of the shoulder blades, or check respiration, as the collars undoubtedly must. I have seen four bullocks, in yokes, drag a heavy dray with 24 hundredweight of wool along one of our indifferent toads, with the most perfect ease. Harness, however, is absolutely necessary for the shaft-bullock, when getting your carts to work.'

— FROM TWO YEARS IN NEW SOUTH WALES, *1827*,
   PETER CUNNINGHAM *(1789-1864).*

The Bullockies' Ball

The team were camped along the gullies,
Soon the news flew round about.
Plans were worked out by Pat Scully,
We gave the boys a grand blow-out.
We had an awning of tarpaulins,
Kegs and casks came quickly rolling,
Then the boys and girls came strolling
To have a burst at the bullockies' ball.

CHORUS
  Oh, my hearties, that was a party, help yourself, free gratis all,
  Lots of prey and buckets of grog to swish away at the
  bullockies' ball.

First came Flash Joe, but Jimmy was flasher,
Hopping Billy, the one-eyed boss,
Brisbane Sal and Derwent Slasher,
Billy the Bull and Paddy the Hoss.
Nanny the Rat, the real May Cassa,
Brisbane Bess and Mother May Call,
All come rolling together
To have a burst at the bullockies' ball.

Soon pint pots began to rattle,
The cry was, 'Pass the rum this way,'

The boys began to blow their cattle,
The ladies, of course, must have their say.
Sal said she'd take cheek from no man
And Dawn to a dish of hash did stoop.
She'd got a smack in the eye with a doughboy,
Put her sitting in a bucket of soup.

Oh then boys, there was the ructions,
Man the tucker and let fly,
Brisbane Bess with a hunk of damper
Caught Flash Joe right in the eye.
Nanny the Rat, the real May Cassa
With a frying pan a dozen slew.
She got a clip with a leg of mutton,
Took a dive in a bucket of stew.

There was Wallowman Doughty Roly Foley,
Said he'd punt them to the rout,
Seized a chunk of roly-poly
But a poultice of pigweed stopped his mouth.
This raised his old woman's dander
And into an awful tantrum flew,
'Fair play' cried she to a bleeding overlander,
'You pumpkin-peeling toe-rag coot!'

— *Traditional*

The Bullockies' Track, Berrima to Sydney 1850

'Lockyersleigh, Paddy's River, Black Bob's Creek, the head of Mittagong Range, Chalker's Flat, the Bargo Hotel, the foot of Razorback, then on to the Cowpastures Bridge. Our ninth camp would often be at the Crossroads—some four miles [6.5 kilometres] from Liverpool. The publican at the Crossroads was a Mr Martin whose better half was alleged to be the prettiest woman in all Australia—that is to say, the carriers thought so; for though we had other work to do than forming mutual admiration societies we had the true Australian appreciation of Beauty's form divine.

'And though our musical education had been neglected there were amongst the old carriers singers who, metaphorically, could move the soul of a crocodile. Such songs as *The Old Bark Hut*, *The Old Bullock Dray*, *The Stockman's Last Bed*, *Black-eyed Susan* and *The Wild Colonial Boy* were the chief classics known to the platform of the campfire.'

— *Chas. MacAlister.*

Bullockies

'On the dry bush tracks, with their frequent intermissions of heavy sand and stony hills, between Bourke and the Queensland border the bullock-driver has a hard time. A long day through blistering heat, flies and dust; then a ride back with tired bullocks, eight or ten miles [13–16 kilometres] to the last water; and tomorrow a long night ride ahead to the next water. There he camps for the night, getting back to the wagons about sunrise next morning. There is often no grass or herbage, and after taking his cattle to water he has to cut scrub to feed them. One can hardly blame the poor bullocky if he helps himself to a nip from the tempting consignment of hotel goods he has on board . . .

'Many teamsters on the western tracks are bound to time, and in making up for some unforeseen delay the cattle suffer, and not infrequently several head are left by the roadside to die. There is a stiff penalty for dilatoriness, ranging up to one pound per day. Sometimes the drivers are docked so much per ton for every day over contract time. On these roads grass and water are precious, and very often a good night for the team is not to be had for love or money. Still, the team must eat and drink to get the load through; so the teamster has to battle for it; and the cunning begotten of long experience on the roads is set against the watchfulness of the landowner. The bullocks are taken quietly to the tanks at night, not

to the one near which the teams may be camped, but to one several miles distant. Then the wires are strapped down, and the hungry animals are slipped in where the feed is best and left till nearly daylight, one of the men sleeping in the paddock with them. Perhaps only half the team will be thus treated at a time, the other half being left on neutral ground, carrying all the available bells to mislead the enemy . . .'

— *EDWARD S. SORENSON.*

Dad and Dave on the Selection

Dad and Dave Rudd first made their appearance in the *Bulletin* in 1895. The author was a young aspiring writer, Arthur Hoey Davis (1868-1935) who wrote under the pen-name 'Steele Rudd'. The first collection of stories was published in book form by the *Bulletin* in 1899 as *On Our Selection*. The son of a Welsh convict father and an Irish mother, the author had grown up on his father's selection on the Darling Downs of Queensland, living there from 1875 to 1885, when he left to work as a clerk in Brisbane. The Rudd family adventures were continued in a sequel *Our New Selection* (1903) — and retold in several popular films and the long-running ABC Radio serial *Dad and Dave*.

'It's twenty years ago now since we settled on the Creek. Twenty years! I remember well the day we came from Stanthorpe, on Jerome's dray, eight of us, and all the things—beds, tubs, a bucket, the two cedar chairs with the pine bottoms and backs that Dad put in them, some pint-pots and old Crib. It was a scorching hot day, too—talk about thirst! At every creek we came to we drank till it stopped running.

'Dad didn't travel up with us: he had gone some months before, to put up the house and dig the water-hole. It was a slabbed house, with shingled roof, and space enough for two rooms, but the partition wasn't up. The floor was earth, but Dad had a mixture of sand and fresh cow-dung with which he used to keep it level. About once a month he would put it on, and everyone had to keep outside that day till it was dry. There were no locks on the doors. Pegs were put in to keep them fast at night, and the slabs were not very close together, for we could easily see anybody coming on horseback by looking through them. Joe and I used to play at counting the stars through the cracks in the roof.

'The day after we arrived Dad took Mother and us out to see the paddock and the flat on the other side of the gully that he was going to clear for cultivation. There was no fence round the paddock, but he pointed out on a tree the surveyor's marks showing the boundary of our ground. It must have been fine land, the way Dad talked

about it. There was very valuable timber on it, too, so he said; and he showed us a place among some rocks on a ridge where he was sure gold would be found, but we weren't to say anything about it. Joe and I went back that evening and turned over every stone on the ridge, but we didn't find any gold.

'No mistake, it was a real wilderness—nothing but trees, goannas, dead timber, and bears; and the nearest house, Dwyers, was three miles [4.8 kilometres] away. I often wonder how the women stood it the first few years, and I can remember how Mother, when she was alone, used to sit on a log where the lane is now and cry for hours. Lonely! It was lonely.

'Dad soon talked about clearing a couple of acres and putting in corn—all of us did, in fact —till the work commenced. It was a delightful topic before we started, but in two weeks the cluster of fires that illuminated the whooping bush in the night, and the crash upon crash of the big trees as they fell, had lost all their property.

'We toiled and toiled clearing those four acres, where the haystacks are now standing, till every tree and sapling that had grown there was down. We thought then the worst was over—but how little we knew of clearing land! Dad was never tired of calculating and telling us how much the crop would fetch if the ground could only be got ready in time to put it in; so we laboured the harder.

'With our combined male and female forces and the aid of a sapling lever we rolled the thundering big logs together in the face of hell's own fires; and when there were no logs to roll it was tramp, tramp the day through, gathering armfuls of sticks, while the clothes clung to our backs with a muddy perspiration. Sometimes Dan and Dave would sit in the shade beside the billy of water and gaze at the small patch that had taken so long to do, then they would turn hopelessly to what was before them and ask Dad (who would never take a spell) what was the use of thinking of ever getting such a place cleared. And when Dave wanted to know why Dad didn't take up a place on the plain, where there were no trees to grub and plenty of water, Dad would cough as if something was sticking in his throat, and then curse terribly about the squatters and political jobbery. He would soon cool down, though, and get hopeful again.

' "Look at the Dwyers," he'd say. "From ten acres of what they got £70 last year, besides feed for the fowls. They've got corn in now, and there's only the two of them."

'It wasn't only burning off! Whenever there was a short drought the waterhole was sure to run dry. Then we had to take turns to carry water from the springs—about two miles [3.2 kilometres]. We had no draught-horse, and even if we had had one there was neither water-cask, trolly, nor dray. So we humped it—and talk about a drag! By the time you returned, if you hadn't drained the bucket, in spite of the big drink you'd taken before leaving the springs, more than half would certainly be spilt through the vessel bumping against your leg every time you stumbled in the long grass. Somehow, none of us liked carrying water. We would sooner keep the fires going all day without dinner than do a trip to the springs.

'One hot, thirsty day it was Joe's turn with the bucket, and he managed to get back without spilling very much. We were all pleased because there was enough left after the tea had been made to give us each a drink. Dinner was nearly over. Dan had finished and was taking it easy on the sofa when Joe said, "I say, Dad, what's a nater-dog like?"

Dad told him, "Yellow, sharp ears and bushy tail."

' "Those muster bin some then that I seen—I don't know 'bout the bushy tail—all the hair had comed off."

' "Where'd y' see them, Joe?" we asked.

' "Down 'n the springs floating about—dead."

Then everyone seemed to think hard and look at the tea. I didn't want any more. Dan jumped off the sofa and went outside; and Dad looked after Mother.

'At least the four acres—except for the biggest of the ironbark trees and about fifty stumps—were pretty well cleared. Then came

a problem that couldn't be worked out on a draught-board. I have already said that we hadn't any draught-horses. Indeed, the only thing on the selection like a horse was an old "tuppy" mare that Dad used to straddle. The date of her foaling went farther back than Dad's, I believe, and she was shaped something like an alderman. We found her one day in about eighteen inches of mud, with both eyes picked out by the crows, and her hide bearing evidence that a feathery tribe had made a roost of her carcass. Plainly, there was no chance of breaking up the ground with her help. And we had no plough. How, then was the corn to be put in? That was the question.

'Dan and Dave sat outside the corner of the chimney, both scratching the ground with a chip and not saying anything. Dad and Mother sat inside talking it over. Sometimes Dad would get up and walk round the room shaking his head, then he would kick old Crib for lying under the table. At last Mother struck something which brightened him up, and he called Dave.

' "Catch Topsy and . . ." he paused because he remembered the old mare was dead. "Run over and ask Mr Dwyer to lend me three hoes." 'Dave went. Dwyer lent the hoes, and the problem was solved. That was how we started.'

— *FROM* ON OUR SELECTION, *STEELE RUDD.*

Hit by a boomerang

In 1825 the settler William Thornley was attacked by natives led by the black bushranger, Musquito. This account from his memoirs is doubly interesting, for it tells what it is like to be hit by a boomerang at close range.

'While I was looking, a native showed himself and, running a little way towards the spot where I stood, cast a boomerang at me. I had never witnessed the casting of this curious native weapon in a hostile manner before and, having had that satisfaction, I certainly have no curiosity to see it cast in that manner again. The boomerang would have struck me if I had not skipped aside in time and, as it was, it was only by a hair's breadth that I avoided it.

'Almost before I could take aim at the native, the boomerang, skimming through the air, returned to the spot from which the native had cast it. The native picked it up and, without waiting, cast it again at me. I saw it whirling towards me with great velocity and, an instant afterwards, I felt myself struck with considerable violence on my left leg which at the moment I thought it had broken. The shock brought me on one knee to the ground. The native gave a cry of exultation, and I immediately fired at him. The discharge of my gun was a signal for a rush from the whole body. About a dozen of them suddenly shot out from among the trees, and, with wild and terrific shouts, rushed towards me.

'Supposing that I was defenceless after the discharge of my gun, they came on swiftly, boldly brandishing their waddies in the air, with the intent of shortly exercising them on my unfortunate skull. I did not lose my presence of mind but, remaining on one knee, I fired off my second barrel and hit the foremost man.

'The second discharge puzzled them, and they halted, not knowing what to make of a gun that could fire twice without reloading. Seeing them hesitate, I drew one of my horse-pistols and treated them to another shot. This completed their dismay, and they all scampered off to the shelter of the trees as fast as they came.'

The Springsure Massacre

The bloodiest massacre of whites by black tribesmen occurred on 17 October 1861 at Cullin-La-Ringo station near Springsure in Queensland. Among the victims were Horatio (H.S.L. Wills), who had chosen to take his family north from Victoria because of the rich promise afforded by the new colony of Queensland. Ironically, Wills had established good relations with the local Aborigines—or so he thought. His son Tom later co-founded 'Aussie Rules' football (see page 389).

What prompted the massacre is unknown, for none of the 19 members of the Wills family and their employees at the station that day survived though one station hand hid in a tree far from the homestead and witnessed much of the killing. The attack was sudden: women victims were killed while they were sewing; a bullocky was found dead near with his team with his whip still in his hand, as if surprised.

Days after the massacre, Oscar dc Satge, a young Frenchman who later became a renowned horseman and pioneer in the region, reached the Richard's station after five days' hard ride from Peak Downs, on his way to visit Wills. 'Mr Richard's story was a tragic one. He told us that less than a week ago Wills, together with his overseer and wife and child and numerous station hands, had been massacred by the blacks . . .,' one of his party wrote. But before suspects could be rounded up for trial, retribution had begun: the native police under Lieutenant Cave had already attacked the local tribe and killed many of them.

Wills' son, absent from the station on the day of the massacre, stayed on at Cullin-La-Ringo and won admiration for continuing to employ local blacks as stockmen.

The Rabbits Run Wild: 1859

Long before the rabbit plague began English settlers had brought rabbits to Australia to augment their food supply, and careful husbandry (and hearty appetites) kept them safely from becoming a pest.

In 1850 however, a Somerset landowner, James Austin, sent out to his brother Thomas a gift of 24 wild rabbits that the latter released on his property at Barwon Park in Victoria to provide shooting for himself and his neighbours. The plan backfired when the rabbits multiplied rapidly—each doe can give birth to 60 offspring each year—and they began to eat his crops.

Within ten years, millions of rabbits had spread through Victoria's Western Districts where the pickings were rich and no indigenous predators existed to cull their numbers. They crossed the Murray around 1872, reached the Murrumbidgee in 1876 and invaded Queensland in 1886. As eastern Australia suffered two devastating droughts in 1875 and 1883, the added depredations of the

rabbits were calamitous. These loveable creatures ate everything in their path—not only the blades of grass but the roots also; they tore the bark off trees and ate seedlings and shrubs, turning paddocks into dustbowls.

In 1887, when the New South Wales government offered a bounty for every rabbit skin handed in, nearly 25,000,000 skins were handed in for reward and the Treasury faced bankruptcy.

In the same year, crude attempts were made to introduce a virus; but the offspring of inoculated animals easily developed immunity and continued to increase.

In 1894, the rabbits hopped across the Nullabor into Western Australia, having conquered the continent. Both Queensland and Western Australia constructed rabbit-proof fences along their borders but the animals burrowed their way under them.

Few single acts by a European has had a more destructive effect on the nation, its land, or its flora and fauna. Deprived of grass, some stations lost half their sheep; poison baits killed off harmless native animals while barely reducing the rabbit armies; without vegetation to hold the soil some areas became permanently eroded.

The only effective remedy was shooting the pests or destroying their burrows, and from 1870 until the late 1940s 'rabbiters' (not to be confused with 'rabbitohs', who sold rabbits for meat in the cities) were employed by most properties.

Farmers had learned to exist with the rabbits, cursing them daily, until the CSIRO developed myxomatosis ('myxo') in the 1950s, which finally killed them off. By the late 1980s, however, rabbits were appearing again in numbers, totally immune to the disease, and the CSIRO began developing an imported rabbit virus, calicivirus, which was released on the mainland (accidentally) in October 1995 and quickly decimated the rabbit population, killing an estimated 10 million rabbits in three states within two months. Within weeks vegetation reappeared in many areas—but in other regions rabbits still flourished.

'The rabbit was a favoured animal on Austin's station at the Barwon. It was a privilege to shoot him—in small quantities—he was so precious. But he soon became, as the grammar says, a noun of multitude. He swarmed on the plains, hopped over the hills, burrowed among the rocks in the rises, and nursed his multitudinous progeny in every hollow log of the forest. Neither mountain, lake, nor river ever barred his passage. He ate up all the grass and starved the pedigree cattle, the well-born dukes and duchesses, and on tens of thousands of fertile acres left no food to keep the nibbling sheep alive.

'Every hole and crevice of the rocks was full of him. An uninvited guest, he dropped down the funnel-shaped entrance to the den of the wombat, and made himself at home with the wild cat and snake. He clothed the hills with a creeping robe of fur, and turned the Garden of the West into a wilderness. Science may find a theory to account for the beginning of all things, but among all her triumphs she has been unable to put an end to the rabbit. War has been made upon them by fire, dynamite, phosphorus, and all deadly poisons; by dogs, cats, weasels, foxes, and ferrets, but he still marches over the land triumphantly.'

— GEORGE DUNDERDALE.

The Lonely Bush

'Words fail me for painting the loneliness of the Australian bush. Mile after mile of primeval forest; interminable vistas of melancholy gum-trees; ravines, along the sides of which the long-bladed grass grows rankly; level, untimbered plains alternating with undulating tracts of pasture, here and there, broken by steep gully, stony ridge, or dried-up creek. All wild and utterly desolate; all the same monotonous grey colouring, except where the wattle, when in blossom, shows patches of feathery gold or a belt of scrub lies green, glossy, and impenetrable. I know of nothing so strange in its way, as to travel for days through endless gum- forest ...'

— FROM AUSTRALIAN GIRLHOOD, *1902*,
   BY ROSA PRAED (1851-1935).

Bushfires

Every 10 years or so, in times of drought, fires devastate the Australian bush. When winds are high the rivers of flame sometimes reach into the outer suburbs of cities, consuming everything in their path with a horrifying suddenness.

One day in the scorching summer of February 1851 lingers in Victoria's lore as 'Black Thursday'. For five weeks the colony had lain under a suffocating heat and hot, dry winds. The bush was like tinder. On Thursday 6 February, when the temperature in Melbourne in late morning reached 47°C in the shade, black clouds

of smoke settled over the city, heavy with ashes and cinders. Dandenong and Mount Macedon were ablaze; in fact the whole colony was burning from Seymour to Kilmore, from Barwon Heads to Mount Gambier across the border in South Australia. 'By some inexplicable means the whole country was wrapped in a sheet of flame—fierce, awful and irresistible . . . farmhouses, crops, fences, haystacks, bridges, woolsheds—everything in its path —were swept away by the fierce onrush of the flames,' ran one account. At least ten people were burned to death, including a mother and her five children, but the exact death toll was probably higher.

On Friday 13 January 1939, 'Black Friday', the most devastating bushfires in Victoria's history ravaged the state, taking 71 lives and destroying more than a thousand buildings. Two hot, dry, windy Februaries linger in memories for their savagery: in 1969 bushfires in south-east Tasmania spread almost to the centre of Hobart and 62 people died; and in 1983 the 'Ash Wednesday' bushfires devastated parts of South Australia and Victoria and took another 71 lives.

Floods: Goodbye Gundagai

'After the great fires of 1851 came floods. In 1852, the Murrumbidgee burst its banks and the thriving town of Gundagai (almost midway between Sydney and Melbourne) was swept away.

'Over eighty persons perished, either through drowning or exposure, and many had hair-breadth escapes amid the swirling waters. People had to swim for their lives in many instances, and to take refuge in the dripping trees for days and nights together ... Through the wholesale devastation wrought by the flood, many of the people were on the brink of starvation, and as there were no railways running inland at the time, the sending of supplies was a matter of slow process ... [When we arrived we found that] the Murrumbidgee was still a banker, and the carcasses of drowned horses and cattle were—several of them—reposing high up among the branches of the oak-trees along the river banks ... It was the worst thing of the kind ever known in New South Wales. However, the lesson learnt by the flood were not ignored—for the present town is high and dry, and well above the flood level.'

— CHAS. MACALISTER.

Bushfire: New England

'The season has been very dry and my husband in consequence started a large mob of cattle away for the Maitland market. The distance overland was four hundred miles [650 kilometres], and he could only accompany them part of the way and then leave them in charge of a trustworthy man, and return home.

'He had been gone about a fortnight when, after a close, sultry night, we were awakened by the smell of burning timber. We soon found that the kitchen, a detached building, was in flames. Calling my young sons and the men employed about the place to help me, we did all we could to save the house. My eldest boys fought valiantly against the heat and smoke and endeavoured to spread wet blankets over the roof, but the weight was too much for their strength. The wind rose and blew the flames towards them, so, with scorched faces and blistered hands, they gave up in despair, and came to my assistance to save what we could from the house, while there was time—but the fire spread so rapidly, fanned by the strong wind, that a few clothes, valuable papers, and a little food was all we secured. The store room held two years' supply of necessaries, with a good stock of ammunition, guns, saddlery, etc. When the flames reached here the explosion was terrible and shook the very earth on which we stood. The fire was carried for yards right across the river, setting alight to the grass and bushes on the other side. My eldest son had a pet monkey chained up at the rear of the building. At the risk of his life, when he remembered his pet, he rushed through the burning grass, etc. and rescued the poor animal, and held it, singed and almost frightened to death, in his arms.

'As I stood gazing at what was once a happy and comfortable home, now fast being reduced to ashes, my poor children homeless, myself alone and unprotected with a young child in my arms, my heart for the first time in my life failed me, and for some time I hardly knew what I did and wept bitterly. But my children gathered round me and for their sakes I collected my strength and began to look round for shelter.'

— *Mary McMaugh, 1870s.*

Bush Children

'Hard-worked, horny-handed little mites they are, most of them, whose knowledge is of cattle and horses, of reptiles, beetles, birds and animals, and their home and playground the trackless bush. They master the secrets and mysteries of life at an early age through constant association with the native fauna, flock and herd, and hearing the talk of their elders. Their most admirable traits are their homeliness, courage, self-reliance and mateship.

'They can ride almost as soon as they can walk. You will see a little mite throw the bridle-rein over the neck of a big horse, and lead him thus to a log or stump, and there put on the bridle and mount; and presently you will see him cantering bareback across the hills. I noticed a little fellow one day trying to mount a rogue. Time after time he brought him side-on to a log, and each time as he prepared to cross his back the old horse sidled away so that he stood at right angles to the log. At last the boy led him into a fork where he couldn't sidle away, and triumphantly mounted.

'It is surprising how soon these children learn the bush, what clever little heads they have for working out the problems of their timbered world. I have met them, boys and girls, riding along mountain spurs, miles away from home, looking for cattle. And if you ask them at any time in what direction home lies, no matter how they have turned and twisted during the day, they will at once point to it like a compass. Fences do not stop them from going as straight as the crow flies either; they strap down the wires with a stick across for the horse to see, and lead or ride him over. Rail fences give a little trouble; but when a loose top rail is found, they jump their cuddies over the bottom one. They can describe a beast minutely, even to a single white spot at the tip of its tail, or a tiny black streak on its off-side horn. They can recognize a beast or a horse at sight, though they may not have seen it for a couple of years or more; and they have a wonderful memory for brands and earmarks. Though they may be otherwise illiterate, they will squat on the road, and with a stick faultlessly portray the brands and earmarks of every station and selection for miles around them.'

— *EDWARD S. SORENSON, 1911.*

Swaggies

'The old battler can usually tell at a glance what state a man belong to by the way he carries his swag. The swags, too, are different. Matilda, of Victoria, has the most taking figure. She is five or six feet long, neat and slim and tapering at the ends. Her extremes are tied together, and she is worn over the right shoulder and under the left arm— much in the way a lubra wears a skirt. The Banana-lander's pet is short and plump. She is carried perpendicularly between the shoulder-blades, and held in position by shoulder-straps. Getting into this, to a new chum, is like putting on a tight skirt. The Cornstalk (the young countryman in New

South Wales) doesn't much care how he rolls his; he merely objects to bulk and weight. Generally it is borne on a slant from right shoulder to left hip, his towel doing duty for shoulder-strap. He chucks it down as though it was somebody else's luggage, and takes it up as if he would much rather leave it behind.

'I was once shocked to see Matilda brutally assaulted by a Murrumbidgee whaler. Stopping at a camping spot, he pitched Billy aside with a growl, then took hold of Matilda by her tentacles, swung her high overhead and banged her on the ground. Then he propelled her violently across the landscape with his boot, unstintedly cursing her in the meantime for not being able to travel on her own.

'Neddy, the tucker-bag, or nosebag, is of more importance than the blue one, and by way of precedence dangles in front, mostly hanging from Matilda's apron-strings. Billy sticks faithfully to the hand that claims him. The exact time when Swaggie, Bluey, Neddy and Billy first entered into partnership would be hard to determine. Go where you will in the backblocks, and no matter how lonely, dry and hopeless the track, you will not fail to meet the firm taking its usual walk and going to its customary picnic. Catechetical formula of such meetings: "How far's the next station?" "What's it like for tucker?" "Anyone died there lately? No! Then it's no use askin' for work." And, as the firm moves on again, the manager mutters: "Hard times—nobody won't die."

'Nearly everywhere in country parts the term "traveller" is more often heard than "swagman". It is applied to the footman, as though he were the only genuine species of the order that has a habit of moving about. The man with horses, the man on the bike, and the men who trek per medium of vehicles are just as much travellers as the person who "pads the hoof"; but the bush doesn't recognize them in the same light at all. Track society has its castes and classes, its ramifications and complications, like any other society, and its lowest ebb is the sundowner. Too many people are prone to judge the fraternity by its low classes. The word "tramp" to them is almost a criminal suggestion; it came from the Old Country with a bad reputation, and is seldom used by the native-born.'

— *EDWARD S. SORENSON, 1911.*

The Back Country

'There is a pleasure in a mad gallop; or in watching the dawn of day on a cattle camp—to see the beasts take shape, and change from an indistinguishable mass of white and black into their natural colours; in the dead of night to find yourself alone with the cattle—all the camp asleep, perhaps only a red spark betokening the camp. I always, when I think of it, find something unearthly in this assemblage of huge animals ready at any moment to burst forth like a pent-up torrent, and equally irresistible in their force. When every beast is down, asleep or resting, just pull up and listen. You will hear a long moaning sound rising to a roar, then subsiding to a murmur like distant surf—or, as I fancy, the cry of the damned in Dante's *Inferno*. When the cattle are like that it is a good sign. But in the moonlight this strange noise, the dark mass of cattle with the occasional flash of an eye or a polished horn catching the light—it always conjures up strange fancies in me: I seem to be in some other world.

'If I could only write it, there is a poem to be made out of the back country. Some man will come yet who will be able to grasp the romance of Western Queensland and all that equally mysterious country in Central and Northern Australia. For there is a romance, though a grim one—a story of drought and flood, fever and famine, murder and suicide, courage and endurance.

'And who reaps the benefit? Not the poor bushman: but Messrs. So-and-So, merchants of Sydney or Melbourne—or the Mutual Consolidated Cut-down-the-drovers'-wages Company, Limited—or some other capitalist. If you showed them the map half of them could not point out the position of their runs. All they know is that their cheques come in regularly from the buyers; and if the expenses pass the limit they, in their ignorance, sack the manager and get another easy enough.'

— *BARCROFT BOAKE (1866-92).*

Boake was a promising poet who later hanged himself with his stockwhip.

Snakes Alive

Australia has 173 types of snake but only a handful of them are poisonous—the most feared are the tiger snake and the brown snake (and the taipan in tropical Queensland). Few are aggressive, all are now protected, and most will go their own way if not confronted, though in the bush the brown snakes that make their way into bedrooms in summer pose a problem.

'Camping out is not all smooth sailing. The tentless swagman at times has to make queer shifts on wet nights. I once shared a hollow log with a dingo—but neither of us had any sleep; we were too interested in watching each other. On another night I slept in the hollow of a tree, and next morning I noticed a big black snake crawling out of the root to sun himself.

'When once you have been scared by snakes you live in dread of them, for they wander on hot nights, and your fire attracts them. They travel for miles before a dust-storm; so when a dust-storm is coming you lie expectant. Every crooked stick resembles a snake, and if you look at it by firelight it seems to dance and to wriggle; I travelled with one man who made it a rule to gather up every little stick before dark. Said he had killed two or three stick-snakes that summer and didn't want to be making a fool of himself any more...

'Perhaps the most remarkable thing about bush children is that they are very rarely bitten by snakes. They roam the day long about creeks and billabongs with bare feet and bare legs, playing in scrubs, wading through long grass and ferns, turning over bark and logs, thrusting their hands into hollows and burrows, and invariably come off unscathed ...'

— *Edward S. Sorenson, 1911.*

The 'Bully'

It was known as 'the Bushman's Bible'. *The Bulletin*, launched in Sydney in 1880 as a weekly journal of news, opinion and literature, was read by all classes but especially by country people who enjoyed its irreverent style, mockery of the silvertails, satirical cartoons and rollicking bush verses and stories. It was first published by a Scot named Traill who three years later sold it to a syndicate including J.F.Archibald, a journalist who was bitterly Anglophobe, deeply Francophile and passionately nationalistic. When A.G. Stephens joined him in 1894 and founded the 'Red Page' which featured book reviews and readers' contributions, the *'Bully'* became a platform for some of the country's best writers. The journal welcomed verse by gifted amateurs and gave rebirth to the bush ballad tradition that was thought to have died with Adam Lindsay Gordon's suicide in 1870—it published the poems (and stories) of Barcroft Boake (who also suicided), 'Banjo' Paterson, Henry Lawson, 'Breaker' Morant, Joseph Furphy, Mary Gilmore, Miles Franklin, Shaw Neilson, Hugh McCrae, among others. Equally outstanding were its illustrators—starting with the American Livingston Hopkins ('Hop') and the Englishman Phil May and progressing to George Lambert, Norman Lindsay, the Dysons, David Low and Percy Leason. The best of these talents were published in book form by a canny Scot, George Robertson of Angus & Robertson, and became the bedrock of Australian literature. Archibald had a nervous breakdown and spent time in Callan Park lunatic asylum (now, ironically, a writers' centre funded by the New South Wales government). 'A.G.', as Stephens was called, left the *Bulletin* in 1906 to open a bookshop (it failed and his stock was auctioned off), went to New Zealand as a last resort, and then founded a journal in Sydney, the *Bookfellow*.

Slow to adapt to changing times, the *Bulletin* barely changed in format (or attitudes) until 1960 when it was bought and converted by its new owners into a smart weekly newsmagazine similar to *Time*, in which form it survives to this day.

'Banjo' versus Lawson

They remain Australia's best-loved writers, legendary figures. Their verse and stories have never diminished in popularity. By one of these strange coincidences that delight the curious, Andrew Barton ('Banjo') Paterson and Henry Lawson were born in the same part of central western New South Wales, and only three years separated them in age. Paterson was the romantic, famous as the handsome horseman and soldier, who lived to a distinguished old age; Lawson was the realist who died relatively young from drink and disappointment. Yet their backgrounds were similar and their lives curiously intertwined. When Lawson died penniless in 1922, he was accorded the honour of a state funeral. Banjo Paterson, like many who live by their pen, also died relatively poor, leaving an estate of only £255 (510 dollars) and his passing during the war in 1941 hardly rated headlines. But their books have never been out of print.

A.B. 'Banjo' Paterson

'Banjo' was born on a farm near Orange, New South Wales, in 1864, the son of a Scottish immigrant father. Henry Lawson was born only 130 kilometres to the south-west, at Grenfell, in 1867, the son of a Norwegian father of limited skills. Both men had hard childhoods, their fathers being often absent, and received their early education at bush schools—but both were blessed with mothers of rare strength of character. Paterson was fortunate in having relatives of some wealth who paid for him to attend Sydney Grammar and then progress to study Law, but Lawson was not so fortunate. Both men began writing for the *Bulletin* in the 1880s and in 1892, when they were the two most popular writers of verse in the journal, they played out, on Lawson's suggestion, a mock feud in verse on the merits and shortcomings of bush life. Banjo later wrote: 'This suited me all right,

Henry Lawson

for we were working on space and the pay was very small . . . so we slam-banged away at each other for weeks and weeks—not until they stopped us, but until we ran out of material. I think Lawson put his case better than I did, but I had the better case, so that honours (or dishonours) were fairly equal.'

The good-natured 'feud' produced some of their best verse (excerpts of which appear here). It is hard to imagine present-day writers, by-and-large a humourless lot, indulging in such good-natured feuding.

Banjo loved the bush as few writers have and saw in bush life certain heroic qualities. Lawson saw in the bush and the Outback only loneliness and an unending struggle for existence. In *Borderland* (later called *Up the Country*) published on 9 July 1892, Lawson—who had never been out to the far West—pictured the bush as:

> *Miles and miles of thirsty gutters*
>   *—strings of muddy waterholes—*
> *In the place of 'Shining rivers'*
>   *—'walled by cliffs and forest boles'.*
> *Barren ridges, gullies, ridges!*
> *Where the everlasting flies*
>   *— Fiercer than the plagues of Egypt*
>   *—swarm about your blighted eyes!*
> *Bush! Where there is no horizon!*
> *Where the buried bushman sees,*
> *Nothing but the sameness of the ragged, stunted trees.*

In due course Banjo replied with *In Defence of the Bush* and *An Answer to Various Bards* (excerpts from which appear below):

In Defence of the Bush

...You found the bush was dismal and a land of no delight,
Did you chance to hear a chorus in the shearers' huts at night?
Did they 'rise up, William Riley' by the camp-fire's cheery blaze?
Did they rise him as we rose him in the good old droving days?
And the women of the homesteads and the men you chanced to meet—
Were their faces sour and saddened like the 'faces in the street',
And the 'shy selector children'—were they better now or worse
Than the little city urchins who would greet you with a curse?
Is not such a life much better than the squalid street and square
Where the fallen women flaunt it in the fierce electric glare,
Where the seamstress plies her sewing till her eyes are sore and red
In a filthy, dirty attic toiling on for daily bread?

Did you hear no sweeter voices in the music of the bush,
Than the roar of trams and buses, and the war whoop of 'the push?'
Did the magpies rouse your slumbers with their carol sweet and strange?

Did you hear the silver chiming of the bell birds on the range?
But, perchance, the wild birds' music by your senses was
despised,
For you say you'll stay in townships till the bush is civilized.
Would you make it a tea garden and on Sundays have a band,
Where the 'blokes' might take their 'donahs', with a 'public'
close at hand?
You had better stick to Sydney and make merry with the 'push',
For the bush will never suit you, and you'll never suit the bush.

An Answer to Various Bards

. . . I 'over-write' the bushmen! Well, I own out a doubt
That I always see a hero in the 'man from furthest out'.
I could never contemplate him through an atmosphere of
gloom,
And a bushman never struck me as a subject for 'the tomb'.
If it ain't all 'golden sunshine' where the 'wattle branches
wave',
Well, it ain't all damp and dismal, and it ain't all 'lonely grave'.
And, of course, there's no denying that the bushman's life is
rough,
But a man can easy stand it if he's built of sterling stuff;
Tho' it's seldom that the drover gets a bed of eider down,
Yet the man who's born a bushman, he gets mighty sick of
town,
For he's jotting down the figures, and he's adding up the bills
While his heart is simply aching for a sight of southern hills.
Then he hears a wood team passing with a rumble and a lurch,
And although the work is pressing yet it brings him off his
perch.
For it stirs him like a message from his station friends afar
And he seems to sniff the ranges in the scent of wool and tar.

And it takes him back in fancy, half in laughter, half in tears,
To a sound of other voices and a thought of other years,
When the woolshed rang with bustle from the dawning
of the day,
And the shear blades were a-clicking to the cry of 'wool away!'
When his face was somewhat browner and his frame was
firmer set,
And he feels his flabby muscles with a feeling of regret.
Then the wool team slowly passes and his eyes go sadly back
To the dusty little table and the papers in the rack,
And his thoughts go to the terrace where his sickly children
squall,

And he thinks there's something healthy in the bush life after
all.

But we'll go no more a-droving in the wind or in the sun,
For our fathers' hearts have failed us and the droving days are
done.
There's a nasty dash of danger where the long-horned bullock
wheels,
And we like to live in comfort and to get our reg'lar meals.
And to hang about the townships suits us better, you'll agree,
For a job at washing bottles is the job for such as we.
Let us herd into the cities, let us crush and crowd and push
Till we lose the love of roving and we learn to hate the bush;
And we'll turn our aspirations to a city life and beer,
And we'll sneak across to England—it's a nicer place than here;
For there's not much risk of hardship where all comforts are in
store,
And the theatres are plenty and the pubs are more and more.

— *A.B. (BANJO) PATERSON.*

Lawson's rejoinder, *The City Bushman,* was a tart one:

The City Bushman

It was pleasant up the county, City Bushman, where you went,
For you sought the greener patches and you travelled
like a gent;
And you curse the trams and buses and the turmoil
and the push,
Though you know the squalid city needn't keep you from
the bush;
And we lately heard you singing of the 'plains where shade
is not,'
And you mentioned it was dusty—'all was dry and it was hot.'

Though the bush has been romantic and it's nice to sing
about,
There's a lot of patriotism that the land could do without—
Sort of British Workman nonsense that shall perish in the
corn,
Of the drover who is driven and the shearer who is shorn,
Of the struggling western farmers who have little time for rest,
And are ruined on selections in the sheep-infested West;
Droving songs are very pretty, but they merit little thanks
From the people of a country in possession of the Banks . . .

— *HENRY LAWSON.*

The Bushman

'On an average the bushman is very wide-awake. Nothing in his native surroundings comes amiss to him; he can cook his dinner, wash his clothes, patch his pants, darn his socks, plait a whip, mend his own harness and boots, build his own house; he is musterer, drover, shearer, fencer, miner, bullock-driver, trapper, horse-breaker, hunter, what-not. He is good-tempered; good-natured, plain-spoken, witty and humorous. He smokes heavily of strong tobacco, has a vigorous appetite, and laughs heartily—like the kookaburra. He is not religious, though I have heard him say grace before meat even in a shearing shed. This is the grace: "One word's as good as ten, wire in. Amen."

'He is well learned in the habits and characteristics of his native fauna and flora. He has acquired many of the traits of the Aboriginal,

notably in bushcraft, and likewise he has developed a keenness of vision in tracking, bee-hunting, possum-shooting, and searching for distant objects. He requires no compass on a cloudy day, knowing the north and south side of plants; he points out the straight-grained and cross-grained trees by the bark; and the locale of water is indicated to him by the convergence of bird and animal tracks.

'Like the Aboriginal, too, he is quick to notice the idiosyncrasies, eccentricities and peculiarities of people, and he names them accordingly. Thus in conversation we hear of "Johnny All-sorts", "Jacky-Without-a-Shirt", "Long Bob", "Billy the Rooster", "Mick the Rager", "Daylight Mac", "Jimmy Short-breeches", "Boko", "The Splinter", "Shovellin' Archie", "Crayfish Dan", "Yorky", "Scotty", "Stumpy", "The Long un", and a family comprising Big Angus, Little Angus, Red Angus, Black Angus, Pole Angus, Baldy Angus, Young Angus, Old Angus, Angus the First, and Angus-Come-Lately.

'His grit and endurance under trying conditions are proverbial. We often hear of men and boys who, after being thrown, crawl after their horses with a broken leg, drag themselves into the saddle and ride many miles home. Men, too, bind up their own broken limbs between bits of rough wood and, using a forked stick for crutch, cover long journeys without food or water. I remember a teamster who fell under his wagon, and the wheels, passing over him, crushed a leg, arm, shoulder and several ribs. He instructed his mate to lash the injured leg to the sound one, and to tie the arm to his side. Then he said "Put me in the cart, and I'll ride as right as pie." There was no hope for him from the start, but he was cheerful and game to the end. In towns people get accustomed to depend on the ambulance and the hospital, and to look to the doctor being in attendance in five minutes. In the bush a man learns to depend on his own resources, and being seldom within reach of a doctor, he never looks for one except when his bones are broken, or when the home remedies have failed in other cases. Mere flesh wounds to him are nothing to trouble about; his only concern is to stop the bleeding. He never knows when he goes out alone into the bush what he may be called upon to endure before he gets back. The boundary rider jogging along his fences, the shepherd, the stockman, the prospector and the scrub-cutter, when unaccompanied by a mate, have always before them the risk of a lingering death.'

'But he loves his wild surroundings with the love of the true child of Nature; for the bush is bright, fragrant, invigorating, interesting: the leaves whisper symphonies to him, and the birds are brilliant and cheery. There all is health and vigour, music and gladness, beauty and laughter—and land of sunshine and happiness. To the old hand the bush is an open book; it is his Bible. Bird and animal life, botanical and physical characteristics are all so many chapters in it, read and studied, re-read and understood . . .'

— *EDWARD S. SORENSON, 1911.*

Paddy Hannan

An Irish immigrant (and future judge in Western Australia), John Kirwan, who prospected for gold at Coolgardie in the 1890s, preserved this account of Hannan's description of his find.

'I arrived in the colony in March 1889, and was at Parkers Range about forty miles [60 kilometres] from Southern Cross, when Bayley reported the discovery of a rich reef at Coolgardie. I joined in the rush.

'Early in June, 1893, news arrived at Coolgardie of a good discovery at a place called Mount Yuille somewhere to the east or north-east. Parties left Coolgardie in search of the find. A few days after the report had been received, my mate, Thomas Flanagan, and I left Coolgardie. We left on June 7. We would have left earlier with the others, but we could not obtain horses, and so we were delayed two or three days. We were lucky enough to pick up some animals in the bush ten or twelve miles [15–20 kilometres] from Coolgardie. The other parties going to Mount Yuille were mostly travelling with teams. Only one or two of the prospecting groups had horses of their own. We were a separate party, as we wished to be free to travel when we liked. We could also by this arrangement if we chose prospect any country during the journey.

'A very large number was in the main party going to Mount Yuille. Only Bayley's claim was working at Coolgardie, and the alluvial had become exhausted just about the time we left, hence the strong desire amongst the men to reach the new find.

'One June 10, three days after leaving Coolgardie, we reached what is now Kalgoorlie. The other parties had gone on in the direction of the reported discovery, but it was only to find later that the report had been false.

'Well, as I have said, when we came on June 10 to Mount Charlotte, my mate and I decided to stop and prospect the country roundabout. To us it looked country where there might be alluvial. We found colours of gold and then got good gold at the north end of Mount Charlotte to down south of Maritana Hill.

'There was another man by the way, Dan Shea was his name, to whom we gave an equal share in our venture.

'We soon realized that we were located on a valuable field. Alluvial gold was in abundance. We got scores of ounces. It was agreed that I should go to Coolgardie and apply for a reward claim. I left Flanagan and Shea to watch our interests, and on June 17 started for Coolgardie. I got there on a Saturday night.

'The news of our find soon got abroad. There was a good deal of excitement. Hundreds of men set out for the scene. The flats and gullies all about our reward claim became alive with diggers dryblowing and finding gold.

Paddy Hannan statue, Kalgoorlie

'The water difficulty, which had been unusually great, was solved. Rain began to fall as I was on my way to Coolgardie to report the find, and continued for some time. The fall was fairly heavy. It was exceedingly welcome to us all and relieved the shortage from which we suffered. The downpour left plenty of water in rock holes and lakes. The supply lasted until November.

'Where the ground was too wet for dryblowing, the men dried the earth by fires and so could work their claims.'

— *FROM* MY LIFE'S ADVENTURE, *1936,* SIR JOHN KIRWAN (1869-1949).

The Riot Where No-One Was Hurt

When the Western Australian government prohibited digging below a certain level the miners went wild and angrily mobbed Premier John Forrest when he visited the fields. Newspaper accounts exaggerated reports of the 'riot'; in fact the only injury suffered by Forrest was an accidental jab by an umbrella.

There have been riots, I know, in the land of the spud,
   Which are not unattended with the spilling of blood,
   As the blackthorn encounters the Constable's crown
   And the stalwart policemen like ninepins go down.
   When the amiable Hindoo is ripe for the fray,
   There are nice little shindies in sultry Bombay,
   Things get lively at times in Hyde Park and the Strand
   When the suffering Communist gets 'out of hand'.
   But except in Westralia—'tis safe to assert
   There was never a riot where no one was hurt.

What a blood-curdling story they pitched us last week,
   Of a tumult colossal, Homeric unique!
   Of a crowd of wild diggers, some ten thousand strong,
   Who bustled and chevied a premier along;
   Of ears that were deafened by salvoes of groans, Of lives that
   were threatened by bludgeons and stones!
   You'd have thought from the published reports of the fray
   Red Hell had broke loose in Kalgoorlie that day,
   And that scores had been trampled to death in the dirt,
   In that terrible riot—where no one was hurt.'

Coolgardie Humour

'The first Mayor of Coolgardie was James Shaw, a Belfast man, a veteran of the Maori war and a one time Mayor of Adelaide. In his capacity of chief magistrate a case came down before him where a man used insulting language towards another, who promptly knocked him down. A fine of £1 for assault was imposed, but when the man who was knocked down asked for costs, Mr Shaw promptly replied, "Certainly not, a man who cannot fight should not use insulting language."

'One man, charged with being drunk and disorderly, was asked what he had to say to the charge. He calmly replied, "I plead guilty to the charge of drunkenness, but cannot truthfully say anything about being disorderly until I hear the evidence."

'A warden friend of mine told me of a blackfellow, Jacky, who was brought before him and asked before he was sworn, "What will happen to you if you tell a lie?"

' "If I tell lie I go to hell," was the prompt answer.

When cross-examined he was asked, "You say you know the meaning of an oath and if you lie you will go to hell. What will happen if you tell the truth?"

' "Then," said Jacky, "we'll lose the bloody case!" '

— *JOHN KIRWAN.*

The Prospector

'The prospector is to the digger what the pilot fish is to the shark.

'The comparison may appear rather strange, but it nevertheless expresses very faithfully the relation between the two classes. The prospector is the digger's provider, and a bold and adventurous character he is. He is a true Bohemian—never settling down long in one place, but always restlessly on the move—seeking, and at rare intervals finding. He means to become suddenly wealthy without long, settled, and laborious toil. The difficulties and dangers undergone by these wanderers beyond the confines of civilization are only equalled by those encountered by the explorers and pioneers, of whom I have already given some account.

'Every goldfield in the colonies has contributed to swell the ranks of the skirmishers in advance of the great army of diggers. I have met with them often in my journeys, and many a night's camp has been enlivened by their yarns. The last time I came in contact with a prospector was at Craigie, in Northern Queensland. His tent was pitched away amongst the gorges some twelve miles [20 kilometres] from the station where I met him, and there he lived all alone, pursuing his avocation, heedless of the numerous blacks who wandered about their fastnesses, and who doubtless kept a watchful eye over him, in the hope of surprising and killing him. Miller (this was the prospector's name) had spent several weeks in this neighbourhood, examining and trying all the likely-looking gullies, with pick, shovel and tin dish, but up to the time of my visit he had been unsuccessful in making any great find. He could manage to get "the colour", that is, small grains of gold, almost anywhere he tried, but only very rarely did he get anything approaching payable gold. Nevertheless, he plodded on day after day in the hope of doing better. On one or two occasions his tent was visited by the blacks in his absence [and they took his food and clothing], and he later abandoned the district, and travelled away to the Etheridge during the wet season, arriving there after a journey of two hundred miles, the greater portion of the time being spent in struggling through interminable boggy and flooded flats and swimming rivers which had overflowed their banks.'

— *A.J. (WILLIAM ALEXANDER) BOYD*

PROSPECTING.

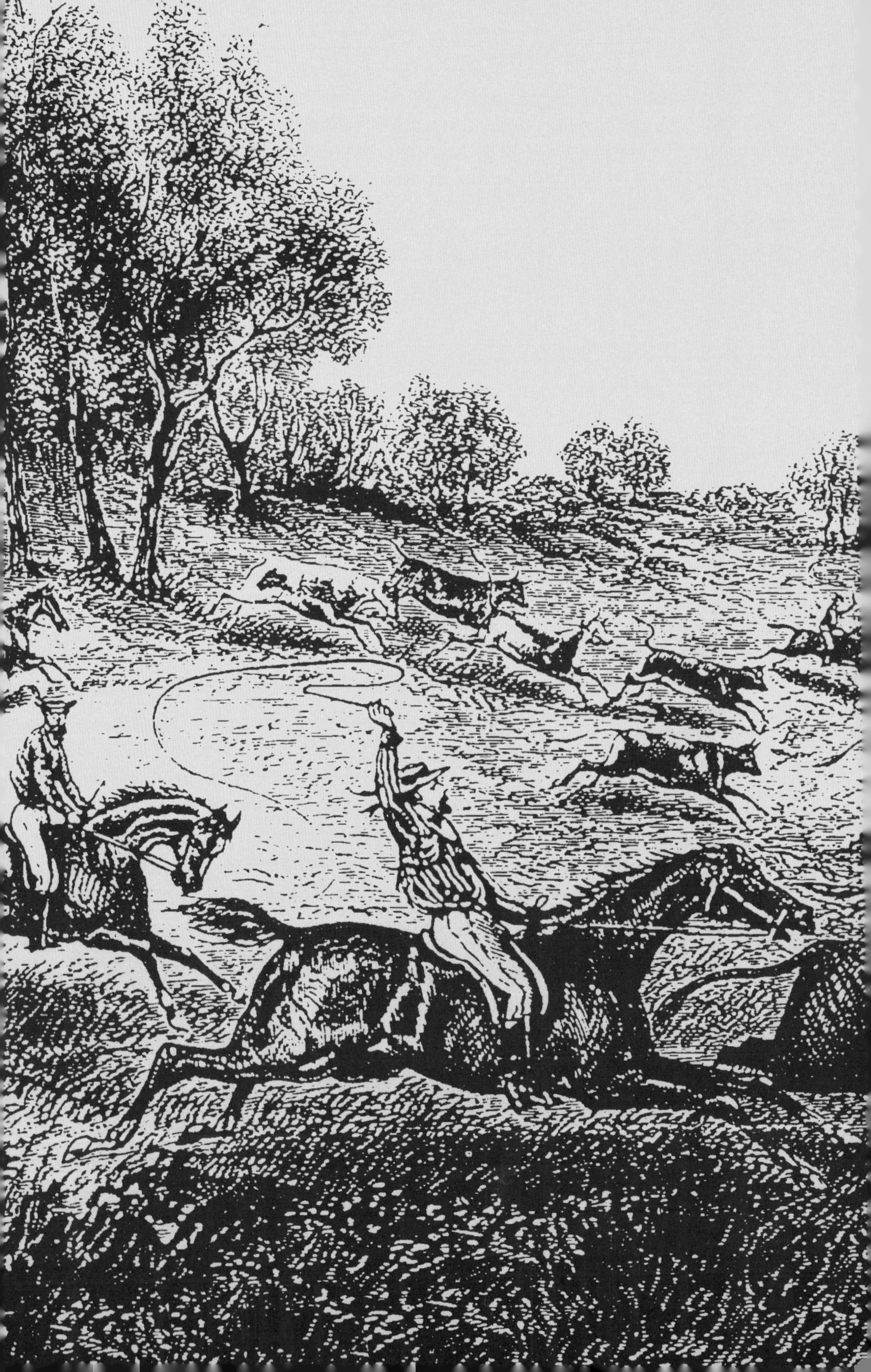

8: *The Overlanders*

IN 1835, SETTLERS AND DROVERS began taking sheep and cattle overland from New South Wales to their new settlements in the Port Phillip district—easy country and a short journey compared to the deserts and distances of the Outback that drovers would conquer before the century's end. In 1988 the stockmen's and overlanders' contribution to Australia's economy, history and folklore was commemorated by the opening of the Stockman's Hall of Fame and Outback Heritage Centre at Longreach, Queensland, where every two years in September the Starlite Stampede is held to commemorate the deeds of the legendary overlander Harry Redford, known widely (and wrongly) as 'Captain Starlight'.

The First Overlanders

In 1838, an English settler, Joseph Hawdon, accompanied by Charles Bonney and a handful of others, drove sheep and cattle from the Murray River to Adelaide, proving that an immense stretch of undiscovered country short of water could be crossed. By 1840, more than 20,000 cattle at any given time were kicking up the dust on the route from Yass to Melbourne.

The 1860s saw the opening of the North. In 1864, the Jardine brothers drove a herd of cattle from Rockhampton to Cape York and in 1870 Ralph Milner overlanded 1,000 sheep from South Australia to the Northern Territory, a journey of more than a year. The stock routes pioneered by these and other hardy horsemen would soon result in three main tracks—one of them from the Gulf Country south to the Darling River and thence to Wodonga in Victoria. The two other main routes would be the Murranji Track—running from Victoria River in the North to Newcastle Waters—and the famous Birdsville Track, used by drovers from the 1880s to the 1970s (when road transport began taking over the transport of cattle). The Birdsville Track runs 500 kilometres south from Birdsville on the Queensland-South Australia border to the rail-head at Marree in South Australia and is best known today as an outback highway, one of the roughest in Australia.

The Riverina

'On those by-gone droving journeys [in the late 1850s–early 1860s], we had great opportunities of noting the splendid grazing qualities of the Murrumbidgee and Riverina country. From Kimo

'From all accounts the overlanders were magnificent fellows.
They looked like banditti; they had the finest Arab horses; they
had big sombreros with eagle plumes waving; bright red flannel
shirts, broad belts filled with pistols and tomahawks. They had
great long beards and moustaches. They were all sorts of men—
foreigners, emancipists and Oxford dons, the lot. What a marvellous picturesque lot they must have been . . .'

— FROM ALAN MARSHALL'S AUSTRALIA, *1981, ALAN MARSHALL (1902-84)*

(Collins) to Buckinbong (Jenkins), in the Murrumbidgee Country, as from Table-top, then owned by Mr. Warby, to Chapman's Urana Station, in the Murray side—the country in the blue-eyed seasons of the later 'fifties was worth the ransom of a thousand kings. The rich trefoil and clover—the lush grasses along the river-banks; the green, open-hearted look of the country; the cattle rolling fat; the unfenced "panorama" of the sunny landscape, was all a grand tonic to the heart and the vision of the drover after the murky, frost-bitten hills of the Tablelands, Riverina was then purely a pastoral paradise. There were no rail-side wheat-depots or elevators; no signs of model farm or state nurseries; and very little farming "on the whole or on the halves," along the banks of the Mighty Murrumbidgee or the Lord Murray.'

— *CHAS. MACALISTER.*

The Drovers

'From the memorable time when those enterprising and picturesquely-garbed men, whose arrival created more excitement than the local earthquake, steered the first mobs of cattle into Adelaide, the overlanders have left their tracks across the pages of Australian history and have passed on to the Big Muster under a halo woven of song and story. From the Gulf and the northern peninsula, from Arnhem's Land and no man's land and from other regions of broad, wild runs, the mobs still come teeming down over hundreds of miles of unfenced country, under conditions very similar to those of early times. When they reach the zone of the small

settler; the modern squattages and townships, then the conditions are different. They are hemmed in on all sides, and where once only King Murri was concerned about their movements, they are now closely watched by boundary riders, mounted troopers and stock inspectors. Every drover must carry a passport, giving date and place of delivery, destination, and the number and description of the cattle and horses. Then the stations ahead have to be notified of their coming on to the runs. This is usually done by the horse-boy who, having to report twenty-four hours in advance, has many a long ride through rain and shine, and through light and shadow, to perform.'

— *EDWARD S. SORENSON.*

The Duracks

By the 1860s the new colony of Queensland—and even territory further west—was holding promise of land unclaimed where a man could still stake out a property for next to nothing, provided he had the beasts to stock it and the courage to reach it.

Much of south-western Queensland remained unoccupied—the land that Patsy Adam Smith called the heart of Australia's folk history, the land of legend. Here, anyone could stake out a run of 100 square miles [259 square kilometres] and if, after nine months, he

had stocked it to at least a quarter of its capacity, he could obtain a 14-year lease for an annual rent of 10 shillings per square mile.

In June 1863, Patrick Durack, his brother Michael and John Costello, Irishmen all, left Goulburn with a small group of stockmen and a herd of 100 horses and 400 cattle (valued at £5 a head) to head for the Queensland border. They followed the Lachlan to Bourke, a thousand kilometres north and 2.5 months' journey away.

They reached Bourke and pushed on through drought-stricken land, losing their stock and almost perishing until saved by blacks. They returned to Goulburn determined to try again—and to bring their women and children with them.

In June 1867, 'Patsy' Durack, his wife and children and brother Michael, set out from Goulburn again, with 200 head of cattle (all strong but docile Herefords) and reached Burke after a three-month trek.

Abandoning his property on the Paroo, Costello joined them and the Overlanders pushed up north to Mobel Creek. Here John Costello rounded up the horses they had abandoned four years before and drove them down to Adelaide, a journey of 1400 kilometres, where he got £15 a head for them, took a boat to Sydney and then rode to Goulburn and Bourke to rejoin the Durack party.

In the Channel Country between the Diamantina and Bullo Creek the Costellos and the Duracks carved out cattle empires over the next decade totalling 10 million acres (4,046,856.4 hectares).

Stockmen

'The finest riders and the wildest spirits are found in the back-blocks. Their most favoured rig-out consists of snow-white, tight-fitting moleskins, coloured shirt, black coat, light cossacks and a gaudily-coloured silk neckerchief. Leggings, once universally worn, have pretty well gone out of fashion, but the long-necked spurs are inseparable from the stockman's heels. They jingle him to dinner, and they keep time to his pirouetting in the dance-room. When he removes his boots at night the spurs are still strapped on them; if he is camping out, he very often sleeps in them. The thinking end of him is decked with an expansive cabbage-tree or a broad-leafed felt hat, something like the sombrero of the cowboy. He is a picturesque fellow, and not a bad sort, with all his whims and fancies. He is good-hearted and hospitable and, though he has a mild contempt for a man who cannot ride a bucking horse down a precipice, he is at all times generous enough to give assistance and advice to a novice, especially to lads who are beginning a station career.

'On many of the big cattle stations [in the west] half the stockmen are Aborigines. They make good horsemen, are marvellously quick in a yard, keen-sighted, and are at home in any part of the bush. These supple-jointed nimble-fingered gentry can pick up the smallest objects from the ground while riding at full speed. They fraternize like brothers with the whites, though at the head station they have separate quarters.'

— *EDWARD S. SORENSON.*

The Overlander

There's a trade you all know well—
   It's bringing cattle over—
   I'll tell you all about the time,
   When I became a drover.
   I made up my mind to try on spec,
   To the Clarence I did wander,
   And brought a mob of duffers there
   To begin as an overlander.

CHORUS:
   Pass the wine cup round, my boys;
   Don't let the bottle stand there,
   For tonight we'll drink the health
   Of every overlander.

When the cattle were all mustered,
   And the outfit ready to start,
   I saw the lads all mounted,
   With their swags left in the cart.
   All kinds of men I had
   From France, Germany, and Flanders;
   Lawyers, doctors, good and bad,
   In the mob of overlanders.

From the road I then fed out,
   When the grass was green and young;
   When a squatter with curse and shout,
   Told me to move along.
   I said 'You're very hard;
   Take care, don't raise my dander,
   For I'm a regular knowing card,
   The Queensland overlander.'

'Tis true we pay no licence,
   And our run is rather large;
   'Tis not often they can catch us,
   So they cannot make a charge.
   They think we live on store beef,
   But no, I'm not a gander;
   When a good fat stranger joins the mob,
   'He'll do', says the overlander.

— *TRADITIONAL BALLAD.*

Young Tom Hamilton

In 1871, Thomas Hamilton left his family's Victorian property to take
up land in the North. He took with him a herd of cattle, a drover, a
boy and several packhorses. He reached Darwin two years later.
'This amazing feat,' writes Michael Cannon, 'was achieved with com-
parative nonchalance, no loss of life and no publicity, only ten years
after the disastrous Burke and Wills Expedition in which seven lives
were lost along the north-south route.'

The Stockmen of Australia

The stockmen of Australia, what rowdy boys are they,
 They will curse and swear a hurricane if you come in their way.
 They dash along the forest on black, bay, brown, or grey,
 And the stockmen of Australia, hard-riding boys are they.

By constant feats of horsemanship, they procure for us our grub,
 And supply us with the fattest beef by hard work in the scrub,
 To muster up the cattle they cease not night nor day,
 And the stockmen of Australia, hard-riding boys are they.

Just mark him as he jobs along, his stockwhip on his knee,
 His white mole pants and polished boots and jaunty cabbage-
 tree.
 His horsey-pattern Crimean shirt of colours bright and gay,
 And the stockmen of Australia, what dressy boys are they.

If you should chance to lose yourself and drop upon his camp,
 He's there reclining on the ground, be it dry or be it damp.
 He'll give you hearty welcome, and a stunning pot of tea,
 For the stockmen of Australia, good-natured boys are they.

If down to Sydney you should go, and there a stockman meet,
 Remark the sly looks cast on him as he roams through the
 street,
 From the shade of lovely bonnets steal forth those glances gay,
 For the stockmen of Australia, the ladies' pets are they.

Whatever fun is going on, the stockmen will be here,
 Be it theatre or concert, or dance or fancy fair.
 To join in the amusements be sure he won't delay,
 For the stockmen of Australia, light-hearted boys are they.

Then here's a health to every lass, and let the toast go round,
 To as jolly a set of fellows as ever yet were found.
 And all good luck be with them, for ever and today,
 Here's to the stockmen of Australia—hip, hip, hooray!

— *Traditional.*

Harry Redford

'My name's Dick Marston, Sydney-side native. I'm twenty-nine years old, six feet in my stocking soles, and thirteen stone weight. Pretty strong and active with it, so they say. I don't want to blow—not here any road—but it takes a good man to put me on my back, or stand up to me with the gloves, or the naked mauleys. I can ride any-thing—anything that ever was lapped in horsehide—swim like a musk-duck, and track like a Myall blackfellow. Most things that a man can do I'm up to, and that's all about it. As I lift myself now I can feel the muscle swell on my arm like a cricket ball, in spite of the—well, in spite of everything.'

Rolf Boldrewood's classic novel *Robbery Under Arms,* told through the words of Dick Marston, who introduces himself in its famous opening lines quoted above, relates the adventures of our best known fictional bushranger, Captain Starlight. Starlight was based to a great extent on the overlander Harry Redford (or Readford), whose true-life adventures included bushranging and cat-tle duffing. In 1870 Redford overlanded 1,000 head of cattle from Western Queensland to Adelaide down the desert track—all of them had been stolen. When he heard that it was John Costello who had set the police on his trail, Redford laughed: 'I'm proud to think it took one of the best bushmen in Australia to dob me in. Those green-horn police would have been hunting for me yet!'

Despite being caught again, red-handed, Redford was found 'not guilty' at a famous trial at Roma and thereafter became an honest man. He once overlanded 3,000 head from the Barcoo to the Northern Territory to form Brunette Downs Station and his feats as

a drover are commemorated still in cattle drives named in his honour. Redford once led a party of Chinese miners safely from Katherine to Camooweal, a distance of more than 1,300 kilometres through desert country threatened by hostile blacks in which hundreds of Chinese had died in previous years in attempting to return from the diggings.

Michael Durack found Harry Redford in the 1890s living at Anthony's Lagoon (bone dry for nine months of the year) on the Kimberley Track, 'a right good old social character, willing at all times to entertain with stories of his youthful prowess.'

Nat Buchanan: 'Old Bluey'

Ginger-haired and 'wiry, like the very devil', Nathaniel Buchanan was the most colourful overlander of them all.

One of that tough breed, the Scots-Irish, he was born in Dublin in 1826 and immigrated to Australia with his family eleven years later. Leaving Sydney for the Californian gold rush, he arrived back penniless and became a drover. In 1859 he joined Will Landsborough's expedition to southern Queensland and four years later established Bowen Downs station.

In 1864, Nat Buchanan overlanded to the Gulf of Carpentaria and took up land near Burkton. Married to Kitty Gordon, he set off with

Nat Buchanan

'Greenhide Sam Croaker' to ride across the Barkly Tableland in 1877 to investigate the country that city speculators were leasing sight unseen; Sydney and Alfred Prout had died of thirst on the tableland the year before but Nat and Croaker crossed it with ease and reached the Overland Telegraph.

The Northern Territory—a vast unknown of approximately 1.3 million square kilometres (about 500, 000 square miles)—struck him as possessing perfect cattle country in the gulf region of grassy river flats and monsoonal rains. 'Might ride over and take a look at it someday,' John Costello told him. (in 1884 Costello sold up his Rockhampton properties, sent his wife and youngsters on a trip to Ireland and then headed for the Roper with his son Michael and 1,700 head of cattle.)

Nat Buchanan took a herd of 1,200 cattle from Aramac in Queensland to the Adelaide River in the Northern Territory in 1878, discovering en route Buchanan's Creek, which became the main stock route for overlanders from Queensland to the Centre. The station he formed, Glencoe, became the first cattle property in the Northern Territory.

In 1883, 'the Overlanders' Year', Nat Buchanan and his relatives, the Gordons and the Cahills, drove a mob of 4,000 cattle in an epic 2,200-kilometre journey from the Flinders River in Queensland to the Kimberley region in northern Western Australia for a Melbourne pastoral company, Osmonds. Tom Cahill recalled Nat's actions when he discovered that the head drover was an incompetent: 'One of the first things he did was to sack the man who was being paid seven pounds a week as pilot . . . The next thing Nat did was to go to each camp and empty the demijohns of rum, that were on the drays, out onto the black soil'. The drovers suffered in silence.

The party reached the Ord River without mishap. In 1885, Buchanan opened up Wave Hill Station with the Gordon brothers and in 1892 pioneered Buchanan's Track to the Murchison goldfields, making his last great overland expedition in 1896 when he tried to find a route from the Barkly Tablelands to Western Australia. 'A legend in his own time,' writes Chris Halls, 'Nat Buchanan probably opened more country to settlement than any other explorer.'

The Overlanders' Year: 1883

The great cattle drives north had begun. Western Australia—nearly 2.6 million square kilometres—now glimmered like gold, and all reports of the Kimberley region confirmed that vast areas there were ideal for cattle. In 1881, Patsy Durack and his brother 'Stumpy Michael' sailed to Western Australia to talk with the explorer Alexander Forrest, who described the Fitzroy and Ord river country as a cattleman's paradise. Reserving 2,500,000 acres [approximately 10,000 square kilometres] in the region for themselves and their partners, the Emanuels, the Duracks selected Michael to investigate the region. His reports were glowing.

In June 1883, the first of four parties led by the Durack men, driving a herd totalling 7,520 cattle, 200 horses and 60 working bullocks, left Thylungra on the Cooper River for the 4,800-kilometre journey to the Kimberleys. The first party was led by Patsy's cousin

John Durack, the second by his brother Jerry, the third by another Durack relative Tom Kilfoyle, and the fourth by another cousin, Michael (known in the clan as Long Michael to distinguish him from Patsy's nuggety brother, Stumpy Michael.)

Their overland saga, recounted by the patriarch's grand-daughter, Mary Durack, in the classic family history, *Kings in Grass Castles*, took two years. Nearly 4,000 cattle died on the way and two drovers, crazed by malaria and drink, shot themselves dead; once Long Michael rode 1,500 kilometres to get water. But they reached the Ord River in September 1885 and founded Argyle Downs station.

Patrick Durack's optimism was rewarded immediately. In mid-1886, word got out that gold had been found at Hall's Creek and thousands of miners were soon buying bullocks for £17 a head— and paying for their meat in nuggets. Surviving an infestation of cattle parasite that resulted in a quarantine of their remaining stock, the Duracks formed a partnership with Denis Doherty and Francis Connor in 1897, cornerstone of a cattle empire that would in time encompass seven million acres.

Patsy Durack lost all his Queensland properties and investments as the economic clouds darkened in 1889; he moved to join his family in Western Australia and died there in 1898. Denis Doherty cabled the news to Patsy's son Michael—with an Irish disregard for brevity: 'Your father died this morning brave to the last, a heart like a lion no complaint despite his sufferings. His thoughts were with you and your brothers' success. I have cabled Ireland. My father will break the news to Bird [Patsy's youngest daughter]. I will wire all your people in Queensland and elsewhere the passing of a generous relative and stalwart pioneer. Follow his course. Be up and doing. He has left you a priceless heritage, an unblemished name.'

Twenty years earlier, Patsy Durack had written the famous words that could serve as his epitaph: 'Cattle Kings ye call us, then we are kings in grass castles that may be blown away upon a puff of wind ...'

Cattle Kings

'The bluff pioneer squatters were Monarchs of all they surveyed; and they were worthy of the best treatment the seasons and the gods could give them. For many of them, like Tyson, John Jenkins, Jimmy Maiden and Mick Keighran, started long before they reached man's estate, with little better stock-in-trade than their innate knowledge of stock and bushcraft, and a stern determination to succeed ...'

— *CHAS. MACALISTER.*

Tyson and Kidman

The properties of the 'Cattle King', Sir Sidney Kidman (1857–1938) stretched so far across the continent that his drovers could drive their herds from northern Australia to Adelaide almost without crossing a neighbour's boundary. His life inspired numerous anecdotes and his only rival was his predecessor James Tyson (1819–98), who even inspired a ballad.

Kidman, born near Adelaide, left school at thirteen after buying a one-eyed horse and setting out on horseback for New South Wales, where he worked as a station hand at Broken Hill. He then bought a bullock team and in 1878, with 400 pounds inheritance, began trading in horses and cattle. In 1886 he bought Owen Springs station near south-west of Alice Springs, first of the large properties that would later total 150,000 square kilometres. He once obtained a fourteenth share in the Broken Hill Proprietory (BHP) mine by bartering ten bullocks, but unwisely sold it for a song, before BHP struck it rich, netting himself only £60 profit; he often stopped to pick up nails from the ground and saved them for future use, though he was also known in later years as a generous benefactor.

Tyson, the son of a district constable at the Appin district of New South Wales (in the Illawarra region close to Wollongong), first ran a station with his brother on the Moulamein (Billabong) River, but lost it in 1851. He then took up droving cattle from the Riverina to the Bendigo goldfields, where he set up as a butcher—and made a fortune, investing it in properties from Victoria to the Darling Downs in Queensland. By 1883, he was wealthy enough to offer Premier McIlwraith's Queensland government a £500,000-loan (a million dollars—but he never married and died without leaving a will.

Andy's Gone With Cattle

The first verse of Henry Lawson, born in rural New South Wales, the son of a Norwegian immigrant, reflected his political sympathies. He called it *The Song of the Republic*. In search of more popular subject matter, Lawson accepted funds from J.F. Archibald of the *Bulletin* to go out to the West in 1892, to the country around Bourke, where he spent nine months, amassing there enough experiences to provide him with material for a lifetime's writing. Few Australian writers have written about the bush and its characters with more humour and feeling than this city man who fought a losing battle with the bottle.

Our Andy's gone with cattle now—
    Our hearts are out of order—
    With drought he's gone to battle now,
    Across the Queensland border.

He's left us in dejection now,
    Our thoughts with him are roving;
    It's dull on this selection now,
    Since Andy went a-droving.

Who now shall wear the cheerful face,
    In times when things are slackest?
    And who shall whistle round the place,
    When Fortune frowns her blackest?

Oh, who shall cheek the squatter now,
    When he comes round us snarling?
    His tongue is growing hotter now,
    Since Andy crossed the Darling.

The gates are out of order now,
    In storms the 'riders' rattle',
    For far across the border now,
    Our Andy's gone with cattle.

Poor Aunty's looking thin and white;
    And Uncle's cross with worry;
    And poor old Blucher howls all night,
    Since Andy left Macquarie.

Oh, may the showers in torrents fall,
    And all the tanks run over;
    And may the grass grow green and tall,
    In pathways of the drover;

And may good angels send the rain
    On desert stretches sandy;
    And when the summer comes again
    God grant 'twill bring us Andy.

Andy's Return

With pannikins all rusty,
  And billy burnt and black,
  And clothes all torn and dusty,
  That scarcely hide his back;
  With sun-cracked saddle-leather,
  And knotted greenhide rein,
  And face burnt brown with weather,
  Our Andy's home again!

His unkempt hair is faded
  With sleeping in the wet,
  He's looking old and jaded;
  But he is hearty yet.
  With eyes sunk in their sockets—
  But merry as of yore;
  With big cheques in his pockets,
  Our Andy's home once more!

Old Uncle's bright and cheerful'
  He wears a smiling face;
  And Aunty's never tearful,
  Now Andy's round the place.
  Old Blucher barks for gladness;
  He broke his rusty chain,
  And leapt in joyous madness,
  When Andy came again.

With tales of flood and famine,
  On distant northern tracks,
  And shady yarns— 'Baal gammon!'
  Of dealings with the blacks,
  From where the skies hang lazy,
  On many a northern plain,
  From regions dim and hazy,
  Our Andy's home again!

His toil is nearly over;
  He'll soon enjoy his gains.
  Not long he'll be a drover,
  And cross the lonely plains.
  We'll happy be for ever,
  When he'll no longer roam,
  But by some deep, cool river,
  Will make us all a home.

— *HENRY LAWSON.*

Blue Heelers

Once the drovers had crossed the Great Divide and the cattle kings had staked out runs in the Outback that dwarfed in size some European countries, the cattle dog came into his own. It took 50 years for breeders to develop a dog that possessed all the instincts necessary to aid the drover—one that moved swiftly yet silently without barking, one that could snap or bite low without wounding the cattle and possessed the instinct to guard—and yet had high intelligence and stamina. The result was a ragamuffin masterpiece—the part-dingo blue heeler, the only pure-bred cattle dog in the world.

The breeder, Robert Kaleski, drew up the standards of pedigree in 1897, but the story goes back to 1840, when a squatter near Muswellbrook, New South Wales, named Hall imported a male and female merle, or short-haired Scottish collie; smart dogs of mottled hue. They were noisy dogs, so he crossed them with a dingo—which had no bark and the result was a silent, strong low biter. Called 'Hall's heelers', their offspring were widely sought after by the early squatters.

In 1870, Harry Davis took a pair to Sydney, where they aroused interest and the Bagust brothers ran some dam dalmatian through them. The result was a sturdy dog with a mottled body, one with remarkable intelligence. Some have black heads and ears (showing the collie strain) others red, as evidence of their dingo blood.

Bushman's Farewell to Queensland

Queensland, thou art a land of pests,
　From flies and fleas one never rests.
　Even now mosquitoes round me revel,
　In fact they are the very devil.

Sand-flies and hornets just as bad,
　They nearly drive a fellow mad:
　The scorpion and centipede,
　With stinging ants of every breed.

Fever and ague with the shakes,
　Triantelopes and poisonous snakes,
　Goannas, lizards, cockatoos,
　Bushrangers, logs and jackeroos.

Bandicoots and swarms of rats,
　Bull-dog ants and native cats,
　Stunted timber, thirsty plains,
　Parched-up deserts, scanty rains.

There's rivers here, you sail ships on,
　There's nigger women without shirts on,
　There's humpies, huts and wooden houses,
　There's men who don't wear trousers.

There's Barcoo rot and sandy blight,
　There's dingoes howling half the night,
　There's curlews' wails and croaking frogs,
　There's savage blacks and native dogs.

There's scentless flowers and stinging trees,
　There's poison grass and Darling peas,
　Which drive the cattle raving mad,
　Make sheep and horses just as bad.

And then it never rains in reason,
　There's drought one year and floods next
　season,
　Which wash the squatters' sheep away,
　And then there is the devil to pay.

To stay in thee, O land of Mutton!
　I would not give a single button,
　But bid thee now a long farewell,
　Thou scorching sunburnt land of Hell.

— *Anonymous.*

The Dying Stockman

A strapping young stockman lay dying;
   His saddle supporting his head;
   His two mates beside him were crying,
   As he rose on his elbow and said:

CHORUS:
   'Wrap me up with my stockwhip and blanket,
   And bury me deep down below,
   Where the dingoes and crows won't molest me,
   In the shade where the coolabahs grow.'
   'Oh, had I the flight of the bronzewing,
   Far over the plains I would fly,
   Straight to the home of my childhood,
   And there I would lay down and die.'

'Then cut down a couple of saplings,
   Place one at my head and my toe;
   Carve on them cross, stockwhip, and saddle
   To show there's a stockman below.

'Hark! There's the wail of a dingo,
   Watchful and weird — I must go,
   For it tolls the death-knell of the stockman
   From the gloom of the scrub down below.

'There's tea in the battered old billy
   Place the pannikins out in a row,
   And we'll drink to the next merry meeting,
   In the place where all good fellows go.

'And oft in the shades of the twilight,
   When the soft winds are whispering low,
   And the darkening shadows are falling,
   Sometimes think of the stockman below.'

— *TRADITIONAL.*

9: *Sheep and Shearing*

'ONE WHO HAS BEEN USED TO THE BRISK, stirring life on a cattle station does not easily adapt himself to the tame, commonplace routine of sheep. The first is poetry, the other prose; yet the prosaic existence is responsible for three parts of the bush doggerel that is written. It affords more time to dream. For all that, sheep-farming is not a lazy man's job. Even on the table-lands of New England, the river-lands of Riverina, and the prairie-lands of the Darling Downs, it is the hardest of all stock-work; while on the runs of the Western Division, in dry times, it is one of the short cuts to constitutional ruin. It is significant that very few Aborigines will work constantly among sheep, while they will live their lives out among cattle. Nevertheless, sheep life has its gleams, and at least twice a year it presents attractive features—when the fleeces are falling, and when the lambs are losing their tails . . .'

— *FROM* LIFE IN THE AUSTRALIAN BACKBLOCKS, *1911,*
EDWARD S. SORENSON.

The Shearers

Sheep farming may seem 'commonplace' after the dramas of cattle stations, but—unlike wheat farming—it has entered Australian folklore. Edward Sorenson's description of shearing (which is still back breaking work, even with the electric shears of today) was published in 1911, but it evokes wonderfully the atmosphere of the shearing sheds and describes the hierarchy therein—two things that have barely changed in a century:

'Shearing is the most important event of the year on a sheep station. For weeks beforehand preparations are made for it, while any other work can be done at little notice. The shearers' hut has to be patched up, the gaps in the shed repaired, gates, fences and yards fixed up, wool tables cleaned and put in place, the press erected (where it is not permanently housed in a modern shed), machinery and a hundred and one other items attended to. Stacks of wood have to be cut in the neighbouring bush and drawn in to huts and homestead; the iron tanks are replenished, or arrangements otherwise made for a water-supply. It is the busiest time of the year, a time of bustle and excitement, which seems to accentuate the loneliness and quietness of the surroundings for the rest of the year. For three or four weeks, or months, you hear the constant click of the shears, the shouting of men, the bleating of sheep, and the barking of dogs; you see the flashing of snowy fleeces, the ringing and rushing of huge flocks, galloping horsemen and clouds of dust. Then one morning the whole busy scene has vanished; there is silence about the huts and shed, and the only living things to be seen are the crows feasting on dead sheep outside the yard.

'The time of starting at any shed is seldom advertised. Such news is carried in the bush by mulga wire—in other words, by travellers passing from place to place. Then, again, a number of sheds will follow in rotation, the shearers and shed hands going from one to the other. Most squatters prefer men fresh from a shed to those who have not recently had a cut, as with the latter there is frequently much delay during the first week with knocked-up wrists. But then men are plentiful and there is a market to catch, or other considerations make it convenient or urgent, there is no waiting for anybody's cut-out and a dozen adjoining stations may be in full swing at the one time. The general cut-out then means a merry time at "mother's" (the wayside hostelry), where a shearers' race meeting and other attractions are held to wind up the season.

'Stands are sometimes booked weeks and months prior to date of shearing, applications being accompanied in many cases with a sovereign as a guarantee of good faith, the amount being refunded at the settling up, or donated to the local hospital if forfeited by non-appearance. Many men after sending their pounds along find as the time draws near that something more pressing, or some unlooked-

for circumstance, will prevent their filling their engagement. This difficulty is easily surmounted if the shearer is not well known. He sells his stand to a mate, or wires one at the place to sell it for him, and thus saves his deposit. Of course, the purchaser must take the name of the man who was originally engaged. Dozens of men in this way impersonate others, and are known by certain names in one district and by different names in other parts.

'A shearer whose cognomen, say, is Bill Brown, will one year be a big, freckled-faced man, with red hair and beard, and next year he will be a little, dark man. Sometimes a Bill Brown is discovered to be Jim Smith, and trouble ensues; but generally the culprits make pretty sure of their ground beforehand. Again, scores of men changed their names after the 1891 strike. Tom Jones, the non-unionist, would efface himself in a far-back locality, and appear long afterwards among the unionists as Bill Smith. Where ever he shore he would hear the vilest epithets hurled at the memory of Tom Jones, and many a threat of vengeance avowed, and the pseudo Bill Smith, to keep up appearances, would do likewise, and express the most caustic opinion of all on his own self. Squatters, as a rule, soon forget the faces of men who have been temporary employees. They are familiar with the names in their books, but they are, year after year, being hoodwinked by Bill Smiths who are in reality Tom Jones.

'On the morning of the roll-call you will see two or three hundred men gathered about the hut. The majority are horsemen or bikemen. Some drive up in spiders, sulkies, titled carts and other traps; the rest are footmen, who come in tired and footsore, carrying heavy swags. Gleaming white tents spring up like mushrooms among the bush clumps and along the creek, thin wreaths of smoke curl up from all manner of places, and the jingling of horse-bells makes music everywhere, mingled with the yowling and ferocious scrimmages that result from the meeting of many strange dogs. These outcampers look on the hut with loathing; some of them, long inured to a gypsy life, would not camp under a roof under any consideration. Others have an equal dislike to the open. One of the latter, on reaching the hut, will first of all examine the vacant bunks, pick the most suitable, and put his swag on it. Everybody recognizes that bunk then as reserved, and if the owner of the swag gets on, he remains in possession till the shed cuts out; but if his name is not called he has to vacate it pretty quickly, or he will find his dunnage thrown on the floor.

'The roll-call is an interesting function. The big crowd of men and boys line up near the hut. A pretty mixed lot they look; they are all shapes and sizes, and as various in their colours and nationalities. Many are joking or laughing; some show absolute indifference—their names are not down, and all they can hope for is a supply of rations when the cook gets his stores; others stand with folded arms, or arms akimbo, watching and waiting with anxious faces, thinking, perhaps, of wives and little ones, miles away, who are waiting for their first pound. No two are dressed alike. There are men in rags, there are many in silk, or starched white shirts, collars and ties, and with polished boots, gold rings and diamond pins, and nuggets of gold dangling from their watch-chains. Gentlemen they look, with soft white skin, men whom you would think had never done a day's hard work. These are some of the big guns, who can do their 150 to 200 a day, who travel from state to state, and are probably shearing nine months out of the twelve. There are battered-looking derelicts, who are also ringers but are heavy drinkers. There are here university graduates, lost heirs to fortunes, sons of big men in England, broken-down school-masters, lawyers, ex-policemen, poets, artists, journalists, cheek by jowl with horny-handed navies, and a few who put a cross for their signatures, all waiting with varying degrees of interest to hear the verdict of the wool king.

'Having checked the names of his men, the manager reads out the terms of agreement. If the shearing is to be conducted under the rules of the PU or AWU [Australian Workers Union], a good deal of time is occupied in signing; but under verbal agreement, which seems to give the most satisfaction, the business is quickly disposed of. The shed hands are then engaged, a few questions asked by the men, and the price list of station stores is produced. This is compared with the list of the town grocer, but the station usually obtains the custom, and expects to, unless the charges are comparatively heavy. Then the cook is chosen.

'The shearing rate in most parts is twenty-four shillings per hundred, with variations according to locality and class of sheep. [24 shillings in modern dollar conversion is $2.40 but nowadays shearers can earn nearly two dollars per sheep— $178 per hundred 'ordinary' sheep and almost double that sum for shearing rams.] The rouseabout's usual pay is from twenty-five shillings a week and

tucker, and in small sheds the station pays the cook the customary four shillings per man per week, and all hands are boxed together. Where the rouseabout receives seven shillings per day and finds himself he pays his share of the bill; when he has a separate hut he puts on his own cook, and is expected to feed all travelling rouse-abouts who call, while shearers feed shearers. Under this system the rouseabout loses, as he gets no pay for wet days. Wet days, too, pre-vent the traveller going on, and he hangs around. Odd ones are occa-sionally given the word to move on by the cook. But these are reg-ular loafers, who would, if permitted, put in an appearance at every meal as long as the shed lasted, and then expect to have their bags filled for the road. Nothing riles a cook more than the tactics of the gentry; his good name and chance of election on future occasions depend largely on keeping down the mess account.

'The men also choose a representative, who becomes responsible head of the mess department, and through whom all negotiations take place as between employer and men, and to whom all disputes are referred. He accompanies the cook to the station immediately after election, and orders stores, utensils, tinware, cutlery, etc. The cook takes immediate charge of these, but the rep. is the responsi-ble party. He must be a financial unionist in a union shed; it is his office to receive the union delegates, distribute tickets, etc.

'The shearers in twos and threes file to the store, returning each with a pair or two of shears, a bottle of salad oil and an oil-stone. The rest of the day is spent variously in arranging bunks, hunting up wool-packs and sheepskins for mattresses, turning at the grindstone, fixing up water-tins and oilstone boards on the stands, and rigging the shears. The blades are pulled back and the knockers filed down, so that the shears will take a bigger blow. This is called "putting Kinchler on them', from the fact that it was first adopted by John Kinsella, who died in Armidale about August 1902. The shears are also fitted with a strap, which passes over the hand. Putting this on requires an expert, one man's services being often requisitioned by half a dozen of his conferes. Many bind basil or sheepskin round the grip, and those who are not endowed with powerful wrists cut strips off the bow and cold chisels, to weaken the spring. It is common for a shearer to spend a whole day in preparing his blades for work.

'A typical backblock hut, where these men are temporarily housed, is a long, narrow structure built of galvanized iron. Bunks are arranged in tiers along the sides, usually two tiers, though sometimes there are three. There is always a rush for the bottom bunks. They are just long enough for the average man to stretch in. The men, for obvious reasons, sleep feet to feet and head to head. The dining-table runs down the centre. It is made of casing, or sheet iron, tacked on to a rough frame, the legs sunk in the ground, while the seats are simply round saplings, or narrow scantling, laid on rough forks, or spiked on to low posts. There is just enough room for a man to walk between them and the bunks. At night two or three evil-smelling slush-lamps flicker and splutter and fizzle along the table, and these, with the odour of drugs, liquor, soiled shed clothes, stale boots and unaired blankets, have not exactly an improving effect on the meal.

'One doesn't need to be fastidious. The men seldom all sit down together. Some are sitting on the bunks, with feet on the stools, puffing fragrant tobacco smoke over the table while others are eating; some are shaving or dressing, others are shaking out blankets and making beds. And there is the everlasting smell of saddles and packs and eucalyptus. Then the late rouseabouts, who have been cleaning up, and benighted musterers come rushing in, hungry and anxious-looking, wondering if there's any blancmange left. They hustle into their places, and one calls out, "Sling th' poisoned baker this way, Texas!" Another shouts, "Chuck us a bun, will yer!" or "Jerk that spot-tified brownie this way, Snoozer!" while some hardened sinner demands, "What d'yer call this, cook? Goat, or a hunk of a cart-'orse? Dog scratch me, it's as tough as Mother Lord Harry!" Tea over, they smoke and yarn, or play cards till ten o'clock. All lights must be out at ten "by the cook's orders". He has to get up early.

'To a quiet man, or one who is fond of reading, the shearers' hut is a den of horror. There are men whose tongues are never still and, as might be expected, these are the ones who seldom say anything worth hearing. There is a rattling of dice and the shuffling and chat-ter of card-players; the repetition of "Fifteen two, fifteen four", and the euchre-players' everlasting "Pass!" "I'm away!" "She's down!" "By me!" and so forth. The man who bangs his fist on the table with every winning card he plays is particularly obnoxious. Occasionally he gets his deserts in the form of a flying boot. There are draught-players, domino enthusiasts, noughts-and-crosses cranks, and fox-and-goose lunatics; there are loud discussions, arguments—mostly about dogs and horses—yarning, singing and whistling, to the accompaniment of half a dozen mouth-organs, tin whistles, Jew's harps, and a crack concertina. It's hard to follow the adventures of Reginald de Clancy through the jungles of the Punjab under such disturbing conditions; it is harder still to compose a soulful epistle to your best girl, pining for her shearer boy down south, or to dash off a fetching little ode to the entrancing beauty of your eyes.

'At ten o'clock a bucket of tea and another of coffee are placed on the floor, and there is a rush for pannikins and buns. You feel glad that there will soon be peace, but it is not unadulterated. When the lights are out you learn the sleeping characters of your shed mates. There are several asthmatical nuisances who cough inter-mittently; about a dozen go pig-hunting, and are pursuing the spot-ted one nearly all night; others fidget and kick and roll, have night-mares and other nocturnal visitations, and yell blue murder in their sleep; a few are troubled with insomnia, and get up at frequent intervals to fill and light their pipes. And there are the town-goers, who come stumbling in about midnight, with noise enough to waken the next man. When that row has subsided the thirty of forty dogs tied up outside begin to corroboree in dismal and melancholy tones. Somebody yells at them to lie down, and one or two get up to throw firewood and jam tins at them. The nights are pretty near all alike, so you don't wonder at the number of tents and bush gun-yahs there are scattered about the neighbourhood.

'On many of the big stations there is separate accommodation for shearers and rouseabouts—detached kitchens and special dining-rooms for each, the sleeping apartments are partitioned off, having two or four bunks in each. There are sitting-rooms, card-rooms and reading rooms. There is no piano yet, but probably that will come along in the near future. These good sheds are often systematically worked by one band of men year after year. Now and again a couple drop out and strangers fill their places. Otherwise a stranger has little chance against the old hands, who are booked for the following year as soon as the shed cuts out. Under this long-range system New Zealanders, after finishing the season in their own country, often complete the year with a run of sheds through Victoria, New South Wales and Queensland.

'The day starts early. The cook's bell, soon after daylight, is the first summons—to "awake and arise". There is more tea and brownie, and the men file to the shed. Stands have been drawn for, water-tins fixed up to dip shears in, oil-bottles hung, and boards nailed conveniently for oil-stones, pipe and tobacco, etc., and each man goes to his place. On one side of the board are narrow pens, one for each man, for the shorn sheep; on the other side a wide catch-pen for every two men. These pairs are called penmates, and they turn the grindstone for each other. They are not always boon companions; they are sometimes deadly enemies. In many sheds there is a double board; in others the catch-pens are in the centre, and there is a board on each side. The big machine-sheds, as a rule, are roomy and substantial structures, though mostly built of galvanized iron. Some of the cocky sheds of old time, with the huge gum-log press, are still standing, covered with bark and walled with slabs. The common backblock shed is not walled, except in part with the low stubs that form the pens. The gap between this fence and the roof, in hot or dusty places, is screened with bagging or hessian, everything is pretty rough and slipshod about these sheds. The yards and pens are built of logs, rails, stubs and boughs; the shed is covered with bushes or cane grass, occasionally further protected with hessian blinds. It is low and flat, so low that a tall man often bumps his head against the cross-beams; and rust, leaves and twigs are continually falling on the board and getting mixed up with the wool. There is not much comfort. It is often many miles away from the station homestead, and being used for but a short time once a year, and having no caretaker between whiles, it is

too risky to build an elaborate and expensive shed. In any case, as shearing can only be done in dry weather, it answers the purpose as well as the rest. The galvanized iron shed is cleaner, but in summer the heat is terrific. For working purposes, and for the sheep, the cane grass or the bough shed is the better.

'Thursday and Friday are the most favoured days on which to start shearing. The first couple of days are the hardest on backs and wrists, and commencing near the end of the week provides a break of a day and a half, and the operators are consequently in good trim when they toe the scratch on Monday morning. The first mob of sheep in is closely examined and criticized, and when the pens are full, hands play among the backs and shoulders to ascertain the quality and density of the wool. When there is a good show of yolk and the fleeces are free of burrs, sand and grass seed, the knights of the blades are jubilant.

'As the overseer, or "man-over-the-board", comes in, the men rise expectantly, and at the first jingle of the bell there is a wild rush into the catch-pens and a scramble for sheep. Struggling animals are dragged out and dumped on to each stand, and at once the shears are clicking from end to end, every man striving for the honour of first fleece. The belly is the first part taken off, the sheep being sat on the board between the operator's legs, its forelegs held back under his left arm. The fleece is opened up along the neck, from the brisket to the left ear, and shorn down the left side well over the spine, to the tail; then the animal is turned, shorn down the off side, finishing off the thigh, and half pitched through the open gate. Then another is grabbed, dragged on to the board, and dumped on its rear extremity with its heart palpitating like a wounded bird's. But they seldom kick, except when a chunk of skin is taken off.

'Then there is a demand for tar. The breathless hurry of every man, the apparent desperate desire to separate fleece and sheep in a certain time, is the first thing that strikes the stranger in a shearing-shed. The ringer, or fastest shearer, soon singles out when hands are in. There are two or three jingling very close to him, and these keep up a perpetual race, while the others try to keep as near as possible, or are running one another. The drummer, or slowest shearer is about the only man who doesn't seem to care when supper-time comes. But his position is not conspicuous at the start.

'A shearer who answered to the name of Dick gained a little notoriety during the first week in a northern shed. Only a couple then had their hands in, and Dick had third highest tally. Swelling with pride and magnanimity, he said to his penmate: "Cut in, Mac, you can lick most of these coves here. You'll be fifth, anyway". The yarn went round, and every man-Jack was doing his level best. One after another, the others passed Dick's tally, finally one shouted across the board: "Cut in, Dick, you'll be last, anyway." And Dick was.

'In most sheds where pinking is desirable the ringer, no matter how good or fast he may be, is restricted to a certain limit, and no one is allowed to go beyond him. This prevents tomahawking, and it explains why a man will make a phenomenal record in one shed and cut only an ordinary tally in another. Of course, the quality and weight of the fleeces, and the size and condition of the sheep, have also a lot to do with the fluctuations of tallies. The easiest of all to cut are lambs and hoggets, and the next best are the ewes. Breed, condition and weight of sheep, density of wool, and the season just passed through have a big influence on the tally barometer. There is a sudden drop when the shears get to work on the wethers, while the hardest and slowest work is done on the rams and ram stags. Each of these latter is counted as two sheep.'

— *E.S. SORENSON.*

'Ringers'

'A run is anything from seventy-five to ninety minutes, when the bell rings for smoke-o, lunch, afternoon tea, or knock off. Shearers drink tea all day, a bucket of it being kept continually hung in the shed, replenished from time to time as required. One or two pannikins only are used, and everybody dips them into the bucket. The sheep are counted out at the end of each run, and the tallies are posted on a board in a conspicuous place every morning. These morning bulletins command a good deal of notice and interest; they are scanned by visitors and swagmen; even the little tar-boy, between runs, derives a lot of satisfaction from comparing one man's tally with another's, and computing the daily earning of the big guns. If the boss is not particular about the sheep being pinked (shorn so closely and evenly that the skin shows plainly), the tallies are at times remarkable. At Barenya station, for instance, on 19 September 1895, twenty-six men averaged 172 each; on the same day eight men averaged 236 each; and on 20 September twenty-six men averaged 175 each. The record for hand-shearing is held by Jack Howe, who shore 327 ewes in 7 hours 20 minutes at Alice Downs (Queensland), in October 1892. His tallies for the last eleven days at the shed were 149, 264, 131, 249, 257, 258, 262, 267, 321, and 190 lambs and 30 wethers. On 16 July 1904, he shore 337 sheep in 8 hours with the machine.

'The following unique records belong to an earlier date. At Belalie, on the Warrego, in 1884, Sid Ross shore 9 lambs in 9 minutes, and at Evesham, in 1886, Jimmy Fishes shore 50 lambs in one run before breakfast (about 75 minutes). At Charlotte Plains, Warrego

River, in 1885, Alex Miller shore 4,362 sheep in three weeks and three days, an average of 203 per day throughout the shed. "Long" Maloney shore 22,000 in one season in South Australia, Victoria and New South Wales. In 1876 Angus M'Innes shore against Jack Gunn, at Parratoo, South Australia, for £50, when the former shore 180 sandback wethers in one day, and but for a timely interference would have exterminated two boundary riders because they had no more sheep in. At Fowler's Bay, in 1874, the lengthy Maloney shore 11 big wethers in 11 minutes, using a pair of Ward and Payne's 38s. At a shed on the Paroo, in 1884, seven—namely, Allan M'Callam, Bamphil (the "Warbler"), Jack Lynch, Jimmy Donaldson ("Maorilander"), "Warrigal Jack", M'Donald (the "Barrier Ringer", "Long Bob" Hobbs, and Jack Reid (the "Victorian")—shore 1,540 sheep in one day, an average of 220 per man. At Parelli, in 1885, another Jack M'Donald, who weighed only 6 stone 9 pounds, shore 187 full-fleeced wethers in 7.5 hours.

'A shearer who used the tongs all over the Commonwealth during the squabble between pastoralists and shearers in 1902, gave the following particulars of his earning: in 1899 he shore 23,538 sheep, receiving £235 7s 7d; in 1900, 22,976 for £229 15s 2½; in 1901, 23,142 for £231 9s 5d; and during the first half of 1902 he shore 10,379, his cheque being £103 15s 10d. This man was a long way below being a champion. A fair team of thirty men can average 100 per day. But bad weather, much travelling, and long breaks between sheds, prevent the majority of fairly smart shearers making enough to carry them though the year. Jimmy Power, who was the champion machine shearer, and whose record is 315 sheep in 7 hours 40 minutes, made at Barenya in 1904, shore 40,000 in one season. His bones are now resting in South Africa. As a rule, better money is made with machines than by hand. The tallies are higher in the aggregate, the work is lighter and cleaner, and the operator has to find neither shears, stone, nor oil, and never loses any of his rest-time at the grindstone. His only expense, so far as the actual work is concerned, is for combs and cutters, which amounts to merely a few pence per hundred sheep.

'Harry Livingstone, the Queenslander, in successive days in 1910, shore 223, 225, 237, 237 and 221. The pay was twenty-four shillings per hundred. The same season thirty-eight men at Cambridge Downs in one day averaged 198½ sheep per man, Harrison, who rung the shed, being top with two hundred and sixty-five.

'Bigger tallies are made in Queensland than in New South Wales, the sheep of the mother State being noted for greater density of wool. Smaller tallies, however, are cut nowadays all round than formerly, on account of the improved breed of sheep, which carry more wool. Merinos in good country are fine sheep to shear, while the introduction of the Vermont strain makes the work more arduous in any locality. The Shropshires and crossbreeds also make heavy work; they are big, whereas the merinos are small, compact animals.

'The sheep in the catch-pens are not taken as they come, but are carefully picked in by the penmates right through. A glance at the back is sufficient to decide which of the penned animals will cut best. The lightest and thinnest-woolled sheep are always grabbed, providing they are clean, and a desperate race ensues when it comes to the last two in the pen. This enclosure is not refilled until the last sheep—the cobbler—is caught, and each of the mates shows his generosity by trying hard to let go first, so as to leave him for the other. It does not follow that when a slow and a fast shearer are penmates the former will get all the cobblers; he can shear as a stiff horse races—only he sprints when the third last is caught. There is also hard cutting among greedy persons for a bell sheep (the one caught just as the bell is about to ring off). It is against the rules to lay hands on a sheep after the bell has rung to knock off, but the men time themselves to a minute, and put on an extra spurt to beat the bell. By this means they shear many sheep in smoke-o and mealtimes, while the majority of blades are idle.

'Every shed in the country, one might say, has had its squabble over the wetness or non-wetness of sheep. No shearer cares to handle wet sheep—except near the cut-out, when he wants to finish and get to another shed.

'A good captain has no trouble with his men. He may "chip" them often, but while his chips are effective, they leave no bitterness. For instance: "You needn't be afraid to take the stocking off them Jack" (referring to the leg wool); "There's no snakes about here."

'The work in and about the shed is under sectional heads. The man-over-the-board, for instance, merely superintends the actual shearing and keeps time. Occasionally he may brand a few bales as they come from the press. The wool-rollers, who skirt, divide and roll the fleeces as they are thrown out by the pickers-up; the piece-pickers, who sort out the first and second pieces, stains, dags, and locks. He also keeps an eye to the pressers as they fill the press-boxes from the bins. These classers hail generally from the metropolis, travelling thousands of miles in a season, going from shed to shed, classing the clips at a pound per thousand fleeces, and very often taking wool-scouring contracts as well. There are plenty of good classers among the bush workers, who class the clips at a few stations in the neighbourhood where they are known, and take any other work offering between shearing, including boundary-riding, tank-sinking, and fencing. The mustering and drafting are usually under the supervision of the manager himself, or his station overseer. In machine-sheds there is an extra boss ("boss" is the common term applied to any man who is over the men), the expert who has charge of the machinery.

'On an ordinary single board there are two pickers-up, one to each half. They are smart youths, and often command men's pay. They are ever darting to and fro, picking up the belly wool, to prevent it mixing with the fleeces, and throwing it into bales, which are hung in convenient positions along by the side of the board, sweeping the stands as soon as a sheep is let go and while another is being caught, and picking up the fleeces and throwing them out on the table. The latter is done quickly and dexterously. It is so picked up that with a single light throw it spreads right out over the table like a blanket, not a wrinkle or turned-over corner showing, and without severing any portion of it. A bad picker-up makes double work for the men at the table, in straightening out fleeces and lapping breaks.

'When the fleeces are falling rapidly along the board, or when several let go simultaneously to the cry of "wool away!" these youths are kept on the run, their canvas shoes or big moccasins making much "wop-wop" (one of their pet designations) as they bound to and fro. Besides keeping the stands clear of wool, they attend to the calls for tar. The pots stand in juxtaposition, each containing tar or sheep-dip, and a stick with a piece of rag or wood bunched on the end of it. Where the Wolseley clippers are used the tar-boy's services are seldom required. Only novices and very clumsy hands tear the skin with these nicely-adjusted implements. The pickers-up are under everybody's thumb. They are ordered about by the man-over-the-board, and the moment they cross out of his kingdom to the wool tables they are subject to the ruling of the classer. Then they are hustled by the shearers, have to clean up when everybody else has left off, and carry out the locks and bellies to the press.'

— *EDWARD S. SORENSON.*

Sheep Dogs

The summer heat and the great size of Australia's sheep stations demanded a sheep dog more suited to these extremes than northern hemisphere dogs. The most popular working dogs used today are the kelpie (named after the Scottish water sprite) and the short-haired border collie. Many theories have been advanced as to the origin of the kelpie (which is said to be part dingo, part fox!) but these have not been proven. It is probable that kelpies are a mixture of Scottish breeds, as is the short-haired border collie.

Kelpies are strong, alert, intelligent and very slow to tire regardless of the heat or cold—and are said to be worth three men when working sheep in the yards. Short-haired border collies are the most popular for sheep dog trials and are used widely as working dogs in the paddocks despite their reputation for being 'softer' than kelpies. Other breeds used are the German collie, characterised by a mottled coat ranging from grey to slate blue or even dull red-brown. The long-coated old English sheep dog is used to some extent in colder regions such as Tasmania.

These dogs, born with a hunting instinct, often show aptitude for rounding up creatures as pups—including chooks and kids—though all require training (some more than others) to respond to shouted instructions such as 'Go Back!', 'Come Behind!' and 'Speak Up!' (bark!), while ignoring the occasional swear word directed at them when they are slow off the mark or misinterpret a command. Country newspapers were famous for publishing 'sheep dog stories' (of which farmers have an endless supply) when the presses were running and the editor was short of copy.

That There Dog of Mine

'Macquarie the shearer had met with an accident. To tell the truth, he had been in a drunken row at a wayside shanty, from which he had escaped with three fractured ribs, a cracked head, and various minor abrasions. His dog, Tally, had been a sober but savage participator in the drunken row, and had escaped with a broken leg. Macquarie afterwards shouldered his swag and staggered and struggled along the track ten miles [16 kilometres] to the Union Town hospital. Lord knows how he did it. He didn't exactly know himself. Tally limped behind all the way, on three legs.

'The doctors examined the man's injuries and were surprised at his endurance. Even doctors are surprised sometimes—though they don't always show it. Of course they would take him in, but they objected to Tally. Dogs were not allowed on the premises.

'"You will have to turn that dog out," they said to the shearer, as he sat on the edge of a bed.

Macquarie said nothing.

'"We cannot allow dogs about the place, my man," said the doctor in a louder tone, thinking the man was deaf.

'"Tie him up in the yard then."

'"No. He must go out. Dogs are not permitted on the grounds."

'Macquarie rose slowly to his feet, shut his agony behind his set teeth, painfully buttoned his shirt over his hairy chest, took up his waistcoat, and staggered to the corner where the swag lay.

'"What are you going to do?" they asked.

'"You ain't going to let my dog stop?"

'"No. It's against the rules. There are no dogs allowed on the premises."

'He stopped and lifted his swag, but the pain was too great, and he leaned back against the wall.

'"Come, come now! Man alive!" exclaimed the doctor, impatiently.

'"You must be mad. You know you are not in a fit state to go out. Let the wardsman help you to undress."

'"No!" said Macquarie. "No. If you won't take my dog in you don't take me. He's got a broken leg and wants fixing up just—just as much as—as I do. If I'm good enough to come in, he's good enough—and—and better."

'He paused a while, breathing painfully, and then went on. "That-that there old dog of mine has follered me faithful and true, these twelve long hard and hungry years. He's about—about the only thing that ever cared whether I lived or fell and rotted on the cursed track."

' He rested again; then he continued: "That-that there dog was pupped on the track," he said, with a sad sort of a smile. "I carried him for months in a billy, and afterwards on my swag when he knocked up . . . And the old slut—his mother—she'd foller along quite contented—and sniff the billy now and again—just to see if he was all right . . . She follered me for God knows how many years. She follered me till she was blind—and for a year after. She follered me till she could crawl along through the dust no longer, and-and then I killed her, because I couldn't leave her behind alive!"

'He rested again.

' "And this here old dog," he continued, touching Tally's upturned nose with his knotted fingers, "this here old dog has follered me for—for ten years; through floods and droughts, through fair times—and hard—mostly hard; and kept me from going mad when I had no mate nor money on the lonely track; and watched over me for weeks when I was drunk—drugged and poisoned at the cursed shanties; and saved my life more'n once, and got kicks and curses very often for thanks; and forgave me for it all; and-and against that crawling push of curs when they set onter me at the shanty back yonder—and he left his mark on some of 'em too; and—and so did I."

'He took another spell.

'Then he drew in his breath, shut his teeth hard, shouldered his swag, stepped into the doorway, and faced round again.

'The dog limped out of the corner and looked up anxiously.

'"That there dog," said Macquarie to the hospital staff in general, "is a better dog than I'm a man—or you too, it seems—and a better man—or any man to me. He's watched over me; kep' me from getting robbed many a time; fought for me; saved my life and took drunken kicks and curses for thanks—and forgave me. He's been a true, straight, honest, and faithful mate to me—and I ain't going to desert him now. I ain't going to kick him out in the road with a broken leg. I—Oh, my God! My back!"

'He groaned and lurched forward, but they caught him, slipped off the swag, and laid him on a bed.

'Half an hour later the shearer was comfortable fixed up. "Where's my dog?" he asked, when he came to himself.

'"Oh, the dog's all right," said the nurse, rather impatiently. "Don't bother. The doctor's setting his leg out in the yard."'

— HENRY LAWSON.

Flash Jack from Gundagai

I've shore at Burrabogie, and I've shore at Toganmain,
  I've shore at big Willandra and upon the old Coleraine,
    But before the shearing' was over I've wished myself back again
    Shearin' for old Tom Patterson on the One-Tree Plain.

CHORUS:
  All among the wool, boys
  Keep your wide blades full, boys,
  I can do a respectable tally myself when I like to try,
  But they know me round the backblocks,
  As Flash Jack from Gundagai.

I've shore at big Willandra and I've shore at Tilberoo,
  And once I drew my blades, my boys, upon the famed Barcoo,
    At Cowan Downs and Trida, as far as Moulamein,
    Bit I always was glad to get back again to the One-Tree Plain.

I've pinked 'em with the Wolseleys and I've rushed with
  B-bows, too,

And shaved 'em in the grease, my boys, with the grass seed
showing through.
Bit I never slummed my pen, my lads, what'er it might contain,
While shearin' for old Tom Patterson, on the One-Tree Plain.

I've been whaling up the Lachlan, and I've dosssed on Cooper's
Creek,
And once I run Cugjingie shed, and blued it in a week.
But when Gabriel blows his trumpet, lads, I'll catch the morning
train,
And I'll push for old Tom Patterson's on the One-Tree Plain.

— *Anonymous.*

Jack Howe

His record stood unbeaten for half a century. On 10 October 1892, at Alice Down station in Queensland, he shore 321 sheep in 7 hours, 40 minutes, using blades—'a pair of glorified scissors', as machine shearers called them. It was not until 1950 that a shearer named Reick topped his score by shearing 326 merinos—but using machine shears! In early July 2002 a young shearer at Hamilton, Victoria, named Damian Hogan broke all records: in 21 hours he shore more than 650 sheep—and was still going strong but ran out of sheep!

In the week before his record-breaking day Jack Howe also broke the weekly record by shearing 1,437 sheep in 44½ hours—a blade tally that remains unbeaten. He was 'The Ringer of Ringers', a legend in the sheds.

Jack Howe was a magnificent looking man—14 stone of muscle, 'with a hand the size of a small tennis racquet,' according to one of his sons. Jack's father, an acrobat famed for spring-vaulting over the back of 14 horses, became a stockman and married a girl who had accompanied the Leslies in pioneering the Darling Downs. Jack Howe senior was also famous for overlanding nine llamas from Sydney to the Downs and shearing them at journey's end—no mean feat, for the 'Peruvians' were more cantankerous than docile sheep and cattle, and spat like machine guns. (Llamas have been widely farmed in Australia in recent decades for their wool.)

Young Jack Howe began shearing in the 1880s, beating the ringer at Langlo by shearing 211 merinos in one day for a bet—a feat that made him a legend along the Barcoo. A dedicated unionist, Howe took up a pub at Blackall in 1901 and bought Sumnervale Station in 1919 but died the next year, aged 59. In a telegram to his widow, Premier Tom Ryan said: 'I have lost a true and trusted friend and Labor has lost a champion.'

South-West Queensland

'These broad, dry acres that graze one sheep to one and a half hectares (and sometimes one to four) are the heart-land of Australia's legend and lore. The properties are measured in hundreds of thousands of hectares, the place names are tattoed in the folk memory of Australia. The rivers run like magic words: The Barcoo, Paroo, Diamantina, Warrego and Cooper's Creek; the towns are redolent of days when Australia rode on the sheep's back: Blackall, Cunnamulla, Charleville, Longreach, Winton, Barcaldine and Julia Creek. You scratch the soul of a people when you talk of the trees that "Banjo" Paterson and Henry Lawson wrote of, the gidgee, she-oaks, iron barks, sandalwoods, ghost gums, wilgas and borees. Brolgas dance on the outskirts of towns and pelicans sail like galleons on the billabongs after floods that come with the rare rain; emus are a danger to motorists as are kangaroos, both flocking in mobs of hundreds across the plains; dingoes and wild pigs menace the un-shepherded lambs.

'Its lingo is as Runyonesque as anything Nathan Detroit ever gritted out in the back alleys of Chicago. "I grabbed my boggi and I ran her down the shipping side and the Sweat Lover says he'll tell the Cocky if I tomahawk another and I said I'll pull the pin and he says he'll put me down the track." Which, translated, means that the shearer took up his handpiece—named after the boggi lizard of inland Australia which it is said to resemble—and ran the clippers down the last side to be shorn while the sheep is on its back. The contractor says he will tell the owner that the sheep is roughly cut. The shearer threatens to cause trouble in the shed by stopping the machines and the contractor in turn threatens to throw him off the property.

'The following is heard at the long, scrubbed, mess table. "The bait-slinger chiakked the blue-tongue but that brownie-gorger called for some roll-me-in-the-gutter for his dodger and sand for his burgoo and the babbler headed for the mulga saying he'd not cook for a sword swaller." Translation: The shearer's cook rebuked the greedy shearer (blue-tongued lizard with tongue incessantly flicking in and out) but that lover of sweet brown-sugar current loaf called for butter for his bread and sugar for his porridge. At which the cook left, saying he'd not cook for a man who ate off his knife.

' "I'm on the board, and a gate-opener is barrowing a bare-belly at smoke-O, and goes for the long blow, when the dreadnought shouts that the Apaches are in and the toma-hawks out!" Translation: I'm on the floor where the shearing is done, the wool-roller kid is learning to shear by finishing off an old sheep for a shearer after the bell has gone. ("Barrowed" sheep are counted in the shearer's tally because they have been started by him before the bell went. This is the most common way a lad can get experience with the shears.)'

— FROM THE SHEARERS, *1982*, PATSY ADAM-SMITH *(1924-2000)*.

Saltbush Bill

Now this is the law of the Overland that all in the West obey,
   A Man must cover with travelling sheep a six-mile stage a day;
   But this is the law which the drovers make, right easily under
   stood,
   They travel their stage where the grass is bad, but they camp
   where the grass is good;
   They camp, and they ravage the squatter's grass till never a blade
   remains,
   Then they drift away as the white clouds drift on the edge of the
   saltbush plains;
   From camp to camp and from run to run they battle it hand to
   hand,
   For a blade of grass and the right to pass on the track of the
   Overland.
   For this is the law of the Great Stock Routes, 'tis written in
   white and black—
   The man that goes with a travelling mob must keep to a half-
   mile track;
   And the drovers keep to a half-mile track on the runs where the
   grass is dead,
   But they spread their sheep on a well-grassed run till they go
   with a two-mile spread.

So the squatters hurry the drovers on from dawn till the fall of
night,
And the squatters' dogs and the drovers' dogs get mixed in a
deadly fight.
Yet the squatters' men, though they hunt the mob, are willing
the peace to keep,
For the drovers learn how to use their hands when they go with
the travelling sheep;
But this is the tale of a Jackaroo that came from a foreign strand,
And the fight that he fought with Saltbush Bill, the King of the
Overland.

Now Saltbush Bill was a drover tough as ever the country knew,
He had fought his way on the Great Stock Routes from the sea
to the big Barcoo;
He could tell when he came to a friendly run that gave him a
chance to spread,
And he knew where the hungry owners were that hurried his
sheep ahead;
He was drifting down in the Eighty drought with a mob that
could scarcely creep,
(When the kangaroos by the thousand starve, it is rough on the
travelling sheep),
And he camped one night at the crossing-place on the edge of
the Wilga run;
'We must manage a feed for them here,' he said, 'or half of the
mob are done!'
So he spread them out when they left the camp wherever they
liked to go,
Till he grew aware of a Jackaroo with a station-hand in tow.

They set to work on the straggling sheep, and with many a stock
whip crack
They forced them in where the grass was dead in the space of
the half-mile track;
And William prayed that the hand of Fate might suddenly strike
him blue
But he'd get some grass for his starving sheep in the teeth of
that Jackaroo.
So he turned and he cursed the Jackaroo; he cursed him, alive or
dead,
From the soles of his great unwieldy feet to the crown of his
ugly head.
With an extra curse on the moke he rode and the cur at his
heels that ran,
Till the Jackaroo from his horse got down and went for the
drover-man;

With the station-hand for his picker-up, though the sheep ran
loose the while,
They battled it out on the well-grassed plain in the regular prize-
ring style.

Now, the new chum fought for his honour's sake and the pride
of the English race,
But the drover fought for his daily bread with a smile on his
bearded face;
So he shifted ground, and he sparred for wind, and he made it a
lengthy mill,
And from time to time as his scouts came in they whispered to
Saltbush Bill—
'We have spread the sheep with a two-mile spread, and the
grass it is something grand;
You must stick to him, Bill, for another round for the pride of
the Overland.'
The new chum made it a rushing fight, though never a blow got
home,
Till the sun rode high in the cloudless sky and glared on the
brick-red loam,
Till the sheep drew in to the shelter-trees and settled them
down to rest;
Then the drover said he would fight no more, and gave the
opponent best.

So the new chum rode to the homestead straight, and told them
a story grand,
Of the desperate fight that he fought that day with the King of
the Overland;
And the tale went home to the Public Schools of the pluck of
the English swell—
How the drover fought for his very life, but blood in the end
must tell.
But the travelling sheep and the Wilga sheep were boxed on the
Old Man Plain;
'Twas a full week's work ere they drafted out and hunted them
off again;
A week's good grass in their wretched hides, with a curse and a
stockwhip crack.
They hunted them off on the road once more to starve on the
half-mile track,
And Saltbush Bill, on the Overland, will many a time recite
How the best day's work that he ever did was the day that he
lost the fight.

— A.B. ('BANJO') PATERSON

10: *Into the Unknown*

Where the Dead Men Lie

Out on the wastes of the Never Never—
    That's where the dead men lie!
    There where the heat-waves dance forever —
    That's where the dead men lie!
    That's where the Earth's loved sons are keeping,
    Endless trust: not the west wind sweeping
    Feverish pinions can wake their sleeping—
    Out where the dead men lie!

Where brown Summer and Death have mated—
    That's where the dead men lie!
    Loving with fiery lust unsated—
    That's where the dead men lie!
    Out where the grinning skulls bleach whitely,
    Under the saltbush sparkling brightly;
    Out where the wild dogs chorus nightly—
    That's where the dead men lie!

Ask, too, the never-sleeping drover:
    He sees the dead pass by;
    Hearing them call to their friends—the plover,
    Hearing the dead men cry;
    Seeing their faces stealing, stealing,
    Hearing their laughter, pealing, pealing,
    Watching their grey forms wheeling, wheeling,
    Round where the cattle lie!

Strangled by thirst and fierce privation—
    That's how the dead men die!
    Out on Moneygrub's farthest station—
    That's how the dead men die!
    Hard-faced graybeards, youngsters callow;
    Some mounds cared for, some left fallow;
    Some deep down, yet others shallow;
    Some having but the sky.

Moneygrub, as he sips his claret,
  Looks with complacent eye,
  Down at his watch-chain, eighteen carat—
  There, in his club, hard by:
  Recks not that every link is stamped with,
  Names of the men whose limbs are cramped with,
  Too long lying in grave-mould, cramped with,
  Death where the dead men lie.

— *Barcroft Boake (1886-92).*

Barcroft Boake, the son of an Irish immigrant, worked as a survey-or's assistant and later as a boundary rider and drover in New South Wales. He called the bush life 'the only life worth living' but much of his verse is gloomy and he hanged himself by his stockwhip in the bushland on Middle Head on the shores of Sydney Harbour in May 1892.

Charles Sturt

He has been called 'a near saint of folklore history', 'the gentlest and bravest of Australian explorers', and 'a father figure and folk hero'. But the stalwart English regimental officer who discovered the mouth of the Murray in 1830 and later led the search for the Inland Sea was also a complex man who fabricated much of his own leg-end, disguised a driving ambition beneath a plausible modesty and once summarily flogged 72 convicts when a couple of them doused him with water. His achievements remain epics of discov-ery and (in his biographer Edgar Beale's analogy), Charles Sturt is still an Australian idol—but a chipped one.

Sturt was born in Madras, India in 1795, educated in England and entered the 39th (Dorsetshire) Regiment in 1813, arriving in Sydney in charge of convicts in 1827. With Governor Darling's back-ing, Sturt and Hamilton Hume and ten companions (eight of them convicts) left Bathurst in December 1828 to explore beyond the Macquarie River. On 1 February 1829 the party reached 'a noble river'—which Sturt named the Darling—whose course they fol-lowed to a point 100 kilometres from Bourke, puzzled that its water was salt and not fresh.

In a second expedition in March of the same year, Sturt reached the dry bed of the Castlereagh (discovered by Oxley in 1818), jour-neyed on to the Darling and discovered that the Macquarie flowed into the Darling, solving a mystery that had perplexed Oxley.

On a further expedition Sturt travelled along the Murrumbidgee, built two boats and floated them downriver until he struck a 'broad and noble river'—the mighty Murray. He followed its course as far

as Lake Alexandrina in present-day South Australia before returning to Sydney in May 1830, after a round-trip of 3,000 kilometres.

Sturt's later attempt to discover the fabled 'Inland Sea' was plagued with disappointment and near tragedy. Leading a well-equipped party complete with boat, he reached the site of present-day Broken Hill in October 1844 before heading west but, after enduring extremes of summer heat that nearly killed him (two of his men died), found only emptiness—endless expanses of rocky terrain, sand dunes, a series of water courses known as Cooper's Creek and finally an impassable desert of sand: the Simpson Desert. Having failed to reach the centre of the continent he returned from his epic journey in January 1846. (The inland sea existed—but it was underground: the Great Artesian Basin whose waters, pumped from bores, now provide water for cattle herds.)

Sturt died in England in 1869, a titanic figure of Australian exploration, yet a man damaged by life's failure to adequately reward him.

Heatwave, Central Australia

'The wind, which had been blowing all the morning from the N.E., increased to a heavy gale, and I shall never forget its withering effect. I sought shelter behind a large gum-tree, but the blasts of heat were so terrific that I wondered the very grass did not take fire. This really was nothing ideal: everything both animate and inanimate gave way before it; the horses stood with their backs to the wind and their noses to the ground, without the muscular strength to raise their heads; the birds were mute, and the leaves of the trees under which we were sitting fell like a snow shower around us. At noon I took a thermometer graded to 127° [Fahrenheit, approximately 54°C], out of my box, and observed that the mercury was up to 125° [Fahrenheit, approximately 51°C]. Thinking that it had been unduly influenced, I put it in the fork of a tree close to me, sheltered alike from the wind and the sun. I went to examine it about an hour afterwards, when I found the mercury had risen to the top of the instrument and had burst the bulb, a circumstance that I believe no traveller has ever before had to record. I cannot find language to convey to the reader's mind an idea of the intense and oppressive nature of the heat that prevailed.'

— *Captain Charles Sturt, from his journals, summer 1845.*

Mitchell

Sturt's rival in early exploration of the inland was his antithesis, except in ambition: a nuggety Scot, Thomas Livingstone Mitchell (1792–1855), who had soldiered under Wellington and arrived in Australia in 1827 as assistant to the Surveyor-General, Oxley, whom he succeeded in the position in the following year. Mitchell, a gifted artist and cartographer, surveyed and mapped the Nineteen Counties around Sydney and in 1831 led the first of the great overland expeditions that would consume the next fifteen years of his life, striking north-west as far as the Namoi and McIntyre rivers. In 1836 he left Orange in New South Wales, marched across country to the Murray to where the Darling River joined it, and then crossed the Murray to the site of the present-day Swan Hill before venturing south into today's Victoria, where he was inspired by the verdant rolling hill country of the Western District to call it 'Australia Felix' (Australia the Content). He reached the coast of Bass Strait at Portland, where he found settlers, the

Henty family, and on the return journey to New South Wales, climbed Mount Macedon and saw in the distance a cluster of tents on the northern shores of Port Phillip Bay—Fawkner's first settlers at the site of the future capital of Melbourne.

In 1845, Mitchell led another expedition to find an overland connection between the settlements in New South Wales and the far north. He led a party of 32 men from Orange, reached the Condamine River and pushed on to the Maranoa country and then ventured due west, discovering and naming the Victoria River. After Mitchell's return to Sydney, Edward Kennedy (who was later, in 1848, to be killed by tribesmen in Cape York) set out to trace the course of the 'mighty' Victoria River but established that it joined the Thomson and became what the natives called 'the Barcoo', the upper part of Cooper's Creek.

Mitchell was an irascible man. In 1851, he fought a duel in Centennial Park with the premier of New South Wales, Sir Stuart Donaldson, and sent a pistol ball through the premier's hat; there were no other injuries. Sir Thomas died four years later in his Scottish baronial mansion on Sydney Harbour, 'Carthona', and there have been odd reportings of the sound of a carriage drawing up outside its gates late at night: apparently Sir Thomas arriving just to check up on things.

Mount Kosciuszko

As early as 1839, Angus McMillan set out from Goulburn to explore the south-east. He crossed the Snowy River with an Aboriginal guide and reached Omeo before returning. (By 1841, he had found a way through the rugged terrain of Gippsland to the sea, opening the region for settlement.)

At almost the same moment, in February 1841, a Polish scientist named 'Count' Strzelecki, with one of the Macarthur boys, ventured into the high Monaro country, which rose grandly into the Australian Alps. Climbing a high mountain peak, he named it after the patriot Kosciuszko (1746–1817), one of Poland's national heroes. For over 150 years the name of Australia's highest peak (2228 metres high) was spelled incorrectly as Mount Kosciusko and nobody noticed it apart from Australia's erudite former prime minister Gough Whitlam, who for many years fought a one man battle to have the spelling mistake corrected. In 1996, the Geographic Names Board finally admitted defeat and restored the missing 'z', forcing all existing road signs to be replaced and maps to be reprinted. It is pronounced 'Kos-yoosko.'

Eyre and Wyllie Cross the Nullarbor

Edward John Eyre (1815-1901), who had arrived in Australia from England in 1833, had already overlanded sheep and cattle from New South Wales to Adelaide several times when he decided in 1840 to explore north from Port Augusta to the southern shores of the 'ghost lake' (Lake Eyre) that today bears his name. Forced by the extreme heat and the aridity of the country from pushing further north, he sent most of his party back to Adelaide and then set off on 27 February 1841 for the west, intending to explore the country as far as Albany in Western Australia. He had with him one European, James Baxter, and three Aborigines. It was a nightmare journey. The party followed the coastline of the Great Australian Bight but the land they traversed was for the most part harsh desert where no trees grew—the Nullarbor Plain. In April Baxter was attacked and killed by two of the Aborigines, who ran away. With his remaining companion, the Aborigine Wyllie, Eyre struggled into Albany on 7 July 1841. In 1845 he returned to England where he published his account of his expeditions. He was acting governor of Jamaica when the black revolt took place there in 1860 and the ruthless measures he took to suppress it saw him recalled from his post to England in disgrace and thrice put on trial. The great Australian explorer spent the last forty years of his life a discredited man.

The Mystery of Leichhardt

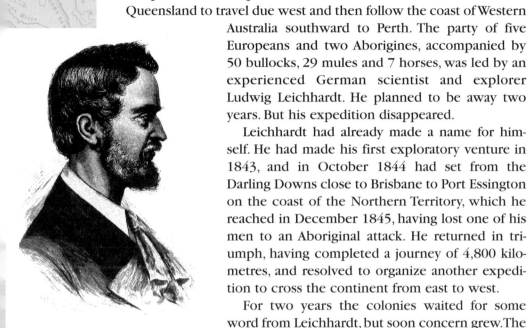

In April 1848 an expedition set out from near Roma in southern Queensland to travel due west and then follow the coast of Western Australia southward to Perth. The party of five Europeans and two Aborigines, accompanied by 50 bullocks, 29 mules and 7 horses, was led by an experienced German scientist and explorer Ludwig Leichhardt. He planned to be away two years. But his expedition disappeared.

Leichhardt had already made a name for himself. He had made his first exploratory venture in 1843, and in October 1844 had set from the Darling Downs close to Brisbane to Port Essington on the coast of the Northern Territory, which he reached in December 1845, having lost one of his men to an Aboriginal attack. He returned in triumph, having completed a journey of 4,800 kilometres, and resolved to organize another expedition to cross the continent from east to west.

For two years the colonies waited for some word from Leichhardt, but soon concern grew. The first search party set out in 1852 and in 1855 A.C. Gregory led a well-organized expedition to the north—his group made important discoveries, but found no trace of Leichhardt's men. Over the next century a total of nine expeditions were mounted to try and ascertain the fate of the explorer, but no strong evidence was discovered and the disappearance remains to this day one of the unexplained mysteries of the Outback. It inspired Patrick White's novel, *Voss*, which was subsequently made into an opera.

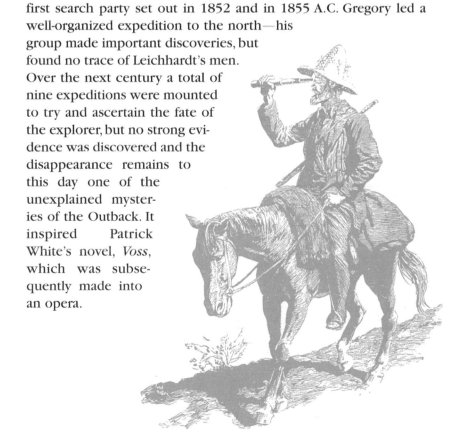

Burke and Wills

'If there really exists within our great continent a Sahara—a desert of sands—we should like to know the fact. If great lakes on whose verdant banks thousands of cattle might feed, tempt men to build new cities—let us know the character and the produce of the land by a true report of a true man.' With this valediction from the Rev. Stone, the Colony of Victoria farewelled the largest expedition of exploration yet mounted in Australia, and the worst led. For Robert O'Hara Burke (1821–61), its tempestuous but charismatic leader, disturbed many by his lack of organization and impulsive nature. John McDouall Stuart's expedition to northern Australia had departed from Adelaide five months before and Burke was determined to beat it. The 'Race' was on.

ROBERT O'HARA BURKE.

Burke's expedition of fifteen men, financed by the Victorian Government, was intended to explore the nature of the continent's interior and make the first crossing of Australia from south to north and back again. To traverse the deserts, Burke's group had 23 horses—and 25 camels, which had been brought out from Afghanistan to carry the 20 tonnes of supplies. To command it the government selected Burke, who was an Irishman, and a former army officer and police superintendent at Beechworth.

The cavalcade left Melbourne in August 1860 and made for Menindee on the Darling before pushing on to Cooper's Creek, first described by Charles Sturt. Here, William John Wills, an English surveyor, was appointed second-in-command. It was now December 1860. Instead of sitting out the worst of the summer at Cooper's Creek and avoiding the 'Wet' of the north, Burke decided to push on to the Gulf of Carpentaria, accompanied by Wills and two others, King and Gray, with transport animals and supplies for three months, leaving Brahe and the main party at the base camp. Burke estimated he would be back at Cooper's Creek in three months.

Burke, Wills, King and Gray crossed the Diamantina near the site of the present Birdsville and reached the impassable marshland on the southern edges of the Gulf in February 1861, after an epic journey of two months. Unable to proceed, they turned back without sighting the sea, and struggled south through flooded country in

W. J. WILLS.

the worst of the Wet—cyclonic storms, ceaseless downpours of rain—their energies sapped by the humidity. When food ran out they ate all their camels except for two, and even had to eat Burke's faithful horse Billy. Gray, weakened by dysentery, succumbed to the rigours of the trek and died, delirious.

They struggled into Cooper's Creek leading their two remaining camels late on 21 April 1861 to find the camp deserted. The main group, after waiting not three but four months for Burke's return, had left only nine hours earlier for Menindie on the Darling River on their six camels and twelve horses, leaving food supplies buried not far from the coolibah tree on which was inscribed the word 'DIG'. The three explorers, physically done in, now knew despair. They dug up the buried food but instead of awaiting Brahe's eventual return, Burke decided on 23 April to lead his two companions not towards Brahe's party but to the police post at Mount Hopeless, 240 kilometres away. Before leaving he destroyed any trace that they had been at Cooper's Creek in case the Aborigines followed them. On 8 May, when Brahe returned to Cooper's Creek camp, he found no evidence that Burke's group had been there and promptly returned to the Darling.

But Burke and his two companions were finding the going tough, and had reached a place called Innamincka, where the tribespeople showed hospitality, offering them food—nardoo, ground from the roots of a bush, which was filling but lacking nourishment—and fish from the river. Wills made his own way back, over three days to Cooper's Creek, found no evidence that Brahe had returned there, deposited his journals and then, incredibly, returned to his companions. But Burke had quarrelled with the natives, who had subsequently left the white men. On the banks of Cooper's Creek, as their food ran out, the patient and gallant Wills and then the headstrong Burke died. Only King, befriended and cared for by Aborigines, was found alive by Howitt's expedition which reached Cooper's Creek in September.

The extraordinary story of Burke and Wills has inspired numerous books, a film and a series of paintings by Sidney Nolan.

John McDouall Stuart

'I am not at all surprised at Stuart's success, for I know him to be a plucky little fellow—cool, persevering and intelligent, as well as an excellent bushman . . . He is entitled to all praise for his exertions . . . He has fairly passed, or I should say, surpassed me, and may justly claim the laurels.'

So wrote Charles Sturt of his former surveyor, Stuart, when the tough little Scottish explorer succeeded in reaching the heart of Australia in 1863. Stuart named the hill on which he planted the Union Jack 'Mount Sturt' in honour of his old leader, but the authorities renamed it Central Mount Stuart to perpetuate the achievements of the modest and neglected hero whom many regard as the greatest Australian explorer of them all.

John McDouall Stuart was born in Edinburgh in 1815 and left Scotland for Australia in 1839. Trained as a draughtsman and surveyor, he joined Sturt's expedition to Central Australia in 1844, but did not begin his independent explorations until 1858, when the South Australian government offered a £2,000 pounds reward to the first individual to cross the continent from south to north, to establish a route for the overland telegraph.

THE GREAT AUSTRALIAN EXPLORATION RACE.

A preliminary foray in 1859 west of Lake Eyre earned Stuart the government's notice and in March 1860 he left to attempt to reach the Gulf of Carpentaria with two companions and 13 horses. He reached the McDonnell Ranges and the geographical centre of Australia on 23 April 1860 and raised the flag, before sickness, lack of water and attacks by Aborigines forced his return in August.

With Burke and Wills' doomed expedition dominating people's minds, Stuart made another attempt, with little fanfare, early in 1861 and reached the Centre only to again be forced to return by lack of water.

Early in 1862 Stuart left Adelaide with a party of ten men and 71 horses and reached the Roper River before pressing on to the shores of the Indian Ocean in July. Nearly blinded by trachoma and his health destroyed by his exertions, Stuart led his expedition back to Adelaide in triumph in December 1862. He had lost not a single man.

John McDouall Stuart's only reward was obscurity. Denied financial assistance, he returned to England, broken in health, and died there in poverty in 1864.

'Stuart's achievement was unsurpassed,' wrote the historian Edward Stokes recently. 'His three transcontinental expeditions transcended those of every other Australian explorer.' C.T. Madigan (conqueror of the Simpson Desert) wrote this tribute to Stuart in the 1930s: 'The persistence of this man, his tenacity of purpose, his journey after journey into the interior . . . his hardships and privations, ending in his crowning success of 1862, mark the greatest achievement of Australian exploration.'

Why then is Stuart's name eclipsed in folk memory by those of his near-namesake Sturt and by Burke and Wills? Possibly because he lacked the romantic image of these men; perhaps because his journals—always meticulous—convey little to the drama of the events they record. Yet in the memories of his companions Stuart remained a giant. One of them, Pat Auld, called him simply: 'A truly brave man—the king of Australian explorers.'

Afghans and Camels

The first camels to reach Australia were landed—for some reason—in Tasmania in 1840 but a camel accompanied Horrocks on his expedition in South Australia in 1846 and two dozen of them formed part of the Burke and Wills expedition. After the 1860s, about 2,000 Afghans arrived in Australia to work with camels, which were found to be the ideal form of transport in the parched expanses of the Outback. In fact, camels were used in all parts of mainland Australia apart from Victoria, and 'Ghan' depots were soon found around Cloncurry in Queensland, Broken Hill, Bourke and Wilcannia in western New South Wales, Port Augusta and Oodnadatta in South Australia, Kalgoorlie in Western Australia and Alice Springs in the Northern Territory. In the 1870s, Afghan camel drivers and their 100 camels carried the supplies and equipment necessary to complete the Adelaide to Darwin telegraph line and later on, the Trans-Continental Railway from Port Augusta to Kalgoorlie. The Afghans' role in the building of the Alice Springs to Port Pirie railway is commemorated in its name: the 'Ghan'.

Australians rode camels in the Middle East campaigns of 1917–18 and formed a high proportion of the Imperial Camel Corps there. Often Light Horse men were sentenced to serve in the camel corps as punishment—and the cameliers' language was said to be more colourful than that of bullockies when faced by beasts who refused to move.

The 'Wet'

From December to March the southern monsoon strikes tropical Australia, turning dry creek beds into raging torrents several kilometres wide, flooding the flat lands and making the ground impassable. Cyclonic storms rage—but there is no lessening in the heat: some days the skies are clear, but when the rain comes the atmosphere becomes heavier, almost suffocating with a humidity that saps all energy and drives men to despair. Visiting the seedy, forlorn port of Broome on the far northern coast of Western Australia for the first time in 1900, Daisy Bates called the Wet season, when the pearling fleet was laid up for three months, 'a season of madness, in which white as well as coloured men went berserk', and the palm-lined alleys separating the Chinese from the Japanese quarters became full of 'howling, drunken madmen.' (Broome is now a stylish tourist resort complete with air-conditioning.)

In December 1882, a 20-year-old Melbourne journalist, George Morrison, a son of the headmaster of Scotch College, decided to walk to Melbourne from the Gulf of Carpentaria, a short hop of nearly 3,300 kilometres. 'Every hour was precious,' he wrote, 'for the rainy season was close at hand, and the sky already darkening.' He was lucky to miss most of the rains but in February, near Thargomindah in Queensland, he struck the floods and for 600 kilometres he records that he waded through water, 'a vast series of swamps and flooded creeks', often up to his waist with nothing on but a shirt. He found the dry country past Echuca in Victoria easy going and strolled into Melbourne none the worse for wear on 21 April. It had taken him 123 days. Morrison later became the *London Times* correspondent in China, surviving the 55-day siege of Peking to become the West's most respected expert on Chinese affairs: 'Chinese' Morrison.

Lasseter's Reef

In 1897, a 17-year-old boy prospecting for rubies in the MacDonnell Ranges near Alice Springs in the 'dead heart' of Australia stumbled on a reef of gold nearly 12 kilometres long. Found days later near death from thirst by a surveyor and nursed back to health, the boy told his rescuer of his discovery. In 1899 the two men mounted an expedition to locate the reef but the surveyor was killed and his partner, struggling back to civilization, failed to interest investors in funding a second attempt to find the gold.

This, anyway, was the story that the prospector told a group of fascinated backers in Sydney 30 years later, in March 1930. His name was Harold Bell Lasseter, a short, pugnacious-looking man of 49, and the stories he recounted of his youthful adventures spellbound his listeners. The first chills of the Depression were blowing,

and another gold rush was just what Australia needed to drag her out of her economic woes. The word 'gold' was still magic, dazzling men's commonsense and blinding their natural scepticism.

A quick check verified Lasseter's claim to be the son of a gold-miner and within 48 hours the businessmen had formed a partnership with him—the Central Australian Gold Exploration Company. All shares were eagerly snapped up. The public was fascinated when the New South Wales government offered free transportation for the expedition's vehicles, and other companies donated trucks, fuel and an aircraft.

In July 1930, the motorized expedition left Alice Springs, driving west along the Tropic of Capricorn line towards Ilpili. The terrain was rough and dry, for the Centre had had no rain for three years. Temperatures reached 50° C in the shade and spinifex and sandhills reduced progress to a crawl. For all his self-confidence and likeable nature, Lasseter seemed at times moody, indecisive, slightly confused, and secretive when asked bluntly how far away the reef lay.

The party's patience was wearing thin when, after going up on reconnaissance in the expedition's aircraft, Lasseter returned, beaming with excitement. He had located the reef, 241 kilometres to the south. The journey there would be impossible for a truck. He would reach its location by camel.

In September 1930, Lasseter and one other companion, a dingo-skinner, left the base camp at Ilpili by camel. Making south, they crossed the dried surface of Lake Amadeus and passed Uluru (Ayer's Rock), the monolith sacred to the Pitjantjatjara tribe, before entering the rugged Petermann Ranges, a region into which few whites had ventured. Here, in October, the two men argued and split up. Lasseter was never seen again by whites.

Search parties that reached the area after his companion's return pieced together Lasseter's possible fate. Local tribesmen said that his camels bolted and he spent a month with them, dying near their camp in January 1931. They buried him, they said, but his body has never been found. In March 1931 a bushman, Robert Buck, found Lasseter's campsite and brought back his diaries and letters; but many believe the diaries to be forgeries. A skull stated to be Lasseter's was later found to be that of another man.

Stories persist that the prospector pushed on further west and lived for years, avoiding all contact with Europeans. Others maintain that they saw him in Perth only months after his supposed disappearance, for items found in the man's hotel room bore Harold Lasseter's name.

And, even today, tribesmen show travellers small nuggets of old, said to come from a fabulous reef ..

Survival

'I think it was in October 1898, that a man named M'Dermott, who
was boundary-riding on Mount Wood, north-west New South Wales,
nearly lost his life through being left too long unvisited. He had
gone out for his horse on a Friday morning, and was riding it bareback, when it stumbled in a rabbit-burrow, within half a mile of the
camp. M'Dermott was thrown, his hip striking a dry, knotty root of
a mulga tree. He was severely injured, and lay there suffering agonies till Monday evening. He fastened a message to his dog's neck
and tried to drive it away, but the dog would not leave him. Now
and again through the hot days it trotted to the creek for water, but
though hungry enough, it never once went near the hut for food.
In the meantime a traveller come to the camp and, thinking
M'Dermott had gone to the homestead for rations, remained there
waiting, with patience of the faithful dog, until he should return.
Mac had cooeed at intervals through the long days and nights, but

no sound came to the traveller's ears. On Monday a boy came out with meat, and the appearance of the place, and the traveller's assurance that he had seen nothing of M'Dermott, at once indicated that something was amiss. No fire had been lit for some time, and the man's saddle was in the hut. Moreover, the hut was untidy, and as Mac never went out for the day without putting things ship-shape, it was at once apparent to the bush boy that Mac had left with the intention of returning shortly, and that something serious had happened to him not far from the camp. His first act was to look to the horses, to see if any were missing. He found the mare with the broken bridle and the hobbles around her neck. That told its tale, and he rode post-haste to the homestead for assistance. Picking up the tracks, the rescue party followed to where he had caught the mare; then they tracked the mare to the rabbit-burrow, where they found M'Dermot all but dead, the hungry dog lying by his side, with the undelivered message still tied to its neck.

'A boundary rider on Gobbagumbalin run, near Wagga, in January 1902, was better served by his brute companion. His leg was broken by a fall from his horse when a long distance from camp. Like M'Dermott, he wrote a message and tied it round his dog's neck. His course being indicated to him, and being menaced with a waddy, and further instructed in abusive language, the animal at once started for home, and the required aid was thus promptly secured.

'Another man, named Frank Dacey, in February 1904, was making his way across Bonnie Doon run when he was taken seriously ill. His small supply of provisions soon ran out, but he managed to make one billy of water last him three weeks. He was able to crawl about near his tent, which had been temporarily pitched, and kept himself alive by eating pigweed. When the water gave out he gradually became weaker, and at last was unable to move. When discovered by a black boy he was in a dying condition, but subsequently recovered in hospital.'

— *Edward S. Sorensen.*

The Kookaburra *Tragedy, 1929*

One week after the disappearance of *Southern Cross* over the northern coast of Western Australia, the Sydney *Sun's* headlines shouted: 'Andy to the Rescue—Smithy's Old Pal Joins Search at Dawn.'

The headlines of 6 April 1929 thrilled Australia. Keith Anderson and his navigator Bobby Hitchcock had both gone to court seeking compensation from their old colleague and Anderson had partly paid for a single-engined Westland Widgeon with $2,000 Smithy had given him off the cuff. He called it the *Kookaburra*. 'I'd give anything to be able to go and look for the boys,' Anderson had told the owner of the pub where Smithy and he had drunk in happier days. The publican told him he would back a rescue flight to the tune of £500 and gave Anderson an advance of £30.

'He is probably better equipped for the task than anyone else in Australia,' stated the *Guardian*. The mechanics at Richmond RAAF base who serviced Anderson's *Kookaburra* the day before, would not have agreed. The plane's compass was defective and the tool kit had disappeared when Anderson and Hitchcock took off for Alice Springs. They had no wireless, no money, and only two packets of sandwiches and a couple of bottles of water; even then the Widgeon was overloaded.

Kookaburra landed at Blayney where the local garage owner donated fuel and, seeing Anderson shivering in the cold, gave him his leather coat to wear. On 9 April a prospector on the northern edge of Lake Eyre, 50 kilometres from Oodnadatta, saw *Kookaburra* grounded on the desert and its two crew members 'trying to fix the engine with a chisel serving as a screwdriver before getting into the air'.

Reaching Alice Springs, Anderson received there a telegram from Civil Aviation asking him to call off the rescue attempt. He disregarded it. He was positive he knew Smithy's and Ulm's whereabouts: somewhere near Glenelg, in the vicinity of the Port George Mission, hundreds of kilometres from the Drysdale that was the focus of operations by the other seven aircraft desperately searching for the plane.

Anderson and Hitchcock took off for Wyndham on 10 April, telling officials that they would follow the telegraph lines north. They failed to arrive.

But on 12 April, as word came through that *Kookaburra* was overdue, an aircraft piloted by Les Holden spotted *Southern Cross* on the Glenelg River mudflats and swooping low saw four tiny figures waving with joy. Dropping food to them, Holden sent the message: 'Found *Southern Cross*.' In Sydney taxis sounded their horns in joy, the Stock Exchange ceased trading and Smithy's old father hoisted a flag in his garden to the delight of reporters.

But within two weeks Australia's joy in finding the crew of *Southern Cross* alive would be clouded by questioning, puzzlement and grief. On 21 April a Qantas aircraft piloted by Lester Brain, one of eight civil and RAAF planes searching for the lost *Kookaburra*, saw smoke from burning scrub at a point in the desolate Tanami Desert, midway between Alice Springs and Wyndham, and flying low to investigate, saw the stranded *Kookaburra* and a body beneath its wing.

The aircraft was at the end of a long, red stretch of cleared scrub that the men apparently tried to make into a take-off strip, and wheel marks in the dust had shown how desperate their efforts had been. A ground party, led by bushmen, setting out from Wave Hill Station, found Hitchcock's body under the wing of the derelict aircraft, and Anderson's 400 metres away. The terrible Tanami scrub was so thick that it took a blacktracker more than an hour to find Keith Anderson's body.

Also found was a rough diary scratched on the tailplane. It told how the two men had hacked a runway on the first day but the strip was too short; weakened by hunger and thirst, they had been unable to make further attempts after 11 April. In desperation they had drunk the compass alcohol. Both had probably died on 12 or 13 April, tormented by heat, flies and thirst.

Eventually the bodies of the two men were recovered and buried—Anderson's with full military honours. But the *Kookaburra* remained in the Tanami, slowly disintegrating until only its rusting air frame and engine remained. In 1978, an expedition mounted by Dick Smith discovered its remains and bore them back to Perth.

Bernard O'Reilly and the search for the Stinson

On Friday, 19 February 1937, a Stinson passenger aircraft flying from Brisbane to Sydney disappeared in a storm. Over the next few days reports reached searchers that the aircraft had been seen and heard near the Hawkesbury, only minutes from Sydney, and had almost definitely crashed into the sea. Wreckage had been seen off Palm Beach. Two states mourned the loss of the two pilots and five passengers.

Listening to the wireless reports of the crash and the search, a young dairy farmer in the lushly-jungled Green Mountains southwest of Brisbane, Bernard O'Reilly, began to form his own opinion. He had heard the Stinson go over his property—as it had done every day since the service began—and felt sure that it had been heading direct to Lismore, its scheduled stop. Farmers in the rugged McPherson Ranges in its flight path told him that they too had heard the plane.

'It dawned upon me that the answer lay somewhere up in the gorges and jungles of the McPherson ranges,' O'Reilly would later write. On an aerial survey map of the country he drew a straight line between where the Stinson had been last seen, and its destination at Lismore. Saddling up his horse and loading up with provisions, he set out on what would be a 40-kilometre trek by horse and foot through impossible mountain country into which few men had ever ventured.

In the rain-drenched mountains two survivors of the crash, one of them in severe pain, huddled near death. Their aircraft, flying on instruments through a cyclone, had been caught suddenly by a 100-mph downwind and tossed like a toy into a mountain side, hitting the trees before falling to the earth below. The two pilots were killed instantly, as were the two passengers on one side of the aircraft; three passengers, Proud, Binstead and Westray, had hauled themselves from the wreckage.

Westray, a young Englishman, volunteered to try and get help. Though no bushman, he followed the course down-stream of a river, knowing it must lead to a lake or the sea. He was never again seen alive.

O'Reilly rode as far as Bethongabel before tying his mare's reins in her stirrups and shooing her off home. He then struck out on foot into the MacPherson Ranges towards the first of the four spurs that lay beneath the airliner's route. The jungle was thick and visibility limited to little more than ten metres by the overgrowth of vines and vicious thorns; his first night was spent in drizzling rain.

Just after noon next day, having climbed Mount Throakban, O'Reilly saw something distinct 15 kilometres away that puzzled him: a burnt tree top. He headed towards it and eight hours later, hearing the faint sound of human cries, came upon the wreckage of the Stinson. There he found Proud, cruelly injured, lying propped against a tree, and Binstead, also injured, close by. The survivors' first words were; 'How about boiling the billy?'

O'Reilly made the two men as comfortable as he could and went off to get assistance, promising to return within a day. It was on this return journey, following Westray's tracks, that he found the Englishman—dead, seated on a rock to which he had crawled, horribly injured, after falling down a chasm, in his efforts to rescue his companions. O'Reilly pushed on, reached the Buchanan homestead and, near collapse, organized a relief party which brought the two survivors in on stretchers.

O'Reilly's discovery of the Stinson survivors on their eleventh day of suffering was a famous episode in its time; 50 years later it inspired an Australian film. Bernard O'Reilly lived the rest of his life in his Green Mountains home after war service, and his lofty retreat is still visited by thousands attracted by the beauty of the fauna and the majesty of the Green Mountains themselves.

Kabbarli

She was called 'Kabbarli' (grandmother) by
the Aborigines of Western Australian
among whom she lived and worked.
European Australians knew her as Daisy
Bates and revered her in her old age as the
prim, dignified old lady who had devoted
her life to the welfare of the Aborigines of
the desert and her long life inspired an
opera with a libretto by Maie Casey. Daisy
Bates' life was a passionate one and full of
contradictions.

Daisy Bates

She was born Daisy May O'Dwyer into
a wealthy Protestant family in Tipperary,
Ireland in 1863, and was noted in her girlhood for her beauty, her vivacity and her
Irish impulsiveness. She travelled widely in
Europe and, suffering from weak lungs,
sailed for Queensland in 1884 to escape Ireland's dampness, in
search of a land with a healthy climate—and perhaps a husband.
The biographers of 'Breaker' Morant (and A.B. 'Banjo' Paterson's
biographer, the late, Dr Colin Roderick) discovered astonishing evidence that she married Morant (Murrant) at Charters Towers in
Queensland in 1884 and surmise that she left him only weeks later
when she realized his wayward nature. The *Australian
Encyclopaedia* repeats this fact, but no mention of Morant appears
in Elizabeth Salter's 1971 biography, *Daisy Bates*. In 1886 she married in Sydney a good natured drover Jack Bates, by whom she had
a son, but tiring of poverty left them both in 1894 to return to
Europe. In London she worked for the crusading journalist W.T.
Stead, whose high ideals and moral courage further inspired her
(and who was later drowned on the *Titanic*) and in 1899 she
offered her services to the *London Times* to investigate reports of
ill treatment of Aborigines in Western Australia. Returning briefly to
her husband, whom she could no longer abide (but whom she
never divorced), she travelled by steamer to the Catholic Mission at
Beagle Bay in the far north, with the active encouragement of the
government. There she became fascinated by the Aborigines and
their simple way of life. She explained: 'In their native state the
Aborigines possess many of the characteristics of the Irish, being
light hearted, quick to take offence and quick to forgive.' Their culture became her passion, as did their welfare, and their rituals
(including a male initiation ceremony) caused her no embarrass-
ment. She lived thereafter among the desert people of Western

Australia and South Australia until the last three years of her life and died in Adelaide in 1951. Her partly-autobiographical book *The Passing of the Aborigines*, rich in observations of Aboriginal culture (many of which have been challenged by later ethnologists and anthropologists) and written with the assistance of Ernestine Hill, was published in 1938. It mourned the 'inevitable' extinction of Australia's native people; but history, happily, has proved her prediction wrong.

Antarctic Deserts

The world's driest continent and greatest desert is not Australia or Asia. It is Antarctica, the vast ice mass of more than 16,000,000 square kilometres, twice the size of Australia's land mass (7,600,000 square kilometres). In winter, Antarctica's size is doubled by the freezing into ice of its surrounding waters which is summer detach into icebergs that drift north, permitting exploration vessels to push through to their coastal bases through the pack ice. Rain almost never falls, but snowfalls are whipped into howling blizzards by gales of up to 300-kilometres per hour, for it is also the world's

Douglas Mawson

windiest continent. Unlike the Arctic, it is virtually uninhabitable.

Yet Antarctica is a place of silent, monumental beauty, and many of those who visit it feel the compulsion to return there. Here are no human dangers, only nature at its most formidable. It was long thought to be part of the Australian continent—one immense Terra Australis Incognita—and, perhaps appropriately, the largest single segment of it belongs to Australia.

Naval explorers from many nations had chartered Antarctica's coastline during the 1800s but no expeditions had explored its interior until the first decade of the 20th century. In Ernest Shackleton's expedition of 1907–09, three Australians, the scientists Douglas Mawson, Edgeworth David and Forbes McKay, climbed its highest peak Mount Erebus and reached the South Magnetic Pole. On his second expedition to the regions, Captain Robert Falcon Scott and his three men perished after reaching the South Pole itself in January 1912, only to discover that the Norwegian Amundsen had beaten them there by one month.

Douglas Mawson, born in England but brought to Adelaide as an infant and educated there and at the University of Sydney, was lecturing in geology when he was appointed at the age of 29 to command the Australasian Expedition to Antarctica in 1911. After a year of extensive scientific work, and as the first penguins returned heralding summer, Mawson and two companions, the Englishman Belgrave Ninniss and the Swiss, Dr Xavier Merz, set off 10 November 1912 on three sledges dragged by 17 huskies to explore the interior. They planned to cover 800 kilometres and return to base no later than 15 January. They set off in winds uncommonly severe and a temperature of -38°C (-36°F). The weather deteriorated, with winds so strong that huddling in their tent at night they found it impossible to light their primus stove. Then tragedy struck. On 14 December, Ninniss and his dog team disappeared down a 250-metre deep crevasse and all were mercifully killed instantly. The two survivors were now over 500 kilometres from the base, and some of their essential supplies were now lost. They began their march to the west, often marching for 12 hours without rest. For food they began to shoot their dogs, for whom no food remained. For nourishment they even ate the livers, unaware that canine liver contains such high levels of Vitamin A that it is toxic to man. Soon all the dogs were dead; and Merz began to sicken on 1 January and by 6 January was in pain and incoherent. He died next day.

Mawson buried his friend and cut the sledge in half. He set off alone, dragging the shortened sledge behind him, making barely two kilometres a day. The ridged ice was a nightmare to negotiate but his exhaustion was briefly lightened by improved weather. He pushed on, wracked by stomach pains, as the blizzards returned. On 1 February 1913, after a lone journey of 200 kilometres, he reached the depot called Aladdin's Cave. For a week he lay in the ice hole, warm and with adequate food, gathering his strength while the elements raged outside. He then pushed on to the coast base at Commonwealth Bay, and saw a speck on the horizon—the ship was putting out to sea. Shades of Burke and Wills! When Mawson struggled into camp his men failed to recognize him—and gave him the shattering news that the ship had left only six hours before. The wireless operator aboard, alerted that the 'Leader' had survived, turned back to Commonwealth Bay. But the winds ands seas rose and she had to put out to steam away.

Mawson spent another long winter in Antarctica. One of his men went mad, for the isolation was too much for him. When he returned to Australia in 1914 with his men, he was acclaimed as a national hero, was knighted in the same year, wrote *The Home of the Blizzard*, and led two scientific cruises to Antarctica in 1921 and 1931. He died in 1959.

Mawson's hut is preserved as an Australian national memorial but he never inspired the love and devotion of his men as did the Irishman Ernest Shackleton, whose second great expedition to the Antarctic on the eve of war in 1914 included a young Australian photographer, James Francis (Frank) Hurley. When their vessel the *Endeavour* was crushed in the ice Shackleton led his men overland, hauling their boats, and then rowed in another epic of navigation and human fortitude with five others 1,287 kilometres to the island of South Georgia, before crossing the mountains with two others to the Norwegian whaling station on the other side of the island to organize a ship to rescue his other groups of men. Shackleton died in 1922—on New Georgia—on another Antarctic expedition and is buried there; Frank Hurley lived until 1962, after an adventurous life as an official photographer in both world wars, a pioneer film-maker in New Guinea and a renowned photographer.

11: *Bush Ballads*

The Shearer's Dream

Oh, I dreamt I shore in a shearin'-shed, and it was a dream of joy,
For every one of the rouseabouts was a girl dressed up as a
boy—
Dressed up like a page in a pantomime, and the prettiest ever
seen—
They had flaxen hair, they had coal-black hair, and every shade
between.
There was short, plump girls, there was tall, slim girls, and the
handsomest ever seen,
They was four-foot-five, they was six-foot high, and every height
between.

The sheds was cooled by electric fans that was over every shoot,
The pens was of polished ma-ho-gany, and everything else to
suit;
The huts had springs to the mattresses, and the tucker was sim-
ply grand,
And every night by the billabong we danced to a German band.

Our pay was the wool on the jumbucks' backs, so we shore till all
was blue—
The sheep was washed afore they was shore (and the rams was
scented too),
And we all of us wept when the shed cut out, in spite of the
long, hot days,
For every hour them girls waltzed in with whisky and beer on
tra-a-a-ays!

There was three of them girls to every chap, and as jealous as
they could be—
There was three of them girls to every chap, and six of 'em
picked on me;
We was drafting 'em out for the homeward track and sharin'
'em round like steam,
When I woke with my head in the blazin' sun to find 'twas only
a shearer's dream.

— *Henry Lawson*

Click Go the Shears

Down by the catching pen the old shearer stands,
   Clasping his shears in his thin bony hands.
   Fixed in his gaze on a bare-bellied yoe,
   Glory, if he gets her, won't he make the ringer go.

CHORUS:
   Click go the shears, boys, click, click, click.
   Wide is his blow and his hands move quick.
   The ringer looks around and is beaten by a blow,
   And curses the old snagger with the bare-bellied yoe.

In the middle of the floor in his cane-bottomed chair,
   Sits the boss of the board, with his eyes everywhere,
   Noting well each fleece as it comes to the screen,
   Paying strict attention that it's taken off clean.

The tar-boy is there and waiting on demand,
   With his blackened tar-pot in his tarry hand.
   Sees an old yoe with a cut upon her back
   This is what he's waiting for, 'Tar here, Jack!'

The Colonial Experience Man, he's there, of course,
   Shining boots and leggings, boys, just off his horse.
   Casting round his eyes like a flaming connoisseur,
   Shaving cream and brilliantine and smelling like a whore.

Shearing is all over and we've all got our cheques,
   Roll up your swags, boys, we're off along the track.
   The first pub we come to we'll all have a spree,
   And everyone that comes along it's, 'Have a drink with me!'

Down in the bar, the old shearer stands,
   Grasping his glass in his thin bony hands.
   Fixes his gaze on a green-painted keg,
   Glory, he'll get down on it before he stirs a leg.

There we leave him standing, shouting for all hands,
   While all around him the other shearers stand.
   His eyes are on the keg which now is lowering fast.
   He works hard, he drinks hard, and goes to hell at last.

— *TRADITIONAL*

Billy Brink

There once was a shearer by the name of Bill Brink,
   A devil for work and a devil for drink.
   He'd shear his two hundred a day without fear,
   And he'd drink without stopping two gallons of beer.

When the pub opened up he was first in,
   Roaring for whisky and howling for gin,
   Saying, 'Jimmy, my boy, I'm dying of thirst,
   Whatever you've got here just give to me first.'

Now Jimmy the barman who served him the rum,
   Hated the sight of old Billy the bum;
   He came up too late, he came up too soon,
   At morning, at evening, at night and at noon.

Now Jimmy the barman was cleaning the bar,
   With sulphuric acid locked up in a jar.
   He poured him a measure into a small glass,
   Saying, 'After this drink you will surely say "Pass".'

'Well,' says Billy to Jimmy, 'the stuff it tastes fine.
   She's a new kind of liquor or whisky or wine,
   Yes, that the stuff, Jimmy, I'm strong as a Turk,
   I'll break all the records today at my work.'

Well, all that day long here was Jim at the bar,
   Too eager to argue, too anxious to fight,
   Roaring and trembling with a terrible fear;
   For he pictured the corpse of old Bill in his sight.

But early next morn there was Bill as before,
   Roaring and bawling, and howling for more.
   His eyeballs were singed and his whiskers deranged,
   He had holes in his hide like a dog with a mange.

Said Billy to Jimmy, 'She sure was fine stuff,
   It made me feel well but I ain't had enough.
   It started me coughing, you know I'm no liar,
   And every damn cough set my whiskers on fire!'

— *TRADITIONAL*

The Sick Stock-Rider

Hold hard, Ned! Lift me down once more, and lay me in the shade,
  Old man, you've had your work cut out to guide
  Both horses, and to hold me in the saddle when I swayed,
  All through the hot, slow, sleepy, silent ride.
  The dawn at 'Moorabinda' was a mist-rack dull and dense,
  The sun-rise was sullen, sluggish lamp;
  I was dozing in the gateway at Arbuthnot's bound'ry fence,
  I was dreaming on the limestone cattle camp.

We crossed the creek at Carricksford, and sharply through the haze,
  And suddenly the sun shot flaming forth;
  To southward lay 'Katawa', with the sand peaks all ablaze,
  And the flushed fields of Glen Lomond lay to north.
  Now westwards winds the bridle-path that leads to Lindisfarm,
  And yonder looms the double-headed Bluff;
  From the far side of the first hill, when the skies are clear and
  calm,
  You can see Sylvester's woolshed fair enough.

Five miles we used to call it from our homestead to the place,
  Where the big tree spans the roadway like an arch;
  'Twas here we ran the dingo down that gave us such a chase
  Eight years ago—or was it nine?—last March.
  'Twas merry in the glowing morn, among the gleaming grass
  To wander as we've wandered many a mile,
  And blow the cool tobacco cloud, and watch the white wreaths
  pass,
  And sitting loosely in the saddle all the while.

'Twas merry mid the blackwoods when we spied the station roofs,
  To wheel the wild scrub cattle at the yard,
  With a running fire of stockwhips and a fiery run of hoofs;
  Oh! The hardest day was never then too hard!
  Ay! we had a glorious gallop after 'Starlight' and his gang,
  When they bolted from Sylvester's on the flat;
  How the sun-dried reed-beds crackled, how the flint-strewn
  ranges ran
  To the strokes of 'Mountaineer' and 'Acrobat'!

Hard behind them in the timber, harder still across the heath,
  Close beside them through the tea-tree scrub we dash'd;
  And the gold-tinted fern leaves, how they rustled underneath!
  And the honeysuckle osiers, how they crash'd!
  We led the hunt throughout, Ned, on the chestnut and the grey,
  And the troopers were three hundred yards behind,
  While we emptied our six-shooters on the bushrangers at bay,
  In the creek with stunted box-tree for a blind!

There you grappled with the leader, man to man and horse to horse,
   And you rolled together where the chestnut rear'd;
   He blazed away and missed you in that shallow water course—
   A narrow shave—his powder singed your beard!
   In these hours when life is ebbing, how those days when life was
   young,
   Come back to us; how clearly I recall,
   Even the yarns Jack invented, and the songs Jem Roper sung;
   And where are now Jem Roper and Jack Hall?

Ay, nearly all our comrades of the old colonial school,
   Our ancient boon companions, Ned, are gone;
   Hard livers for the main part, somewhat reckless as a rule,
   It seems that you and I are left alone.
   There was Hughes, who got in trouble through that business with
   the cards,
   It matters little what became of him;
   But a steer ripp'd up Macpherson in the Cooraminta yards,
   And Sullivan was drown'd at Sink-or-Swim.
   And Mostyn—poor Frank Mostyn—died at last a fearful wreck,
   In the horrors of the Upper Wandinong,
   And Carisbrooke, the rider, at the Horsefall broke his neck,
   Faith! The wonder was he saved his neck so long!
   Ah! Those days and nights we squandered at the Logans' in the
   glen—
   The Logans, man and wife, have long been dead,
   Elsie's tallest girl seems taller than your little Elsie then,
   And Ethel is a woman grown and wed.

I've had my share of pastime, and I've done my share of toil,
   And life is short—the longest life a span;
   I care not now to tarry for the corn or for the oil,
   Or for wine that maketh glad the heart of man.
   For good undone, and gifts misspent, and resolutions vain,
   'Tis somewhat late to trouble. This I know—
   I should live the same life over, if I had to live again;
   And the chances are I go where most men go.

The deep blue skies wax dusky, and the tall green trees grow dim,
   The sward beneath me seems to heave and fall;
   And sickly, smoky shadows through the sleepy sunlight swim,
   And on the very sun's face weave their pall.
   Let me slumber in the hollow where the wattle blossoms wave,
   With never stone or rail to fence my bed;
   Should the sturdy station children pull the bush flowers on my
   grave,
   I may chance to hear them romping overhead.

— *ADAM LINDSAY GORDON (1833-70)*

Gordon's Leap

Adam Lindsay Gordon, (1833–70) balladist, horseman and trooper, shot himself on the day his most popular collection of ballads was published.

Gordon, the son of an Anglo-
Scottish army officer, arrived in
South Australia in 1853 and served
for two years in the mounted
police before resigning to buy a
property and work with horses.
His feats as a rider made him a
figure of legend long before his
ballads saw him hailed as a force in
Australian literature. In sheer daring nothing rivalled his gallop
round the cliff edge of Blue Lake
at Mount Gambier—the extinct
crater whose cliffs drop nearly 70
metres to the unfathomable waters below.

'The poet and some sporting friends from Victoria were riding
in the neighbourhood, and the conversation turned on feats of
horsemanship witnessed in the vicinity,' wrote a friend, pen-named
'Bruni', in the Australasian years afterwards. 'Gordon was immediately inflamed with a desire to perform a feat that he felt none of
his friends would dare emulate. He carried 'Red Lancer' over a
fence, and by leaping from rock to rock, cleared a chasm more than
40 feet wide, the noble horse seeming to be inspired with the fearless courage of its rider.' Another described how Gordon jumped
his horse over a fence several times, challenging the other riders to
follow him. None did. 'The slightest mistake would have hurled
horse and rider into the lake two hundred feet below.' (The champion buck-jumper Lance Skuthorpe repeated Gordon's leap in the
1890s.)

Soon after, Mick Kelly of Kyneton, playing on Gordon's well-
known poor eyesight, challenged the balladist to repeat the performance in Victoria by jumping a fence around a dam; again, horse
and rider did the impossible. Unable to resist a challenge, Gordon
was preparing to ride his horse off a bridge into the Yarra when the
authorities put an end to the plan. When he shot himself in the
depths of depression at Brighton, Victoria, in 1870, colonists
mourned the loss of their first national poet.

Banjo Paterson and 'Clancy'

'Banjo' (Andrew Barton) Paterson (1864–1941) became Adam Lindsay Gordon's successor and remains Australia's best loved balladist of the bush. A lawyer by training, he was also a famous as a horseman, war correspondent, journalist and soldier.

Who was the 'Clancy' whom Banjo Paterson immortalized in verse? Some maintain that he was—like the 'Man from Snowy River'—totally fictional, a composite of various horsemen and bushmen whose qualities Paterson admired. The descendants of Thomas Michael McNamara, a drover known in the 1890s as 'Glancy', maintain that their grandfather was the hero of the ballad. Glancy McNamara who, like Banjo, got his nickname from his horse ('The Glance') was born in 1848, one of 13 children of an immigrant Irish couple. His father and Banjo's shared a property at West Wyalong at one time and there the two young men would have met. Glancy McNamara was well-known as a drover in the north of the state and lived to the ripe old age of 95; his grandson, Norman McNamara, remembers Glancy yarning about the good old days and says that the Overflow was a tributary of the Lachlan. Moreover, Norman maintains that the ' Man from Snowy River' was Jimmy Troy, a noted horseman who married Glancy's sister Teresa.

As for the famous line that sparked the poem, Banjo Paterson was to write: 'This ballad had its being from a lawyer's letter which I had to write to a gentleman of the bush who had not paid his debts. I got an answer from a friend of his who wrote the exact words: "Clancy's gone to Queensland droving and we don't know where he are." So there it was—the idea, the suggestion of the drover's life, the metre, the exact words for a couple of lines of verse, all delivered by Her Majesty's mail at a cost of a postage stamp.'

The ballad was published in the *Bulletin* in 1889, its author being described as a 'modest young man of Sydney'. After writing *Clancy of the Overflow*, Banjo related to a friend: 'I woke up to the fact that I was becoming known as a writer of verse, and from that time forth I seem to have caught on with Australian readers everywhere. I often receive letters from men out back who have read my pieces. You see, I understand them and their lives, and they know it.' He sometimes said that the 13/6d he got from the *Bulletin* for the piece was better value than the 6/8d he got for his legal opinion.

Clancy of the Overflow

I had written him a letter which I had, for want of better
  Knowledge, sent to where I met him down the Lachlan, years ago;
  He was shearing when I knew him, so I sent the letter to him,
  Just on spec, addressed as follows, 'Clancy of the Overflow'.

And an answer came directed in a writing unexpected
  (And I think the same was written with a thumbnail dipped in
  tar);
  'Twas his shearing mate who wrote it, and verbatim I will
  quote it:
  'Clancy's gone to Queensland droving, and we don't know where
  he are.'

In my wild erratic fancy visions come to me of Clancy
  Gone a-droving 'down the Cooper' where the western drovers go;
  As the stock are slowly stringing, Clancy rides behind them
  singing,
  For the drover's life has pleasures that the townsfolk never know.

And the bush hath friends to meet him, and their kindly voices
  greet him
  In the murmur of the breezes and river on its bars,
  And he sees the vision splendid of the sunlit plains extended,
  And at night the wondrous glory of the everlasting stars.

I am sitting in my dingy little office, where a stingy
  Ray of sunlight struggles feebly down between the houses tall,
  And the foetid air and gritty of the dusty, dirty city,
  Through the open window floating, spreads its foulness over all.

And in place of lowing cattle, I can hear the fiendish rattle
  Of the tramways and the buses making hurry down the street;
  And the language uninviting of the gutter children fighting
  Comes fitfully and faintly through the ceaseless tramp of feet.

And the hurrying people daunt me, and their pallid faces haunt me
  As they shoulder one another in their rush and nervous haste,
  With their eager eyes and greedy, and their stunted forms and
  weedy,
  For townsfolk have no time to grow, they have no time to waste.

And I somehow rather fancy that I'd like to change with Clancy,
  Like to take a turn at droving where the seasons come and go,
  While he faced the round eternal of the cashbook and the journal—
  But I doubt he'd suit the office, Clancy, of The Overflow.

— A.B. ('BANJO') PATERSON [1889]

Banjo Paterson wrote of his famous ballad—some say the greatest Australian ballad of them all—*The Man from Snowy River*, which was first published in the *Bulletin* in 1890:

'It was written to describe the cleaning up of the wild horses in our district, which was rough enough for most people, but not nearly as rough as they had it on the Snowy. To make any sort of job of it I had to create a character, to imagine a man who would ride better than anybody else, and where would he come from except from the Snowy? And what sort of horse would he ride except a half-thoroughbred mountain pony? Kipling felt in his bones that there must have been a well in his mediaeval fortress, and I felt equally convinced that there must have been a man from the Snowy River. I was right. They have turned up from all the mountain districts—men who did exactly the same ride and could give you chapter and verse for every hill they descended and every creek they crossed. It was no small satisfaction to find that there really had been a 'Man from Snowy River'—more than one of them.'

The Man from Snowy River

There was movement at the station, for the word had passed
    around
      That the colt from old Regret had got away,
      And had joined the wild bush horses—he was worth a
      thousand pound,
      So all the cracks had gathered to the fray.
      All the tried and noted riders from the stations near and far
      Had mustered at the homestead overnight,
      For the bushmen love hard riding where the wild bush horses
      are,
      And the stock-horse snuffs the battle with delight.

There was Harrison, who made his pile when Pardon won the
    cup,
      The old man with his hair as white as snow;
      But few could ride beside him when his blood was fairly up—
      He would go wherever horse and man could go.
      And Clancy of the Overflow came down to lend a hand,
      No better horseman ever held the reins;
      For never horse could throw him while the saddle-girths would
      stand—
      He learnt to ride while droving on the plains.

And one was there, a stripling on a small and weedy beast;
      He was something like a racehorse undersized,

With a touch of Timor pony—three parts thoroughbred at
least—
And such as are by mountain horsemen prized.
He was hard and tough and wiry—just the sort that won't say
die—
There was courage in his quick impatient tread;
And he bore the badge of gameness in his bright and fiery eye,
And the proud and lofty carriage of his head.

But still so slight and weedy, one would doubt his power to stay,
And the old man said, 'That horse will never do
For a long and tiring gallop—lad, you'd better stop away,
Those hills are far too rough for such as you.'
So he waited, sad and wistful—only Clancy stood his friend—
'I think we ought to let him come,' he said;
'I warrant he'll be with us when he's wanted at the end,
For both his horse and he are mountain bred.

'He hails from Snowy River, up by Kosciusko's side,
Where the hills are twice as steep and twice as rough;
Where a horse's hoofs strike firelight from the flint-stones every
stride,
The man that holds his own is good enough.
And the Snowy River riders on the mountains make their home,
Where the river runs those giant hills between;
I have seen full many horsemen since I first commenced to
roam,
But nowhere yet such horsemen have I seen.'

So he went; they found the horses by the big mimosa clump,
They raced away towards the mountain's brow,
And the old man gave his orders, 'Boys, go at them from the
jump,
No use to try for fancy riding now.
And, Clancy, you must wheel them, try and wheel them to the
right.
Ride boldly, lad, and never fear the spills,
For never yet was rider that could keep the mob in sight,
If once they gain the shelter of those hills.'

So Clancy rode to wheel them—he was racing on the wing
Where the best and boldest riders take their place,
And he raced his stock-horse past them, and he made the
ranges ring
With the stockwhip, as he met them face to face.
Then they halted for a moment, while he swung the dreaded
lash,
But they saw their well-loved mountain full in view,

And they charged beneath the stockwhip with a sharp and sudden dash,
And off into the mountain scrub they flew.

Then fast the horsemen followed, where the gorges deep and black
Resounded to the thunder of their tread,
And the stockwhips woke the echoes, and they fiercely answered back
From cliffs and crags that beetled overhead.
And upward, ever upward, the wild horses held their way,
Where mountain ash and kurrajongs grew wide;
And the old man muttered fiercely, 'We may bid the mob good-day,
No man can hold them down the other side.'

When they reached the mountain's summit, even Clancy took a pull—
It well might make the boldest hold their breath;
The wild hop scrub grew thickly, and the hidden ground was full
Of wombat holes, and any slip was death.
But the man from Snowy River let the pony have his head,
And he swung his stockwhip round and gave a cheer,
And he raced him down the mountain like a torrent down its bed,
While the others stood and watched in very fear.

He sent the flint-stones flying, but the pony keep his feet,
He cleared the fallen timber in his stride,
And the man from Snowy River never shifted in his seat—
It was grand to see that mountain horseman ride.
Through the stringybarks and saplings, on the rough and broken ground,
Down the hillside at a racing pace he went;
And he never drew the bridle till he landed safe and sound,
At the bottom of that terrible descent.

He was right among the horses as they climbed the farther hill,
And the watchers on the mountain, standing mute,
Saw him ply the stockwhip fiercely; he was right among them still,
As he raced across the clearing in pursuit.
Then they lost him for a moment, where two mountain gullies met
In the ranges—but a final glimpse reveals
On a dim and distant hillside the wild horses racing yet,
With the man from Snowy River at their heels.

And then he ran them single-handed till their sides were white
  with foam;
  He followed like a bloodhound on their track,
  Till they halted, cowed and beaten; then he turned their heads
  for home,
  And alone and unassisted brought them back.
  But his hardy mountain pony he could scarcely raise a trot,
  He was blood from hip to shoulder from the spur;
  But his pluck was still undaunted, and his courage fiery hot,
  For never yet was mountain horse a cur.

And down by Kosciusko, where the pine-clad ridges raise
  Their torn and rugged battlements on high,
  Where the air is clear as crystal, and the white stars fairly blaze,
  At midnight in the cold and frosty sky,
  And where around the Overflow the reed-beds sweep and sway
  To the breezes, and the rolling plains are wide,
  The Man from Snowy River is a household word today,
  And the stockmen tell the story of his ride.

— *A.B. ('Banjo') Paterson [1890]*

Banjo Paterson wrote the words to *Waltzing Matilda*, now known as Australia's unofficial national anthem, during a visit in March–April 1895 to the Riley property at Winton, Queensland, 170 kilometres north-east of Longreach. He was unofficially engaged to the owner's niece, Sarah Riley, and one day the couple called on the Macpherson's station, Dagworth, on the Diamantina. There Banjo heard young Christina Macpherson picking out an old Scottish tune—*The Bonnie Woods of Craigielea*—on an autoharp, and boldly offered to write new words for it. He drew inspiration from a local yarn about a cattle duffer or a swaggie who had drowned in a creek. ('Matilda' was a German army expression for a swag—a rolled blanket or overcoat slung over the shoulder.) Banjo's publishers, Angus & Robertson, were pleased enough with it to buy it outright from him for 5 pounds (10 dollars). They later leased it to Inglis and Co., who reprinted it in leaflet form to advertise Billy Tea after the wife of the Inglis manager, Marie Cameron, tinkered with the words and the tune to produce the version we sing today. Banjo lost out, in more ways than one. Soon after their visit to Winton and Dagworth, Sarah Riley broke off their engagement, irked, according to legend, by the attentions Banjo had paid to Christina! Copyrights expired in 1992 on the famous verse and its myriad variations. The tune of the 'Queensland version' has a bouncier melody than the slow one sung in the South.

Waltzing Matilda

Once a jolly swagman camped by a billabong,
  Under the shade of a coolibah-tree,
  And he sang as he watched and waited till his billy boiled
  'Who'll come a-waltzing Matilda with me?'
  Waltzing Matilda,
  Waltzing Matilda,
  Who'll come a-waltzing Matilda with me?'
  And he sang as he watched and waited till his billy boiled,
  'Who'll come a-waltzing Matilda with me?'

Down came a jumbuck to drink at the billabong:
  Up jumped the swagman and grabbed him with glee,
  And he sang as he shoved that jumbuck in his tucker-bag,
  'You'll come a-waltzing Matilda with me.
  Waltzing Matilda,
  Waltzing Matilda,
  You'll come a-waltzing Matilda with me.'

Up rode a squatter, mounted on his thoroughbred;
  Down came the troopers, one, two, three:
  'Who's that jolly jumbuck you've got in your tucker-bag?
  You'll come a-waltzing Matilda with me!
  Waltzing Matilda,
  Waltzing Matilda,
  You'll come a-waltzing Matilda with me.
  Who's that jolly jumbuck you've got in your tucker-bag?
  You'll come a-waltzing Matilda with me!'

Up jumped the swagman and sprang into the billabong;
  'You'll never catch me alive!' said he;
  And his ghost may be heard as you pass by that billabong,
  'You'll come a-waltzing Matilda with me!
  Waltzing Matilda,
  Waltzing Matilda,
  You'll come a-waltzing Matilda with me!'
  And his ghost may be heard as you pass by that billabong,
  'You'll come a-waltzing Matilda with me!'

— A.B. ('BANJO') PATERSON

'Breaker' Morant

'The Breaker'—Harry Morant (1864–1902) —was an Anglo-Irish immigrant who worked as a drover in Queensland and achieved a name as a horseman and horse-breaker and a following with his bush ballads, published under his pen-name the 'Breaker' in the *Bulletin* the 1890s. Good looking, dashing but irresponsible (something of a bounder), he is said to have married Daisy O'Dwyer, known to history as Daisy Bates, in Charters Towers in 1884, but the marriage, if it ever existed, did not last. A skilled horseman, he volunteered to serve with the mounted troops leaving for South Africa in 1899 (to escape his creditors, some said). There he took part in the relief of Kimberley (1900) and in 1901, when the Boers resorted to guerilla warfare, Morant joined an irregular unit, the Bush Veldt Carbineers, specially formed to fight the Boer commandos on their own terms, using their own methods. When a fellow officer was found dead, his body apparently mutilated, Morant and his men became known for sometimes shooting prisoners. (The Boers generally wore no uniforms other than those taken off dead British troops; 'armed civilians' were traditionally punished by summary execution, a practice the Germans initiated in France in 1870 and perfected in Belgium in 1914). Both sides broke all the rules of war in the bitter closing year of the conflict and it appears that the British Commander-in-Chief, General Lord Kitchener, finally decided to make an example of some of his troops—preferably colonial ones, not British. Found guilty by a British court martial of executing prisoners, Morant and a fellow Australian officer were shot by a Scottish firing squad in 1902. The Breaker faced his end without flinching, his last words being 'Shoot straight, you bastards!'

The 'Breaker'— Harry Morant

The execution caused a storm in Australia and still provokes argument. From that date no Australian soldier has been subjected to capital punishment for military offences in time of war. The myth of Harry Morant still rides through our lore, and his life and death has inspired numerous books and a famous film.

West by North Again

We've drunk our wine, we've kissed our girls, and funds are
    sinking low,
    The horses must be thinking it's a fair thing now to go;
    Sling the swags on Condamine and strap the billies fast,
    And stuff a bottle in the bags and let's be off at last.

What matter if the creeks are up—the cash, alas, runs down!
    A very sure and certain sign we're long enough in town.
    The nigger rides the book, and you'd better take the bay,
    Quart Pot will do to carry me the stage we go today.

No grass this side the border fence! And all the mulga's dead!
    The horses for a day or two will have to spiel ahead;
    Man never yet from Queensland brought a bullock or a hack
    But lost condition on that God-abandoned Border track.

When once we're through the rabbit-proof—it's certain since
    the rain—
    There's the ships o'grass and water, so, it's West by North again!
    There's food on Tyson's country—we can 'spell' the mokes a
    week,
    Where Billy Stevens last year trapped his brumbies on Bough
    Creek.

The Paroo may be quickly crossed—the Eulo Common's bare;
    And, anyhow, it isn't wise, old man! To dally there,
    Alack-a-day! Far wiser men than you and I succumb,
    To woman's wiles, and potency of Queensland wayside rum.

Then over sand and spinifex and on, o'er the ridge and plain!
    The nags are fresh—besides, they know they're westward-
    bound again.
    The brand upon old Darkie's thigh is that upon the hide,
    Of bullocks we must muster on the Diamantina side.

We'll light our camp-fires where we may, and yarn beside their
blaze;
    The jingling hobble-chains shall make a music through the days.
    And while the tucker-bags are right, and we've a stick of weed,
    A swagman shall be welcome to a pipe-full and a feed.

So, fill your pipe! And, ere we mount, we'll drink another nip—
    Here's how that West by North again may prove a lucky rip;
    Then back again—I trust you'll find your best girl's merry face,
    Or, if she jilts you, may you get a better in her place.

— *HARRY MORANT ('THE BREAKER') (1864-1902)*

On the Road to Gundagai

Oh, we started down from Roto when the sheds had all cut out.
  We'd whips and whips of Rhino as we meant to push about,
  So we humped our blues serenely and made for Sydney town,
  With a three-spot cheque between us, as we wanted knocking
  down.

CHORUS:
  But we camped at Lazy Harry's, on the road to Gundagai.
  The road to Gundagai! Not five miles from Gundagai!
  Yes, we camped at Lazy Harry's, on the road to Gundagai.

Well, we struck the Murrumbidgee near the Yanco in a week,
  And passed through old Narrandera and crossed the Burnett
  Creek.
  And we never stopped at Wagga, for we'd Sydney in our eye.
  But we camped at Lazy Harry's, on the road to Gundagai.

Oh, I've seen a lot of girls, my boys and drunk a lot of beer,
  And I've met with some of both, chaps, as has left me mighty
  queer;
  But for beer to knock you sideways, and for girls to make you
  sigh,
  You must camp at Lazy Harry's, on the road to Gundagai.

Well, we chucked our blooming swags off, and we walked into the
  bar,
  And we called for rum-an'-raspb'ry and a shilling each cigar.
  But the girl that served the pizen, she winked at Bill and I—
  And we camped at Lazy Harry's, not five miles from Gundagai.

In a week the spree was over and the cheque was all knocked
  down,
  So we shouldered our Matildas, and we turned our back on
  town,
  And the girls they stood a nobbler as we sadly said good-bye,
  And we tramped from Lazy Harry's, not five miles from
  Gundagai.
  And we tramped from Lazy Harry's, not five miles from Gudagai.

— *TRADITIONAL*

The Dog on the Tuckerbox

I'm used to punchin' bullock teams
  Across the hills and plains,
  I've teamed outback this forty years
  In blazin' droughts and rains,

I've lived a heap of troubles down,
Without a bloomin' lie,
But I can't forget what happened to me,
Nine miles from Gundagai.

'Twas gettin' dark, the team got bogged,
The axle snapped in two,
I lost me matches and me pipe,
So what was I to do?
The rain came on, 'twas bitter cold,
And hungry too was I,
And the dog sat on the tucker box
Nine miles from Gundagai

Some blokes I knows has stacks o' luck
No matter 'ow they fall,
But there was me, Lor' luv-a-duck,
No blessed luck at all.
I couldn't make a pot o' tea,
Nor get me trousers dry,
And the dog sat on the tucker box
Nine miles from Gundagai.

I can forgive the blinkin' team,
I can forgive the rain, I can forgive the dark an' cold,
An' go through it again.
I can forgive me rotten luck,
But hang me till I die,
I can't forgive that plurry dog,
Nine miles from Gundagai.

— *TRADITIONAL*

Another popular version of this famous old ballad has the reprise:

> *...And the dog shat in the tuckerbox,*
> *Five Miles from Gundagai!*

But it is the image of loyal dog guarding his master's tucker-box (five or nine miles from Gundagai) that is immortalized in a famous statue above the wishing well on the road outside Gundagai.

Gundagai itself, roughly mid-way between Sydney and Melbourne, has inspired numerous ballads—one of which is *Nine Miles from Gundagai* written by Jack Moses (1866–1945), a friend of Henry Lawson and first published in 1938. Jack O'Hagan's song of the same name was a favourite of the troops in the 1939-45 war ('There's a track winding back ...') and its music became the theme of the long-running ABC radio serial *Dad and Dave*.

The Swagman and His Mate

From north to south throughout the year,
   The shearing seasons run,
   The Queensland stations start to shear
   When Maoriland has done;
   But labour's cheap and runs are wide,
   And some the track must tread,
   From New Year's Day till Christmastide
   And never get a shed!
   North, west, and south—south, west and north—
   They lead and follow Fate—
   The stoutest hearts that venture forth—
   The swagman and his mate.

A restless, homeless class they are,
   Who tramp in border land.
   They take their rest 'neath moon and star—
   Their bed the desert sand,
   On sunset tracks they ride and tramp,
   Till speech has almost died,
   And still they drift from camp to camp
   In silence side by side.
   They think and dream, as all men do;
   Perchance their dreams are great—
   Each other's thoughts are sacred to
   The swagman and his mate.

With scrubs beneath the stifling skies,
   Unstirred by heaven's breath;
   Beyond the Darling Timber lies,
   The land of living death!
   A land that wrong-born poets brave,
   Till dulled minds cease to grope—
   A land where all things perish, save,
   The memories of Hope,
   When daylight's fingers point out back,
   (And seem to hesitate),
   The far faint dust cloud marks their track,
   The swagman and his mate.

And one who followed through the scrub,
   And out across the plain,
   And only in a bitter mood
   Would see those tracks again;
   Can only write what he has seen—
   Can only give his hand—

And greet those mates in words that mean
'I know', 'I understand'.
I hope they'll find the squatter 'white',
The cook and shearers 'straight',
When they have reached the shed to-night—
The swagman and his mate.

— HENRY LAWSON

My Four Little Johnny Cakes

Hurrah for the Lachlan, boys, and join me in a cheer;
   That's the place to go to make a cheque every year,
   With a toadskin in my pocket, that I borrowed from a friend,
   Oh, isn't it nice and cosy to be camping in the bend!

CHORUS:
   With my four little johnny-cakes all nicely cooked,
   A nice little codfish just off the hook;
   My little round flour-bag sitting on a stump,
   My little tea-and-sugar bag a-looking nice and plump.

I have a loaf of bread and some murphies that I shook,
   Perhaps a loaf of brownie that I snaffled off the cook,
   A nice leg of mutton, just a bit cut off the end,
   Oh, isn't it nice and jolly to be whaling in the bend!

I have a little book and some papers for to read,
   Plenty of matches and a good supply of weed;
   I envy not the squatter, as at my fire I sit,
   With a paper in my hand and my old clay a-lit.

And when the shearing-time comes round, I'm in my glory then;
   I saddle up my moke and then secure a pen;
   I canter thro' the valley, and gallop o'er the plain;
   I shoot a turkey or stick a pig, and off to camp again.

— TRADITIONAL

The Banks of the Condamine

Oh, hark the dogs are barking, love, I can no longer stay,
    The men are all gone mustering, and it is nearly day;
    And I must be off by the morning, before the sun doth shine,
    To meet the Sydney shearers on the banks of the Condamine.

Oh Willie, dearest Willie, I'll go along with you,
    I'll cut off all my auburn fringe and be a shearer, too.
    I'll cook and count your tally, love, while ringer-o you shine,
    And I'll wash your greasy moleskins on the banks of the
    Condamine.

Oh, Nancy, dearest Nancy, with me you cannot go,
    The squatters have given orders, love, no woman should do so;
    Your delicate constitution is not equal unto mine,
    To stand the constant tigering on the banks of the Condamine.

Oh Willie, dearest Willie, then stay back home with me,
    We'll take up a selection, and a farmer's wife I'll be;
    I'll help you husk the corn, love, and cook your meals so fine
    You'll forget the ram-stag mutton on the banks of the
    Condamine.

Oh Nancy, dearest Nancy, please do not hold me back,
    Down there the boys are waiting, and I must be on the track;
    So here's a good-bye kiss, love, back home here I'll incline,
    When we've shore the last of the jumbucks on the banks of the
    Condamine.

And when the shearings over, love, I'll make of you my wife;
    I'll get a boundary riding job and settle down for life,
    And when the day's work's over, in the evenings calm and fine,
    I'll tell you of those sandy cobblers on the banks of the
    Condamine.

— *Traditional*

Bullocky Bill

As I came down Talbingo Hill,
    I heard a maiden cry,
    'There's goes old Bill the Bullocky—
    He's bound for Gundagai.'

A better poor old beggar,
    Never cracked an honest crust,
    A tougher poor old beggar,
    Never drug a whip through dust.

His team got bogged on the Five-Mile Creek,
  Bill lashed and swore and cried,
  'If Nobbie don't get me out of this
  I'll tattoo his bloody hide.'

But Nobbie strained and broke the yoke,
  And poked out the leader's eye,
  And the dog sat on the tucker-box,
  Five miles from Gundagai.

— *ANONYMOUS*

The Old Bullock Dray

Oh! The shearing is all over, and the wool is coming down,
  And I mean to get a wife, boys, when I go down to town.
  Everything that's got two legs presents itself to view,
  From the little paddy-melon to the bucking kangaroo.

CHORUS:
  So it's roll up your blankets, and let's make a push,
  I'll take you up the country and show you the bush.
  I'll be bound you won't get such a chance another day,
  So come and take possession of my old bullock-dray.

Now, I've saved up a good cheque and I mean to buy a team,
  And when I get a wife, boys I'll be all serene;
  For, calling at the depot, they say there's no delay
  To get an off-sider for the old bullock dray.

Now I'll teach you the whip, and the bullocks how to flog,
  You'll be my off-sider when we're stuck in a bog;
  Lashing out both left and right and every other way,
  Making skin, hair and blood fly round the old bullock-dray.

Oh! We'll live like fighting cocks, for good living I'm your man.
  We'll have leather-jacks, Johnny-cakes, and fritters in the pan;
  Or if you want some fish, why, I'll catch you some soon,
  For we'll bob for barramundies round the banks of a lagoon.

Oh! Yes, of beef and damper I make sure we have enough,
  And we'll boil the bucket such a whopper of a duff;
  And our friends will all dance to the honour of the day,
  To the music of the bells, around the old bullock-dray.

Oh! We'll have plenty girls, we must mind that.
  There'll be 'Buck-jumping Maggie' and 'Leather-belly Pat',
  There'll be 'Stringybark Peggy' and 'Green-Hide Mike',
  Oh, yes, my colonials, just as many as you like!

Now we'll stop all immigration, we don't need it any more;
  We'll be having young natives, twins by the score.

And I wonder what the devil Jack Robertson would say,
If he saw us promenading round the old bullock-dray.

Oh! It's time I had an answer, if there's one to be had,
I wouldn't treat that steer in the body half as bad;
But he takes as much notice of me, upon my soul,
As that old blue stag off-sider in the pole.

Oh! To tell a lot of lies, you know it is a sin,
But I'll go back up the country and marry a black gin
'Baal gammon white ferrer,' that is what she'll say,
'Budgery you and your old bullock-dray!'

FINAL CHORUS:
So it's roll up your blankets, and let's make a push
I'll take you up the country and show you the bush.
I'll be bound you won't get, such a chance another day
So come and take possession of the my old bullock-dray.

— TRADITIONAL

The Lights of Cobb and Co.

Fire lighted, on the table a meal for sleepy men,
A lantern in the stable, a jingle now and then;
The mail coach looming darkly by light of moon and star,
The growl of sleepy voices—a candle in the bar;
A stumble in the passage of folk with wits abroad;
A swear-word from a bedroom—the shout of 'All aboard!'
'Tchk-tchk! Git-up!' 'Hold fast, there!' and down the range we go;
Five hundred miles of scattered camps will watch for Cobb
and Co.

Old coaching towns already 'decaying for their sins',
Uncounted 'Half-Way Houses', and scores of 'Ten Mile Inns";
The riders from the stations by lonely granite peaks;
The black-boy for the shepherds on sheep and cattle creeks,
The diggers on the Lachlan; the huts of Furthest West;
Some twenty thousand exiles who sailed for weal or woe;
The bravest hearts of twenty lands will wait for Cobb and Co.

The morning star has vanished, the frost and fog are gone,
In one of those grand mornings which but on mountains dawn;
A flask of friendly whisky—each other's hopes we share—
And throw our top-coats open to drink the mountain air.
The roads are rare to travel, and life seems all complete;
The grind of wheels on gravel, the trot of horses' feet,
The trot, trot, trot and canter, as down the spur we go—
The green sweeps to horizons blue that call for Cobb and Co.

We take a bright girl actress through western dust and damps,
  To bear the home-world message, and sing for sinful camps,
  To wake the hearts and break them, wild hearts that hope and ache—
  (Ah! when she thinks of those days her own must nearly break!)
  Five miles this side the gold-field, a loud, triumphant shout:
  Five hundred cheering diggers have snatched the horses out:
  With 'Auld Lang Syne' in chorus through roaring camps they go—
  That cheer for her, and cheer for Home, and cheer for Cobb and Co.

Three lamps above the ridges and gorges dark and deep,
  A flash on sandstone cuttings where sheer the sidings sweep,
  A flash on shrouded wagons, on water ghastly white;
  Weird bush and scattered remnants of 'rushes in the night';
  Across the swollen river a flash beyond the ford:
  'Ride hard to warn the driver! He's drunk or mad, good Lord!'
  But on the bank to westward a broad, triumphant glow—
  A hundred miles shall see tonight the lights of Cobb and Co.!

312 An Anthology of Classic Australian Folklore

Swift scramble up the siding where teams climb inch by inch;
    Pause, bird-like, on the summit—then breakneck down the
    pinch
    Past haunted half-way houses—where convicts made the
    bricks—
    Scrub-yards and new bark shanties, we dash with five and six—
    By clear, ridge-country rivers, and gaps where tracks run high,
    Where waits the lonely horseman, cut clear against the sky;
    Through stringy-bark and blue-gum, and box and pine we go;
    New camps are stretching 'cross the plains the routes of Cobb
    and Co.

Throw down the reins, old driver—there's no one left to shout;
    The ruined inn's survivor must take the horses out.
    A poor old coach hereafter! —we're lost to all such things—
    No burst of songs or laughter shall shake your leathern springs,
    When creeping in unnoticed by railway sidings drear,
    Or left in yards for lumber, decaying with the year—
    Oh, who'll think how in those days when distant fields were
    broad,
    You raced across the Lachlan side with twenty-five on board.

Not all the ships that sail away since Roaring Days are done—
    Not all the boats that steam from port, nor all the trains that
    run,
    Shall take such hopes and loyal hearts—for men shall never
    know,
    Such days as when the Royal Mail was run by Cobb and Co.
    The 'greyhounds' race across the sea, the 'special' cleaves the
    haze,
    But these seem dull and slow to me compared with Roaring
    Days!
    The eyes that watched are dim with age, and souls are weak
    and slow,
    The hearts are dust or hardened now that broke for Cobb and
    Co.

— HENRY LAWSON

How McDougal Topped the Score

A peaceful spot is Piper's Flat. The folk that live around—
  They keep themselves by keeping sheep and turning up the
  ground;
  But the climate is erratic, and the consequences are,
  The struggle with the elements is everlasting war.
  We plough, and sow, and harrow—then slip down and pray for
  rain;
  And then we all get flooded out and have to start again.
  But the folk are now rejoicing as they ne'er rejoiced before,
  For we've played Molongo cricket, and McDougal topped the
  score!

Molongo had a head on it, and challenged us to play,
  A single-innings match for lunch—the losing team to pay.
  We were not great guns at cricket, but we couldn't well say no,
  So we all began to practise, and we let the reaping go
  We scoured the Flat for ten miles round to muster up our men,
  But when the list was totalled we could only muster ten.
  Then up spoke big Tim Brady: he was always slow to speak,
  And he said— 'What price McDougal, who lives down at
  Cooper's Creek?'

So we sent for old McDougal, and he stated in reply,
  That he'd never played at cricket, but he'd half a mind to try.
  He couldn't come to practise—he was getting in his hay,
  But he guessed he'd show the beggars from Molongo how to play.
  Now, McDougal was a Scotchman, and a canny one at that,
  So he started in to practise with a paling for a bat.
  He got Mrs Mac to bowl to him, but she couldn't run at all,
  So he trained his sheep-dog, Pincher, how to scout and fetch
  the ball.

Now, Pincher was no puppy; he was old, and worn, and grey;
  But he understood McDougal, and—accustomed to obey—
  When McDougal cried out 'Fetch it!' he would fetch it in a trice,
  But, until the word was 'Drop it!' he would grip it like a vice.

And each succeeding night they played until the light grew dim:
  Sometimes McDougal struck the ball—sometimes the ball struck
  him.
  Each time he struck, the ball would plough a furrow in the
  ground;
  And when he missed, the impetus would turn him three times
  round.

The fatal day at length arrived—the day that was to see
  Molongo bite the dust, or Piper's Flat knocked up a tree!

Molongo's captain won the toss, and sent his men to bat,
And they gave some leather-hunting to the men of Piper's Flat.

When the ball sped where McDougal stood, firm planted in his
track,
He shut his eyes, and turned him round, and stopped it—with his
back!
The highest score was twenty-two, the total sixty-six,
When Brady sent a Yorker down that scattered Johnson's sticks.

Then Piper's Flat went in to bat, for glory and renown,
But, like the grass before the scythe, our wickets tumbled down.
'Nine wickets down for seventeen, with fifty more to win!'
Our captain heaved a heavy sigh, and sent McDougal in.

'Ten pounds to one you'll lose it!' cried a barracker from town;
But McDougal said, 'I'll tak' it, mon!' and planked the money
down.
Then he girded up his moleskins in a self-reliant style,
Threw off his hat and boots and faced the bowler with a smile.

He held the bat the wrong side out, and Johnson with a grin
Stepped lightly to the bowling crease, and sent a 'wobbler' in;
McDougal spooned it softly back, and Johnson waited there,
But McDougal, crying 'Fetch it!' started running like a hare.

Molongo shouted 'Victory, he's out as sure as eggs',
When Pincher started through the crowd, and ran through
Johnson's legs.
He seized the ball like lightning; then ran behind a log,
And McDougal kept on running, while Molongo chased the dog!

They chased him up, they chased him down, they chased him
round and round, and then,
He darted through the sliprail as the scorer shouted 'Ten!'
McDougal puffed; Molongo swore; excitement was intense;
As the scorer marked down twenty, Pincher cleared a barbed-
wire fence.

'Let us head him! Shrieked Molongo. 'Brain the mongrel with a bat!'
'Run it out! Good old McDougal!' yelled the men of Piper's Flat.
And McDougal kept on jogging, and then Pincher doubled back,
And the scorer counted 'Forty' as they raced across the track.

McDougal's legs were going fast, Molongo's breath was gone—
But still Molongo chased the dog—McDougal struggled on,
When the scorer shouted 'Fifty' then they knew the chase could
cease;
And McDougal gasped out 'Drop it!' as he dropped within his
crease.

Then Pincher dropped the ball, and as instinctively he knew,
  Discretion was the wiser plan, he disappeared from view;
  And as Molongo's beaten men exhausted lay around,
  We raised McDougal shoulder-high, and bore him from the
  ground.

We bore him to McGinniss's where lunch was ready laid,
  And filled him up with whisky-punch, for which Molongo paid.
  We drank his health in bumpers and we cheered him three
  times three,
  And when Molongo got its breath Molongo joined the spree.

And the critics say they never saw a cricket match like that,
  When McDougal broke the record in the game at Piper's Flat,
  And the folk are jubilating as they never did before;
  For we played Molongo cricket—and McDougal topped the
  score!

— *THOMAS E. SPENCER (1845-1911)*

12: *The Australian Slanguage*

Australian Accent

VISITORS AND LINGUISTICS EXPERTS find it remarkable that all Australians speak with basically the same accent and intonation—the Great Australian drawl, most noticeable in our stretched vowels, and discarded consonants which produce an effect described as 'not unpleasant'. Linguists trace our accent—and much of our slang—to Cockney origins, but none can explain the sameness of the sound we make with so few regional variations.

A lot of experts have puzzled over Australian speech and wondered why it's much the same, over such a huge continent. John Manifold's wife was an expert on this ... she took a tape-recorder all over Australia, taking down local speech. She told me Tasmanian was slightly different; she'd pinned down some differences between Queensland and Victoria, but she told me the only place that seemed to have a different distinct dialect all of its own (she meant dialect, not simply local words) was the Snowy region of Victoria. Why? As usual, nobody knows.

— *ALAN MARSHALL (1902-84), WRITING OF THE 1950S AND 1960S*

Now and then—but this is rare—one hear such words as 'piper' for paper, 'lydy' for lady, and 'tyble' for table fall from lips,' wrote Mark Twain in 1895. 'There is a superstition prevalent in Sydney that this is an Australianism, but people who have been "home" —as the native reverently and lovingly calls England—know better. It is "costermonger". All over Australia this pronunciation is nearly as common among servants as it is in London among the uneducated and the partially educated ....'

The American visitor had been puzzled when the chambermaid in his Sydney hotel announced one morning: 'The tyble is set, and here is the piper; and the lydy is ready to tell the wyter to bring up the breakfast.'

Arriving in wartime Australia in 1942 an American correspondent described Australians as speaking 'in a monotone, harsh to strange ears, without vibrancy or variety', but found that their 'complete friendliness' eased the ordeal of listening to their voices. A British naval officer in 1941 records that he found our accent odd—apart from that of some Australian officers whom he described as speaking nicely'- because 'they came from Melbourne'. The broad, slow, nasal Australian drawl may soon only be heard outside the cities. Many young Australians nowadays end their sentences on a high, questioning note—the interrogative: a puzzling speech trait some say was once common in Brisbane, but no-one knows why it is now so widespread.

Australian Slanguage

Akubra
Brand of bushman's hat made from rabbit skins; now widely used to describe any form of man's hat.

the Alice
Alice Springs

Anzac
Originally, a soldier of the Australian and New Zealand Army Corps formed in Egypt late in 1914, which first saw action on Gallipoli, 1915; later referred to any Australian or New Zealander who served in World War I, 1914–18, and even to those who served in the Middle East, 1940–42. A convenient collective noun for the forces of both nations.
'Although tarnished over the years, the Australian image of the healthy, bronzed Anzac still lingers as part of our folklore.' SYDNEY MORNING HERALD, *1974.*

she's apples
everything is under control.

arvo
afternoon.

Aussie Rules
Australian Rules (Australian Football League) football.

back-blocks
remote areas; unsuitable land.

bag
to knock or disparage.

bagman
in itinerant worker, mounted; a swagman on a horse.

Bananalander
A Queenslander.

bandicoot
native animal; also 'silly as a bandicoot'.

bangtail muster
cutting the tail hair of cattle or sheep to aid in identifying them when doing a head count.

banker
overflowing river.

Barcoo buster
a westerly gale in Queensland's outback.

Barcoo rot
scurvy-like affliction suffered widely by bush people last century, caused probably by inadequate vitamins.

bare-bellied Joe (or Yoe)
a sheep that has lost its belly wool and is thus faster to shear.

barney
fight or brawl; 'A barney first com-

mences with a little bit of skiting, but calling names is not enough, and so it ends in fighting'. (1858).

barrack
to shout encouragement; to banter.

battler
someone who keeps trying and deserves better of life (as in affectionate term 'Little Aussie Battler').

big noter
a skite; self important.

billabong
A watercourse, often horse-shoe shaped, filled from the overflow from a river.

billy
tin can used for boiling water.

bimbo
an effeminate swaggie.

to put the bite on
to scrounge a loan.

bitser
mongrel dog.

Black Stump
mythical tree stump that marks the end of habitation in the outback; term first used in 1826.

Blinky Bill (and Nutsy)
Dorothy Wall's accident-prone koalas who appeared in the Sunday comics for decades.

bloke
A man; also the 'Bloke': a boss in a shearing shed.

bloody
Widely used descriptive word also known as the Great Australian Adjective. 'The word bloody is a familiar oath in that country. One man will tell you that he married a "bloody young wife", another, a "bloody old one", and a bushranger calls out "Stop, or I'll blow your bloody brains out!" (*TRAVELS IN NEW SOUTH WALES, 1847*)

blow-in
an unexpected guest.

bludger
Someone who does little or nothing and expects to get paid for it.

blue
A quarrel: also nickname for a red-haired person.

blue heeler
Australian cattle dog renowned for its quick reflexes in dodging kicking cattle, and its intelligence and loyalty.

bluey
a blanket; also a parking fine (when they were printed on blue paper).

to hump the bluey
to carry a swag.

boss of the board
supervisor of the shearing shed.

bodgie
worthless; term for an Australian juvenile delinquent in the 1950s.

boggi
Shearer's handpiece, similar in shape to a boggi lizard.

Boggo Road
Boggo Road gaol in Brisbane.

bolter
A runaway convict.

bonzer
terrific; excellent .

boomer
a large kangaroo.

boomerang
Aboriginal weapon that returns to the thrower; thus anything that comes back, as in 'his cheque boomeranged'.

getting the boot
to be sacked.

bot
to sponge off.

back of Bourke
the beginning of the great outback.

bowyang
string that bush workers tied around their trouser legs, some said 'to keep out the snakes'.

broad-guage
In shearing, a 'wide comb' that exceeds 65 mm from outside top to outside bottom tooth; once illegal in Australia, it was also known as the 'New Zealand comb'.

broken-mouthed
An 8-toothed sheep that is losing its teeth and going gummy.

bronze
backside (as in 'get off your bronze!').

brumby
a wild horse named from either booramby (native word for horse) or from James Brumby, an early settler known for his horses.

Buckley's chance
Not much chance at all (as in 'You've got Buckley's chance'!) from either William Buckley, a convict who escaped and lived for 30 years with the Aborigines of Melbourne or from the famous Melbourne store, Buckley & Nunn (as in 'You've got two chances—Buckley's and none!').

Bullamakanka
another mythical region, past the Black Stump or near Woop Woop.

bull dust
fine dust on country roads; also a term for nonsense.

to drop your bundle
to give up.

bunyip
mythical monster said to lurk in waterholes and billabongs; it eats anything.

bushranger
originally a runaway convict (1801); later a mounted and armed robber.

bushwacker
city term for a country person

The Cabbage Patch
Derisive late-19th Century New South Wales term for the junior state, Victoria—because it was small and green, 'and only good for growing vegetables'.

back to the cactus
to return home.

canary
a convict (from his yellow uniform).

the cat
the cat-o-nine-tails.

chalkie
a schoolteacher; also a clerk who used to chalk up the prices at the Stock Exchange.

charlies
women's breasts.

chiack
to banter or tease.

Chesty Bond
Figure introduced by Bond's advertising in 1938 and still used as a trademark; symbol of the Australian male who always fought in his singlet.

chooms
Englishmen.

not much chop
not much good, or no good at all as in 'Mac's no great chop' ('Tom Collins', *Such is Life*, 1904)

clip
all the wool shorn in one shed or on one property.

cobber
a mate 'confidant, closest friend, mate or chum' (term first widely used around 1900).

cobbler
a sheep that is difficult to shear, often wrinkled, and thus usually left until last in the pen.

cockatoo
Australian parrot; also a lookout at an illegal game.

cocky
a small farmer who scratches a living from the soil; a term for farmers in general.

cocky's joy
golden syrup.

colonial
patronizing term used by the British to describe Australians, New Zealanders and Canadians; it lapsed at the end of World War I.

Condamine
cattle bell with a distinctive high note first made in the Condamine region of Queensland.

coo-ee
Aboriginal cry adopted by Europeans as a call of recognition; also 'to be within coo-ee of a place'.

Coolgardie
safe used to keep meat fresh in the bush—it allowed the air to circulate through a wire frame that was kept cool by a dampened cloth.

copper tail
one of the less privileged; the opposite of a silver tail.

the Corner
the area where the borders of New South Wales, Queensland and South Australia meet.

cornstalk
a native-born white Australian, so called 'from the way they shoot up' (term first used around 1827).

corroboree
Aboriginal tribal ceremony.

cove
a bloke, a male.

Cracking hardy
putting on a brave front.

crawler
an obsequious bloke; 'A country [Australia] where the strongest reproach was to be a crawler.' (term first used around 1857).

crook
feeling lousy; sick as a dog (as in 'things are crook in Tallarook').

croppy
an Irish convict of the 1790s and early 1800s, so called because the Irish rebels of 1798 cropped their hair short like the French revolutionaries.

crow-eater
a South Australian (late 19th Century term).

currency
Australian-born (as opposed to Sterling, or British-born).

cut lunch commando
a public servant; a soldier who seldom served in the front lines (used during World War II, 1939–45).

dag
in rural areas: a wag or an amusing person; in cities it means a dull or boring one.

dagging
cutting away the flyblown wool from a sheep's backside.

damper
unleavened bread made from flour and water and baked in the ashes of a camp fire.

dead cert
a certainty; a sure thing.

Dead Heart
The centre of Australia (from Ernest Giles' book of that title, 1906).

deener
one shilling coin in the old currency, superseded by the ten cent piece in 1966.

deucer
a shearer who can shear 200 sheep in a day.

digger
gold miner of the 1850s and 1860s; also the affectionate nickname for Australian or New Zealand soldiers. The word 'Digger' first became generally adopted by troops in both forces in France and Flanders, mid-1917, and was probably first used by New Zealanders whose gum-diggers were well-known for their toughness. Banjo Paterson records New Zealand troops shouting 'Hullo, Diggers!' to Australians in 1914. '"Digger" has taken the place of the time-honoured "Cobber" in the parlance of the Australian soldier".' (January 1918) New Zealand soldiers in the 1939-45 war called themselves 'Digs'; Australians remained Diggers.

dingbat
an idiot; also an army batman.

the dingbats
the delirium tremens (DTs); to go

crazy (also originally a New Zealand phrase).

dingo
native dog, one that can't bark; thus a treacherous man, a coward (as in 'them townies must be a fair lot o' dingoes'). (1908)

dinkum (also *fair dinkum*)
genuine; the real thing; also hard work (as in 'an hour's hard dinkum', Rolf Boldrewood, *Robbery Under Arms* 1882)

donnybrook
a fight (Irish in origin).

drongo
an idiot; slow-witted, as in 'it wasn't his fault he was a drongo'.

dreadnought
a shearer who can shear more than 300 sheep in one day.

drummer
a lazy shearer; in the old days they used to be drummed out of the shed.

'Ducks on the pond!'
warning shout in a shearing shed when women are seen approaching (in other words: 'moderate your language').

duffer
an unproductive mine, as in 'to sink a duffer'; also a cattle thief.

dumper
a large wave that dumps surfers to the bottom.

dunny
an outside lavatory.

ethnic
any immigrant who doesn't speak English (outmoded by the 1990s).

euchred
done in; exhausted.

fair go
call in a two-up game; also a protest or plea for decent treatment, as in 'Fair go!'.

drinking with the flies
drinking alone in a pub.

enzedder
Australian term for a soldier of the New Zealand forces (1914–18)

floater
a meal sold from a stand, now found only in Adelaide—a meat pie floating in a bowl of pea soup, invented by an English cook named Gibbs; it was filling but hardly nourishing

flyer
a female kangaroo (1826); 'The males are called "foresters, and the females "flyers".' (1834)

flying fox
an overhead cable-way often used in mining.

Flying Doctor
the aerial medical service pioneered by the Rev. John Flynn in the outback in the 1920s.

furphy
a rumour (from the wheeled water tanks made by Furphy & Co around which troops gathered in army camps in 1914-15, and from where all rumours flowed).

the 'Gabba
the Queensland Cricket Association ground at Woolongabba.

galah
native bird renowned for its absurd antics, like hanging upside down on telephone wires; thus, a fool.

galoot
an even bigger fool.

galvo
galvanized iron.

the Gap
a sheer cliff near South Head in Sydney and a popular spot for suicides.

garbo
garbage collector.

geebung
an Australian-born money grubber (1859).

the Ghan
famous train running from Port Augusta (South Australia) to Alice Springs.

gibber
a boulder, as in a gibber desert.

to give it a go
to give something a try

goodonyer
term of approval (as in 'good on you').

grasshopper
Canberra term for weekend visitors to the capital: 'they eat everything in sight and never have a drink'

gumsucker
19th century term for a Victorian or an Australian.

up a gumtree
completely lost or confused.

the gun
the top shearer.

gunyah
Aboriginal hut.

coming a gutser
to fall or fail.

hatter
a miner of bushman who worked alone; they became well known for talking to themselves (as in 'mad as a hatter').

giving it the herbs
adding extra power or putting on extra speed (from cooking—adding more herbs).

Hexham greys
Large mosquitoes found in the Hunter River estuary; some legends say they are strong enough to carry off sheep.

hooroo!
Farewell; now almost obsolete.

Hughie
God; when pleading for rain, bushmen cry 'Send her down, Hughie!'.

humpy
Aboriginal dwelling or lean-to.

illywacker
a sharp operator, spieler or confidence man.

jack of it
to be exasperated .

jacking up
objecting.

jackeroo
a city boy or an Englishman working on a property. 'Young gentleman getting the "colonial experience" in the bush are called jackeroos by station hands.' (1873)

jilleroo
a young female version of a jackeroo.

jackass
a kookaburra, renowned for its cackling laugh; someone who laughs at anything.

Jacky
19th century term for an Aborigine

Jimmy Grants
British immigrants, late 19th century.

Joes
Police on the Victorian goldfields named after Governor Joseph Latrobe; also sheep.

Joe Blakes
snakes; also the delirium tremens (DTs), the shakes due to heavy drinking

jumbucks
sheep, from an Aboriginal word for a white mist, which a flock of sheep resembled, first used in 1824 (also jimba, jambock, dombock).

kangaroo
Australia's leaping marsupial and national icon.

Kangaroos
Australia's Rugby League team.

kangaroos in his top paddock
loony; gone in the head.

kelpie
The great Australian sheep dog, bred from short-haired Scotch collies in the 1870s in New South Wales, and named after the Scots term for a spirit or ghost

kipper
an Englishman; an English sailor (naval term).

Kiwi
a New Zealander.

knockabout
a general labourer engaged around a squatter's homestead

knock-back
a refusal for closer intimacy, usually from a woman.

knocker
one who disparages or cuts down others.

Koori people
one of the Aborigines' preferred names for the own people.

lair
a show-off.

to be lambed down
a shearer who is defrauded by publicans after cashing his cheque.

larrikins
noisy lairs, usually irreverent, found in cities.

learner
in shearing, a shearer is regarded as a learner until he has shorn 5,000 sheep.

lurk
a dodge, scheme or dishonourable plot.

mallee
the scrub.

mallee root
tree roots found in Victoria's Mallee region that are long-burning and make a hot fire .

mate
English word for a man's friend that Australians adopted.

mateship
the Australian male's strong trust in his fellow man, more particularly in his close friends. 'What makes Australians unique? Three things: Anzac; Mateship; Ned Kelly.' (Australian writer Russell Braddon, 1988)

matilda
a swag, German in origin (German soldiers in the late-19th century carried a rolled blanket over their shoulders dubbed a 'Matilda'. (Waltzing Matilda: to carry your swag over your shoulder)

merino
the strong Spanish breed of sheep inured to extremes of heat and cold, which when interbred, produced extraordinary amounts of long-fibred wool; the basis of Australia's wealth for more than a century

Pure Merinos
derogatory term for the privileged settlers in early 1800s who benefited from land grants; they predated the squatters.

Mick
an Irish Catholic.

mickey
an unbranded bull calf.

middy
a glass of beer (10 oz in New South Wales, 7 oz in Western Australia), in size between a pony and a schooner ('Why do they call a "pot" a "middy"? Because it's halfway between nothing and a pint.')

Ming
Sir Robert Menzies (whose surname is pronounced 'Mingis' in Scotland), longtime prime minister of Australia (1939–41; 1949–66). He reminded his enemies of the villain of the popular Buck Rogers comic strip of the 1930s, Ming the Merciless

mob
herd of cattle or sheep; group of men or army unit, as in 'What mob are you from'.

putting the mockers on
wishing someone bad luck.

molly dook
a left-hander.

monte
a sure thing (in betting).

mopoke
native bird with a mournful cry; hence a dreary individual.

motzer
a large win.

mulga
the scrub or the outback.

Murrumbidgee Whaler
A lazy swagman, one who by repute

spends six months of the year snoozing under gumtrees on the banks of the Murrumbidgee instead of working.

nasho
a National Service man.

Game as Ned Kelly
courageous; the ultimate Australian compliment.

the Never Never
the far outback, the back of beyond (from Mrs Aeneas Gunn's book We of the Never Never, 1908).

new chum
an English immigrant, a term widely used at the turn of the century.

New South
Truck drivers' term for New South Wales.

keeping nit
keeping a lookout.

no-hoper
a horse or a man who proves hopeless.

nong
an idiot.

ocker
an ill-educated Australian slob similar to an English alf.

offsider
originally a bullock driver's assistant, walking on the offside of the team.

the outback
the parched and uninhabited regions of Australia

on the pea
gone crazy (the result of sheep eating the poisonous Darling Pea plant).

on the pear
seasonal work eradicating prickly pear by poison from farmland.

Piccadilly bushman
An Australian businessman who lives in London.

piccaninny
West Indian name for a baby, applied by whites to Aboriginal children.

Pig-iron Bob
name bestowed on R.G. Menzies when, as federal attorney-general, he invoked federal powers to break the waterside workers' embargo on exporting pig-iron to Japan in 1935.

rough end of the pineapple
getting the rough end of a deal; poor treatment.

pink-eye
Aboriginal term for walkabout.

pinking
shearing the sheep so close that their skin shows.

plonk
cheap wine (probably from 'vin blanc' drunk by the diggers in France).

tall poppy
a successful person—in Australia widely resented, particularly if he or she is conceited

pozzie
army term for a dug-out safe from shells.

stirring the possum
creating a bit of mischief to get some reaction.

coming the raw prawn
asking too much of someone.

the Push
a group of larrikins in Sydney's working class Rocks area; also a libertarian group of hard-drinking pseudo-intellectuals who flourished in Sydney in the 1950s and 1960s.

Rafferty's Rules
making up the rules as you go along.

rainbows
Australian Imperial Forces (AIF) term for reinforcements or for units who arrived overseas later in the war (as in 'You always see a rainbow after the storm').

not a brass razoo
skint; not a cent in your pocket.

rye-buck
feeling tops; in good spirits.

ringer
the fastest shearer.

ringbark
to kill a tree by stripping off a ring of bark around the tree.

rort
a good lurk until its discovered (as in 'rorting the system' in tax evasion); also having a good time (as in 'the party was a good rort').

rouseabout
the worker in a shearing sheds who cleans up; an unskilled worker.

saddling paddock
a place to pick up women; originally the bar in the Theatre Royal, Melbourne.

sandgroper
a Western Australian.

sandy blight
trachoma, once a common eye disease.

schooner
a large glass of beer (15 oz in New South Wales).

the scrub
the remote areas of the bush; areas of stunted trees and poor soil.

settlers' friends
greenhide and stringybark, which made useable rope and twine.

sheila
an Australian female; not derogatory at all, but hardly used any more (from the Irish word for a girl—shelagh)

shepherd's companion
the willy wagtail, which often rides on the sheep's back pulling out wool for its nest.

shiralee
a swag

shouting
paying for drinks all around—an Australian custom that confuses visitors as in 'Is it my shout or yours?').

six bob-a-day tourists
Australian soldiers in the 1st and 2nd AIF; they received six shillings a day as a private, the highest pay (in 1914) of any troops in the war, though close to an Australian worker's average earnings.

skite
a show-off, a boaster.

open slather
no restrictions, an open go.

the Big Smoke
Aboriginal name for towns (used as early as 1848)

smoko
a regular break in the working day.

snagger
a rough shearer.

spider
in Victoria a glass of lemonade with a scoop of ice cream added.

a good sort
a good looking female.

southerly buster
the cool breeze that often whips up at dusk after a day of heat wave in Sydney during summer.

the Speewah
mythical station in the Outback where Crooked Mick hangs out, figuring often in the humorous writings of Alan Marshall and Bill Wannan.

the Speck
mainland term for Tasmania.

come in spinner!
shout in the game of two-up; also the title of a famous novel set in Sydney in the 1940s made into a TV series in 1990.

spruiker
a persuasive talker, like a spieler at a sideshow.

squatter
originally an American term for settlers in the backblocks; in Australia, the settlers who took up land—to which they had no title—as sheep runs from the 1820s to the 1840s establishing themselves as 'the squattocracy'.

sundowner
a swagman or a bagman who arrived at a station at dusk for a bed and a meal, when it was too late to ask them to do any work. They usually departed at dawn.

swy
the game of two-up.

Thommo's
famous gambling den in Sydney that survived for decades, close to police headquarters.

The Top End
Northern Australia.

traveller
a swagman.

trey bit
a three-penny piece.

tucker
food.

tyke
a Catholic.

waler
a horse from New South Wales, a favourite of Australian mounted troops.

walkabout
Aboriginal custom of going bush, to renew contact with the land.

on the wallaby (track)
humping your bluey on the bush roads.

walloper
Policeman.

waratah
state emblem of New South Wales—a brilliantly coloured red flower.

warrigal
Aboriginal term for untamed; often applied to dogs or horses.

the Wet
period of torrential monsoonal rain in summer in northern Australia.

widgie
a female bodgie.

willy willy
Aboriginal for spiralling winds.

wombat
slow-moving, inoffensive native marsupial of nocturnal habits; anyone who has the same characteristics.

wowser
self-appointed guardians of morality; killjoy.

Woop Woop
Another mythical town somewhere near Bullamakanka.

yabbie
freshwater crayfish found in creeks.

Yacker (yakka)
Talk or conversation; also work (as in 'hard yakker').

yowie
mythical ape-like creature about as believable as a bunyip.

zack
a sixpenny bit

Humping the Bluey

It is just about the best life that a fellow could wish for, 'carrying his swag' or 'humping the bluey' as the colonials call it, going all over the country with all your belongings strapped on your back—that is, your blanket, a change of underclothing 'if you have got any', and a billy can ...

— *JOHN SIMPSON KIRKPATRICK, 1910*

Remittance Man

Banished to the Antipodes by their scandalized families, the 'remittance men' were a cross-section of battlers, n'er-do-wells, hapless younger sons of the British aristocracy and outright rogues. Often an object of scorn or amusement to Cornstalks, the 'remittance men' were literally paid by their parents or relations to stay away from home. The nephew of the Marquess of Salisbury (Britain's prime minister in the 1890s), Cecil Balfour, who had bounced cheques all over England, died of drink in Australia at an early age.

Gentleman George in his youthful days was the pride of the Eighth Hussars,
He's only a bronzed old teamster now in the land of the red galahs ...

— *ANONYMOUS*

New Chums

To the Australian-born—the Cornstalks or 'natives'—from the 1830s on, already ferociously proud of their land and their own strange accent, all English migrants were 'New Chums', whether they were high-born or working class. The term was superseded by the descriptive 'Pommie' early in the twentieth century, but still occasionally surfaces in conversation.

Many young well-born Englishmen preferred to work for a living and took to Australian ways with gusto. Charles Dickens, Charles Kingsley and Anthony Trollope all had sons who settled in Australia. George Morrison recalls Lord Gladstone's nephew cattle-droving to Darwin in the 1880s.

The Great Australian Adjective

'Alas, alas, the word "bloody" is on every lip and in every speech,' wrote the English war correspondent (and future Poet Laureate of England) John Masefield in March 1917, in a letter to his wife. He had been posted to the Australian sector and had followed the advance of the Anzac Corps as the Germans withdrew to the Hindenburg Line, leaving the city of Bapaume behind them.

'It is said that an Australian patrol first found that Bapaume was empty,' Masefield wrote. 'The officer in charge of it came back to his Colonel and said:

' "They've hopped the bloody twig. They're out of it."

'Colonel: "Who? The Boche? Out of Bapaume?"

'Officer: "Yes. The bloody place is empty."

'Colonel: "You're a bloody liar."

'Officer: "Bloody liar be damned. You give me the bloody battalion and I'll take the bloody place right now!"'

— *John Masefield, 1917*

Which he did. Bapaume—the objective of the great Somme offensive of 1916 with its 450,000 British and Dominion casualties—was entered by a patrol of Victorians, with barely a shot fired.

'One of the witnesses, a fettler, came into the inquiry room and tripped on a mat and said, "What bastard put that bloody mat there?" and he slung it out the door "Bull" Mitchell on the inquiry board said to him, "None of your bloody swearing here, you just remember that you're on a bloody inquiry, and bloody well behave yourself."'

— *from* Folklore of Australia's Railwaymen, *1969, Patsy Adam Smith.*

Anzac Vocabulary

'The stay in Egypt naturally meant an influx of Egyptian or Australianized Egyptian words. "Saida" (or Sayeeda) became the common greeting "Good-day", "good-night", "good-bye", all became "sayeeda". The term passed very quickly to the Australians themselves and to their distinctive hat. "Where's your sayeeds hat?"

'"Bukshee" is another importation from the Egyptian. "Backsheesh" is "something for nothing"; "alms". The children—ay, and men and women, too—beseech the foreigners for "backsheesh"— a gift, a tip. So a "bukshee feed" would be a meal scored for nothing or at someone else's expense. "Bukshee stripes" betoken the fact that the wearer holds a certain rank but doesn't draw the equivalent pay.'

— *from the* Anzac Memorial Book, *1920*

Comic Characters

Ginger Meggs first appeared as a character in a comic strip by J.C. Bancks called *Us Fellas* in 1921. 'Ginge' quickly became the leading character and took over the strip, which was renamed as Ginger Meggs in 1939. His mates, Ocker and Benny, and their battles with Tiger Kelly, later drawn by Jim Hensley, delighted two generations of Australia.

Ginger's only rival was Fatty Finn, a strip by Syd Nicholls, which began in 1923 and lasted until 1977.

Blinky Bill and Nutsy, the bushland heroes of a strip by Dorothy Wall, a New Zealander who moved to Sydney when she was twenty, first appeared in book form in 1933 and was the first of a series of titles.

Snugglepot and Cuddlepie were the creation of May Gibbs (1876–1969), who was born in England but raised in Western Australia. The first book of their adventures appeared in 1918—and their complete adventures in 1940—but they first appeared in May Gibbs' first book, *The Gumnut Babies*, published in 1916.

Bib 'n Bub, May Gibbs' comic strip, was published from 1924 to 1967.

The Magic Pudding, written and illustrated by Norman Lindsay, was published as a book in 1918. Recounting the misadventures of Bill Barnacle, Bunyip Bluegum and Sam Sawnoff in their attempts to keep the cantankerous magic pudding from the paws of the hungry, it has never been out of print.

Barry McKenzie, hero of a comic strip (for adults) detailing the exploits of a naïve, beer-guzzling Australian marooned in cynical, world-weary London, was invented by the satirist Barry Humphries (creator of Edna Everage) and drawn by Nicholas Garland. It was first published in the London magazine *Private Eye* in 1963 and appeared in book form in his homeland in 1971. 'Bazza' was as popular in England—where his crude but funny behaviour confirmed readers' perceptions of the typical Aussie—as in Australia, where he inspired two films.

The Faces on the $100 Note: Melba

She was the first Australian to win international renown on the stage or off it, and she had a gift for strong language that would turn a bullocky pale. She was born Helen (Nellie) Porter Mitchell, the daughter of a Scottish building contractor in 1861 in the well-to-do suburb of Richmond, Victoria, and educated in Melbourne where she received tuition in singing. Her talent as a soprano was furthered by private lessons in 1879, but in 1882 she accompanied her widowed father to Mackay, Queensland, where she married a sugar planter, Charles Armstrong, in December of that year. After giving birth to a son she left her husband and returned to Melbourne early in 1884, resumed her singing lessons, and sailed with her father for London in 1886. In Paris she was trained by Madame Cecchi and, as Madame Melba (naming herself after her birthplace), made her operatic debut in *Rigoletto* in Brussels in 1887. It was a triumph, and the beginning of her remarkable career that carried her to London, Milan, Paris, St Petersburg and the United States. She toured Australia in 1902–03, performing to overjoyed audiences, and thereafter made Australia her home while touring the opera houses of the world. To Dame Clara Butt, who was also visiting Australia, Melba, who had the Australian facility for not beating round the bush, told her ,'It's a wonderful country, and you'll have a good time,' but advised her: 'All I can say is—sing 'em muck. It's all they can understand!' Melba was created a Dame of the British Empire in 1918 for her services to her homeland and her love of Australia was passionate, but some Australians were disconcerted by Melba's judgement of their cultural taste when Butt's book appeared in 1928—Melba denied using the words and threatened a libel action! Melba died in Sydney in February 1931 and is buried at Lilydale, her home north of Melbourne. Her life has inspired numerous biographies and a Hollywood film.

... and Monash

Only eight months after Melba died, Australians mourned the passing (in October 1931) of their greatest soldier, General Sir John Monash, a man recognized as one of the few Great War commanders with genius. He, too, was born in Melbourne, in 1865, and while studying civil engineering at Melbourne University worked for Nellie Mitchell's father, David Mitchell. He met Nellie but found her somewhat coarse.

Monash was the only son of German-Jewish immigrants and by dint of hard work and brilliant gifts was a millionaire and a pillar of the Melbourne establishment when war came in 1914. A colonel in the militia who had never heard a shot fired in anger, overage and overweight, a cultured man with a love of soldiering but a hatred of war, he nevertheless volunteered for overseas service and commanded the 4th Brigade on Gallipoli with distinction, but was not to enter the fighting again until June 1917, when his command of the 3rd Division at Messines was recognized as brilliant. Monash was appalled by the British strategy (and the stupidity of their generals) on the Western Front that resulted in hideously heavy casualties for little gain, and in May 1918 was given command of the entire Australian corps, which he led in a series of short, sharp, decisive battles which he planned with extraordinary attention to

detail, from the great offensive by the Australians and Canadians at Amiens on 8 August 1918 ('the Black day of the German Army') to October 1918, when the Australians were instrumental in breaking the Hindenburg Line. Monash looked on the Diggers like a proud father, and they revered him. Perhaps only in Australia could a German Jewish civilian rise to supreme command of an army. His face appears with Melba's on the new $100 banknote, in itself testament to the high place these two figures occupy in our short history.

13: *Conflict and Strife*

Eureka Stockade, 1854

The flame that exploded into open rebellion at Ballarat had been burning for years, for all to see, on the Victorian gold-fields.

The diggers—men from all nations who had flocked to Melbourne and taken the dusty road to Ballarat with few possessions other than what they carried—were outraged by the heavy licence fee dictated by the government, an imposition that few of them could afford and most successfully evaded. A new governor, Charles Hotham, ordered the fees to be collected. Constant raids on miners' camps by the troopers (the 'Traps' or 'Joes') inflamed feelings and brutal treatment of licence evaders were common. The licence system was a gross injustice; most authorities agreed about that; and most agreed that the presence of so many Irish among the diggers made an act of defiance inevitable.

When a digger was killed by the owner of the Eureka Hotel and the publican (whom many reviled as a confederate of the corrupt gold commissioners) escaped punishment, a mob of diggers burned the pub down in revenge in October 1854. From that moment on, events moved swiftly to a climax. Several diggers were

arrested. To a protesting mob of their mates, the commissioner read the *Riot Act* and called in military detachments.

To force the diggers to pay their licence fees, the government decided to use force. While the mass of the diggers began forming groups and rumours of unrest reached Melbourne, the government ordered two regiments and police reinforcements to Ballarat. On 29 November 1854, nearly 12,000 diggers gathered for a mass meeting on Bakery Hill to decide their action. Here the Irishman Peter Lalor and two equally impassioned companions, the German, Vern, and the red-haired Italian, Raffaello Carboni (or Carboni Raffaello, as he called himself in his famous account of the uprising), called on the men to stand together and resist the government by force. Under a cloudless blue sky and a blue-and-white flag of their own devising—the 'Southern Cross' flag—hundreds burned their licences and took an oath to fight for justice. Arms were handed out.

This was treason. Men called not only for the abolition of fees but for manhood suffrage and short parliaments and none shouted for these more loudly than those who had left oppressive homelands for freedom in Australia. Eureka would become a test case for freedom, a battle fought on behalf of future generations of Australians by foreign-born men.

NOT TRANSFERABLE.

£2 £2

GOLD LICENSE.—THREE MONTHS

No. 134. 17th October,

The Bearer, *Carboni Raffaello*, having paid the Sum of TWO POUNDS on the General Revenue of the Colony, I hereby License him to mine or dig for Gold, reside at, or follow any trade or calling, except that of Storekeeper, on such Crown Lands within the Victoria as shall be assigned to him for these purposes by any one duly authorised in that behalf.

This License to be in force for THREE Months ending 16th January, and no

REGULATIONS TO BE OBSERVED BY THE PERSONS DIGGING FOR GOLD OR OTHER EMPLOYED AT THE GOLD FIELDS.

1. This License is to be carried on the person, to be produced whenever demanded by any Commissioner Officer, or other duly authorised person.
2. It is especially to be observed that this License is not transferable, and that the holder of a transferred is liable to the penalty for a misdemeanour.
3. No Mining will be permitted where it would be destructive of any line of road which it is necessary and which shall be determined by any Commissioner, nor within such distance round any store or dwelling necessary to reserve for access to it.
4. It is enjoined that all persons on the Gold Fields maintain a due and proper observance of Sundays.
5. The extent of claim allowed to each Licensed Miner is twelve feet square, or 144 square feet. &c., &c.

V. R.

Colonial Secretary's Office Melbourne, 13th December,

£400 REWARD

Whereas Two Persons of the Names of

Lawlor & Black

LATE OF BALLAARAT,

Did on or about the 13th day of November last, at that place, use certain TREASONABLE AND SEDITIOUS LANGUAGE, And incite Men to take up Arms, with a view to make war against Our Sovereign Lady the QUEEN:

NOTICE IS HEREBY GIVEN

That a Reward of £200 will be paid to any person or persons giving such information as may lead to the Apprehension of either of the abovenamed parties.

DESCRIPTIONS.

LAWLOR.—Height 5 ft. 11 in., age 35, hair dark brown, whiskers dark brown and shaved under the chin, moustache, long face, rather good looking, and is a well made man.
BLACK.—Height over 6 feet, straight figure, slight build, bright red hair worn in general rather long, brushed backwards, red and large whiskers, meeting under the chin, blue eyes, large thin nose, ruddy complexion, and rather small mouth.

By His Excellency's Command,

WILLIAM C. HAINES

BY AUTHORITY: JOHN FERRES, GOVERNMENT PRINTER, MELBOURNE.

On 30 November, the military made a move against the stockade and shots were fired at them—open rebellion had come. Captain Thomas, commanding the units of the 12th and 40th Regiments and the police troopers (about 276 men) resolved to wait until the morning of Sunday 3 December, hoping that the increasing number of diggers deserting the cause would result in Lalor's bloodless surrender. Many of the English and Scottish Protestant diggers, fearing a bloody outcome, had indeed melted away, leaving a hard core of only 150 diggers, mainly Irishmen. But the Southern Cross flag still flew defiantly over the stockade and no attempt was made by Lalor's men to parley or disband.

Just before dawn on Sunday 3 December, the redcoats and troopers moved silently against the stockade, hoping to take the rebels by surprise. Before they reached the timbers they were swept by musket shots, but the battle was over in fifteen minutes. Storming the defences with fixed bayonets the troops fought briefly without quarter, killing or wounding 34 of the diggers at the cost of 15 casualties. Peter Lalor, who was severely wounded in the arm but carried from the scene by companions and hidden by them, maintained that the police, but not the soldiers, continued to shoot down diggers even when the latter had thrown down their crude weapons. The troops jubilantly felled the flagpole and trampled the Southern Cross flag in the bloodied dirt. Of the 14 diggers whose bodies lay on Bakery Hill, many of them terribly mutilated by musket shot and sword; eight were Irish, two were German, one an Englishman, one a Scot, one Australian-born. Eight more wounded rebels later also died.

Governor Hotham's last mistake was to order 13 of the ringleaders tried for High Treason. When Lalor—with one arm amputated—and his companions stood for trial before an Irish judge (appropriately, on 1 April 1855) all were acquitted. Licence fees were abolished. Sweeping reforms were made to the electoral boundaries

and suffrage, and eight goldfields representatives were admitted to the legislative assembly in 1855. Property qualifications were changed so that men 'without property' could stand for election. By 1857, the vote was extended to almost all adult males in Victoria (one year after South Australia had done so) and by the decade's end New South Wales and Queensland had followed suit. The secret ballot (the 'Victorian ballot') was introduced, making Australia one of the most democratic societies in the world. Though the majority of Victorians had little sympathy with the Eureka Rebellion, the iniquities of autocratic rule had been exposed. If Australia has been free of bloody confrontation between government and citizens, much is due to the lessons learned from Eureka. Peter Lalor, who emerged as a strong political leader, was later offered a knighthood; he refused it. His grandson and namesake, a captain in the Australian Imperial Forces, carried Peter Lalor's sword at the landing on Gallipoli on 25 April 1915 and was killed in the first day of fighting.

A Ballad of Eureka

This ballad was one of Victor Daley's best known works. Born in
Ireland in 1858 Daley immigrated to Australia in 1878 and wrote
under the pen-name 'Creeve Rowe'. He died in 1905.

Stand up, my young Australian,
  In the brave light of sun,
  And hear how Freedom's battle,
  Was in the old days lost—and won.
  The blood burns in my veins, boy,
  As it did in years of yore,
  Remembering Eureka,
  And the men of 'fifty-four.

The old times were the grand times,
  And to me the past appears,
  As rich as seas at sunset,
  With its many-coloured years;
  And like a lonely island,
  Aglow in sunset light,
  One day stands out in splendour—
  The day of the Good Fight.

Where Ballarat the Golden
  On her throne sits like a Queen,
  Ten thousand tents were shining
  In the brave days that have been.
  There dwelt the stalwart diggers,
  When our hearts with hope were
  high ...
  The stream of Life ran brimming
  In that golden time gone by.

They came from many countries,
  And far islands in the main,
  And years shall pass and vanish,
  Ere their like are seen again.
  Small chance was there for weak-
  lings,
  With these men of iron core,
  Who worked and played like giants
  In the year of 'fifty-four

The tyrants of the goldfields,
  Would not let us live in peace;
  They harried us and chased us,
  With their horse and foot police.

Each man must show his licence
  When they chose, by fits and starts:
  They tried to break our spirits,
  And they almost broke our hearts.

We wrote a Declaration
  In the store of Shanahan,
  Demanding Right and Justice,
  And we signed it, man by man,
  And unto Charles Hotham,
  Who was then Lord of High,
  We sent it; Charles Hotham
  Sent a regiment in reply.

There comes a time to all men,
  When submission is a sin;
  We made a bonfire brave, and
  Flung our licences therein.
  Our hearts with scorn and anger,
  Burned more fiercely than the flame,
  Full well we knew our peril,
  But we dared it all the same.

On Bakery Hill the Banner,
  Of the Southern Cross flew free;
  Then up rose Peter Lalor,
  And with lifted hand spake he:
  'We swear by God above us,
  While we live to work and fight,
  For Freedom and for Justice,
  For our Manhood and our Right.'

Then, on the bare earth kneeling,
  As on a chapel-floor,
  Beneath the sacred Banner,
  One and all, that oath we swore;
  And some of those who swore it,
  Were like straws upon a flood,
  But there were men who swore it,
  And who sealed it with their blood.

We held a stern War Council,
    For in bitter mood were we,
    With Vern and Hayes and Humffray,
    Brady, Ross, and Kennedy,
    And fire-eyed Raffaello,
    Who was brave as steel, though
    small—
    But gallant Peter Lalor,
    Was the leader of us all.

Pat Curtain we made captain,
    Of our Pikemen, soon enrolled,
    And Ross, the tall Canadian,
    Was our standard-bearer bold.
    He came from where St Lawrence,
    Flows majestic to the main;
    But the River of St Lawrence,
    He would never see again.

Then passed along the order,
    That a fortress should be made,
    And soon, with planks and palings,
    We constructed the Stockade.
    We worked in teeth-set silence,
    For we knew what was in store:
    Sure never men defended,
    Such a feeble fort before.

All day the German blacksmith,
    At his forge wrought fierce and
    fast;
    All day the gleaming pike-blades,
    At his side in piles were cast;
    All day the diggers fitted,
    Blade to staff with stern goodwill,
    Till all men, save the watcher,
    Slept upon the fatal hill.

The night fell cold and dreary,
    And the hours crawled slowly by.
    Deep sleep was all around me,
    But a sentinel was I.
    And then the moon grew ghostly,
    And I saw the grey dawn creep,
    A wan and pallid phantom,
    O'er the Mount of Warrenheip.

When over the dark mountain,
    Rose the red rim of the sun,
    Right sharply in the stillness,
    Rang our picket's warning gun.
    And scarce had died the echo,
    Ere, of all our little host,
    Each man had grasped his weapon,
    And each man was at his post.

The foe came on in silence,
    Like an army of the dumb;
    There was no blare of trumpet,
    And there was no tap of drum.
    But ever they came onward,
    And I thought, with indrawn
    breath,
    The Redcoats looked like Murder,
    And the Blackcoats looked like
    Death.

Our gunners, in their gun-pits,
    That were near the palisade,
    Fired fiercely, but the Redcoats,
    Fired as if upon parade.
    Yet, in the front rank leading,
    On his men with blazing eyes,
    The bullet of a digger,
    Struck down valiant Captain Wise.

Then 'Charge!' cried Captain Thomas,
    And with bayonets fixed they
    came,
    The palisade crashed inwards,
    Like a wall devoured by flame.
    I saw our gallant gunners,
    Struggling vainly, backward reel,
    Before that surge of scarlet,
    All alive with stabbing steel.

There Edward Quinn of Cavan,
    Samuel Green the Englishman,
    And Haffele the German,
    Perished, fighting in the van.
    And with them William Quinlan,
    Fell while battling for the Right,
    The first Australian Native,
    In the first Australian fight.

But Robertson the Scotchman,
  In his gripping Scottish way,
  Caught by the throat a Redcoat,
  And upon that Redcoat lay.
  They beat the Scotchman's head in,
  Smiting hard with butt of gun,
  And slew him—but the Redcoat
  Died before the week was done.

These diggers fought like heroes,
  Charged to guard a kingdom's gate.
  But vain was all their valour,
  For they could not conquer Fate.
  The searchers for the wounded
  Found them lying side by side.
  They lived good mates together,
  And good mates together died.

Then Pater Lalor, gazing
  On the fight with fiery glance,
  His lion-voice uplifted,
  Shouting, 'Pikemen, now advance!'
  A bullet struck him, speaking,
  And he fell as fall the dead;
  The fight had lost its leader,
  And the pikemen broke and fled.

The battle was not over,
  For there stood upon the hill,
  A little band of diggers,
  Fighting desperately still,
  With pistol, pike, and hayfork,
  Against bayonet and gun.
  There was no madder combat,
  Ever seen beneath the sun.

Then Donaghey and Dimond,
  And Pat Gittins fighting fell,
  With Thaddeus Moore, and
  Reynolds:
  And the muskets rang their knell,
  And staring up at Heaven,
  As if watching his soul's track,
  Shot through his heart so merry,
  Lay our jester 'Happy Jack'.

The sky grew black above us,
  And the earth below was red,
  And, oh, our eyes were burning,
  As we gazed upon our dead.
  On came the troopers charging,
  Valiant cut-throats of the Crown,
  And wounded men and dying
  Flung their useless weapons down.

The bitter fight was ended,
  And, with cruel coward-lust,
  They dragged our sacred banner,
  Through the stockade's bloody dust.
  But, patient as the gods are,
  Justice counts the years and waits—
  That banner now waves proudly,
  Over six Australian States.

I said, my young Australian,
  That the fight was lost —and won—
  But, oh, our hearts were heavy
  At the setting of the sun.
  Yet, ere the year was over,
  Freedom rolled in like a flood:
  They gave us all we asked for—
  When we asked for it in blood.

God rest you, Peter Lalor!
  For you were a whiteman whole;
  A sword blade in the sunlight,
  Was your bright and gallant soul.
  And God reward you kindly,
  Father Smith, alive or dead:
  'Twas you that give him shelter
  When a price was on his head.

Within the Golden City,
  In the place of peace profound,
  The Heroes sleep. Tread softly:
  'Tis Australia's Holy Ground.
  And evermore Australia,
  Will keep green in our heart's core,
  The memory of Lalor
  And the men of 'fifty-four.

— VICTOR DALEY (1858–1905)

Southern Cross

The constellation of stars only seen in the southern hemisphere has been adopted by Australia and New Zealand as their symbol and appears as stars on a blue background on both nations' national flags. It appeared on the flags of the Australian patriots in the 1840s, and most famously on the digger's flag at Eureka (the tattered banner now hangs in the Ballarat Museum and Art Gallery). In 1967, the Southern Cross replaced the cross of St George on the White Ensign of the Royal Australian Navy.

'Blood on the Wattle'

This famous phrase came from a line of Henry Lawson's poem Freedom on the Wallaby, published in 1891, at the beginning of a decade of social strife:

So we must fly a rebel flag,
As others did before us,
And we must sing a rebel song,
And join in rebel chorus.
We'll make the tyrants feel the sting,
O' those that they would throttle;
They needn't say the fault is ours,
If blood should stain the wattle.

The Shearers' Strike

Australia had ridden to prosperity on the sheep's back for nearly a century before strife occurred between station owners and shearers.

By the late 1880s, only 400 of the 3,000 shearing sheds on properties ranging the length of eastern Australia were not 'union sheds', for William Guthrie Spence had been tireless in promoting the cause of unionism among rural workers. The shearers' strike began in Queensland in 1884 when shearers refused to accept a cut in wages or to let non-unionist shearers onto properties. If some sneaked through the strikers' cordon they were dunked in the water tanks.

The pastoralists, pleading low returns on wool, refused to negotiate and the Queensland Government, alarmed by the loss to the colony's revenues if wool could not be got to markets, sent in the militia to escort non-unionists to the sheds. In March 1891, the strikers at Clermont clashed with police and the colony's newspapers spoke of insurrection. Next month, police arrested a number of leaders at the strikers' camp at Barcaldine and sentenced twelve of them—under an archaic law—to three years' gaol for unlawful assemblage.

The colony appeared to many to be in a state of siege, the strikers—now well armed—vowing to fight if the army moved against them. The shearers finally gave in as the 1890s wore on, but only the advent of the Commonwealth arbitration system managed to restore stability to the industry in the early years of the new century.

The Turbulent Decade: the 1890s

First came the boom, then came the bust. The 1880s were prosperous years for businessmen and bankers, speculators and swindlers. The Australian colonies celebrated the first century of British civilization in the antipodes with a spending spree that by decade's end seemed to be getting out of control. 'In the late 1880s and early 1890s the whips of adversity lashed the backs of the Australian colonists,' wrote an American historian. 'At some point, not precisely identified, but along in the 1880s, investment of capital for development, both on private and public account, passed from sound investment to over-capitalization . . . and thence into rank speculation.'

The growth in building, railways construction and pastoral investments could not be sustained. Three million colonists by the late 1880s owed a total of £150 million to British banks. When British investors panicked—and who could blame them—and withdrew funding, the results were calamitous. Banks crashed, speculators were wiped out and recession and then the Depression followed, making the 1890s a dark decade in Australia's history. This was the decade of the great maritime strike, the birth of the Australian Labor Party (1890) and strident nationalist and republican sentiment.

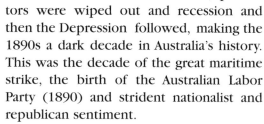

The Star of Australasia

Henry Lawson, in one of his many gloomy moments in 1895 (during the depths of the 1890s Depression, a time of strikes, union battles and the campaign for Federation), felt that Australia would never achieve a sense of nationhood before it went through the flames of war:

We boast no more of our bloodless flag, that rose from a nation's slime;
Better a shred of a deep-dyed rag from the storms of the olden time.
From grander clouds in our 'peaceful skies' than ever there were before
I tell you the Star of the South shall rise— in the lurid clouds of war . . .

— *FROM HENRY LAWSON'S* THE STAR OF AUSTRALASIA, *HENRY LAWSON.*

The Union Boy

When I first arrived in Quirindi, those girls they jumped with joy,
Saying one unto the other, 'Here comes a union boy!

'We'll treat him to a bottle, and likewise to a dram,
Our hearts we'll freely give, too, to all staunch union men.'

I had not long been in Quirindi, not one week, two or three,
When a handsome pretty fair maid she fell in love with me.

She introduced me to her mother as a loyal union man,
  'Oh mother, dearest mother, now he's gently joined the gang!'

'Oh daughter, dearest daughter, of this can never be,
  For four years ago-oh he scabbed it at Forquadee.'

'Oh mother, dearest mother, now the truth to you I'll tell,
  He's since then joined the union, and the country knows it
  well.'

'Now Fred, you've joined the union, so stick to it like glue,
  For the scabs that were upon your back, they're now but only
  few.

'And if ever you go blacklegging or scabbing it likewise,
  It's with my long, long fingernails I'll scratch out both your eyes.

'I'll put you to every cruelty, I'll stretch you in a vice,
  I'll cut you up in a hay machine and sell you for Chinese rice.'

Come all you young and old men, oh, wherever you may be,
  Oh it's hoist-oh the flag-oh, the flag of unity!

Then scabbing in this country will soon be at an end,
  And I pray that one and all of you will be staunch union men.

— *Traditional*

Rothbury

Oh Norman Brown, oh Norman Brown
  The murdering coppers they shot you down,
  They shot you down in Rothbury town,
  To live forever, Norman Brown ...

— *Anonymous*

Norman Brown was the only fatality of the Rothbury coal miners' strike but five others fell wounded when police opened fire on the crowds in November 1929. The New South Wales government's attempt to reopen the mines with non-union labour had led to bloodshed—'something unusual in Australian industry history,' said the miners' federation. Within weeks, miners gathered to form a workers' army to fight, 'our capitalist class enemy'. Rothbury was Australia's grim introduction to the Depression.

  Australia's economic state was worsening long before the Wall Street Crash of 28th October 1929, which precipitated the world economic depression—'the Slump' that was to last almost an entire decade. On 30th October 1929 , the new Labor prime minister, Jimmy Scullin, who had taken office only one week before, announced a conference to draw together the striking coal miners and mine-owners of Rothbury in the Hunter Valley.

In November 1929, talks broke down and the New South Wales government announced that it would run the mines itself, if necessary with non-union labour. On 16th December, an army of 8,000 striking miners were camped at Rothbury, and 3,000 of them smashed down the mine's gates, hurling stones at the police on guard. One policeman shouted 'Out with your guns and into them!'; another cried 'No, don't fire!' but several of them fired. Three miners were wounded and others were bashed to the ground by truncheons.

At the mine head, a mob of miners refused to retreat and five police opened fire, hitting another three. One of them, Norman Brown, later died in Maitland Hospital. His death gave the strikers a martyr for their grievances, and non-union workers were set upon and bashed. Refusing to bend to the strikers, the New South Wales government held out, until on 22nd May the coal miners—deprived of the dole and starving—agreed to return to work. The wounds remained deep.

The 'Big Fella'

John Thomas Lang (1876–1975) was one of the stormiest Labor leaders of them all. Born in Sydney of Irish stock he was elected to State parliament in 1913 and led Labor to victory in 1925. As premier for just two years he introduced child endowment and widows' pensions, restored the 44-hour week and abolished fees for secondary education—among other extraordinary reforms. Elected premier again in 1930, he was confronted by the onset of the world economic depression and proposed in February 1931 to cease payment of interest on British loans and reduce interest payments on local loans—moves

that angered conservatives already fearful of a socialist takeover and which led to the growth of a semi-fascist 'New Guard' to oppose him. At the opening of the Sydney Harbour Bridge in February 1932 a New Guard officer on horseback cut the ribbon with his sword before Lang could do the honours. In May, the governor sacked Lang for refusing to remit money to the federal government, sparking a crisis that threatened to spill over into violence. In elections held soon afterward Lang was defeated. Lang was expelled from the Australian Labor Party in 1943 but readmitted in 1971, just before his death, when he was already a living legend. He died an embittered man. He was a brother-in-law of Henry Lawson (both men had married Bredt sisters) and often had to see the writer safely home in a cab.

The 'Big Fella' was a term also extended to Gough Whitlam, Australia's immensely tall Labor Prime Minister from 1972 to 1975. Like Lang he was dismissed from office by the monarch's representative. Whitlam too was a reformer, but unlike Lang, he never succumbed to bitterness; his caustic anger at the time of his dismissal was enough, and he had too great a heart.

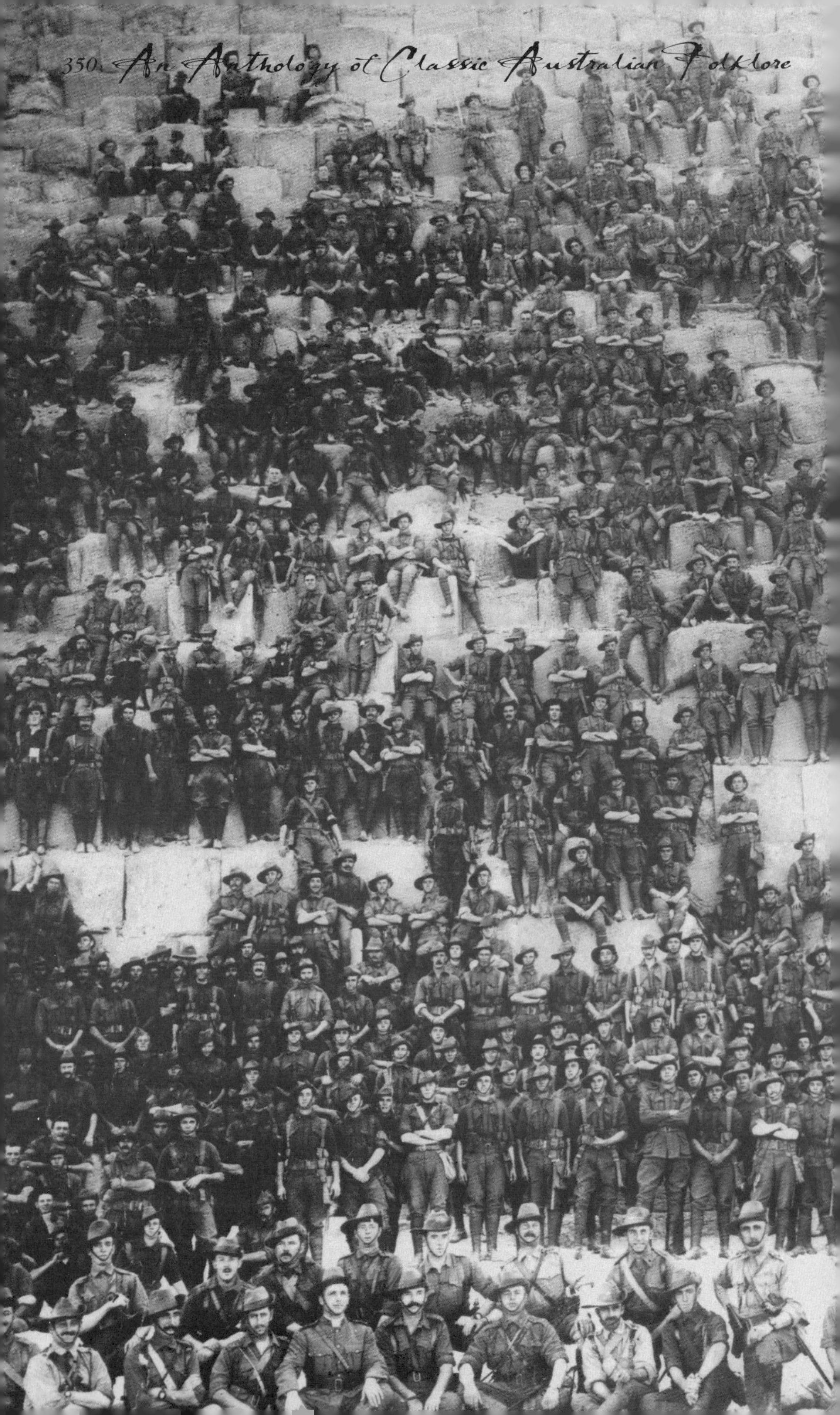

14: *Legends of War*

Ballad of the Cornstalk

He hung up the stock-whip and laid by the shears—
   It maybe for months and it may be for years;
   It may be for ever—but restless was he:
   'I'm tired of the Bush and I'm off for a spree!

I'm going to the war, and I don't know what it's for,
   But the other chaps are going with the Bush Contingent men,
   But if I should stay behind, there'll be trouble on my mind,
   For my girl would throw me over when they come back agen.'

— HENRY LAWSON (WRITTEN WHEN AUSTRALIAN VOLUNTEERS
   SAILED FOR SOUTH AFRICA TO FIGHT THE BOERS, 1899-1902)

*Left: Australians in Egypt prior to the Gallipoli landings,
1915. Australian War Memorial photograph A 2875*

The First A.I.F

Within five weeks of the death of an Austrian archduke in a Bosnian town called Sarajevo, Europe was at war and the German armies marching through Belgium. On 4th August 1914 Britain declared war on Germany and her empire rallied to her cause, pledging arms and men. Volunteers from sheep stations, from banks and schools and railway yards flocked to join the 'expeditionary force' (the Australian Imperial Force or AIF as it became) and were heartbroken if they were rejected. Physical standards were high. Only Australia's fittest were accepted.

But even Australia's best were regarded as second best when compared with the stolid, well disciplined British Tommy. Though our men looked magnificent under their wide-brimmed slouch hats, they marched badly, thought some, as they swung from barracks and army camps to the waiting transports. 'They'll leave the real fighting to the British Army, and use this crowd for lines of communications,' was one remark overheard. Others conjectured that these 20,000 civilian soldiers would spend the war—which would be 'over by Christmas'—to garrison India to relieve England's manpower shortage. Even General Ian Hamilton, visiting Australia early in 1914, had written privately that it would take 'three colonials' to equal one British soldier, and thought the Australian Light Horse—for all the enthusiasm they displayed in manoeuvres at Lilydale—compared poorly in drill to the New Zealanders he had seen.

Yet by 1918 this colourful army of Australians would be called 'the shock troops of the British Empire' by their foe, Ludendorff. The French would call them 'The Lords of Battle'. And John Masefield, who had seen them on Gallipoli and loved their spirit, would call them 'the finest army that served in the Great War'. And Australians would modestly agree.

The 'diggers' would become the first heroes whom Australia—as a

AWM Photo A3351

nation—had produced, and figures embodying all the qualities Australians had revered for a century: impudence, endurance, wild courage and mateship carried to even the jaws of death.

They would suffer the heaviest battle casualty rate of any army, on any front, in the war of 1914-18: 221,000 men were recorded dead, wounded or missing out of a total of 332,000 who served overseas (65 per cent), dwarfing even the cruel casualty rate of their brothers-in-arms, the New Zealanders, who fought beside them in every battle.

They suffered: 60,000 killed—50,000 of them in two and a half year's slaughter in France and Flanders, an ordeal in which they never lost a battle or failed to reach an objective.

Despite army discipline, they remained incorrigibly civilian, losing none of their humour or humanity. They were truly the stuff of legend.

The Anzacs

In camp in Egypt as the two divisions—nearly 40,000 men—of the 'Australian and New Zealand Army Corps' assembled, a stores clerk, tiring of writing this long title on forms and requisition sheets, suggested a rubber stamp be authorized using the formation's initials: 'A.N.Z.A.C.' His officers thought it a good idea, and so did their English general, Birdwood ('Birdie'), and the troops liked the word. Soon 'Anzac' would describe every Australian and New Zealander soldier in the war, and would enter the vocabulary.

'A finer set of men than the "Anzacs" after their three months training upon the desert sands could hardly be found in any country ...They walked the earth with careless and daredevil self-confidence. Gifted with the intelligence that comes from freedom and healthy physique ... they could be counted upon to face death, but hardly to salute an officer ...Their language habitually violent, continued unrestrained in the presence of superiors . . . Except in action, the control of such men was inevitably difficult ...'

— HENRY W. NEVINSON, ENGLISH WAR CORRESPONDENT, 1915

'The Australians there have given a lot of trouble from their want of discipline and their strange habits: at Christmas they made a raid from Mena and painted Cairo red. But they are improving and [General Maxwell] says they are splendid raw material ...'

— BRITISH PRIME MINISTER ASQUITH,
    WRITING IN ENGLAND, JANUARY 1915

Rising Sun

In 1914 all Australian soldiers in their democratic army, from private to lieutenant-colonel, wore on cap and collar the same badge—a 'Rising Sun' of burnished brass. With minor variations in design it has been worn by Australian soldiers now for a century.

Eager to give the Commonwealth military forces a distinctive emblem, Major-General Sir Edward Hutton, the English-born General Officer Commanding (GOC), saw an eye-catching display of bayonets above a barracks door and adapted it for the badge of a regiment departing for South Africa in 1902, the Australian Commonwealth Horse. In 1904 he ordered all Australian army units to wear the badge.

To 'Curly' Hutton, Australia owes its famous Light Horse regiments. In 1903, reflecting on the effectiveness of the colonial mounted infantry in South Africa, he ordered that all mounted regiments—even the Lancers—be converted to light horse. They were in fact infantry on horseback, trained to ride to the scene of battle, dismount, tether their horses, and fight like foot soldiers. And he allowed them to wear an emu plume.

Slouch Hat and Lemon-Squeezer

The name 'slouch hat' seems typically Australian, ideally coined for the casual soldiers who wore the wide bush hat as part of their uniform. But the term is an English one, dating back to the 1600s, describing any hat whose brim is not worn straight. In 1899, the six Australian colonial military forces agreed to adopt the bush hat for all troops other than artillery (who continued to wear the sun helmet of the British forces). They wore them in the Boer War (quickly discarding the British sun helmets they were issued on arriving there). In 1914, the Australians pinned ('looped') their brims up on

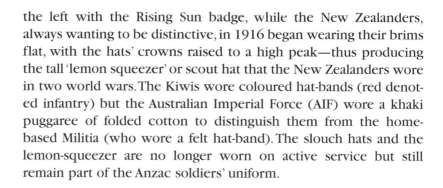

the left with the Rising Sun badge, while the New Zealanders, always wanting to be distinctive, in 1916 began wearing their brims flat, with the hats' crowns raised to a high peak—thus producing the tall 'lemon squeezer' or scout hat that the New Zealanders wore in two world wars. The Kiwis wore coloured hat-bands (red denoted infantry) but the Australian Imperial Force (AIF) wore a khaki puggaree of folded cotton to distinguish them from the home-based Militia (who wore a felt hat-band). The slouch hats and the lemon-squeezer are no longer worn on active service but still remain part of the Anzac soldiers' uniform.

Colour Patch

The Australian Imperial Force that sailed in 1914 had no regimental badges similar to these worn by British, Canadian and New Zealand battalions, for all ranks wore the same simple badge—the Rising Sun—which made identifying men from different battalions difficult if not impossible.

In camp in Egypt the battalion lines were marked by a system of coloured flags to enable the troops to find their tents—green was the colour used to denote New South Wales units, red for Victorian—and when it was decided to issue some sort of identification to the battalions, the two-colour flags were reproduced in miniature as 'colour patches' to be worn on the upper sleeve. Thus were born the 'battalion colours'—the small patches of coloured felt in various shapes (depending on division) that could be recognized in an instant, and were treasured by all who wore them.

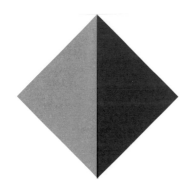

The units of the 2nd AIF adopted the colour patches worn by their predecessors, but added a thin grey border. In both world wars Diggers' wives and families wore miniatures of their men's colours, and at service of remembrance unit wreaths are beribboned with the colours that mean little to most civilians but meant the world to their wearers.

In 1988 the government authorized regular army units to wear colour patches incorporating, where possible, the colours of their original formations, to be worn on the puggaree (band) of their slouch hats.

Gallipoli: The Fatal Shore

So the troops had a distinctive name, uniform, badge and colour patch; but whether they would prove worthwhile soldiers was still unknown.

Gallipoli is now so deeply entrenched in Australia's history and folk memory and legend that even today, despite millions of words and hundreds of books inspired by the campaign, the truth still hides or wears a hundred faces.

The campaign was a mistake, a disaster from its inception, and slid, mismanaged and malign, into a monumental tragedy, one that claimed 400,000 allied and Turkish casualties. Of these, 40,000 were Australian—barely 10% of the total—yet so powerful a presence was exerted by the Anzacs that they seem to dominate accounts of Gallipoli. 'The Australians and New Zealanders,' wrote the English historian James Morris, 'more than any other troops, gave the campaign its aura of epic allure.'

In January 1915, when the British War Cabinet gave their assent to a plan to force the Dardanelles Straits (the sea link from the Mediterranean front to the embattled Russians), the Turks, whose forts on the Gallipoli Peninsula threatened any fleet attempting the force the Straits, seemed a minor enemy. The disastrous failure of the Allied fleet to force the Dardanelles minefields in March (three battleships were sunk in one day) left only one alternative: an invasion of Gallipoli peninsula to capture the forts and allow the fleet passage to Constantinople.

All this was a long way from Australia, and from the battlefields of Belgium that were the original destination of the 40,000

AWM Photo G635

From the painting by G.W. Lambert in the Australian War Memorial

Australian and New Zealand troops training in Egypt. When Prime Minister Asquith asked the secretary of war, Field Marshal Lord Kitchener, whether the unruly Australians were 'good enough' to use on Gallipoli, the old soldier grunted 'Good enough if a cruise on the Sea of Marmara is all that is contemplated.' These untried civilian soldiers formed the only sizeable force available at short notice. The risk was taken to use them in the easiest part of the invasion: to land on the beach near Gaba Tepe, on the mid-west coast far north of the British beaches, and strike inland across the plain to sever the Peninsula and cut off the Turkish retreat. Surveying the coast just north of Gaba Tepe, General Birdwood, the commander of the Australian and New Zealand Army Corps (the Anzacs), noticed cliffs rising up to a rugged mountain range, and hoped that the navy would not land his men there in error, for he saw that it was 'impossible country.'

The Landings, 25 April 1915

When the Australians, strangely silent for such usually rowdy soldiers, clambered from transports into the small boats in the pre-dawn darkness, all was going according to plan: a miracle of organization, for an invasion mounted after only two months' planning. But as the pinnaces chugging ahead headed for the shore, a naval officer noticed that they were making a northerly course, one that would take them too far north of the beach near Gaba Tepe headland. Just as dawn was breaking, at 4.29 a.m., the first boat grounded on the shingle and shadowy figures could be seen on the cliff tops.

Suddenly bullets started hitting the men in the boats. There was no broad beach whatever. Only a stretch of shingle below sloping cliffs. 'Tell the colonel the damn fools have landed us a mile too far north!' a naval officer shouted, but by now the firing had become a crescendo and boatloads of Australians were clustering at the base of the cliffs, puzzled by the geography of the place. They had been landed at Ari Burnu headland, nearly three kilometres (two miles) off course.

And then the Anzac legend was born. Led by officers, groups of Australians calmly shrugged off their packs and began to haul themselves up the cliff side and the rest followed without hesitating. On reaching the top of Ari Burnu, they found a higher plateau facing them, and climbed that too. From its summit they looked out in the growing light on a nightmare landscape of ridges, gullies and ravines, covered in scrub. Sighting Turks scurrying inland they went after them, firing, and falling from enemy fire, companies splitting up into platoons and sections. All day long, as the navy calmly landed more than 20,000 troops, battles raged all over the terrain, the main one in the south on a plateau near Lone Pine, where massive Turkish counter-attacks and heavy bombardments slowly forced the ragged Australian line back. But the line held. By nightfall, Australia had had its first experience of war. 'How we prayed for this ghastly day to end,' wrote one Anzac officer.

Unaware of the extent of the front line and conscious of at least a thousand dead and wounded, Birdwood recommended evacuation. From the commander-in-chief came the reply: 'You have got through the hardest part. Dig, dig, dig.'

Daylight revealed the magnitude of the Australian achievement. The line was still holding and the troops' spirits were rising with the hour. Life in the beach-head began to shake out into a pattern. There was no fresh water, so this was carried up in tins from the beach. From hastily dug trenches and pozzies the troops sniped at the Turks or sheltered from the incessant shelling. For the next eight months 'Anzac Cove' would be their home. When the navy offered to evacuate the force, Birdwood replied that his Australians were quite happy where they were!

Whether they could withstand a concerted attack was revealed on 19 May: in a day-long offensive mounted to drive the Anzacs into the sea, 10,000 Turks were cut down by rifles and machine-gun fire for the loss of 628 Australians and New Zealanders, who were now so firmly entrenched that nothing could move them. The stench of death in No Man's Land was so overwhelming that five days later a truce was called, and the Anzacs helped the enemy bury the thousands of corpses. From that moment on, all hatred seems to have died between the men of the two armies, and Anzac and Turk—despite the bitter fighting that followed—maintained a healthy respect for each other, and even some affection.

The Anzac Legend

It was not until 8 May 1915 that Australians at home read of the landings on Gallipoli. Opening the papers with some trepidation, for none, in truth, was sure what mischief the boys had been up to, people read that the Australians had been acclaimed as heroes, and all subsequent reports spoke of their pluck and humour and toughness. The legend would grow of Anzac invincibility, of the 'careless, cheerful, mocking' troops who feared no enemy.

But there would be no inquiry into the terrible error that placed Australia's first army in the jaws of disaster, landed at the wrong spot; even today, war memorials carry the battle honour Gaba Tepe, though the headland remained just a distant landmark to most Anzacs looking south from their lofty positions on the heights above Anzac Cove.

Nor would most Australians read in detail of the fiasco of the August offensives, when the Australians stormed and held Lone

Pine for three days of hell and the New Zealanders tripled the size of the bridgehead by stealth and cold steel in one night, while the British Army sat supine at Suvla Bay unable to advance, unwilling to retreat, dooming the campaign for good.

Even today, military historians who pick their way over the tortuous terrain of Anzac—as the whole beach-head is still known—puzzle how any troops could have endured eight long months there. It says much about the Australian character that we saw in it a victory of sort. A nation without a sense of national pride found it on a foreign shore.

'They all seem to address their officers as Bill or Dick and though wonderfully brave have absolutely no discipline.'

— HON. WALTER GUINNESS, BRITISH STAFF OFFICER, GALLIPOLI, 1915

'The Nek': 1915

The shattering climax of the Australian film *Gallipoli*, thought by many to be fictional, was in fact a meticulous recreation of the most tragic action of the entire campaign.

The attack by the 3rd Light Horse Brigade's 8th and 10th Regiments on 'The Nek'—a narrow ridge barely wider than a tennis court which led onto the slopes of 'Baby 700'—was intended as one of the major feints or diversions mounted to distract the Turks on 7 August 1915, the second day of the great August offensive. The distance between the Australian and Turkish lines was barely 40 metres: a few minutes' sprint by men charging with fixed bayonets against trenches held by 'only a handful' of Turks.

But the Turkish trenches were held in strength and protected by machine-guns. And the naval bombardment of the enemy position suddenly ceased at 4.23 a.m.: seven minutes before schedule. Undeterred by the sight of dazed but reorganizing Turks lining the parapet, the first wave of the 8th Light Horse surged from their trenches at 4.30 p.m. only to be cut to pieces by a tornado of almost point-blank fire. Two minutes later a second wave of Victorians charged into the murderous fusillade and met the same fate.

As the Western Australians of the 10th Light Horse filed into the trenches now filled with wounded Victorians, their commander, Colonel Brazier, picked his way to Brigade headquarters to plead for a cancellation of a third attack. He was told that the attack must proceed.

At 4.45 p.m., the Western Australians rose from their trenches and charged to their deaths. Mates had shouted farewells to mates; men had already made their compact with their maker. If the Victorians could die bravely, so too could the boys from the West. 'With that regiment went the flower of the youth of Western Australia, sons of

From the painting by G.W. Lambert in the Australian War Memorial

the old pioneering families, youngsters—in some cases two or three from the same home—who had flocked to Perth at the outbreak of war with their own horses and saddlery in order to secure enlistment in a mounted regiment of the AIF,' wrote Charles Bean in the official history. Men known and popular, the best loved leaders in sport and work in the West, then rushed straight to their death. Gresley Harper and Wilfred, his younger brother, the latter of whom was last seen running forward like a schoolboy in a foot-race, with all the speed he could compass . . .'

Realizing at last that further attacks were pointless, the fourth wave was ordered to wait in their trenches, but at 5.15 p.m. an officer ordered the flank to attack. 'By God, I believe the right has gone!' shouted an officer when he heard the tell-tale stutter of machine-guns, and his NCOs immediately led the rest to their doom.

In a patch of scrub no larger than a tennis court lay 368 dead and wounded Australians.

Simpson and his Donkeys

Of all the legends of Gallipoli none is more revered than that of Simpson and his donkeys, who together brought in the wounded in the first weeks of the Gallipoli Landing. As the historian Peter

Cochrane has written in his biography of Simpson (1992): 'Within weeks of his death, the story of Simpson and his donkey was being told in Australia, and it has been told ever since. The legend became part of Australian folklore. It acquired an official presence in national rituals of remembrance, in schooling, and in sermons from the pulpit.'

An earlier biography of Simpson published on the 50th anniversary of Gallipoli (1965), subtitled 'The Good Samaritan of Gallipoli', portrayed him as an Australian saint. The truth is very different, and far more interesting. First, his name was not Simpson. It was Kirkpatrick. Second, he was English, not Australian (except by adoption, for he had turned his back on England years before).

Far from being saint-like in speech, he wrote and spoke like the working-class man he was, hating the inequalities of wealth in the land of his birth and loving the freedom and opportunities he found in Australia. Before he enlisted, John Simpson Kirkpatrick was a fervent socialist. To his mother in South Shields in north-east England he wrote: 'You will see the difference between the two countries—the working man out here votes for a Labor government ... and the man at home has (sic) not got the sense for that, he must go and vote for the first big Liberal capitalist that puts up for the seat ...'

Kirkpatrick enlisted in 1914 as a medical orderly under the name of Simpson. Landing on Gallipoli on the first day, he became distressed by the agonies of the wounded. Rounding up several stray donkeys he daily brought wounded Australians down to the aid stations on the beach. On 19 May he was killed by a Turkish bullet. Australians in the trenches were seen to weep at the news.

'The Diggers', France

'It's funny,' an Australian sergeant wrote in March 1917, 'when they want something dashing or dangerous accomplished they always pick on the Australians and New Zealanders,' but when accounts of the battle are published, he reads that the 'British' have done the fighting. In 1916 another Australian wrote home to his English-born father that his impression of the English Tommy was a favourable one: 'While not so tall as the average Australian he is neat and clean' and much less foul-mouthed and 'objectionable' than his comrades; but by October 1917 he was telling his father that 'the colonials and the Scotch regiments are absolutely the best troops in the British army ...'

It was in late 1917 that the Australians adopted the New Zealand nickname for themselves, 'Diggers', and claimed it as their own. They disliked the British term 'colonials' and regarded the Gallipoli

AWM Photo K22

men as the only real Anzacs. (In World War II, the New Zealand infantry called themselves 'digs', to differentiate themselves from their friendly rivals in a hundred brawls and battles, the Aussies.)

Philip Gibbs wrote of the Australians he saw in Amiens before and during the Somme: 'I liked the look of them, dusty up to their eyes in summer, muddy up to their ears in winter— scornful of discipline for discipline's sake, but desperate fighters, as simple as children in their ways of thought and speech (except for frightful oaths), and looking at life … with frank, curious eyes and a kind of humorous contempt for death and disease, and English Tommies, and French girls, and "the whole damned show" as they called it… They behaved as the equals of all men, giving no respect to generals or staff officers, or the devils of hell. There was a primitive spirit of manhood in them, and they took what they wanted, and were ready to pay for it in coin or in disease or in wounds …'

These same Australians were just about to enter their greatest ordeal: the capture of Pozieres, on the Somme, 1916. Taking it, they held it against unending bombardment and counter-attack. In little more than one square mile (1.6 square kilometres) of battle front, nearly 23,000 Australians were killed and wounded in three months …

The 'Austral-aise'

Fellers of Australia,
Blokes an' coves an' coots,
Shift yer b—y carcasses,
Move yer b—y boots.
Get a b—y move on . .
Gird yer b— loins up,
Get yer b— guns,
Set the b— enemy,
And watch the blighters run.

The first version of this famous verse, recited with gusto by Australian troops in World War I (and World War II) was originally 'written as a joke on the editor of the *Red Page*' and submitted to the *Bulletin* in 1908 when the journal invited Australia's poets to pen the words for a new national anthem. They were expecting a new *Marseillaise*—and they got this. It was so popular that it was reprinted in leaflet form as a marching song for the Australian Imperial Force and even used in recruiting campaigns a generation later during the Korean War in 1951.

Its author C.J. Dennis (1876 –1938), born in South Australia to parents of Irish descent, was known as a writer of humorous verse, editor of the 'cheerfully malicious' weekly the *Gadfly*, and a lover of the Australian bush (he lived at Toolangi outside Melbourne nearly all his life, first in a tent, later in a house). His collection of verse written in the same comic vernacular of working class Melbourne,' *Songs of a Sentimental Bloke*, appeared in book form in 1915 and sold 50,000 copies in under two years, and the Bloke's adventures were equally popular when made into film (twice), and a generation later, as a musical comedy and then a television series. The Songs began with the Bloke's immortal lament over his problems with Doreen:

The world 'as got me snouted jist a treat;
Crool Forchin's dirty left 'as smote me soul;
An all them joys o' life I 'eld so sweet
Is up the pole . . .

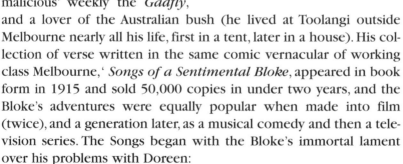

The Light Horse

'Not only do your men fail to salute me, but they laugh at my orderlies.'

— *British general, complaining about the Australians' poor discipline to their colonel, Egypt, 1915*

'I have never ceased wondering how Australia has continued to produce such a splendid lot of horses. During the fighting at Romani, in the hottest month of the year, the horses of one regiment were without water for 52 hours, and during the raid on Maghdaba most of them were without water for 36 hours, having done nearly 50 miles, and been under the saddle all the time.'

— *Major-General Harry Chauvel, 1916*

Australia sent overseas close to 120,000 horses—the famed 'Walers'—in the 1914-18 war, but none returned, because of Australia's stringent quarantine restrictions. When the government ordered them sold to civilian contractors in the Middle East at war's end, the Light Horse men, many of them in tears, quietly shot their chargers to save them a life of misery and ill treatment.

'They were no second-raters, those Australians and New Zealanders. Enviously we watched those Australian cavalrymen, crowded under the occasional tree as they snatched a moment of shade for themselves and their horses. The empty saddles caught the sun and shone like mirrors, while the Anzacs, always eager for a fight, smoked and joked with each other. The semi-desert appeared to be suddenly filled with life.

'The order came to mount. They formed up and as they trotted off heavy tell-tale wisps of dust rose and hung in the air. The whole panorama of mounted movement drove forward and my thoughts and my envy went a-riding with them.'

— *English Yeomanry Officer, 1917*

In December 1917, Allenby's armies entered the great prize, the Holy City of Jerusalem. In Bill Gammage's famous collection of soldiers' letters The Broken Years (1974), the following is one of the many anecdotes recorded:

'Had a good look around Jerusalem,' one Australian trooper wrote to a mate. 'Don't think much of the crib. Of course the old historic sites are interesting, but the yarns about lots of 'em are guess work, and some all balls . . . the Cognac sold there is murder.'

The Charge at Beersheba: 1917

Blocking the road to Palestine and the great goal Jerusalem was the fortress of Gaza, site of two bloody defeats that had resulted in the sacking of General Murray (who had unwisely claimed his second defeat as a success) and his replacement by General Sir Edmund Allenby—the 'Bull'. Allenby decided to lull the Turks into believing that another frontal attack would be made on Gaza, but his main thrust would be against the extreme left of their defence line, the fortified desert village of Beersheba. If he could seize Beersheba, he could turn the Turkish line and render Gaza untenable.

From the painting by G.W. Lambert in the Australian War Memorial

AWM Photo B1414

On 27 October 1917, Allenby opened his attacks on Gaza while under cover of night, the Queenslander Lt-General Harry Chauvel's Desert Mounted Corps began to move to Beerhseba. On 31 October, the British infantry and artillery began their attacks on the village and the Anzac Mounted Division inched forward to storm the outer defences. All day long the battle raged. Yet the capture of Beersheba would be an empty victory if its defenders destroyed its 17 vital wells. Without fresh water for their parched and weary horses, the Desert Mounted Corps would be immobilized.

From his lofty command post overlooking the battlefield, Chauvel studied aerial maps of Beersheba's defences. In the south-eastern sector there were no barbed wire belts or deep ditches to obstruct cavalry, but the approaches were commanded by Turkish field guns. At 3 p.m., only two hours before night would fall, Chauvel made his decision. 'Put Grant straight at it,' he ordered.

Brigadier-General William Grant's 4th Australian Light Horse Brigade, consisting of the 4th and 12th Regiments, would charge straight for the wells, across seven kilometres of fire-swept ground.

'A wave of such subtle excitement swept through the mounted ranks as communicated itself to the beasts they rode,' recorded the writer Frank Dalby Davison. 'There was a pressing and jostling in their ranks as the regiments, squadron by squadron, rode out from cover and wheeled.'

At 4.30 p.m., Grant led the great lines forward, first at a trot, then at a canter. In the last rays of the setting sun, the Light Horse, breaking into a gallop, thundered into the wildest ride they had ever ridden and the last great cavalry charge in history.

It was madness, for the Light Horse were not cavalry possessing sabres like the British 'heavies' or equipped with deadly lances (which were also dreaded by infantry). They were armed only with rifle and bayonet and the latter was a pygmy, stabbing weapon. As the Australians thundered forward observers saw them draw their bayonets—sharpened to a razor's edge—and the setting sun caught the blades in a flash of gold. Shrapnel burst above them and men fell from the saddle, first in ones and twos, and then in dozens, but in minutes the horsemen were leaping over the Turkish trenches and jumping from the saddle to rout out the defenders. Two regiments rode straight for the wells, taking the Turks so completely by surprise that only two of the wells were destroyed.

At 5 p.m., Chauvel got word that Beersheba had fallen and that 1,000 Turks and Germans were prisoner. Fifteen of the wells were intact. The light horse regiment had lost 63 men—31 killed and 32 wounded. 'They are not soldiers at all—they are madmen,' a captured German officer complained.

Gaza, outflanked, fell on 7 November 1917. The road to Jerusalem was open.

'Crucifixion', 1918

In Digger legend, there are numerous references to a particularly cruel form of British army punishment called No.1 Field Punishment, known to the Tommies as 'Crucifixion', in which an offender was lashed by his hands and feet for several hours a day to a wagon wheel. The sight was enough to enrage Australians, who became notorious for cutting the prisoners free, but this account by a young English soldier, Aubrey Wade, is a rare published description.

'Close by the road where the crucifixion took place there ran a narrow road which led to a stream where it was usual for all the artillery in the area to water their horses. At evening stable-time the Australians rode through with their animals on their way to water, and it so happened on the third day of the wheel torture that the victim had been strung up on a wagon in full view of the road, which was an oversight, no doubt, on the part of the sergeant-major.

'The Aussies, coming along at the trot, pulled up dead and stared in blank amazement. They simply could not understand it. The corporal who appeared to be in charge of them (for so much as they were ever in anyone's charge) dismounted, handed over his horse and strode across to the scene of punishment while all of us watched him with the keenest anticipation. Then the Aussie spoke: "Who in hell's name tied you up like this, digger?" And without

waiting for a reply he cut through the new brown straps with his jack-knife, releasing the prisoner who stood looking at him dazedly, while the guard discreetly found something urgently waiting to be done at the guard-room. "Who tied you up, digger?" came a chorus from the watching Australians. "Show us the b—d." I prayed for the appearance of the sergeant-major. But no sergeant-major came. The corporal remounted. "We'll be here again to-morrow," he called, and with that he led his grinning troop away ...

'The next day, to the minute, the process was repeated. Again the victim was released in a jiffy by the Aussies, four more brand-new straps were ruined and the sergeant-major hid himself in fear of his life. But the crucifixion was not called off; the next afternoon the prisoner was led out and strapped tight, and we gleefully awaited the appearance of the Australians. This time they were a little later than usual, but they came right enough just as the sergeant-major emerged from the field in which the tents lay. He walked right into them before realizing that they were the companions of the corporal who was busily engaged in cutting gun-straps to ribbons. Pushing between their horses he yelled at the corporal.

"'Hello, b—d,' said the corporal pleasantly, looking round. "Come down to watch the fun?" he continued, in a soft drawl which infuriated the sergeant-major. His hand flew to the riding-crop tucked under his arm, but the Australian gazed at him steadily and contemptuously. The other riders drew closer. Then the corporal went up to the sergeant-major and told him that for two pins, more or less, he'd tie him to the tails of their horses and gallop him over half France. And for tying a poor digger up like that he ought to be strung up by an extremely susceptible part of his anatomy and flogged to death for a b—d. And every time they came that way they'd cut the prisoner down, and then they'd think about cutting the sergeant-major's throat. The rescuers formed a ring of horses round the two protagonists so that the sergeant-major should not miss one word that was for the good of his soul. It was a great day.'

— FROM THE WAR OF THE GUNS, *1936, AUBREY WADE*

'Villers-Bret'

'The bone of contention was Villers-Bret [the town of Villers-Bretonneux]. With that in his possession Fritz would have had Amiens "in his pocket", but in front of Villers the Australians held the line, and never was line held better. The wild brown men from the open spaces, "the diggers", lean, hard-muscled, hard-swearing, thieves of horses and haters of discipline, free-handed with their colonial riches of six shillings per day, musical-voiced (their intonation of "deown" was a delight), were the finest and the worst soldiers that ever entered France.'

'Villers-Bret was held intact by an army of great-hearted men who were afraid of nothing on earth. I knew them in action and out of action, in the front line, in the observation-posts, with the guns, riding up at night with the ammunition, mending lines to the shriek of shells and the roar of explosions; I and the rest of us made friends for ever of the loose-belted Aussies.'

— *FROM* THE WAR OF THE GUNS, *1936, AUBREY WADE*

Villers-Bretonneux, defended by the Australians, was the key to Amiens. Exhausted, they handed the town over to British troops, who lost it next day (24 April 1918). Two Australian infantry brigades promptly recaptured the village in a famous night attack on 25 April 1918, going forward in the darkness without an artillery bombardment or tanks. The recapture has been described as one of the finest feats of the war. From Villers-Bret the Australians (and the Canadians) launched the great offensive of 8 August, 1918 that

broke the enemy line—the 'Black Day' of the German Army. On 30 August, as General Monash pushed his men to the limits of exhaustion, an Australian brigade stormed the slopes of Mont St Quentin, a German position regarded as impregnable, and after a day of bloody fighting secured it. Four weeks later the exhausted and understrength Australian Corps—only two of the five divisions were now strong enough to send into battle— led the attack on the Hindenburg Line north of St Quentin, breaking through the 10 kilometre-deep defences on 5 October. They were four of the greatest victories of the war.

Villers-Bretonneux, rebuilt after the war (some of the funds were donated by Australian schoolchildren, mainly from Victoria) is in many ways a small piece of Australia. The French have long memories. Visitors walk down the Rue de Melbourne and in every schoolroom is emblazoned a plaque with the words 'N'oublions jamais l'Australie' ('Never Forget Australia'). Every Anzac Day for more than 80 years the schoolchildren lay wreaths on the memorial in the great Australian National War Cemetery on the outskirts of the town and sing *Waltzing Matilda*— in English.

'Hopit!'

In the last days of May 1941, as the doomed seven-day battle to hold Crete against German airborne forces ended and the British, Australian and New Zealand infantry trudged beneath remorseless Stuka attack to the southern coast for evacuation by the fleet, the isolated New South Wales, Victorian and Western Australian battalions defending Retimo against German paratroopers finally received their orders to retreat. It came in a coded message that only Australians could understand:

'Waratahs, Bulli. Puckapunyals, St Kilda. Gropers, Albany. Begin Hopit'. In other words, head for your favourite southern beach! It came too late. Overwhelmed by tanks, Retimo's defenders were forced to surrender, though many made for the mountains from where they made it back to Egypt or to Turkey with the help of Cretan villagers. More than 10,000 Anzacs were lost in the Greece and Crete campaigns.

The Rats of Tobruk, 1941

'There'll be no Dunkirk here. If we should have to get out, we shall fight our way out. There is to be no surrender, and no retreat.' With these words Major-General Leslie Morshead, commanding the 9th Australian Division in Tobruk in April 1941, ordered his men to defend the perimeter of the sea port as Rommel's Afrika Korps closed in. It marked the beginning of a great siege in which the beleagured garrison—the majority of them Australian—would take a savage toll of the enemy.

The Italian town—and fortress—of Tobruk had been captured by the Australians (6th Division) in January 1941, barely three weeks after they had stormed Bardia in their first great land battle of the World War II, taking in the advance nearly 65,000 Italian prisoners for minimal loss.

With the 6th Division and the New Zealanders holding the line in Greece (and later Crete) where they were soon fighting against overwhelming odds, General Wavell asked Morshead to hold Tobruk for at least eight weeks, until a counter-offensive could relieve the garrison; the siege of Tobruk was to last, like Gallipoli, eight months, through the heat and thirst of summer, and would result in the first outright defeat inflicted on the German-Italian Axis forces since the beginning of the war. But on Radio Berlin Dr Goebbels ridiculed the hard-pressed defenders, calling them 'Ali Baba Morshead and his Forty Thousand Thieves' who were caught 'like rats in a trap'. So the heroes of the siege—the infantry of the 9th Division—dubbed

From the painting by G. W. Lambert in the Australian War Memorial

themselves 'The Rats of Tobruk', the name by which the division was known in all its subsequent battles from Libya to El Alamein and Borneo. The 'Rats' are few in number now, but they were the pride of the Desert Army, moulded by Leslie Morshead into a legendary fighting formation.

Of the original garrison of 40,000 troops caught in Tobruk, the hard core of combat troops consisted of 14,000 Australians and 9,000 British, many of the latter being artillery and tank corps. It was the tornado of fire from the Australian infantry and the precision of shelling from the British gunners that stopped dead Rommel's first attack on 11 April; his third attack two days later, a wild battle on Easter Sunday, was similarly repulsed (and saw Australia's first Victoria Cross of the war won by Corporal Jack Edmondson).

In the grim months that followed the disasters of Greece and Crete, the splendid defence of Tobruk showed the world that the Axis was not unbeatable, and gave heart to Australians everywhere. For instead of sitting tight behind his defences, Morshead ordered the 9th Division to mount constant attacks and hit the enemy hard, particularly at night: neither the Germans nor the Italians had ever known war to be fought this way, and their morale fell alarmingly while that of their besieged enemies rose. The diggers were ordered to make themselves 'Masters of No Man's Land', and this they did, venturing out silently after nightfall in patrols and returning with prisoners and bloodied bayonets.

Tobruk

There's places that I've been in,
  I didn't like too well,
  Scotland's far too blooming cold,
  And Cairo's hot as Hell:
  The Pilsner beer is always warm …
  In each there's something crook;
  But each and all are perfect to,
  This place they call Tobruk.

We reckon El Agheila,
  Was none too flash a place,
  El Abiar and Beda Fomm,
  Weren't in the bloody race.
  At the towns this side Benghasi,
  We hadn't time to look—
  But I'll take my oath they're better than ,
  This place they call Tobruk.

I've seen some dust storms back at home,
  That made the housewives work:
  There, there's enough inside our shirts,
  To smother all of Bourke.
  Two diggers cleaned their dug-out,
  And their blankets out they shook:
  Two colonels perished in the dust,
  In this place they call Tobruk.

The shelling's nice and frequent,
  And they whistle overhead,
  You go into your dug-out,
  And find shrapnel in your bed;
  And when the Stukas dive on us,
  We never pause to look,
  We're down our holes like rabbits in,
  This place they call Tobruk.

I really do not think this place,
  Was meant for me and you,
  Let's return it to the Arab,
  And he knows what he can do:
  We'll leave the God-forsaken place,
  Without one backward look—
  We've called it lots of other names,
  This place they call Tobruk.

— ANONYMOUS (SEPTEMBER 1941)

Tobruk became the symbol of the British Commonwealth's vow to stand and fight to the finish and Churchill ordered all available resources to its aid. The British, for the first and only time in the desert war, maintained standing patrols over the battlefield at heavy cost to the outnumbered Hurricanes and the Navy—including Australia's obsolete old destroyers of the 'Scrap Iron Flotilla'—kept the supply lines open, taking out the wounded and ferrying in supplies and reinforcements, but at such heavy cost in ships that the Naval C-in-C recommended that if Tobruk were again besieged it would be better to evacuate it.

By August 1941 the 9th Division was so weakened by insufficient food and the rigours of constant bombing, shelling and attacks, that the Australian Prime Minister demanded their evacuation; after much shilly-shallying by Prime Minister Churchill, this was accomplished by September, the Diggers being replaced by fresh British troops and a Polish brigade.

But when British tanks and the New Zealand Division finally broke through to link up with Tobruk's garrison in late November

1941, there were still Australians manning its defences, among them the unlucky 2/13th Battalion which, taken off by destroyer, had had to turn back to the port under heavy air attack, and was still defending its sector of the perimeter.

The defence of Tobruk cost 3,300 Australian casualties, 800 of whom are buried in the cemetery that lies in the town. Rommel later described the Australians who defended Tobruk in 1941 as 'magnificent troops'.

In June 1942, when the 9th Division was the last Australian formation still in the Middle East, Tobruk fell to Rommel only two days after he attacked the perimeter, and four days later the diggers were ordered south from Syria to turn back the Afrika Korps. From July to September they helped to fight Rommel to a standstill and on 23 October, when Montgomery launched his great counter-offensive, the 9th Division entered its greatest ordeal, the battle of El Alamein. On 4 November the Axis army began its retreat. Churchill was to write: 'The magnificent forward drive of the Australians . . . had swung the entire battle in our favour.' In early 1943 the Rats of Tobruk and the victors of Alamein sailed home to Australia, to fight a new enemy in New Guinea and Borneo, the Japanese.

Kokoda

In July 1942, the Japanese came in force suddenly to the northern coast of Papua-New Guinea. Landing at Buna and Gona, they struck inland across the plain of waist-high kunai grass towards Kokoda, a small village, possessing little more than a rubber plantation and a small airstrip, that lay in the hills near the base of the towering Owen Stanley Mountains.

From Kokoda, a rough track led over the ranges to the foothills near Port Moresby. Having failed to seize Moresby by seaborne invasion—turned back at the battle of the Coral Sea two months earlier—the Japanese would take it by a land approach, a 'seven-day march', risking the perils of crossing some of the worst terrain in the world.

In the Owen Stanley Ranges the peaks were lost in clouds of perpetual mist where men could freeze, while in the valleys that fell to the jungle floor and to roaring torrents, vegetation grew so thick that no sunlight penetrated. The 'Track', winding and precipitous, was in parts nearly vertical and lost in darkness, with no sound but the dripping of moisture. It was a nightmare world, alien to anything the Japanese or Australians had ever known.

Here, the war's first outright defeat would be inflicted on Japanese land forces by diggers untrained in jungle warfare.

AWM Photo 13288

Facing the 5,000 Japanese at Kokoda was an under-strength battalion of militia, the 39th, whose average age was 18. In an epic four-week fighting retreat the several hundred youngsters contested the enemy's advance along the Track, falling back to Isurava, where on 23 August the first strong reinforcements reached them—the desert-hardened men of the Australian Imperial Force's (AIF's) 7th Division. Even the veterans were exhausted by their climb and pushed hard by the relentless enemy: by 31 August the Australians had fallen back to Eora Creek, and the retreat was not yet over. Digging in on Imita Ridge, within sound of the aircraft engines on Moresby's airfields, the Australians waited for the attack. It never came. They had taken a far heavier toll of the Japanese than they suspected. Within sight of the ocean, the enemy began to fall back to Buna.

On 26 September 1942, the Australians, puzzled, advanced, finding signs only of a starving and demoralized enemy. They pushed on, burying hundreds of Japanese and Australian bodies, reaching, in late October, Eora Creek, now rendered almost impregnable and defended to the death by the enemy. For six days the Australians attacked, suffering heavily, until the defence was broken by a wild bayonet charge by the 2/3rd Battalion of the 6th Division.

The advance now became a pursuit, the diggers giving the enemy no rest. On 2 November Kokoda was reached and the Australian flag was raised. Nearly two weeks later they reached the raging Kumusi River, bridged it and passed seven exhausted battalions over it in four days. The Owen Stanleys had been crossed; ahead lay the coastal plain and the bitter, bloody, three-month battle to dislodge the Japanese from their bunkers in the coastal swamps of Gona and Buna. Thousands of Diggers had gone down with malaria and jungle fever; battle casualties were close to 1,700. But 10,000 Japanese were dead or wounded and among their dead was General Horii, conqueror of Rabaul, swept away to drown in the Kumusi.

Kokoda was an Australian epic. Born in the shambles of a retreat, and fought in rain and mud, Kokoda—and the successful Australian repulse of a Japanese landing at Milne Bay on the eastern tip of New Guinea in August-September 1942—were the first two allied land victories against the Japanese in the World War II.

'Weary' Dunlop

Edward Dunlop was born in 1907 in northern Victoria and educated at Benalla High (school of another famous Australian, Captain 'Hec' Waller of the Scrap Iron Flotilla). Massively built and 193 centimetres tall, he was an international Rugby Union champion and earned the nickname 'Weary' from the famous Dunlop Tyre advertisements: 'They Wear Well'. After studying medicine at the University of Melbourne, he was working in London hospitals at the outbreak of war in 1939 and joined the 2nd Australian Imperial Force (AIF) in the Middle East as a doctor in 1940. Captured in Java with a brigade of the 7th Division in March 1942, he became a legend among the Australian prisoners-of-war in Japanese hands. In the jungle hell of the Burma–Thailand Railway he stood up to the Japanese to demand improved conditions for his men, despite beatings and threats of execution, and operated on sick prisoners-of-war without adequate medicines or surgical tools, savings countless lives. He survived to resume his medical practice in Melbourne, generally unknown to most Australians until the publication late in his life of his war diaries, which revealed the hideous conditions in which he worked as a captive of the Japanese—and in which 7,777 Australian soldiers died of illness, malnutrition and punishment from 1942 to 1945. On his death in 1993, Sir Edward Dunlop was accorded a State Funeral. He ranked with another tall and towering figure, Sir Roden Cutler VC, who died in 2002: the image of the hero.

30th ANNIVERSARY OF
FIRST TASMAN FLIGHT
1928 ⋆   ⋆ 1958

8D.

AUSTRALIA

15: *Up and Away: Legends of the Air*

Ross Smith

Australia was the only dominion during the 1914–18 war to form her own air force—the Australian Flying Corps (AFC), which took to the air with four ricketty aircraft in 1914. By the end of the war the AFC had raised four squadrons which fought in the Middle East and on the Western Front. When the British War Office called for volunteers from the Australian Imperial Force (AIF) to train as pilots in the Royal Flying Corps (RFC), noting that 'the Australian temperament is especially suited to the flying services', hundreds of Diggers volunteered.

The war had begun Australia's love affair with flying and some of the wartime pilots were to become legendary figures in post-War aviation. The greatest of them all, Captain Ross Macpherson Smith of Adelaide (1892–1922), decided to fly home in style. He had served on Gallipoli in the Light Horse before transferring to the AFC's squadron in Egypt in 1917 and quickly became famed as a combat pilot, seemingly fearless. He became Lawrence of Arabia's personal pilot, and flew the only Handley-Page bomber in the Middle East, surviving the war to be awarded the Military Cross (MC) and bar, and three Distinguished Flying Crosses (DFC and two bars). He piloted a Handley-Page in the first flight from Cairo to Calcutta and then, with a genial English co-pilot, Major-General 'Buffy' Borton, flew as far as Timor. On 12 November 1919, he took off from England in a Vickers-Vimy bomber with an all-Australian crew (his brother Keith, and sergeants Bennett and Shiers) to compete for the prize offered to the first airmen to fly the 20,000-kilometre distance from England to Australia. The Australians flew in their giant, open-cockpit aircraft through the worst of winter weather, sleet and snow, surviving forced landings and sandstorms in the desert to touch down at Darwin on 10 December, after a flight of 28 days. Ross and Keith Smith were both knighted, but Sir Keith was killed with Lieutenant Bennett at the outset of a round-the-world flight in 1922.

Left:
Charles Kingsforth Smith, first pilot to fly the Pacific and Tasman

Harry Hawker

The Australian aviator Harry Hawker (1889–1921), who had travelled to England in 1911 and set distance and altitude records there, was the first pilot to attempt to fly the Atlantic in 1919, taking off from Newfoundland with a British co-pilot in a single-engine Sopwith, carrying a dinghy strapped to the fuselage, but was forced to ditch in the ocean. He was rescued from the sea but killed two years later in an air crash. His name lives on in the factory he founded, which manufactured the famed Hawker Hurricane fighter of Battle of Britain fame.

'Smithy', Ulm and the Southern Cross

Australians were the first airmen to fly the Pacific, an expanse three times the breadth of the Atlantic. They were two adventurous young AIF veterans, Charles Kingsford Smith and Charles Ulm, who struck up a friendship at Mascot airfield. They raised money from Sydney newspapers, caught a steamer for the United States and there purchased a three-engined Fokker, a magnificently strong aeroplane, which they named *Southern Cross* and in which they trained on long flights to stay at the controls for 12 hours at a stretch. With two American crewmen (navigator and radio operator), Smithy and Ulm

Charles Kingsford Smith and Charles Ulm pose before the 'Southern Cross'

took off in *Southern Cross* from California on 31 May 1928, fought their way through tropical storms, landed to refuel on the fly-speck island at Hawaii, and then took off for the second leg to Fiji (where no airstrips existed; 'Smithy' landed the giant aircraft on a cricket field and they had to take off from a beach). They then took off on 8 June for the last leg to Queensland. By now wireless reports of the dramatic flight had captured the world's attention and millions prayed for the airmen's safety. They landed at Brisbane early on 9 June, after a flight of 20 hours from Fiji, to find themselves national heroes, the flight acclaimed as the greatest aviation feat in history. They then flew the Tasman, stormier even than the Pacific, and the New Zealanders went wild over them. 'Smithy' and Ulm went on to found one of the world's first airlines (the first ANA), and set new records introducing 'air mail' on the England-Australia route. Charles Ulm crashed over the Pacific attempting to open a new air route in 1934.

On 1935 the mighty tri-motor *Southern Cross* was purchased from Smithy by the Australian government (it now stands as a memorial to its pilots at Brisbane Airport).

Five months later, in November 1935, Sir Charles Kingsford Smith disappeared off the Burma coast, while flying from England. Neither his and nor Ulm's planes have ever been found, but their names live on in the story of aviation, the trail-blazing years when Australia led the world, leaving other nations on the ground, gasping with disbelief.

The Record Breakers

Bert Hinkler

Another wartime pilot, the Queenslander Bert Hinkler, made the first solo flight from England to Australia in 1928 and in 1931 made a spectacular flight from New York to London—via Jamaica, Brazil and west Africa! Two years later he was killed in Italy attempting an England-Australia speed record. In 1939, Smithy and Ulm's former crewman, P.G. Taylor, became the first man to fly the Indian Ocean.

In 1920, a daredevil Australian Flying Corps (AFC) pilot P.J. 'Ginty' McGinness and his former navigator Bill Hudson Fysh, formed at Winton, Queensland, an air service for the outback—the

Queensland and Northern Territory Air Service (QANTAS). It survives today as the world's oldest airline—after the Dutch line KLM. It is also the world's safest, having never lost an aircraft on its international routes (though to avoid tempting the gods to respond with wrath, this latter fact is never mentioned in advertising or promotion).

The Flying Doctor

A Presbyterian minister, the Reverend John Flynn (1880–1951), was responsible for founding Australia's famous Flying Doctor service in the outback. Born in Victoria and ordained in 1911, he was commissioned in the next year to visit the Northern Territory and central Australia to report on conditions there. As a result of his report a team of travelling padres and medical centres were established, the beginnings of the Australian Inland Mission. With the ever-widening use of wirelesses in the outback and the introduction of air services, Flynn formed in 1928 the A.I.M. Aerial Medical Service at Cloncurry, Queensland which, linked by radio, became the Royal Flying Doctor Service (RFDS), bringing medical—and spiritual—help to the remote people of the lonely outback. 'Flynn of the Inland' died in Sydney in 1951 and his ashes are buried at the base of Mount Gillen near Alice Springs. In the 1990s, the 37 aircraft of the RFDS attended to 150,000 cases of illness and flew near 9,000,000 kilometres annually. Like the 'School of the Air' by which children are instructed in their lessons by radio, it is a uniquely Australian innovation.

The 'Ace' Clive Caldwell (left) with Australian and British pilots, 1942

AWM Photo 11944

The R.A.A.F.

In 1921 Prime Minister Billy Hughes authorized the birth of a permanent air defence, the Royal Australian Air Force (RAAF). It first chief was Colonel Richard Williams, who had led the famed No. 1 Squadron Australian Flying Corps (AFC) successfully in the Middle East. Disdaining the stylish light grey-blue uniform of the Royal Air Force for the new service, 'Dick' Williams decided that the Australians must—as usual—look distinctive and ordered them uniforms of navy blue.

When war came in 1939, the RAAF consisted of 3,000 officers and men, manning barely a dozen squadrons of obsolete aircraft. When it ended in 1945, the RAAF totalled 180,000 men and women and was close to being the fourth largest air force in the world. The bulk of them fought in the Pacific against the Japanese but thousands of Australians served in the British service (Royal Air Force) and in RAAF squadrons in RAF Fighter, Coastal and Bomber Command (where they suffered heavier casualties than infantry) and in the Middle East air forces. The RAAF recently re-introduced uniforms of the dark blue that the men of 1939-45 had made famous.

Fred Spofforth, the 'Demon' bowler

THE DEMON

16: *Good Sports*

The Races

'As far back as 1805 our early compatriots held race-meetings on the 'Officers' Racecourse', now better known as Hyde Park, Sydney; but the first meeting of any consequence was promoted by Sir John Jamieson, of Regentsville, near Penrith, in 1824; and the fine old sportsman who promoted the meeting, found refreshments on a most liberal scale for the large gathering of 5,000 people who attended. An old ticket-of-leave man who was present at the races gave us a vivid account of the great riot which took place at the end of the day's sport, between the 'Currency Lads' (as native-born Australians were then called), and Sir John Jamieson's servants. The servants, who were nearly all convicts, were disappointed at the defeat of their master's horse "Benalong" in the Big Race, and they started a great row with the winner. The battle of fists and sticks lasted well into the night, and both sides claimed the victory. We have spoken of Charlie Smith, the owner of "Chancellor", and of Bailey, the importer of "Emigrant" and breeder of "Jorrocks" and other great horses; and there were many such stud masters in our annals in the merry days of old. The names of those men and the most famous of their stock are as well known as the first of the month to most Australians.'

— FROM A NINETEENTH CENTURY ACCOUNT

A Back-Block Settlement

When the Mickety-Mulga Wholloper met the Cobbity shearers'
  Cook,
    There was trouble upon the station, you can bet,
    For the Cook he had a debt which he'd recorded in the book,
    And he swore the Wholloper hadn't paid it yet.
    And the Wholloper swore he didn't owe the Cook a blessed
    cent,
    For he always paid his shearing-shed account,
    And in case the Cook did not perceive precisely what he meant
    He'd be pleased to fight his gills for the amount!

Then the Cook he cast reflections on the Wholloper's family tree,
    Said his male relations mostly lived in gaol,
    All but Jimmy, hanged in Goulburn, as the rest deserved to be,
    While the ladies were particularly frail!

And the adjectives he used for illustration they were grand,
And he coined 'em in his own especial mint,
But they were of such a nature, you will easy understand,
As would hardly bear repeating here in print!

So we made a ring around 'em and the battle was begun,
And the language it was forcible and free,
And a better mill was never seen before upon a run,
Nor a better could a sportsman wish to see.
And the Cook he landed Wholloper a beauty on the jaw,
Saying 'Now, will you admit you owe them beans?'
But immediately afterwards the hash-constructor saw,
What the art of concentration really means!

For the Wholloper he countered with a daisy on the neck,
And he followed with another on the point,
And before the Cook recovered he became a perfect wreck,
With a Grecian nose completely out of joint;
Still they kept the fun a-going, and the blows were freely shared,
And they made it very merry for a while,
But at length the Cook was beaten and the referee declared,
They had fought it in a gentlemanly style!

Now there's nothing could be nicer or more beautiful to see
Than the meeting of them two upon the morn,
For with features bruised and swollen they were friendly as
could be
And shook hands as though the pair were brothers born.
And the shearers and the rouseabouts as edict they enforced,
That the winner'd squared all overdue amounts,
And in terms of approbation, too, they cheerfully endorsed
Such a simple way of settling all accounts!

— W.T. GOODGE (1862-1909)

The Melbourne Cup

'They come a hundred thousand strong, as all the best authorities say, and they pack the spacious grounds and grand-stands and make spectacle such as is never to be seen in Australasia elsewhere.

'It is the 'Melbourne Cup' that brings this multitude together. Their clothes have been ordered long ago, at unlimited cost, and without bounds as to beauty and magnificence, and have been kept in concealment until now, for unto this day are they consecrated. I am speaking of the ladies' clothes; but one might know that.

'And so the grand-stands make a brilliant and wonderful spectacle, a delirium of colour, a vision of beauty. The champagne flows,

everybody is vivacious, excited, happy; everybody bets, and gloves and fortunes change hands right along, all the time. Day after day the races go on, and the fun and excitement are kept at white heat; and when each day is done, the people dance all night so as to be fresh for the race in the morning. And at the end of the great week, the swarms secure lodgings and transportation for next year, then flock away to their remote homes and count their gains and losses, and order next year's Cup-clothes, and then lie down and sleep two weeks, and get up sorry to reflect that a whole year must be put in somehow or other before they can be wholly happy again.

'The Melbourne Cup is the Australasian National Day. It would be difficult to overstate its importance. It overshadows all other holidays and specialized days of whatever sort in that congeries of colonies. Overshadows them? I might almost say it blots them out. Each of them gets attention but not everybody's; each of them evokes interest, but not everybody's; each of them rouses enthusiasm, but not everybody's; in each case a part of the attention, interest, and enthusiasm is a matter of habit and custom, and another part of it is official and perfunctory. Cup Day, and Cup Day only, commands an attention, an interest, and an enthusiasm which are universal—and spontaneous, not perfunctory. Cup Day is supreme—it has no rival. I can call to mind no specialized annual day, in any country, which can be named by that large name—Supreme. I can call to mind no specialized annual day, in any country, whose approach fires the whole land with a conflagration of conversation and preparation and anticipation and jubilation. No day save this one; but this one does it.'

— *MARK TWAIN, 1897*

Archer's Wins

'The annual event of the most general interest in Australia is the Melbourne Cup Meeting. The only thing in the world that can compare with it as a national excitement is the English Derby Day; but although the people who witness that race outnumber the whole of the population of Victoria, the interest taken in the Australian holiday is, I venture to assert, more general and more widely-spread.

'From the Gulf of Carpentaria to d'Entrecasteaux Channel, from Perth to Sydney, from Cape York to Invercargill, the whole population are eager to ascertain what horse has the best chance of the victory. Conversation is not confined to bookmakers or sporting men. Solid taciturn people, in far-away stations on Queensland or Adelaide plains, know all about the entries, and calculate by the knowledge of previous "performances" which their infrequent newspaper brings to them, the chances of their favourites. Men who have never laid a bet in their lives grow pale with excitement as they talk of the stables in whose fortunes they are interested. Journeys of hundreds of miles are cheerfully undertaken by "squatters" residents in "backblocks" of the far interior. "To see the Cup run for" is a sacred duty, and there are men who date events from Banker or Barwon's "year", though they have never paid or received a penny, or entered a betting-room. During the first ten days in November, Melbourne is crowded with strangers. The city has the aspect of a town possessed by an enemy, or of a fair of nations. It is more than a race meeting, it is a gathering of the clans. The fair of Nishni Novgorod, Mecca during the Ramadan, might be held to compare with it. Racing is emphatically the national sport of Australia, and it is by no means impossible that Australians will breed the best horses in the world. As it is, the victory of Darriwell, on the 4th November, has only been once excelled at the same weight and distance.

'The first Melbourne Cup was run for in 1861. It was 20 sovereigns, 10 sovereigns forfeit, and 5 sovereigns if declared, with 200 sovereigns added. The stake 930 sovereigns. Distance 2 miles. The favourite was Mr Keighran's Mormon, a Victorian bred horse. Mormon started at 3 to 1, while the winner Archer was at 100 to 8. Flatcatcher led from the start, but at the turn Fireaway passed both horses, and in the struggle for places a serious accident occurred. Despatch, Medora and Twilight fell in a heap. It appeared that Despatch crossed her legs, and Medora fell on her, Twilight getting a terrific fall over both of them. The three jockeys were all more or less injured. Henderson was stunned, while Morrison sustained a compound fracture of the forearm, and Hayes broke his left collarbone. Archer now came through his horses, and Cutts cantered the crack home, winning by half a dozen lengths. Prince beat Antonelli on the post for third place. Time 3 minutes, 52 seconds.

'For the second Cup, Archer started first favourite at 2 to 1, in the largest field of horses ever seen on the course up to that time. The race was a struggle between him and his old rival Mormon, but notwithstanding an extra stone weight, Archer won by ten lengths, and in five seconds less time than that of the previous year.'
— *THE VICTORIAN REVIEW, 1880*

Aussie Rules

Australian Rules football—now known as AFL (Australian Football League) and once known to all as VFL (Victorian Football League)—was invented in New South Wales by H.C.A. Colden Harrison and his cousin T.W.S. (Tom) Wills, as a means of keeping their players fit over the winter months. Sydney showed little interest and the first 'serious' match was played in Melbourne in the same year between Melbourne Grammar and Scotch College. Based at least partly on Irish football, it was played on a huge ground with a total of 80 players. Pandemonium followed. In the first three games neither side managed to score at all.

When Harrison and Wills reduced the team to 20 players each, the game took off (though not in New South Wales, where Rugby later became firmly established). The Victorian Football Association (VFA) was formed in 1877 and the breakaway Victorian Football League (VFL, now the AFL) in 1897. The game was taken up in Western Australia, South Australia and Tasmania, attracted large crowds in Queensland and in the 1980s was introduced to New South Wales. First codified in 1858, the Melbourne Football Club rules of 1859 are the oldest surviving rules of Australian football. It is now Australia's national game but it remains strongest in Victoria, where it is an obsession: in 1970 the Grand Final between Carlton and Collingwood drew a crowd of 122,000. This dynamic game has been described as a 'fast-moving spectacle incorporating elements of gaelic football, soccer, the two Rugby codes, and hurling' .

League and Union

The tough English football game invented at Rugby School was played with enthusiasm by the first settlers and established itself as 'the only game' in New South Wales. By 1907, however, Rugby Union players were being so often injured and having to take time off work to recover—without any form of compensation—that a group of them met at Victor Trumper's sports store to discuss their grievances. They resolved to break away from the Union and form a new league of professional players who would be guaranteed payment for matches played, plus expenses. Soon most of the top players joined the Rugby League but Rugby Union—known as 'the gentleman's game'— is still played widely.

'The Ashes': England Goes Down in Flames

When the deciding Second Innings between England and Australia began at Kennington Oval on Tuesday 29 August 1882, the home team was confident of victory, and betting was 60 to 1 on the English.

Australia opened the batting and racked up 122 runs before England went to bat. The Australian bowler, the tall, lanky Fred Spofforth (1853-1926) from Sydney, was fighting mad over W.G. Grace's 'ungentlemanly' action in knocking the bails off Jones' wicket when the latter had left the crease to pat down some turf, late in the innings. Spofforth had vowed to his mates in the pavilion that he would not let England win.

England's Eleven needed only 85 runs to win the innings when they commenced batting. Their two opening bats had racked up 15 runs when Spofforth bowled their captain out, and minutes later bowled out his replacement. Tension began to mount.

England scored another 36 runs before Ulyatt was caught at the wicket from another ball by Spofforth, and soon the great W.G. Grace was caught for 32 from a ball from Bannerman. England was now six wickets down, but still needed only 32 runs to win.

Spofforth and Boyle began bowling as they had never bowled before. Lyttleton went down for 12, bowled by Spofforth, and then Lucas—for a 'duck'. Four bats left and only 15 runs to win. England's chances were still good, despite 'Demon Fred' Spofforth's tally.

Spofforth then bowled Read for a 'duck' and the suspense became unbearable: one spectator collapsed and another was seen eating part of his umbrella. Taking over the bowling from Boyle, Spofforth bowled out another Englishman.

With two batsmen left—but still short of only 19 runs to win— Barnes was then caught by Murdoch, Australia's captain, from a ball by Boyle.

England's last man, Peate, walked onto the oval knowing that he held the fate of the match in his hands. He hit Boyle's first ball for two runs—only eight more runs to win!—missed the next, and was clean bowled! England had lost.

There were several seconds of silence and then the crowd went wild. They cheered Australia to the skies and scores of them, jumping the fence, carried Fred Spofforth shoulder high to the pavilion. Good losers to the end, the English inserted an obituary notice in London's Sporting Life several days later mourning the death of English cricket and notifying readers that its 'ashes' would be taken to Australia.

When Ivo Bligh led the England team to Australia for the summer tests early in 1883 a couple of young Australian girls burnt a stump and presented its ashes in an urn to the touring captain. Accepting them in good grace, he kept the ashes on his mantelpiece the rest of his life, bequeathing them to England's Marylebone Cricket Club (MCC) on his death in 1927, one year after the death of 'Demon Fred' Spofforth. The Ashes—which by tradition never leave England whatever the outcome of the England–Australia Tests—still stand on display in the Long Room at Lord's, the home of cricket.

Victor Trumper

V Victor he, in name and deed, pride of Austral seas,
I In a blaze of glory such as few recall.
C Clinking strokes that blind us, dazzle and remind us,
T Trumper, Victor Trumper, is the peer of all;
O Onward still where'er he be, England or Australia,
R Reeling out his hundreds while the crowds acclaim.
T Timing, driving, glancing, hooking that entrancing,
R Rushing up the pathway to the Hall of Fame;
U Under all this triumph what do we discern—
M Modesty, refreshing as a desert rain,
P Pride, well-curbed and glowing,
E Earnest and straight-going,
R Round his brow the victor's wreath will long remain.

— *ANONYMOUS*

Victor Trumper (1877–1915) was acknowledged as the greatest batsman of his era. Born in Sydney he was outstanding at the crease even as a schoolboy and played aged 17 for New South Wales against the touring Marylebone Cricket Club, scoring a respectable 67. In the 1897–98 season he made 1,021 runs in eight innings and in the 1899 tour of England made 135 'not out' at Lords, followed by 300 not out against Sussex! In the 1902 tour he scored 2,750 runs. He played 401 first class innings in his life and scored a total of 16,939 runs and was only 37 when he died tragically of Bright's disease.

Les Darcy

Born into an Irish-Australian family in Maitland, New South Wales, James Leslie Darcy (1895–1917) was working as a blacksmith's apprentice when he started boxing at the age of 15. He had his first major fight against Holland in 1914, when he lost on points—but he won the two return bouts. In 1915 Les Darcy won the Australian middleweight title and next year the heavyweight title. In 50 fights he had won 46 of them and he became a national hero. Attempting to enlist in the Australian army (AIF) he was rejected, so he stowed away on an American freighter, determined to win world recognition as a professional boxer. Australians called him a shirker and were angered when he took out US citizenship, though he enlisted in the United States forces. He died suddenly of meningitis in the United States in May 1917. His body was returned for burial in Australia giving Australians their chance to pay respects to a champion unfairly maligned.

The Lifesavers

Until 1903 swimming during the day from Sydney's beaches was technically illegal—a holdover from the Victorian view that the human body was scandalous. When a bunch of carefree Manly youths stripped down to their pants one hot day in September 1902 and plunged into the surf, they were arrested. Determined to put an end to this ridiculous by-law, the editor of the *Manly Daily*, W.H. Gocher, announced that he was taking to the waters on the following Sunday. No policeman arrived. On his third attempt he was arrested, charged with indecency—and had the charge dismissed.

In 1903 Manly Council repealed the by-law, ordered flags to be erected to define safe swimming areas, and opened their beaches to daylight bathers, provided swimmers clothed themselves in garments from neck to knee 'so as to secure the observance of decency' (in the words of the new local government act).

On all beaches inexperienced swimmers were constantly having to be rescued by stronger ones, so in February 1906 a group of keen surfers formed Australia's first 'life savers' club at Bondi. These volunteers tested the ocean for dangerous currents and patrolled the swimming areas between the flags while keeping a lookout on towers for cruising sharks (whose presence was notified by ringing a bell). By the end of the year the first reel and line was in service and the first rescue with it occurred in January 1907 when a young Queenslander was brought in. His name was Charles Kingsford Smith, the future aviation pioneer 'Smithy' of Southern Cross fame.

Phar Lap

Like many famous Australian races horses—including Carbine and Rising Fast—Phar Lap was New Zealand-born and bred. Called by many the world's greatest race horse, he was a chestnut gelding foaled at Timaru Stud, and was bought by a Victorian trainer who liked his breeding pattern for a knock-down price of 160 guineas. Phar Lap—a Singhalese word for thunder—was a big horse but in his first Australian race in February 1929 he ran unplaced. It was not until April that his improving performance against other 3-year-olds made punters sit up and take notice of him. He won the Derby in the spring of 1929 but was still regarded as average until the VRC Autumn Carnival of 1930 when he won the St Leger, the King's Plate and the Governor's Plate, repeating this outstanding performance at the AJC carnival in Sydney. His winning runs continued in South Australia and by the eve of the Melbourne Cup in November 1930 Phar Lap was the favourite. In the four days of the VRC Carnival the mighty Phar Lap won every race he entered, but his victory in the Melbourne Cup—on day two—was the most memorable. A shot was fired at Phar Lap during his morning training run on the Saturday before the Cup, and tension on Cup Day was high. Despite being burdened with the heaviest weight any four-year-old had ever carried in the Cup—9 stone, 12 pounds (62.6 kilograms)—Phar Lap never looked like losing. He tore into the lead on the home turn 'in half a dozen long strides, and coasted over the line three lengths clear' of the next horse. The crowd went wild. The champion was taken to the United States, where he won the famous Caliente in California and seemed set to rewrite horseracing history, but only weeks later, on 4 April 1932, it was announced that Phar Lap had died suddenly in America—of enteritis. Of the 57 races he had ridden, he had won 31 of them.

His body was returned to Australia, where it was discovered how he accomplished this extraordinary record: his mighty heart (which Sydney claimed) was twice the size of most race horse's. Phar Lap's body stands on permanent display in Melbourne's Museum of Victoria.

Up there, Cazaly!

It was the barrackers' shout at football matches in the 1920s and the battle cry of Australian infantry in the Western Desert campaigns in 1941 (though few of them, apart from Victorians, knew its origin). Ray Lawler included it in his play *The Summer of the Seventeenth Doll*, and Australians still shout it out as a term of encouragement or amazement.

Roy Cazaly (1893–1963), Tasmanian-born, was probably the best high mark Aussie Rules has ever known, soaring in the ruck to incredible heights to the crowd's delight. He started playing in the Victorian Football League (VFL) with St. Kilda in 1910, aged 16, but first leaped to prominence in 1921 when he joined South Melbourne, forming with 'Skeeter' Fleiter (ruck) and 'Napper' Tandy

(rover) one of the game's most formidable ruck-rover teams. While Fleiter, a heavier man, shielded him and shouted 'Up, Cazza, Up!' Cazaly would take a deep breath and make his oxygen-assisted leap to the ball—one of his mates said he seemed to 'dwell' above the ground. Melbourne crowds took up the cry.

Cazaly joined Hawthorn as coach in 1942 when the club was in the doldrums; in 1943 it won more games than it lost (9 to 6), ending equal fourth on the ladder. He came out of retirement when he was 51 to play with Camberwell and late coached in his home-state, Tasmania.

452 not out!

"PUBLIC HERO"

NUMBER ONE

D.G. Bradman made the world's highest score in first class cricket at the Sydney Cricket Ground yesterday, being 452 not out when the New South Wales second innings was closed for 761 for eight wickets.' So ran a report of Donald Bradman's astonishing achievements in a Sydney paper on 7 January 1930.

Don Bradman—'The Don'— would become Australia's greatest cricketing hero. Born in Cootamundra in 1908, he scored his first century playing for Bowral High School at the age of 12. In 1928, after playing in Sheffield Shield matches, he was selected for the Australian team. He was to play in every England–Australia test match until his retirement as captain after the 1948 test (missing only one Test, because of illness). His average was 99.94 runs—and he went out for a duck in the last test innings he played!

By 1994 the Australian Test captain Allan Border had equalled Bradmans's score of 452 in one match and had become the highest scoring batsman in Test history, with a total of more than 11,000 runs.

'Snowy' Baker, Champ in 29 Sports

There will never be another 'Snowy' Baker.

Born Reginald Leslie Baker, in Sydney in February 1884, he was one of six children of an Irishman from County Limerick who had come out for the gold rush and stayed to rise high in Sydney council. All six children showed an aptitude for sport, but Reginald— nicknamed 'Snowball' or 'Snowy' in true Australian tradition because of his thatch of un-Irish, pure-blond hair— was a schoolboy swimming and diving champion at the age of ten; at 17— already running in New South Wales track events, and rowing brilliantly, he played for Australia against the visiting English Rugby team.

Coached in cricket by Victor Trumper, Baker was also playing in the state water polo team when he was selected for the 1908 London Olympics, in which he won a silver medal in boxing and competed in the fancy diving and 200-metre swimming relays.

Returning to Australia, Snowy teamed up with Hugh D. McIntosh to form Stadiums Ltd and pioneer the golden age of Australian boxing. (He was to referee 1,300 fights in his long career). He won the Australian middleweight title, and the light, middleweight and heavyweight championships of New South Wales in addition to the middle and heavyweight championships of Victoria.

Snowy Baker was also a championship rider and a pioneer film maker who travelled to Hollywood after the war with his horse 'Boomerang' to star in cowboy movies under the name Rex Snowy Baker. In America he taught Rudolph Valentino how to ride and Douglas Fairbanks how to crack a whip (and according to some legends, in the 1930s, taught Shirley Temple and Elizabeth Taylor how to stay on a horse).

Back in Australia, Baker wrote a book on physical fitness, opened a gymnasium, wrote a sports column for the Evening News and included hockey, fencing and yachting in his list of versatile sportsman in our history.

The Olympics

Australia stands with Great Britain and Greece as the only nations that have competed in every Olympic Games since the modern Olympiads were born in 1896. Australians have traditionally been an outdoors race, playing sport for fun as much as exercise or profit, and Australian record-breakers have astonished the world, particularly in swimming and athletics (track and field).

In the 1896 Games Australia's Edwin Flack won two events, starting the tradition.

But for most Australians, the Melbourne Olympics of 1956 were—until the Sydney 2000 Olympics—the most unforgettable Games of them all. The first to be held in the Southern hemisphere, they saw Australia scoop up no fewer than 13 gold medals—more than double the number won at Helsinki four years before.

For two sunny weeks in November and December 1956, while television (introduced only weeks before) and newspapers told of Russian tanks crushing Hungary's bid for freedom and of the Anglo-French-Israeli invasion of Egypt, Australians watched spellbound as more than 3,000 competitors from 67 nations competed for gold, silver and bronze.

Australia's team of 243 men and 44 women was second in size only to that of the United States' 298 competitors, and it included names that would become legendary. Swimmer Murray Rose and sprinter Betty Cuthbert won two gold medals each. Gold medals also went to swimmers Lorraine Crapp, Dawn Fraser, Jon Hendricks and David Thiele, and to Shirley Strickland (hurdles).

Australia also won gold medals in four team events—the women's relay (100 metres), the 2,000-metre cycling tandem, the women's freestyle relay (100 metres) and the men's freestyle relay (200 metres). Eight silver and 14 bronze medals brought Australia's total to 35 medals in the 1956 Olympics—a dramatic jump from the 11 won in 1952.

The Rome Olympics of 1960 were to bring the nation another 22 medals, including eight gold, placing Australia fifth from the top of the list of 84 competing nations, her total exceeded only by Russia, the United States, Italy and Germany. After Australia's poor showing in the 1970s Games—particularly at Montreal—a massive infusion of federal and state government money was poured into sports and sports training, and the results were soon to show.

Other 'Golden' Olympics came in the Centenary Olympics of 1996 in Atlanta, USA, when Australia won 41 medals including 9 gold—a medals total exceeded only by the United States (101 medals), Germany (65), Russia (63) and China (50) - and in the 2000 Sydney Olympics, when Australia's total was 58 medals, including 16 gold (and 149 medals in the Paralympics).

17: *Tall Tales—and True*

The Infamous Lynch

'The series of atrocious murders committed by the infamous Lynch, who was hanged at Berrima Gaol in 1844, form about the most blood-curdling chapter of horrors in our history. It is said, to begin with, that Lynch murdered his own father (a convict like himself), though of this no absolute proof was tendered. But the crimes Lynch admitted perpetrating were enough for a myriad of demons to have consummated.

'He confessed to having killed at least nine persons—most terrible, cold-blooded crimes. His victims were the whole family of the Mulligans—father, mother, son and daughter—all well known to the author; a man named Fraser and his son; one Ireland (better known as "Cobbawan Jack"); a black boy, and one Landrigan, his last victim, a new-chum labourer; a record against which the fratricidal deed of Cain, the first murderer, is but a fleabite. The weapon generally used by Lynch in his murders was a shingler's tomahawk, and it was his boast that he could kill a man with a single blow. In the author's boyhood, he saw Lynch (in 1842), on several occasions, when the murderer, a wiry, muscular fellow, about 5 feet 6 inches in height and 10 stone in weight, was employed at a job of fencing, along with an old ticket-of-leave man, one Mr Redmond, at Mr Hillas's 'Bunnaby' Station; and, by the way we have often thought that Mat Redmond must have been born under a lucky star to have escaped the murderous attentions of Mr Lynch. Before coming to 'Bunnaby', Lynch had finished his period of assignment at Mr Atkinson's near Berrima. There he had for mate a youthful convict, one 'Boy Tom', whom it was alleged Lynch murdered. At all events, Lynch and 'Tom' left Berrima in company one day, and 'Boy Tom' was never afterwards heard of. But we hope, though the chances are all the other way about, that 'Tom' didn't fall, like so many other unfortunates, a victim to the monster under review. This was some six weeks before Lynch came to 'Bunnaby'. After finishing his contract there, Lynch took the track for Sydney.

'On the road he fell in with "Cobbawn Jack" (Ireland) and a black-boy, who were in charge of a horse team belonging to the late Mr Thomas Cowper (brother of Sir Charles Cowper), which was bound for Sydney with a freight of cheese and bacon, etc., for sale. Lynch journeyed along in their company, and one night at the camp at Razorback, near Picton, under the pretence of looking for the

straying horses of the team, he took the blackboy with him, and at the first opportunity killed the lad with a single blow of his deadly tomahawk. Returning to the camp, he induced 'Cobbawn Jack' to also join in the 'search' for the horses, and at a favourable moment gave the man his deathblow. He then burned the two bodies, and yoking the team, the miscreant made tracks for Sydney, intending to sell the property and pocket the proceeds. Near Liverpool, however, to Lynch's surprise, he was met by Mr Cowper, the owner of the team. To Cowper's inquiry, Lynch said that Ireland and the boy had gone into the bush after whip-handles, and he was only driving the team until they overtook him. Mr Cowper, strange to say, accepted this story, and on leaving, told Lynch that he would expect the team at a certain place in Sydney on an appointed day. Lynch, however, travelling day and night, got to Sydney long before the date appointed, and having quickly disposed of the team and produce, he started up country again. At Bargo Brush he fell in with a teamster named Fraser, and his (Fraser's) son, and on the second night of their acquaintance, the miscreant killed both father and son, the boy in the scrub and the father while sleeping; and, as in Cowper's case, Lynch then appropriated the bullock-dray and freight of which he had so dreadfully deprived poor Fraser.

'A few weeks after his last terrible crime Lynch made his way to Berrima district, going to Mulligan's farm at 'The Ploughed Ground'. The Mulligans, though previously acquainted with Lynch, had no idea what sort of a fiend they were entertaining; but, alas, they were not to remain long deluded, for Lynch, in one night, killed every member of the family; but we will not dwell on the horrible details of those diabolical crimes. The murderer collected the bodies of his four victims, and burned them in one heap ...'

— *FROM* OLD PIONEERING DAYS IN THE SUNNY SOUTH, *1907*
    CHAS. MACALISTER

The Cannibal Convicts

Alexander Pearce (1790–1824) was transported for stealing six pairs of shoes—but is best remembered for eating six of his friends. He described the last one as 'delicious'.

None of the eight convicts who escaped from the hell of Macquarie Harbour was born a monster, but the 'System' and the privations they suffered made them that. Pearce, a nuggety Irishman from Country Monaghan, had arrived in Van Diemen's Land in 1820 and was sentenced to Macquarie Harbour for going bush as an Assigned Servant. His seven confederates included an ex-soldier sentenced to 14 years for perjury and several on seven-year sentences

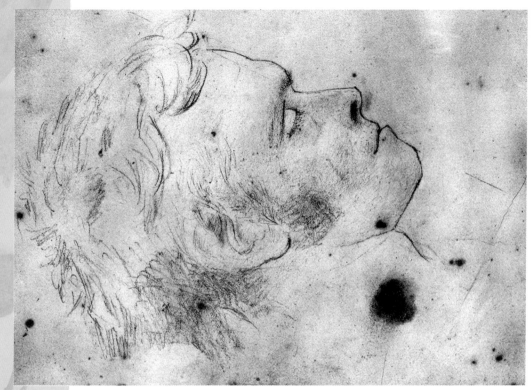

Alexander Pearce, the 'cannibal'
(Mitchell Library Collection, State Library of New South Wales)

for petty theft. Stealing a boat on 20 September 1822, the eight men rowed across the harbour and then headed by foot across the island, hoping to steal a ship on the Derwent and sail for home. They faced some of the most impossible mountain country in Australia— peaks and chasms and almost impenetrable bush so forbidding that not even natives could live there.

After a week in these conditions, frozen by the cold, and starving after three days without food, Greenhill, an English ex-seaman and Travers, his Irish mate, suggested eating one of the party. To the others' horror they killed the ex-soldier and feasted on him. Two of the weaker members of the group, fearing that they would be next, decamped and headed back to Macquarie Harbour; they were found near the shore, dying of malnutrition.

The remaining five ate their fill and pushed on, fording the swollen Franklin River and hacking their way over the mountains until they reached the Loddon Plains. Without weapons to catch game, Greenhill killed another man, whose flesh kept them going for several days, and then killed two more. When Pearce noticed that Greenhill was eyeing him hungrily over the camp fire, he waited until the Englishman fell asleep and killed him with an axe, snacking off the body.

After nearly eight weeks Pearce finally reached a shepherd's hut, whose owner, an Irishman refused to turn him in. He fell in with two bushrangers but the trio were captured in July 1823 and taken to Hobart in chains. There Pearce confessed all, but the authorities refused to believe his story and returned him to Macquarie Harbour. He arrived there as something of a celebrity and escaped again in November, accompanied by a convict named Cox. After three days the two men argued and Pearce killed his companion, and began eating him too. Two days later the 'Monster' was found by soldiers. Taken again to Hobart, he was hanged immediately.

Fisher's Ghost

It has been called Australia's most famous ghost story. In June 1826 a farmer at Campbelltown, New South Wales, named Frederick Fisher, disappeared. He was a former convict, but a law-abiding man. Soon after he vanished his apparition was seen by a wayfarer—a ghostly figure, sitting on a railing post, silently pointing towards a nearby creek. The local police sergeant decided to investigate and saw traces of blood on the railings where the 'ghost' had been sitting. When the nearby creek was dragged Fisher's body was found there, and a neighbour, George Worrall, was later charged with Fisher's murder. He confessed to the crime and was hanged in 1827. The creek is now known as Fisher's Ghost Creek.

More Ghosts

Bill Beatty, in his book *A Treasury of Australian Folk Tales and Traditions*, tells of reportings of other strange apparitions and hauntings, all of which can possibly be explained as natural phenomena or figments of excited imaginations: the Headless Horseman which is said to appear and stampede fear-stricken cattle; the Phantom Mail, a lantern on a stage coach seen on the One-Tree Plain near Hay that horsemen have pursued but never caught; the Kiama ghost that led searchers into the bush to the charred bones of a wayfarer and his dog, both killed by criminals; the Glengallan Gates on a property in Queensland that mysteriously open on the approach of horses, which tremble with fear; the Black Horse of Sutton (near Bowral), said to be the ghost of a farmer thrown by his horse and killed while riding to Goulburn; the headless ghost of Mad Dan Morgan, which was reported to have appeared at the famous landmark Hanging Rock, near Woodend, where a party of schoolgirls are said to have disappeared one summer day a century ago; the Guyra Ghost, which in 1921 is said to have shaken a worker's home like an earthquake and rained rocks on its roof on the night an 87-year-old woman disappeared without trace. Even the governor-general's residence in Canberra, Yarralumla, is said to have a ghost—an Aborigine seen walking in its grounds, and who on cold winter nights occasionally stares through the French doors at the goings-on inside . . .

The Bunyip

'Everyone who has lived in Australia has heard of the Bunyip. It is the one respectable flesh-curdling horror of which Australia can boast. The old world has her tales of ghoul and vampire, of Lorelei, spook, and pixie, but Australia has nothing but her Bunyip.

'No Australian traveller ever saw the Bunyip with his own eyes; and though there are many stockman's yarns and black's patters [talk] which have to do with this wonderful monster, they have all the hazy uncertainty which usually envelops information of the legendary kind. Some night, perhaps, when you are sitting over a camp fire brewing quart-pot tea and smoking store tobacco, with the spectral white gums rising like an army of ghosts around you, and the horses' hobbles clanking cheerfully in the distance, you will ask one of the overlanding hands to tell you what he knows about the Bunyip. The bushman will warm to his subject as readily as an Irishman to his banshee. He will indignantly repel your insinuation that the Bunip may be after all as mythical as Alicc's Jabberwock; and he will forthwith proceed to relate how a friend of his had a mate, who knew another chap, who had once in his life had a narrow escape from the Bunyip, and had actually beheld it— and in a certain lagoon not a hundred miles from where you are squatting. He himself has never set eyes upon the Bunyip, nor has his mate, but there is not the smallest doubt that the other chap has seen it. When facts come to be boiled down however, 'the other chap's' statements will seem curiously vague and contradictory; and if the details are to be accepted as they stand, a remarkable contribution to natural history must be the result.

'The Bunyip is the Australian sea-serpent, only it differs from that much-disputed fact or fiction in that it does not inhabit the ocean, but makes its home in lagoons and still deep water-holes. For rivers and running creeks it appears to have an aversion. No black fellow will object to bathe in a river because of the Bunyip, but he will shake his woolly head mysteriously over many an innocent-looking waterhole, and decline to dive for water-lily roots or some such delicacy dear to the Aboriginal stomach, on the plea that "Debil-debil sit down there".

'Debil-debil and Bunyip are synonymous terms with the black fellow while he is on the bank of a lagoon, though "Debil-debil" in the abstract represents a much indefinite source of danger, and has a far wider scope of action than most mythological deities. "Debil-debil" is a convenient way of accounting, not only for plague, sickness, and disaster, but also for peace, plenty and fortune. The blacks never will volunteer information.'

— *Mrs Campbell Praed, 1890s*

They were Tough Men on the Speewah

'Don't talk to me about Pecos Bill and Colorado Jack and that giant of the lumber camps who picked his teeth with the trunk of a spruce! The heroes of American folk tales are sissies compared to the men of Australia's mythical station, the Speewah. Why, Crooked Mick of the Speewah, a man who would sooner have a fight than a feed, used Ayers Rock to stone the crows and he was no giant by the Speewah standards.

'No, give me the Australian folk heroes every time. Tales of them have been told from Cape York to the Otways, from Brisbane to

Broome. Where teamsters met or drovers gathered, tales of the Speewah were handed on and men pushing their way outback claimed they had reached its boundaries and there were some who said they had worked there.

'When I worked on the Speewah . . .'

'Talk about mud! You should have been on the Speewah . . .'

'Call this a drought! Why, on the Speewah . . .'

'Yes, Old-timer, strange things happened on the Speewah. The kangaroos there were as tall as mountains and the emus laid eggs that men blew and used for houses. But where the Speewah is, no one knows. The men from the Darling said it was back o' Bourke and the men of Bourke said it was out West and the men of the West pointed to Queensland and in Queensland they told you the Speewah was in the Kimberleys.

'Tom Ronan, a bushman of Katherine, Northern Territory, told me in a letter:

' "It was, I think, originally, the place a bit 'farther out', over the next range" where cattle were a bit wilder, horses a bit rougher and men a bit smarter than they were anywhere else. With the growth of backblocks folklore, its position in the scheme of things became more definite: It was the land of running creeks and shady trees and good, green horse feed, the bushman's 'Field of Asphodel', the place where all good bagmen—and some weren't so good—went when they died.

'In the early years of this century an old drover named Jim Dillon  settled down on a bit of country out sou'-west from Wyndham, Western Australia, and called it the Speewah and it still appears on the map as such, thus giving rise to some argument as to whether it was not the original Speewah from which all outlandish places and events took their origin.'

'Whatever its origin, it is possible, from the stories told about it, to get a picture of this mythical station and of some of the men who ran it. The hundreds of stories told about the Speewah are fairly consistent when it comes to giving an idea of its size and though many men feature in the tales one or two crop up regularly, giving the impression that they were "Permanents" known to all the "casuals" who came out with yarns about them.

'Firstly, there is "Crooked Mick" who tried to strangle himself with his own beard in the Big Drought. He was a gun shearer; five hundred a day was nothing to him. Once, the boss, annoyed because of Crooked Mick's rough handling of some wethers, strode up to him on the board and barked, "You're fired". Crooked Mick was shearing flat out at the time. He was going so fast that he shore fifteen sheep before he could straighten up and hang his shears on the hook.

'His later days were saddened by a serious accident. He was washing sheep when he slipped and fell into a tank of boiling water. Big Bill, who was standing beside him, whipped him out, tore off his clothes then seized two wethers and cut their throats. He ripped the hides off the wethers and wrapped them, flesh side in, round Crooked Mick's body and legs. When they got him to a doctor three weeks later the doctor took one look at him and said, "Boys, you've made a wonderful job of him. It would take a major operation to remove these skins. They're grafted to him."

'According to Big Bill they took Crooked Mick back to the Speewah and shore him every year after that.

' "He made twenty-two pounds of wool," Bill said. "Not bad." Big Bill, who built the barbed wire fence, was the strongest man on the Speewah, they said. He made his fortune on the Croydon goldfields cutting up mining shafts and selling them for post holes. He was originally put on to fence the Speewah but gave it up after a day digging post holes. He left his lunch at the first hole when he started in the morning, then at midday he put down his crowbar and set off to walk back for his lunch. He had sunk so many holes he didn't reach his lunch till midnight. That finished him.

' "A bloke'd starve going at that rate," he said.

'Then there was Uncle Harry who rode the crowbar through Wagga without giving it a sore back. He was a modest man who carted five tons of tin whistle through country that was practically unknown at the time. Once, when Big Bill was boasting about his strength, someone asked Uncle Harry had he ever done any heavy lifting.

'"No," he said modestly, "I can't claim that I'm a strong man. Weight lifting was never in my line. However, I once carried a very awkward load off the barge towed by the Tolarno. It was near the Tintinnalogy shed and, mind you, I'm not claiming this load was heavy, only that it was very awkward. I carried, and the banks were steep, too, a double-furrow plough, a set of harrows and eight loose melons. As I say, it wasn't the weight, only the awkwardness of it that makes it worth telling."

'Slab-face Joe was the bullocky on the Speewah. He drove a team so long he had a telephone fitted on the leaders with a line going back to the polers. When he wanted to pull up he rang through to the black boy he paid to ride the lead, and told him to stop the leaders. Half an hour afterwards Slab-face would stop the polers. Once when he rang through he got the wrong number and wasted a day trying to raise "Complaints".

'His team was as strong as they come. When Slab-face Joe was shifting a shed from the Speewah out-station it got bogged in the Speewah creek. Then Slab-face really got that team into it. They pulled so hard they pulled a two-mile bend in the creek and they weren't extended.

'"The Boss" featured in many tales of the Speewah. He had a snout on cockatoos and covered an old red gum with bird lime to catch the flock that was eating his grain. After they landed on the tree he yelled out, "Got you", and they all took off at once. They tore that tree out by the roots and the last he saw of it, it was two miles up making south.

'Hundreds of men worked on the Speewah. In fact, there were so many that they had to mix the mustard with a long-handled shovel and the cook and his assistant had to row out in a boat to sugar the tea. When shearing was on the boss had to ride up and down the board on a motor bike.

'The Speewah holding itself was a tremendous size. When Uncle Harry was sent out to close the garden gate he had to take a week's rations with him, and a jackeroo, going out to bring in the cows from the horse paddock, was gone for six months.

'It was mixed country. There were mountains, salt-bush plains, and thick forests of enormous trees. Crooked Mick, bringing in a mob of three thousand sheep through the big timber, suddenly found himself in pitch darkness. For three days and nights that wretched man punched those sheep along without being able to see one of them. Then daylight snapped on again and Crooked Mick looked back. He had come through a hollow log.

'Some of the hills were so steep on the Speewah that when a man rode a horse down one of them the horse's tail hung over his shoulder and down the front of his chest, giving him the appearance of having a lank, black beard.

'The Speewah was cursed with every plague. Rabbits were there in millions. They were so thick you had to pull them out of the burrows to get the ferrets in and trappers had to brush them aside to set their traps. On some of the paddocks they had to drive them out to get room to put the sheep in.

'Galahs, too, were bad. When the Big Drought broke, the Speewah remained dry as a bone though the rain fell in torrents above it. The first clap of thunder had scared the galahs into flight and they were so thickly packed as they winged over the station that not a drop reached the ground. A mob of them, swooping under Crooked Mick's hut to avoid a hawk, lifted it off the ground with the wind of their wings and carried it for thirty miles. Mick finished his breakfast while going through a belt of cloud at twenty thousand feet, the galahs still pounding along just beneath him.

'The kangaroos were as big as elephants on the Speewah—some were bigger. They say that Crooked Mick and Big Bill were once climbing a hill of fur grass when they slipped and fell into a kangaroo's pouch. The hill got up and made off with Crooked Mick and Big Bill arguing the toss as to how they would get out.

'For six months those two men lived on kangaroo meat and water they got by sinking a bore in the sand that had collected in the bottom of the pouch. Then some silly cow, out with a gun, shot that kangaroo when it was in the middle of a leap. Crooked Mick and Big Bill, who were ploughing at the time, left that pouch like meteors. They were thrown fifty miles and the skid they made when they hit the earth gouged the bed of the Darling.

'Women never feature in the Speewah tales. I have only heard one story in which a woman was supposed to have worked on the Speewah and I'm not inclined to think it was a lie. She was a cook and her name was Gentle Annie.

'The story was told to me by an old man with pale, watery eyes who lived in a hut on the Murray, and, in telling of it, he kept glancing uneasily over his shoulder towards his hut in which I could hear a woman banging pots around and singing in a husky voice.

'According to this old man the Speewah had gone, disappeared, been burnt off the map, and all because of the one and only woman who had ever worked there. Gentle Annie, so he told me, had limbs like a grey box and a frame like the kitchen of a pub. She was always singing and when she sang there was always a change for the worse in the weather. She cooked jam rolls a hundred yards long and her suet puddings had killed twenty shearers.

'Once, at the shearing shed dance, she seized Crooked Mick by the ear as she was dancing the waltz cotillion with him, and kissed that horrified man squarely somewhere about where his mouth lay concealed in hair.

'What a kiss that was! Its like has never been seen before or since. The whole shed rocked upon its foundations and a blue flame streaked away from the point of contact and tore three sheets of galvanized iron off the roof. A thunderous rumble rolled away across the plains and the air was full of the smell of sulphur, dynamite, gunpowder and Jockey Club perfume.

'Ten fires started up at once and the roar of them was like a thousand trains going through a thousand tunnels.

'For three months men fought that bushfire without a wink of sleep. They were famished for a drink of tea. As soon as they lit a camp fire to boil the billy the flames of the bushfire engulfed it.

'As a last, desperate measure, Crooked Mick ran ahead of the fire at sixty miles an hour holding a billy of water back over the flames till it boiled. The tea he made saved the man but not the Speewah.

'Then Big Bill came galloping up on Red Ned, the wildest brumby ever foaled. He drew one enormous breath, then gave one enormous spit and the fire went out with a sizzle.

'"What happened to Gentle Annie?" I asked the old man.

'"I married her," he said with that uneasy glance at his hut.

'I knew then he was a liar. No man who worked on the Speewah ever got married. It was too sissy.

'Well, that was the Speewah where the grandfather clock in the homestead hall had stood in the same place for so long that the shadow of the pendulum had worn a hole in the back.

'Stories of the Speewah are our folklore. While there is still time we should collect and treasure them. They are more than just tall stories of the bush. They are the unwritten literature of men who never had the opportunity to read books and who became tellers of tales instead. They are stories of the Australian people.

— *ALAN MARSHALL (1902-84)*

Two Tales that Never Die

'I was always fond of stories from the bush. Now it turned out, as I noticed over many years, that there were two stories that came up time after time, and it didn't matter where you were, Western Australia, Queensland, you'd hear these two—to my mind they are the wildest-known yarns in this country.'

— *ALAN MARSHALL (1902-84)*

'The first is about a boundary rider on one of these huge stations. He was over ten miles from the station, when he noticed a galah fly out from the hollow of a dead tree. Now it was nesting season, and he knew there'd be baby galahs there and he wanted one for a pet. So he stopped and stood up in the stirrups but he couldn't reach it. I should say broken limbs like that stuck upwards, with a really sharp jagged edge. He wouldn't give up, so he dropped the horse's reins and he stood up in the saddle, and he reached down the hollow limb and got hold of the baby galah, when the horse moved off—and left him hanging with his elbow caught on the jagged edge. He was trapped; there was no hope anybody would come to look for him, the only hope would be if the horse went home and they started looking, but the horse stood there grazing. And of course he was in the most terrible agony; but he managed to get out his Joseph Rogers pocket knife, managed to open it with his teeth— and he cut off his arm at the elbow, and he dropped. Now the

stories all vary from this point. In some he used a torniquet and
reached the homestead where he died on the step; in others his
skeleton was found at the bottom of the tree, and so on and so on.
But I always noticed the bit about the horse grazing was in every
version.

'The other story was about a sleeper-cutter that was working by
himself in very rough country; usually they worked in pairs, but
men on their own would look for smaller trees they could manage
on their own. He'd be looking for red-gums that were fairly straight,
and he'd chop down the tree and then split it into two sleepers,
using a maul and three wedges. He'd belt the wedges in with the
maul and his axe; the maul was wood with an iron ring round it, and
you were careful to hit each wedge in turn, until you heard the omi-
nous crack—I've heard this myself many a time—and soon it would
split. Now what happened with this fellow was, it was green wood
and as he hit, one of the outside wedges fell inside the split—which
made the other two tighter than ever. Now he did a very stupid
thing—though I've seen men do it myself—he put his hand in to
pull the wedge out, and as he did that one of the outside wedges
slipped out and shot up in the air and the split closed on his hand.
He was trapped, without hope of any sort—nobody for miles—and
of course in the most dreadful pain. He tried to reach his axe—he
meant to cut off the hand—but he couldn't reach the axe with his
feet; and years later when they found the skeleton there was a hole
over a foot deep that his feet had made. Here again I heard many ver-
sions of how he came to be found, and how he was identified; but
the main story and the deep hole never varied.

'I always wondered where these things really happened. My
father actually showed me the hollow tree in the bush where the
galah man died; and whenever I heard the story later the man was
usually named—and the place, which could be all over Australia.

'Now I used to write a page regularly for a magazine called
Permewan's Review, a trade paper very popular with bush people
in most parts of Australia, and this page I had was called 'Let's Sit on
the Sliprails', and it was full of bush incidents I'd heard, and wrote
about. We had a lot of controversies—are bullocks stronger than
draught horses? How many posts could a man cut in a day? What
sort of tree supplies most palings, and so on. Actually somebody
could make a wonderful book out of the stuff we used; I ran that
page for fifteen years and I became an authority on bush lore of all
sorts.

'I used to be amazed at the wonderful letters I got from all sorts
of people, but once, when I printed the two stories I've just told
you, the letters came thick and fast for months afterwards. From
Western Australia, Victoria, everywhere—people told me the names
and the places; they'd seen the trees, they knew somebody who

knew the men. I remember one man who begged me to go to Wentworth in New South Wales because he would point out the galah tree to me; but most surprising, I had a long letter from somebody in Claremont in Queensland who said the sleeper-cutter story had been printed as a news item in the Claremont paper, and I remember the date too—5 January, 1902. And most interesting, the other story had been mentioned as happening in Rockhampton.

'Later on, when I used to do lecture tours all over the place I used to talk about bush lore, and very often I ended with these two stories; and once again, letters used to come in afterwards from people who knew one man or the other. The whole thing began to fascinate me, and later on I didn't end the lecture with the stories— I ended with what I'm telling you now—about the amazing reaction from people. I thought that must put an end to the letters, but it didn't. People still wrote to put me right and to show me the old grey dead tree where the skeleton's hand was found trapped; and people still wrote in complaining that other people were liars.'

— *ALAN MARSHALL (1902-84)*

The Minister of Murder

His name was Thomas John Ley (1880-1947) and he was the only Australian Minister for Justice who was himself sentenced to 'hang by the neck' for murder.

Born in Somerset, England, Ley emigrated to Australia with his widowed mother and siblings in 1886. Living in poverty in Sydney, he left school aged ten but studied assiduously for the law and was admitted as a solicitor in 1914, by which time he had entered local politics and served as mayor of Hurstville, though rumours persisted of questionable dealings. Ley was a bully—and something worse: a psychopath, a man whose unctuous, smarmy manner could turn to angry murderous threats and deeds if thwarted. Winning a seat in New South Wales for the National Party, Ley was appointed Minister of Justice in 1922 and three years later stood successfully for Federal parliament; his Labor opponent mysteriously disappeared, presumed murdered, though his body has never been found. In 1928, when Ley was beset by rumours of more crooked business dealings, one of his critics—a business partner, Hyman Goldstein—was found dead at the foot of the cliffs at Coogee. Ley decamped for London with his mistress but soon came to the notice of police for petty crime and Black Market activities. In 1947, suspecting that his mistress was having an affair with a local barman, Ley had the young man killed. He was found guilty of murder and sentenced to hang in March 1947 but reprieved as insane and died of a stroke in Broadmoor Prison four months later. His papers (and his ashes) are among the curious possessions of the National Library of Australia.

The PoWs

World War II provides the last great horror story of Australian history. More than 22,000 Australians fell into the hands of the Japanese after the collapse of Allied defences in Malaya, Indonesia (Dutch East Indies) and the Pacific Islands in 1942. They suffered a terrible fate. The official history, *Australia in the War of 1939-1945*, tucks their tragic story into an appendix, and records that a total of 7,777 Diggers died of illness, starvation, overwork, execution or ill-treatment. The figures look like a row of crosses marking their lonely graves. Add numbers of captured civilians, nurses and naval personnel—and captured coastwatchers, commandos and airmen who were often beheaded by the enemy—and total Australian fatalities rise to more than 8,000.

The majority of Diggers died during the construction of a railway linking Burma to Thailand through pestilential jungle—a crazy Japanese project initiated in mid-1942 to supply their hard-pressed armies in Burma.

In mid-1945 the Japanese decided to move 1,500 British and Australian prisoners at Sandakan in northern Borneo inland to Ranau, a nightmare 270-kilometre journey by foot across mountains. Those who fell by the track were summarily shot, bayoneted or bashed to death. Of 783 Australians who set out, only six survived. The men left behind at Sandakan, too sick to walk, were killed and the camp was burned.

18: *Nicknames*

*N*icknames are as Australian as Bondi Beach or mallee roots, and we take them so much for granted that few people wonder how the custom grew. A Welsh-born journalist in Sydney, Taffy Davies—in England and Australia anyone Welsh is inevitably dubbed 'Taffy'—was astonished by the Australian habit of giving practically everything a nickname and compiled two valuable collections in the 1970s, from which these excerpts are taken:

Give a man a surname that people can make a joke about (no matter how bad the joke!) and they'll do it. Bloke's name is Bell; he'll cop Ding Dong or Tinker as sure as eggs. Chap by the name of Pitty was promptly named Watta; Bean is the nickname of a man named Coffey; another fellow's name is Fowler, so inevitably he's called The Chook. And so on...

A man without a nickname is a man without a friend— or without an enemy. Because some nicknames, of course, are definitely not for use to a bloke's face. You could end up in dead trouble...

— *From Taffy Davies,* Australian Nicknames, *1977*

Nicknames have been around the Australian scene ever since Captain Cook took one look at the best harbour in the world and decided instead to put his money on Botany Bay. Silly Coot. But you know who was on board with him, don't you? Exactly. Sir Joseph Banks, a man who was later to acquire the nickname Father of Australia. All right, I know—W.C. Wentworth was also called the Father of Australia, but old Banksy was there first so we'll have to give it to him.

Anyway, who was hot on the tail of Captain Cook and Father? Right again—the Reverend Sam Marsden, the Flogging Parson himself, not to mention Bully Bligh.

Some of the most famous people in Australia's history are as well known by their nicknames as by their real names. Don't doubt it. I'll bet you've heard of The Little Digger and The Big Fellow, of Oppy and Pig-Iron Bob.

Try a few sporting figures—The Don, The Demon Bowler and Tiger Bill from cricket; the Lithgow Flash from athletics; Rocket Rod and Muscles from tennis; Superfish, that well-known swimmer. They come from all walks of life. I'll take another bet: I would offer as a sporting proposition that more people know a certain Mr Paterson as Banjo than know his real name. Do I win? Thought so. His real name? Andrew Barton Paterson, but who remembers?…

— *From Taffy Davies, Australian Nicknames, 1977*

Naval nicknames

In the Navy anyone surnamed Clarke is nicknamed 'Nobby', anyone called Miller (or Rhoades) gets 'Dusty', all Murphys are known as 'Spud', and Wilsons get 'Tug'—whether they like it or not. In the army anyone called Burrows or Austin (an Austin first imported rabbits) gets 'Bunny'.

A sailor's 'housewife' (pronounced hussuf) is not what it seems: it's a sewing kit issued for repairs to uniforms. The old destroyer HMAS Waterhen, sunk in 1941, was known to all as 'The Chook.'

Seafarers had to invent an entire new language to describe their ships and its parts, as shown in the rare engraving opposite dating from the 1820s—and most of it is double-Dutch to landlubbers.

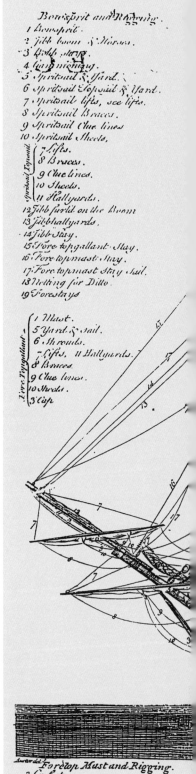

...tion of a Merchant-Ship with all her

...ts, Yards, Sails & Rigging.

...ore particularly designed for that

...hich is the Subject of the Poem.

Fore Mast

Main Mast

Mizen Mast

Mizen Topgallant
1 Mast.
5 Yard & Sail.
6 Shrouds.
7 Lifts.
8 Braces.
9 Clue-lines.
10 Sheets.
2 Cap.
25 Stay.

Mizen Topmast & Rigg
3 Cross Trees.
25 Stay and staysail Hallya
6 Shrouds.
4 Back Stays.
5 Yard and Sail.

Mizen Remad
7 Lifts.
8 Braces.
9 Clue-lines.
16 Bunt-lines.
10 Sheets.
17 Bow-lines.
11 Hallyards.

Mizen Mast & Rigging
5 Yard & Sail.
3 Top.
25 Stay.
26 Stay Sail
6 Shrouds.
27 Brails
10 Sheet & reef.
5 Cross Jack Ya.
21 Crow-foot.
19 Lannyards.

Maintop Mast & Rigging.
3 Cross trees. 25 Middle staysailstay & Hallyards.
6 Shrouds. 4 Back stays.
25 Stay, & Staysail Hallyards.
5 Yard & Sail.
7 Lifts.
8 Braces.
9 Clue-lines. 10 Sheets.
16 Bunt-lines.
11 Hallyards.
17 Bow-lines. 12 Reef Tackles.

Maintopsail

Main
9 Clue-Garnetts.
16 Bunt-lines.
23 Leech-lines.
17 Bow-lines.
7 Lifts.
8 Braces.
24 Horses and Stirrups.

Parts of the Hull
A. Head.
B. Rails.
C. Cutt Water.

...and Jears,
...ks...
...e-Garnetts.
...t-lines.
...ch-lines.
...w-lines.
...ces:
...ses and Stirrups.

Nicknames have been bestowed on the highest—Smithy and the Lone Eagle—and the lowest—Squizzy Taylor. Nor do Australians restrict nicknames solely to people.

Sydney Harbour Bridge has long been known insultingly as The Coat-hanger and Sydney Opera House was, at one point of its mocked-up building, known as The Danish Blue, after its Danish designer.

Racehorses? Couldn't miss. The Red Terror was the most famous of them all: Phar Lap; The Bull was what they called Archer, winner of the first two Melbourne Cups; and in more recent times Gunsynd is known as The Goondiwindi Grey.

We put nicknames to town and cities—Silver City (Broken Hill) and The City of Churches (Adelaide) will do for openers—and Australia itself is known as The Lucky Country.

People who come from interstate will score one of the following: Sandgroper for a Western Australian; Apple Islander for a Tasmanian, Banana Bender for a Queenslander. A Crow Eater comes from South Australia, Cabbage Patchers hail from Victoria and Cornstalks come from New South Wales, though they are also known around the county as Yellowtails on account of their fast driving and the fact that the most you see of them is the yellow number plate as yet another car vanishes over the horizon.

Nicknames come in peace—Mr Eternity used to chalk the single word 'Eternity' in an immaculate copperplate on the streets of Sydney; and in war—The Rats of Tobruk, The Man with a Donkey, The Fuzzy-Wuzzy Angels, even 'G for George' that famous Lancaster bomber…

We all know that Max Walker is Tangles and Rod Marsh is Bacchus. But who are Candles, Bilko and Mary? The first two are not difficult: they are Ray Bright, for obvious reasons, and Craig Sergeant, after the old TV character Sergeant Bilko (remember?). But Mary? That's Geoff Dymock. Now if you ask why, I'll tell you—it's because he comes from Maryborough…

There are plenty more. Mick Malone is known as Solo, from the rhyming slang for alone; Rick McCosker is called Bish because his middle name is Bede, which is close enough to the real name of the famous Indian cricketer Bishan Bedi; Kerry O'Keefe gets Skull, because he is said to be somewhat gaunt of visage, and Gary Cosier's red hair has brought him Jaffa…

But when it comes to teams I suppose Melbourne must bear away the biscuit. Is there a footie side in the city that doesn't have a nickname? I can't think of one.

Some of them are used all over Australia. Once upon a time I used to cheer for a Wagga Wagga side known officially as Turvey Park but known further out as the Bulldogs. But Bulldogs are found everywhere, as are Magpies and Roosters and Tigers…

— *From Taffy Davies*, More Australian Nicknames, *1978*

19: *Ragbag*

ragbag
being a collection
of bits and pieces
informative
or amusing,
in **a**lphabetical
order

L. JOHNSON & CO

Alamein

Name of several decisive battles fought in Egypt from July to November 1942 in which Australia's 9th Division ('The Rats of Tobruk') played a crucial part. Compared with Gallipoli, Tobruk and Kokoda, 'Alamein' is little known to most Australians, yet it was the turning point in the Mediterranean and north African campaigns.

In the searing heat of July 1942 the Australians were rushed down from Syria to defend the Alamein line, 'the last ditch' before Alexandria, which was about to fall to Field-Marshal Rommel's German and Italian forces. Constantly frustrated in attempts to break the Allied line, Rommel was subjected to a massive offensive from 23 October to 4 November 1942; again, the Diggers were chosen for the toughest fighting. 'We could not have won the battle in 12 days without that magnificent 9th Australian Division,' wrote the victor, General Montgomery, in tribute to them

Alps, Australian

It still sounds incongruous that Australia, a land of parched plains, deserts and dried watercourses, possesses snowcapped mountain ranges and ski slopes only several hours travel from Sydney, Melbourne and Canberra. Part of the east coast's Great Dividing Range (which is, in fact, not a mountain range at all, but a series of massive serrated plateaux), the Alps encompass 25,000 square kilometres, beginning at the Brindabella Range overlooking Canberra and extending into Victoria to the vicinity of Mount Donna Buang. The highest peak is Mount Kosciuszko (2,228 metres) in New South Wales, named in 1840 by the explorer and naturalist Count Strezelecki after Poland's national hero.

The Snowy Mountains form part of the Alps and the Snowy River itself begins on the slopes of Mount Kosciuszko. Other once-mighty rivers that begin in the Alps are the Murray and Murrumbidgee.

Aussies

The nickname for Australians is also used for a classic dog, the Australian terrier, which should not be confused—under any circumstances!—with another famous local breed, the silky terrier: Australian silkies are a popular pet, but not a working dog.

The 'Aussie' was bred originally to help eradicate rabbits and rats and is one of the few breeds fast and courageous enough to attack snakes, leaping high and attacking them from behind. For these reasons alone it is a prized member—and faithful guardian—of many bush families. Small, fast, alert and with a blue-grey shaggy coat, its origins can only be guessed at, although they seem to have evolved from a number of imported British dogs—Cairn, Dandie Dinmont, Irish, Yorkshire and Scottish terriers. 'The breed first appeared at a dog show for the first time in 1899, in Sydney, although it had been a mainstay of Outback stations for some 20 years,' states the Readers Digest *Book of Dogs*, from which this information is drawn. When shown in Great Britain in 1906 these small ragamuffins 'aroused little interest' and were not officially recognised as a breed until 1936.

Bondi Beach

Bondi Beach is a name synonymous with Australia. Biggest and broadest of the southern beaches, featured on many tourism posters, it is often the first place visited upon arriving in Sydney. Bondi Surf Lifesaving Club, founded in 1907, proclaims itself Australia's oldest lifesaving club but Manly and Bronte bitterly

A view of Mount Kosciuszko in the Australian Alps, from a lithograph by Bowman, 1886

contest this, claiming that they were founded as early as 1903, the year after the 'indecency' ban was lifted on public swimming in day-light hours.

The phrase 'faster than a Bondi tram' or 'shooting through like a Bondi tram' is typical Australian humour: the winding tram trip from Sydney city to Bondi was one of the slowest in Australia.

Boxing troupes

For 60 years Jimmy Sharman's boxing troupes toured country areas and were regulars at Easter shows in the cities, offering something new in entertainment: a chance of putting on the gloves and being knocked flying by a professional boxer. Many of the boxers were Aboriginals and few newcomers to the ring could land a hit on them. The first Jim Sharman founded the show in Wagga Wagga in 1911 and his son and namesake continued touring the troupe until 1971 when government regulations put an end to it. 'Country boys like a bit of a punch-up,' Jim Sharman junior explained. His own son, another Jim Sharman, is an acclaimed theatre director.

Circuses

For a century 'going to the circus' was as much a part of Australian life as visiting the sideshows at the annual Easter shows. The story of circuses in Australia is a story of families, many of whom followed their parents into circus life for generations.

Australia's first circus, in which acrobats, clowns and horseriders perfomed, opened in Launceston in 1847. A former convict, James Ashton, a skilled equestrian, founded his own circus in 1851—it was just one of many then in existence but was destined to be Australia's most enduring. After the death of his wife, the childless Ashton remarried and produced twelve children, all of whom followed their father in his business. In 1855 the three Wirth brothers, musicians, arrived from Bavaria; one of them, Johannes Wirth, had four sons, all of whom worked for Ashton's. In 1875 another four brothers, the St Leon boys, all of them gymnasts, also formed a circus. The Wirth brothers set up their own circus in Sydney in 1882

and were joined by their mother and two sisters. Tours of rural areas resulted in high profits and soon several circuses and their equipment and tents were on the road at any given time. By the early 1900s circuses were featuring performing animals—elephant, tigers, lions and bears.

Wirth's Circus moved to a new building, Olympia, in Melbourne in 1907. Walter St Leon's travelling circus ended its country touring dramatically in 1912 when it sank, along with the steamer carrying it, on the Darling River; the family survived and settled on the Darling, at Wentworth, where they had links. In 1917 the Sole family who had left Gus de Leon's circus two years earlier and acquired a range of wild animals, founded their own company. Ashton's and Sole's would outlive all others.

Crocodiles

The largest of living reptiles, crocodiles, are found throughout northern Australia's coastal regions; of the two species, freshwater and saltwater (estaurine) the latter can reach up to eight metres in length and have often attacked humans. The saltwater crocodile can go to sea and has been found as far from the mainland as the Fijian Islands; it inspires a certain fear and has entered Australian folklore through Paul Hogan's *Crocodile Dundee* movies and the late Steve Irwin's *Crocodile Hunter* series.

Cyclone Tracy

Described as 'the most devastating natural disaster ever to strike an Australian city', a cyclone named 'Tracy' struck Darwin on Christmas Day, 25 December 1974, and over six hours devastated it, destroying homes and causing the death of 50 people in the city and 16 at sea. Darwin was rebuilt after the disaster; its buildings are now solid and cyclone-proof.

Droughts

Summers of searing heat without rainfall are nothing new to Australia. But summers are getting hotter, rainfall less frequent, forcing city water supplies to dwindle as dams empty, and driving farmers from the land. The first recorded drought occurred less than two years after the first colony was founded at Sydney; crops shrivelled in the earth over 1789-90 and starvation loomed. Other droughts came to New South Wales in 1803, 1809-10, 1813-15, 1824, 1826-27, 1837-39, 1847-59—and have persisted ever since.

Over the years 1895–1903 (known as 'the 1902 drought') all of Australian suffered, as it did in 1911–15, 1918–20, 1922–29 and 1939–43. With droughts come bushfires when high temperatures (often exceeding 40 degrees celsius) combine with strong winds and tinder-dry vegetation. The 'Black Friday' series of bushfires in Victoria in January 1939 claimed 71 lives, the same toll exacted by the devastating 'Ash Wednesday' fires of February 1983 in South Australia and Victoria.

The drought that has devastated Australia since summer 2001 is the worst since 1980–82.

Expatriates

Australians who have achieved fame overseas, principally in the United Kingdom and the United States, include the singers Joan Sutherland and Kylie Minogue, actors Mel Gibson and Nicole Kidman (both of whom were American born), Errol Flynn, Keith Michell, Peter Finch and the late Heath Ledger; writers (and former war correspondents) Alan Moorehead and Chester Wilmot; novelist Russell Braddon (whose experiences as a young prisoner-of-war of the Japanese is recounted in *The Naked Island*), writer (and former fighter pilot) Paul Brickhill (author of three bestsellers of the 1950s, *The Great Escape*, *The Dam Busters*, *Reach for the Sky*, all of which were filmed), and the London celebrities: critic and writer Clive James, poet Peter Porter, feminist and tearaway Germaine Greer.

Famous leaders of the Royal Air Force in World War Two (1939–45) include the Australian-born air marshals Arthur Coningham of Queensland, the Western Australian Peter Drummond (both leaders were killed in post-war air crashes), William Mitchell ('Ginger Mitch'), Arthur Longmore, and Don Bennett (commander of The Path Finders). The ace pilot in the Dam Buster squadron, the Australian 'Micky' Martin, who flew his giant Lancaster bomber at treetop level, miniature toy koala pinned to his flying jacket, survived to become an RAF air marshal.

Flags

Despite a competition for a new flag launched after Federation in 1901 and the adoption of an ensign showing the five stars of the Southern Cross, the seven-pointed Federation star and the British 'Union Jack' in its upper quarter on a red background, Australia had no official flag until 1953, when Parliament decided that the national flag should be dark blue, evoking the night sky. The 'red ensign' flown for half a century was discontinued and is now flown only on merchant shipping.

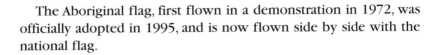

The Aboriginal flag, first flown in a demonstration in 1972, was officially adopted in 1995, and is now flown side by side with the national flag.

Floods

Floods have alternated with droughts and bushfires throughout our recorded history. In mid-winter 1852, Gundagai, on the Murrumbidgee, was swamped by floods that claimed he lives of 89 of the town's 250 people. The year 1870 saw floods in most Australian colonies—even the Murray, normally sluggish at its journey's end, reached record levels in South Australia. In January and February 1893 a cyclone brought floods to Brisbane, took 11 lives and left three ships stranded in the Botanic Gardens, including one of the colony's two iron gunboats. This was the worst Brisbane flood until the 'terrible year' for nationwide floods, 1974, when 12 people were drowned in Brisbane.

In February 1955 the Hunter River burst its banks and flooded 20 towns; much of Maitland was submerged under 1.5 metres of water and 22 people drowned. The drama was recreated in the award-winning 1970s film *Newsfront*.

Larrikins

'The stranger will not be able to discover a new species, but only an old one met elsewhere, and variously called loafer, rough, tough, bummer, or blatherskite, according to his geographical distribution. The larrikin differs by a shade from those others, in that he is more sociable toward the stranger than they, more kindly disposed, more hospitable, more hearty, more friendly. At least it seemed so to me, and I had opportunity to observe, in Sydney, at least. In Melbourne I had to drive to and from the lecture-theatre, but in Sydney I was able to walk both ways, and did it. Every night, on my way home at ten, or a quarter past, I found the larrikin grouped in considerable force at several of the street corners, and he always gave me this pleasant salutation:"Hello, Mark"!'

— *MARK TWAIN, 1897*

The Sydney larrikins (as usual) were flamboyant. In 1891, only four years before Mark Twain visited our shores, an Englishman, Edward Kinglake wrote:'The typical male specimen … is generally a weedy youth, undersized and slight, but like all Australians, who are cast in a lanky, not thickset mould, he is wiry and active. He has a repulsive face, low forehead, small eyes, a colourless skin, and irregular dis-coloured teeth. His hat is either small, round or hard, or a black slouch. He pays attention to his dress, which is always of dark colour and very tight-fitting, the coat of the shortest, the trousers like fleshings, and his boots very high-heeled and small …'

Another bemused reporter described the larrikin as wearing tight cutaway coats with velvet collars, decorated with pearls and buttons, with a red sash, and high-heeled shoes of patent leather or kid with pointed toes; while their girls—their 'donahs'—favoured dresses of violent colours, jackets of plush or velvet, lace-up boots, and hats with ostrich feathers. Despite the difficulty of movement, brawls were common between different gangs. One gang in Sydney consisted solely of one-legged men.

Long Tan

The most famous battle fought by Australians in Vietnam took place on 18 August 1966 near their base at Nui Dat: pop stars were putting on a concert there while 108 infantrymen were fighting for their lives only five kilometres east. It began with an ambush of a company of Australian infantrymen (D Coy, 6th Battalion, RAR) in the Long Tan rubber plantation and ended in a stunning victory when the outnumbered Diggers repulsed a force of 1,200 Viet Cong and North Vietnamese in an engagement fought in monsoonal rain, aided by superb artillery barrages from Nui Dat, ammunition drops from helicopters, and, after three hours of intense battle, the dra-matic arrival of reinforcements in armoured carriers as night was falling. Australian casualties were 18 killed, 24 wounded. Enemy dead numbered 245 and at least 250 wounded.

Australia's war in Vietnam (1962–72) was the longest in our history. More than 50,000 Australians served there and suffered 3,000 killed and wounded.

Macadamias

Almost every crop introduced to Australia grows abundantly but our 'only major native contribution to commercial food crops' (according to *The Australian Encyclopaedia*) is a nut. The macadamia nut is found on two of the seven species of a genus of protea found mainly in southern Queensland and is now widely grown for domestic consumption and export.

The 'Push'

Some of the larrikins were no more dangerous than the 'bodgies' of the 1950s but some drifted into petty crime and others into major crime. No gangs were more feared than Sydney's 'Push', who frequented the seedy alleyways, pubs, sly-grog shops and sailors' haunts of the wharves area of the Rocks. Henry Lawson wrote a famous ballad in which a hayseed from the bush made a monkey of the 'Captain of the Push.'

As the night was falling slowly down on city, town and bush …
From a slum in Jones' Alley sloped the Captain of the Push;
And he scowled towards the North, and he scowled towards the South,
As he hooked his little finger in the corners of his mouth.
Then his whistle, loud and shrill, woke the echoes of the 'Rocks',
And a dozen ghouls came sloping round the corners of the blocks …

It is said that the larrikin gangs came to an end when the government introduced compulsory military service for males in 1911—a large number of youths played truant but most responded well to the easy discipline of the peacetime army and became fine soldiers in the coming war.

Riverboats

Australia lacks great rivers like the Mississippi with its legendary riverboats that have inspired novels, Broadway musicals and Hollywood movies, but the country's largest river system, the Murray–Darling, saw a brief golden age for river transport in the late nineteenth century. Following the pioneers such as Captain Cadell (see page 112) steamboats multiplied on the river, towing barges laden with goods for inland settlements, and returning with wheat and wool. By the 1870s Echuca was Australia's largest inland port and more than 100 steamers and their barges were plying the Murray and Darling and its branches: 6,500 kilometres of waterway. There were many snags other than fallen trees and branches: in years of drought steamers were stranded on mudflats or left high and dry. The mouth of the Murray often sanded up (the problem is still with us), cutting off quick access to Adelaide, and the extension of the railways along the Murray led to the disappearance of most riverboats by the early 1900s.

Sentimental Bloke, The

The book of comic verse by the journalist C.J. Dennis (1876–1938) about the tribulations of a love-smitten Sydney lad—'the Bloke'— was a national bestseller on publication in 1915 and the filmed version released in 1919 was equally popular. It fell out of favour in the sophisticated 1920s and 30s and came to be regarded as a curiosity; few people nowadays could understand the slang. Historians mourned the loss of the film, though an incomplete version shown in cinemas in 1955 sparked a national hunt for old films. It was not until 1973 that an Australian archivist found the negative of the complete film almost by accident in a film library in New York; its six cans had been incorrectly labelled *The Sentimental Blond*!

ME PAL 'E TROTS 'ER UP AN' DOES THE TOFF
'E ALLUS WUS A BLOKE FER SHOWIN' OFF.
"THIS 'ERE'S DOREEN," 'E SEZ. — "THIS 'ERE'S   THE KID."
— I DIPS ME LID —

Sharks

More than half of the world's 350 species of sharks are found in Australian waters. They share with their relatives, rays, whose poisonous sting is usually fatal, an unusual quality, apart from the fear they inspire: they have cartilage instead of bones. Many sharks are harmless and have been killed without reason, but man-eating (carnivorous) sharks cruising in harbours or off beaches still inspire panic. Ironically, over the past 150 years only about 100 fatal attacks have occurred in Australia (about the same number as are killed in road accidents every month on Australian roads). In April 2008 a teenage boy died after being attacked by a shark off Ballina beach in New South Wales.

Stolen Generations

Owing to a flaw in the Federal constitution of 1901 in which the six colonies (states) retained control of the welfare of their Aboriginal communities, infants of mixed European and Aboriginal parentage were, between 1910 and 1970, forcibly taken from their Black mothers, and handed over to the care of non-Aboriginal schools, orphanages or adoption agencies. These cruel and misguided separations blighted many lives. In a 1967 referendum voters approved overwhelmingly the Federal government's determination to take control of Aboriginal affairs from the states—and to give Aborigines full citizenship. In 2008 the new Federal Labor government publicly apologised to Australia's indigenous peoples for wrongs inflicted on them in the past, particularly to the innocent victims in the 'Stolen Generations'.

HMAS Sydney discovered

By 2001, the 60th anniversary year of the loss of HMAS *Sydney*, which had been sunk in battle without survivors in 1941, the tragedy had become not only one of national interest but almost an obsession, particularly in Western Australia with its 400-year maritime heritage. In that year the 'Finding Sydney Foundation' was founded and these dedicated people lobbied successfully for the Federal government to fund the cost of a new search by an expert, an American, David Mearns, who used up-to-date scientific methods and a vessel, the *Geosounder* equipped with powerful sonar sounders that could be lowered almost to the seabed (and were capable of functioning and sending back sonar signals up to four kilometres underwater). He began a new search of the site of the *Sydney-Kormoran* action—an area of 1,800 square nautical miles, nearly 140 miles (over 200 kilometres) off the Western Australian coast between Carnarvon and Geraldton, on 3 March 2008. For nine days the *Geosounder* patiently 'swept' the ocean floor in five-kilometre-wide sonar strips. On 12 March the search team discovered a wreck on the seabed more than two kilometres below: it was identified as *Kormoran*. *Sydney* would have to be close by.

On the morning of 16 March *Geosounder* located the wreck of the *Sydney* approximately eleven miles south-east of the German vessel, 2,468 metres below the surface.

Astonishing photographs were taken by a remote-controlled robot, and brought tears to the eyes of many. David Mearns reported that the images 'are remarkable for both their stunning clarity and their brutal documentation of the punishment suffered by *Sydney* and her crew.' *Sydney* was standing upright on the ocean floor, as if still facing her foe. She was missing her bow, which lay 500 metres away; shattered by German torpedos, it had broken from the hull, dooming *Sydney* and her surviving men to a watery grave within minutes. The photos showed the cruiser in a remarkable state of preservation, her bridge and gun turrets smashed, her port side (which had first faced the enemy) peppered with shell holes; even her starboard—right - side showed massive shell hits suffered when she turned and attempted to ram *Kormoran*; her shattered lifeboats lay near her on the sea bed. Glenys McDonald aboard *Geosounder* wrote: 'As the day unfolded the extent of the damage to our beloved ship was alarmingly clear… [the Germans'] concentrated firepower was incredibly destructive and accurate… HMAS *Sydney* gave up many of her secrets today, may she now rest in peace.'

By closely studying the damage inflicted on both ships historians can piece together the battle in detail. No attempts will be made to raise the two warships or disturb the dead.

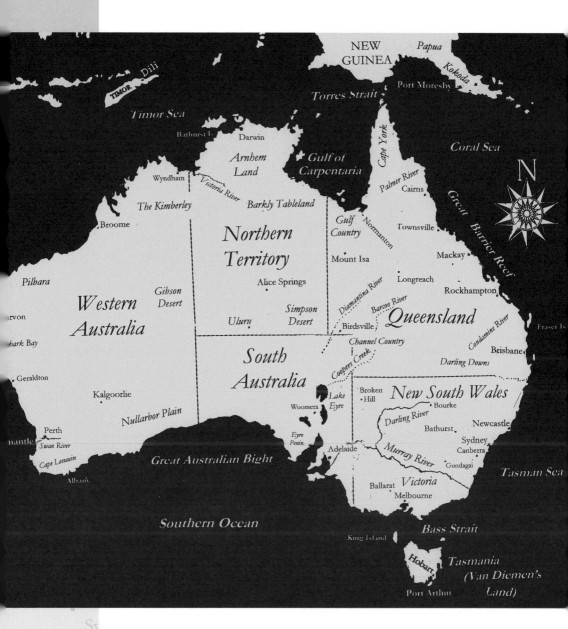

Acknowledgements

The compiler of this book acknowledges his debt to a lifetime of reading the writings of Bill Wannan, Bill Scott, Bill Beatty, Ron Edwards, Alan Marshall and John Manifold, which inspired this volume; and a particular debt to those essential reference works, *The Oxford Companion to Australian Literature* (William H.Wilde; Joy Hooton; Barry Andrews), 1985, and *A Dictionary of Australian Colloquialisms* (G.A.Wilkes), 1978, which inspired the chapter on 'Slanguage' in this volume.

Bibliography

Newspapers consulted on microfilm, and books by the following authors have provided either information or extracts quoted in this anthology:

Adam-Smith, Patsy, *The Shearers*, 1982

Adam-Smith, Patsy, *Folklore of Australia's Railwaymen*, 1969

Boldrewood, Rolf, *Robbery Under Arms*, 1889

Boxall, George, *The Story of the Australian Bushrangers*, 1899

Boyd, A.B, *Old Colonials*, 1882

Clune, Frank, *Wild Colonial Boys*, 1948

Dunderdale, George, *A Book of the Bush*, 1898

Gammage, Bill, *The Broken Years*, 1974

Gordon, Adam Lindsay, *Bush Ballads and Galloping Rhymes*, 1882 ed.

Harding, Edward (Editor), *Alan Marshall Talking*, 1978

Hughes, Robert, *The Fatal Shore*, 1988

Kirwan, John, *My Life's Adventure*, 1936

Lawson, Henry, *Selected Poems*, 1918

Lawson, Henry, *Prose Works*, 1940

MacAlister, Charles, *Old Pioneering Days in the Sunny South*, 1907

Marshall, Alan, *The Complete Short Stories*, 1977

Masefield, John, *Letters from the Front*, 1984

Paterson, A.B., *Collected Verse*, 1923

Pownall, Eve (Editor) *Mary of Maranoa*, 1964 (text by Mary McMaugh)

Praed, Rosa, *My Australian Girlhood*, 1902

Sorenson, Edward, *Life in the Australian Backblocks*, 1911

Stewart, Douglas and Keesing, Nancy, *Australian Bush Ballads*, 1955

Trollope, Anthony, *Australia and New Zealand*, 1873

Twain, Mark, *Following the Equator* (1897; republished 1973)

Wade, Aubrey, *The War of the Guns*, 1936

The author and publishers are indebted to the following for giving permission to reprint copyright material: Curtis Brown Australia Pty Ltd (for writings by Alan Marshall); the Estate of Patsy Adam-Smith; Barbara Mobbs (for permission to use Norman Lindsay's drawing on page 191).

A NOTE ON THE ILLUSTRATIONS
The illustrations and decorations have been drawn principally from nineteenth century and early-twentieth century books and periodicals, with the exception of the following: Pages 52, 53, 352, 356, 357, 361, 363, 366, 367, 372, 376, 382, 383: reproduced courtesy Australian War Memorial. The illustration on p347 is by Ambrose Dyson. The drawing on pages 311 and 316 are by Percy Leason.

Index

Aboriginal folktales 9-17
Aboriginal languages 85
Aboriginal weapons 90
Adelaide 112, 140, 275
Advance, Australia Fair 107
Afghans 276
Airmen 379-383
Alice Springs 276, 277
Alps, Australian 418-419
Andy's Gone with Cattle 233
Antarctic 285
Anzacs 353
Ash Wednesday bushfire 199
Ashes, The 390

Ballarat 154, 159, 337-339
Banjo Paterson 208, 295
Banks, Sir Joseph 28,
Banks of the Condamine 308
Barcoo River 269
Barington, George 69
Bass Strait 37, 40
Batavia shipwreck 23-25
Bates, Daisy 284
Beersheba battle 366
Bendigo 154
Bennelong 67
Bib and Bub 333
Billy Brink 291
Blackbirding 109
Black Friday bushfire 199
Black Thursday bushfire 198
Bligh, William 28-30, 75
Blue Heelers 235
Blue Mountains 81
Bondi 393
Boomerangs 96, 194
Botany Bay 64
Botany Bay songs 60-63
Bounty mutiny 28-32
Boyd, Ben 100
Brady, Matt 120
Breaker, The 302
Bradman, Sir Donald 395
Broome (WA) 174, 376
Brumbies, 320
Bryant, Mary 35
Buchanan, Nat 228
Bulletin, The 207, 364
Bullockies' Ball 187
Bullocky Bill 308
Bullocks 186
Bunyip Aristocracy 160
Bungaree 94
Bunyips 403
Burke and Wills 273
Bushfires 198, 200
Bushrangers 115-137

Cabbage Tree hats 92
Cadell, Francis 112
Castaways 44
Cataraqui shipwreck 40
Catchpole, Margaret 6
Cazaly, Roy 394

Chain gangs 102
Chinese in Australia 166, 228
Chisholm, Caroline 99
Circuses 420
Clancy of the Overflow 296
Click Go the Shears 290
Cobb & Co 163
Cockatoos (farmers) 179
Cook, Captain James 27
Coolgardie 213, 216
Condamine, 308
Convicts 59-105
Coopers Creek 272
Cornstalks 9
Cricket 313, 390, 395
Crocodiles 421
'Crooked Mick' 404
Currency Lads 78
Cyclones 276
Cyclone Tracy 421
Cyprus mutiny 84

Dad 'n Dave 190
Dampier, William 25
Darcy, Les 392
Darling River 112, 266, 272
Death March (Sandakan) 412
Diamantina River 272
Diggers (gold) 153-176
Diggers (soldiers) 352-377
Dog on the Tuckerbox 304
Donohoe, John 118
Drovers 221
Dunbar shipwreck 46
Dunlop, Colonel 'Weary' 377
Dunn, Gilbert and Ben Hall 124
Durack family 222
Dutch navigators 20-27
Dying Stockman, The 237

Emancipists 78
Emden sunk 49
Eureka rebellion 159, 337
Eumerella Shore 150
Expatriates 422
Explorers 266-275
Eyre, Edward John 270

Farewell to Old England 63
First Fleet 59
Fishers's Ghost 402
Flash Jack from Gundagai 255
Flinders, Matthew 36
Floods 199, 422
Flying Doctor 382
Flying Dutchman 26
Football 389

Gallipoli campaign 356
German settlers 144
Ghan, The 276
Ghosts 402

Gilt Dragon wreck 22
Ginger Meggs 333
Gippsland 142
Gold escorts 167
Gold rushes 153
Gordon, Adam Lindsay 294
Green Mountains (Qld) 282
Gundagai flood 199

Hall, Ben 123
Hannan, Paddy 213
Hargraves, Edward 153
Hawker, Harry 380
Hayes, Bully 110
Heatwaves 267
Hill End 157
Hinkler, bert 381
Horseracing 385, 386-389
Howe, Jack 257
Humping the Bluey 331

Immigrants 103
Irish convicts 71-73

Jackeroos 181
Jenolan Caves 14
Jerilderie Letter 134

Kalgoorlie 214
Kangaroos 64
Kelly, Ned 129
Kiandra 165
Kidman, Sir Sidney 232
Koalas 64
Kokoda battles 375
Kookaburra tragedy 280
Kormoran sunk 52
Kosciuszko, Mount 269

Lambing Flat (Young) 166
Lang, Jack 348
Larrikins 423
Lasseter's Reef 277
Lawson, Henry 208
Leichhardt, Ludwig 271
Leslie, Patrick 44
Ley, T.J. 412
Lifesavers 392
Light Horse 365
Long Tan battle 424

Macadamias 424
Magic Pudding 333
Mahogany Ship 21
Man from Snowy River, The 297
Manly Beach 392
Marie shipwreck 43
Mawson, Sir Douglas 285
Melba, Nellie 334
Melbourne 141, 155
Melbourne Cup 386
Merino sheep 75, 239-262
Mitchell, Major 268
Monash, General 335

Index continues on page 432

Montez, Lola 162
Moonlite, Captain 128
Morant, Harry 302
Morgan, Mad Dog
Mount Gambier (SA) 294
Murray River 112
Murrumbidgee river 112
Musquito 121
Myall Creek massacre 95

Neva shipwreck 38
Nicknames 413
Ninety-Mile Beach (Vic) 42
Norfolk Island 65, 88
Northern Territory (NT) 229
Nullarbor Plain 270

Olympic Games 396
O'Reilly, Bernard 282
Overlander, The 225
Overlanders 219

Pacific islanders 109-111
Palmer River 170
Palmer River Song 169
Pandora shipwreck 33
Parkes, Sir Henry 100
Paterson, Andrew Barton
(Banjo) 295
Pearling 173
Phar Lap 393
Pitcairn island 34
Platypus 14, 65
Police 168
Port Arthur 87
Portuguese 19-21
Price, John 89
Prospectors 174, 216
Punishments 86, 93
Push, The 424

Queensland 109, 144, 190,
236

Rabbits 196-198
Redcoats 73-75, 87, 338
Redford, Harry 227
Reibey, Mary 67-68
Riverboats 112, 425
Riverina 148,
Rocks, The 413
Rothbury 346

Saltbush Bill 260
Scottish Martyrs 70
Scots 105

Scrap-Iron Flotilla 54
Selectors 147
Sentimental Bloke 364, 425
Sharks 426
Shearers 239-257
Shearers Dream 289
Shearers' Strike (1890s) 343
Sheep 75, 239-257
Sheep dogs 252
Simpson and his Donkey 361
Sirius wreck 65
Slang 317
Smith, Sir Ross 379
'Smithy' (Charles
Kingsford Smith) 380
Snakes 206
Snowy Mountains 165, 166
Somme battles 363
Southern Cross flag 160, 422
Southern Cross flights 338-
339
'Speewah, The' 404
Sports 385-389
Springsure massacre 195
Squatters 139-147

Stockmen 224
Stuart, John Macdouall 274
Sturt, Charles 266
Swaggies 202, 306
Swan Hill 112
Sydney 35, 36, 46, 64, 66 et al
Sydney, HMAS battles, 41-53
Sydney, HMAS,
wreck found 428

Tambaroora Gold 161
Tanamai Desert 281
Thompson, Barbara 45
Thunderbolt, Captain 122
Timor 56-58
Tobruk siege 372
Tolpuddle Martyrs 82
Tom Thumb 36
Torres Strait 20 173
Trumper, Victor 391
Turon river 156

Ulm, Charles 380
Uluru (Ayers Rock) 278
Unions 343-346
Vandemonians 161
Vaux, James Hardy 79
Victoria 141, 154
Villers-Bretonneux 370

Walhalla 175
Waltzing Matilda 301
Waratah disappearance 46
Wars 351-377
Wet, The 276
Wild Colonial Boy 117
Women of the West 183

Yarra, HMAS 55

Zuytdorp wreck 26

A DESCRIPTION of a wonderful large WILD MAN, or monſtrous GIANT,
BROUGHT FROM BOTANY-BAY.